Un-Forgetting:
Re-Calling Time Lost

—

Stephen David Ross

Copyright © 2009

Published by Global Academic Publishing
For *International Studies in Philosophy*

International Studies in Philosophy Series, Monograph V

Library of Congress Cataloging-in-Publication Data

Ross, Stephen David.
 Un-forgetting : re-calling time lost / Stephen David Ross.
     p. cm. -- (International studies in philosophy monograph series ; 5)
  Includes bibliographical references and index.
  ISBN-13: 978-1-58684-274-1 (alk. paper)
  ISBN-10: 1-58684-274-9
 1.   Memory (Philosophy)   2. Philosophy—History. I. Title.
  BD181.7.R66 2009
  128'.3--dc22   2009019365

Published by Global Academic Publishing
Binghamton University, LNG 99
Binghamton, New York 13902-6000 USA
Phone: (607) 777-4495; Fax: (607) 777-6132
E-mail: gap@binghamton.edu
Website: http://academicpublishing.binghamton.edu/

Contents

ics of memory. Obligations to remember. Thick, thin relations. Shared memory. Nancy. Community. Unworking. Universal ethical community. Impossible. Collective identity. Sin and forgiveness. Returning. Deleuze. Nietzsche. Eternal return. Margalit. South Africa. Truth and Reconciliation Commission. African perspective. Soyinka. Reparations. Reconciliation. Senghor. Black African poet. Sosso-Bala (balafon). Unsolicited metaphor. Burden of memory.

Kant. Lyotard. Sign of history. Can never be forgotten. Progress. Losses. End of art. Science never ends. Irreversible progress. Predict future. Without prophecy. Improvement of humanity. Irreversible. Can never be forgotten. Knowledge advancing toward perfection. What is Enlightenment? Maturity and immaturity. Have courage to use your own understanding. Peirce. Method of inquiry. *A priori* method. Kant. Maturity. Understanding. Freedom. Can predict the future—and everyone must agree. Can know what is to come—and make you believe. Art stands still at a certain point—and has already died. What if art cannot stand still? Lyotard. Inhuman. Two sorts. Development. Infinitely secret one. Anamnesis. Humanism. Guardians. Maturity is dangerous. Dogma. Public, private (official) reason. Foucault. Reason's madness. Hegel. Remembering and forgetting. Death of gods. Images in pantheon of one consciousness. Nancy. Proust. Combray. Death of gods. Madeleine. Writing search of lost time. Embodied in time. Foucault. What is Enlightenment? Reading Kant. Realms of obedience and reason. Caesura. Critique. Baudelaire. Modernity. Attitude. Critical ontology of ourselves. Experiment. Going beyond limits. Cixous. Lispector. *Imund.* Impurity. Heterogeneity of root. Imund with joy. Lyotard. Infinity of heterogeneous finalities. Conflict of faculties. Sign of history. Permanent anamnesis in caesura of forgotten.

Nietzsche. Frog perspectives. Higher value for life. Christianism as decay. History. Life. Herd. Animal. Animals forget. Strength. Power to forget. Animal ahistorical. Historical. Ahistorical. Suprahistorical. Excess of history. Eternal return. Monumental.

Foucault. Insurrection of subjugated knowledges. Archaeology. Genealogy. Oblivion. Forgetting. Caesura. Forgotten traces. Movement. Becoming. Power. Resistance. Archive. Truth of history. Humanity proceeds from domination to domination. Genealogy. Gray, meticulous. *Herkunft. Entstehung.* Descent. Emergence. Platonic modalities of history. Parody. Systematic dissociation of identity. Sacrifice of subject of knowledge. Exteriority. Counter-memory. Forgotten time in first time. Emulation. Resemblance. Signatures. Natural history. Image. Boundless forms of meaning. Ferry. Modern, secular humanism. Foucault. Analytic of finitude. Man. Human sciences. Psychoanalysis. Ethnology. Continuous history. We are difference. Archaeology tracing of forgetting. Genealogy insurrection. Counter-memory disparition of memories and histories.

Ricoeur. Memory. Image. Imagination. Uncouple memory from imagination. Heidegger. World worlds. Earth lets earth be earth. Self-disclosing openness of destiny of historical people. Opposition of world and earth. Striving. Double concealment. Spinoza. No one knows what body can do. Striving. *Conatus.* Expression. Images. Inadequate knowledge. Adequate knowledge. Imagination and memory. Affects. Necessity of contingency. Finiteness and eternity. Leibniz. World of creatures, garden full of plants. Matter teems. Vitality and expression. Wonder as unforgetting. Emptiness as *anamnēsis.* Bergson. Images. Body. Perception. Synthesis of memory. Deleuze. Difference. Disparateness. Intensity. Singularities. Stratification. Whitehead. Concrescence. Prehensions of prehensions. Feelings of feelings. Categoreal obligations. Matter creative, intense, transformative. Filled with desire. Intensity the other of all meaning. Subjective intensity.

Ricoeur. Phenomenology, ethics of memory. Three levels. Pathological-therapeutic. Pragmatic. Ethical-political. Wounds and scars of memory. *Memory, History, Forgetting.* Faithfulness. Heidegger. Happening of truth. Earth self-secluding. Equipmentality. Abundance of reliability. Ricoeur. Aporias of memory. Certeau. Writing. History. Marginalization. Ricoeur. *Phaedrus. Pharmakon.* Imprinting. Genuine memory. Forgetting. Forgiveness. Happy memory. Three traces.

Written. Psychical. Cerebral, cortical. Philosophy. Neuro-sciences. Forgetting as dysfunction, distortion. Enigma of forgetting. Blanchot. Disaster. Ricoeur. Forgiveness. Reciprocity and exchange. Caesura of time. Wounds of being. Fault. Forgiveness and love. Derrida. Judaism, Christianities, Islams. Ricoeur. Imprescriptibility. Forgiving. Giving. Exchange. Giving back. Truth and Reconciliation Commission. Disproportion between forgiveness and admission. Arendt. Forgiving and promising. Action requires forgiveness. Punishment. Inheritance. Treasure of Resistance. Kafka parable. Certeau. Historiography. Subject. Writing. Ricoeur. Forgiveness. Repentance. Eschatology. Happy memory. Happy forgetting. Asymmetry between remembering and forgetting. Augé. *Oblivion*. Three figures of forgetting. Forget present. Forget past and future. Embrace future. Ricoeur. Work of forgetting. Idle forgetting.

Freud. Psychopathology of everyday life. Forgotten. Repression. Still expression. Images. Censorship. Doorkeeper. Threshold. Dreams. Absurd, meaningless, meaningful. Explanation mere fiction. Psychological technique. Interpreting dreams. Scientific. Wish-fulfillment. Intentions, meanings, *as if* of dreams. Misdirection. Manifest, latent content. Doubly repressed. Distortion. Forgetting as remembering. Psychic, political repression. Meaning in interpretation and revelation. Daily forgetting as reality present in everyday life. Displacement. Substitution. Underlying intention. Truth endless forgetting, digging, interpretation. Double displacement. Realities, signs appear obliquely, proliferate by misalignments and indirections. Mechanism of forgetting. Chains of names withdrawn from memory. Resistance. Performances, psychic life, world determined in unknown ways. Pathology. Superstition. Paranoia. Outer world full of projections. Wonderful. Uncanny. *Déjà vu*. Repetition. Repression expressive. Generosity work of mourning, melancholia.

Withdrawal, concealment, errancy. Marks of being. Masks of appearance. Forgettings of recollection. Heidegger. Forgetting ethics. Lyotard. Forgotten law. Jews. Heidegger's silence. Animals paradigm of victim. Adams. Butchering. Heidegger forgets animals. Derrida's critique. Abyss between humans and animals. Heidegger and Levinas do not sacrifice sacrifice. Virility. Levinas. Face of animal. Separation. Diachrony. Animality. Western history sedentary. Possession. Other becomes same. Generosity. Other's mortality. Derrida. Bodies expressive. Responsibility impossible. Sacrifice imperative duties. Impossibility condition of possibility of justice. Levinas. *Time and the Other*. Distance of time. Iterability. Diachrony. Otherwise than being. Proximity. *God* other word. Witness to infinite. Anarchy. Betrayal. Forgetting. Revelation by violation. Human alterity. Time. Relationship of subject with other. Solitude. Heidegger. Hitler. Eschatology. Destiny. Time and history irreparable. Judaism and remorse. Christianity and freedom. Liberalism and materiality. Transcendence of bodies. Flesh. Theology. Secularization. Heidegger. Levinas. Art stops before other. Shadow. Wicked. Egoist. Cowardly. If face beyond knowledge, art refuses grasping. Caesura of doubling. Hyde. Art as gift, giving, moving. Levinas. Exteriority of face. Extra-ordinary. Love. Not name. Infinite. Rupture. Forgetting. Witness to forgetting.

Derrida. Forgetting. Derrida's death. Good mourning. Speaking to your ghost. Inheritance. Nothing in particular. Bearing witness as inheritance. More than one. Mourning. Idealization. Simulacrum. *Mimesis*. Iterability. Double injunction. "Double bind." Undecidability. And so forth. Founding. Conserving. Archive. Psychoanalysis. Different archival prostheses. Gift. *Gabe. Es gibt*. Impossibility of gift. Absolute forgetting. Absolves. Unbinds absolutely. Death of child. Derrida's mother. No limit to forgiveness. No measure. Forgetting. Madness of given and desired forgetting. *Perhaps. Zusage*. Being European. Not identical with itself. Derrida's work of mourning. *Philia, Eros*. Absolute sacrifice. Violence. Guarding. *Arrivance*. Arrival of *arrivant, perhaps*. Carnophallogocentrism. Animals. Women. Death. Hospitality. Performativity. Forget Derrida.

Scarry. Pain. Inexpressible. Levi. Atrocities unheard. Forgotten. Trauma. Memory imperfect. Bearing witness. Refuses judgment of prisoners, including Special Squad. Visible marks of own degradation. Slaves. Domesticated animals. Degradation. Morrison. Meaninglessness of kindness. Lyotard. Impossible to speak about cruelty and degradation. Scarry. Torture. Jackson. Pain sufferers feel misunderstood. Daniel. Pain needs voice. Bodily terror. Winkler. Rape terror. Bodily knowledge. Daniel. Transformation in work. French. Cambodian camps. Buddhist karma inspires degradation. Compassion. Scarry. Mimetic creation. Language shattered by pain, requires making. Torturer and tortured. Pain and imagination.

Blanchot. Disaster. Forgotten. Is it a disaster, calamity? Enigmatic. Joy in midst of disaster? Forgetfulness. Without memory. Beyond remembering and forgetting. Levinas. Other higher. Deleuze and Guattari. Becomings. Deleuze on Marx. Repetition. Eternal return. Zarathustra. Borges. *As if. Perhaps.* Bhabha. Invisibility. As forgetting. Anzaldúa. As bordering, splitting. Blanchot reading Levinas. Paradox. I and other. Infinity as interruption. Disaster as forgotten call. Calling of other. Disastering. Betrayal. As welcome. Responsibility. Call of saying. Unknown name. Holocaust. Death. Disastering as giving. Do not forgive. Forgetfulness. Disaster disastrous. Is disastering. Is not disastering. Is forgetting. Has no name. Perhaps. As if disaster were joy. As if forgetting were remembering. Exposition beyond itself.

EDITORIAL ASSISTANT

Elizabeth Wheeler

INTRODUCTION

The Forgotten

What we can forget we must remember.
What we cannot remember we must not forget.

The Forgotten is the Law. (Lyotard, *HJ*)

*I*n the unforgettable story of Er, at the close of Plato's *Republic*, when souls gather themselves to return to life, they cross the plain and drink of the river of *Lēthē*, of oblivion and forgetting. Heidegger reminds us repeatedly that truth is unforgetting in Greek, *alētheia*, and that forgetting is something positive in its own right. Forgetting is constitutive of being.

The story of Er is told as if it were a story recounted by Socrates of a story he has heard from others at the close of a dialogue— another story—reported by Plato, one of many stories Plato tells of a man whose words and deeds he remembers even when he was not present. One might say that Plato's dialogues recall a Socrates who as protagonist is from the first forgotten as a historical figure, forgotten in the way in which the gods are remembered in the myths told of them. And perhaps we may think of Plato's stories as myths, Socrates' stories as myths inside myths, except that they come with the proper names *Plato* and *Socrates* whereas myths come with other proper names, *Greek* and *aboriginal*, for example.

The proper names serve to recall that which in its appearance is forgotten—I mean recalled as if forgotten. Do you remember the Titans, Prometheus, the house of Atreus? Do you remember Lord Krishna, Vishna, or the Tengu? Or do I mean, have you forgotten? Do we write in order to remember what we have forgotten, or do we write in order to forget, as if to forget. In the caesura of *anam-nēsis*. Interrupting.

Plato writes dialogues that recall Socrates as if to remember what we could not forget, but the Socrates who is recalled is not the Socrates we might wish to remember, but to forget—by writing, speaking of him not as if alive but as a dramatic protagonist. Not the living Socrates but the dead one, more dead than as if once living and perhaps forgotten, living as never having lived, never having touched another's flesh and blood—still *as if* alive, *as if* himself remembering, speaking, saying—but not writing. Socrates never wrote a word. Plato wrote thousands of words about the Socrates who never wrote a word, as if to recall the writing of a man who never wrote, whose thoughts are thereby lost to posterity. Which of these writings and nonwritings is remembering and which forgetting? Or are the writings and the nonwritings together forgetting and remembering, unremembering as if by way of unforgetting? Do these stories take place as if in the caesura between forgetting and remembering, life and death, giving and having?

The myth of Er is told at the moment in which we might say the theme of justice returns for the final time in Plato's *Republic*, no less incredibly for its many recollections. Justice is better in all ways than injustice. As if one might need to prove this for it to be true. As if one could prove it in order to make it true. As if one might easily forget this most moving of truths, so that proof would allow it to be remembered.

> I am going to say that the just, when they become older, hold the offices in their own city if they choose, marry from what families they will, and give their children in marriage to what families they please, and everything that you said of the one I now repeat of the other, and in turn I will say of the unjust that the most of them, even if they escape detection in youth, at the end of their course are caught and derided, and their old age is made miserable by the contumelies of strangers and townsfolk. They are lashed and suffer all things which you truly said are unfit for ears polite. (Plato, *Republic*, 613ce)

This is so unbelievable that of course we cannot remember it. To the contrary, we remember how often the unjust and wicked triumph. We remember it because they do and because they succeed in naming the triumph. The spoils are to the victors, including the name and garb and remembrance of justice. This is surely one of the most overwhelming forgettings possible for humanity: to forget what is given from the good as justice and to imagine that injustice might take its place *as justice, in justice*. We cannot remember what we cannot believe, and so what is unbelievable as truth is and must be forgotten.

I do not mean to say that Socrates is wrong, that in fact the unjust rise and the just fall. I mean to say something closer to forgetting, that in the rise and fall of justice and just human beings and acts, in the injustice for which all things pay restitution as Anaximander says,[1] the form in which injustice appears is as forgetting. We pay restitution not to what we know, what we remember, but to what we have forgotten, to injustice as forgetting. We live as if in a human justice that has forgotten the injustice of all things. Some call it *amnesty*.

And if we have forgotten such things in life, all things and their injustices, if we have forgotten the good in recalling it, we have forgotten much more and much less when it comes to what awaits us after death. Who before Socrates recalled the myth of Er? Who after Socrates remembers what he remembers?

> Well, these, I said, are nothing in number and magnitude compared with those that await both after death. And we must listen to the tale of them, said I, in order that each may have received in full what is due to be said of him by our argument. (Plato, *Republic*, 614b)

Why do we need to recall what we can show and prove by argument? Why must we listen to tales of the wise? That has been the question of philosophy from the time of Plato and before. Philosophy arrays itself against the remembering and dreaming that was knowing before philosophy came on the scene. In *Meno*, Plato aligns philosophy with remembering—I mean, of course, with forgetting. But that is for me the point of *Meno*, and I will recall it in due course. For the moment we are still telling stories some remember. As if to forget.

Er recalls reviving after death—as if, perhaps, he had not died, as if he were still full of life—to find himself among souls who met together from heaven and earth, and who told stories of what they remembered of heaven above and the earth below. So the entire tale told by Er is his recollections, his memories, of the tales and stories and memories of others. Death is full of memory. Er's death is especially full of memory, full of remembering what must be forgotten.

> [W]hen he himself drew near they told him that he must be the messenger to mankind to tell them of that other world, and they

charged him to give ear and to observe everything in the place. (614d)

> And they told their stories to one another, the one lamenting and wailing as they recalled how many and how dreadful things they had suffered and seen in their journey beneath the earth—it lasted a thousand years—while those from heaven related their delights and visions of a beauty beyond words. (614e)

We may recall this beauty beyond words from another place— I cannot say another time: it is a story forgotten as if beyond time:

> a nature which in the first place is everlasting, not growing and decaying, or waxing and waning; secondly, not fair in one point of view and foul in another, or at one time or in one relation or at one place fair, at another time or in another relation or in another place foul, as if fair to some and foul to others, or in the likeness of a face or hands or any other part of the bodily frame, or in any form of speech or knowledge, or existing in any other being, as for example in an animal, or in heaven, or in earth, or in any other place; but beauty absolute, separate, simple, and everlast- ing, which without diminution and without increase, or any change, is imparted to the ever-growing and perishing beauties of all other things. (Plato, *Symposium*, 210–211a [Jowett trans.])

This is a beauty beyond words, and perhaps it is the beauty re- membered from heaven—and forgotten. Perhaps this beauty ever- lasting, beyond time, must be forgotten so that we can grow and decay, wax and wane. Beauty absolute, separate, simple, and ever- lasting is forgotten—an immemorial loss beyond measure—so as to be imparted to the beauties of all other things. We remember these things in such a forgetting. We remember and forget in the stories we tell.

Even so, in this archaic, timeless place the deeds of space and time are recalled to judgment. It is an immemorial time, and "To tell it all, Glaucon, would take all our time" (615) all the time there was or might be, all that might be forgotten. Even so, the sum is this:

> [A]fter every judgment they bade the righteous journey to the right and upward through the heaven with tokens attached to them in front of the judgment passed upon them, and the unjust to take the road to the left and downward, they too wearing be- hind signs of all that had befallen them. (614d)

> For all the wrongs they had ever done to anyone and all whom they had severally wronged they had paid the penalty in turn tenfold for each, . . . and again if any had done deeds of kindness

and been just and holy men they might receive their due reward
in the same measure. (615)

The measure of injustice, the restitution for which all time pays
due, answers beyond time, gives time surpassing time, inheritance
beyond possession. And more, we who live through time bear
traces, marks, tokens, signs of where we have been and what we
have lived. These are inscribed upon our bodies even where we
might have forgotten them. Remembering and forgetting are the
expressive forms and signs in which we belong to time and surpass every time.

Judgment beyond time is harsh, and this world of death threat-
ens disaster. Yet the beauty beyond words returns in words.

> [T]hey saw there at the middle of the light the extremities of its
> fastenings stretched from heaven, for this light was the girdle of
> the heavens like the undergirders of triremes, holding together
> in like manner the entire revolving vault. And from the extremi-
> ties was stretched the spindle of Necessity, through which all the
> orbits turned. Its staff and its hook were made of adamant, and
> the whorl of these and other kinds was commingled. (616bc)

Words and music beyond music and words, beyond what was and
is and will be, the memory and beauty of time beyond time as if it
were to be forgotten.

> And there were three others who sat round about at equal inter-
> vals, each one on her throne, the Fates, daughters of Necessity,
> clad in white vestments with filleted heads, Lachesis, and
> Clotho, and Atropos, who sang in unison with the music of the
> Sirens, Lachesis singing the things that were, Clotho the things
> that are, and Atropos the things that are to be. And Clotho with
> the touch of her right hand helped to turn the outer circumfer-
> ence of the spindle, pausing from time to time. Atropos with her
> left hand in like manner helped to turn the inner circles, and
> Lachesis alternately with either hand lent a hand to each. (617cd)

The fates, daughters of necessity, are images of time and memory
and history—remembered and forgotten. For they sing together of
what was and is and will be, sing in unison of what cannot be
gathered together. What is can be only in the death of what was.
What was can be remembered only in its passing away. "Souls
that live for a day, now is the beginning of another cycle of mortal
generation where birth is the beacon of death" (617e). Birth is the
unforgetting of death, the light in darkness. Perhaps I mean the
darkness in light, for the depths are too beautiful to remember.

It is time for souls who have encountered this beauty beyond to forget—I mean remember. They must forget so that they can remember, so that they can live and die in memory of this forgetting and this forgotten.

> And after this again the prophet placed the patterns of lives before them on the ground, far more numerous than the assembly. They were of every variety, for there were lives of all kinds of animals and all sorts of human lives, ... But there was no determination of the quality of soul, because the choice of a different life inevitably determined a different character. But all other things were commingled with one another and with wealth and poverty and sickness and health and the intermediate conditions. (618ab)

I interrupt in the name of animals to mark their forgetting. Plato remembers animals, does not forget that human beings share the earth and sky with them and the gods.[2] We today forget, animals and others. We remember to sacrifice.

> Through butchering, animals become absent referents. Animals in name and body are made absent *as animals* for meat to exist. Animals' lives precede and enable the existence of meat. If animals are alive they cannot be meat. Thus a dead body replaces the live animal. Without animals there would be no meat eating, yet they are absent from the act of eating meat because they have been transformed into food. (Adams, *SPM*, 40)
>
> a structure of overlapping but absent referents links violence against women and animals. . . . Just as dead bodies are absent from our language about meat, in descriptions of cultural violence women are also often the absent referent. (42)
>
> I propose a cycle of objectification, fragmentation, and consumption, which links butchering and sexual violence in our culture. . . . the rape of women that denies women freedom to say no, or the butchering of animals that converts animals from living breathing beings into dead objects. (47)

This is a forgetting I would recall even as it appears oblique to Plato—but not perhaps to his memory. In our culture—and many others—butchering and sexual violence are linked through two forgettings, the invisible mark of virility and the objectification of animals transformed into dead meat. Forgetting here is not the mark of infinity but of domination. We are made to forget by what rules over us, so that its force is invisible. More of this later, though surely the rule of the best philosopher-king shares this forgotten hegemony.

And perhaps the tale of Er recalls it to our memory. Perhaps what he remembers as the souls return to life is a world without domination—all were commingled with one another and with wealth and poverty and sickness and health and the intermediate conditions—that we must forget in order to live.

Here is all variety, too great to calculate, joined and mixed together, as if entwined beyond any choice. Here, in beauty beyond recall, souls must choose—what cannot be chosen—a choice that cannot be made, that cannot be a choice:

> [H]e said that it was a sight worth seeing to observe how the several souls selected their lives. He said it was a strange, pitiful, and ridiculous spectacle, as the choice was determined for the most part by the habits of their former lives. (619e)

This is a choice that cannot be a choice and a memory that cannot be remembered, culminating in a forgetting that is a return to life, that must be forgotten.

> [T]hey all journeyed to the Plain of Oblivion (*Lēthēs pedion*), through a terrible and stifling heat, for it was bare of trees and all plants, and there they camped at eventide by the River of Forgetfulness (*Lēthēs potamon*), whose waters no vessel can contain. They were all required to drink a measure of the water, and those who were not saved by their good sense drank more than the measure, and each one as he drank forgot all things. (621ab)

Each one forgets all things in the memory of coming to be. This is a story of forgetting and remembering that is itself a remembering and forgetting. Socrates is explicit.

> And so, Glaucon, the tale was saved, as the saying is, and was not lost. And it will save us if we believe it, and we shall safely cross the River of Lethe, and keep our soul unspotted from the world. But if we are guided by me we shall believe that the soul is immortal and capable of enduring all extremes of good and evil, and so we shall hold ever to the upward way and pursue righteousness with wisdom always and ever, that we may be dear to ourselves and to the gods both during our sojourn here and when we receive our reward, as the victors in the games go about to gather in theirs. And thus both here and in that journey of a thousand years, whereof I have told you, we shall fare well. (621bd)

We must be guided by one who does not remember, telling a story not to be forgotten. It will save us if we believe it—does it matter if it is true if we remember it, or will we be saved by it in the forgetting? If we are guided by Socrates, who we will never forget—do we remember? Must we remember for one thousand years, or longer? Must we remember forever—if that is possible?

Finally, then, is there a choice, do we have a choice, between remembering and forgetting, living and dying, or is this nonchoice the condition of every choice? Does it inhabit the caesura between choice and nonchoice, remembering and forgetting?

Derrida speaks of this caesura in the context of the political:

> 1. *Either* to admit that the political is in fact this phallogocentrism in act.... This structure can be combated only by carrying oneself beyond the political, beyond the name "politics," and by forging other concepts, concepts with an altogether different mobilizing force. Who would swear that this is not in progress?
>
> 2. *Or else* keep the "old name," and analyse the logic and the topic of the concept differently, and engage other forms of struggle, other "partisan" operations, and so forth.
>
> If there were a single thesis to this essay, it would posit that there could be no choice.... (Derrida, *PF*, 158–9)

There can be no choice between the old and the new, between remembering and forgetting, but there is a temptation to choose.

> Temptation indeed. It is that of the book you are reading—there can be no doubt about it—but it is also the temptation this same book owes itself to resist, ... we cannot, and we *must* not, exclude the fact that when someone is speaking, in private or in public, when someone teaches, publishes, preaches, orders, promises, prophesies, informs or communicates, some force in him or her is also striving *not* to be understood, approved, accepted in consensus—not immediately, not fully, and therefore not in the immediacy and plenitude of tomorrow, etc. (Derrida, *PF*, 217–9)

Memory, taken as something present—here is what I remember, in its truth—insists on possession, takes claim of what might resist. Language resists, insists on dispossession. The word, the phrase, the memory, exposition insist on a choice where there can be no choice. The word has a history and will have a future, and between the two—the word right now in the present is always between—there is no choice, no choice between the old meaning and the new one, the one tomorrow. We are always in the caesura between the old and the new, remembering and forgetting. That is what it is to be, to inherit what we are and remember in a forgetting.

The temptation, then, is to remember what we forget, to claim that we remember when we forget, to imagine that we do not forget—most of all, perhaps, to insist on forgetting what we have forgotten. We insist that we remember and know and can be understood without forgetting, when forgetting is the very possibility of remembering. Indeed, even this is too weak. For-getting is not the condition of re-membering: it is re-membering itself. For-getting is for-giving, generosity beyond itself.

> 1. *Either* to admit that memory is this violence and domination in act, a structure that can be combated only by carrying oneself beyond—forgetting—remembering and forgetting, by forging other concepts.
> 2. *Or else* keep—remember—the "old names" and analyse the logic and the topic of the concept differently, engage in other forms of struggle.
> There can be no such choice.
> This is the temptation we may hope to resist. When someone is speaking, in private or in public, when someone claims to remember what is known or true, when someone teaches, publishes, preaches, orders, promises, prophesies, informs, or communicates what he or she remembers, some force in him or her is also striving to forget, to be not understood, approved, accepted in consensus.

The temptation is to remember too much when we are constituted by remembering—I mean by forgetting. The temptation is to keep what we inherit when we cannot and must not do so.

In Derrida's words again:

> That we *are* heirs does not mean that we *have* or that we *receive* this or that, some inheritance that enriches us one day with this or that, but that the *being* of what we are *is* first of all inheritance, whether we like it or know it or not. And that, as Hölderlin said so well, we can only *bear witness* to it. To bear witness would be to bear witness to what we *are* insofar as we *inherit*, and that— here is the circle, here is the chance, or the finitude—we inherit the very thing that allows us to bear witness to it. (Derrida, *SM*, 54)

We inherit the very thing that allows us to forget it. To bear witness is to a forgetting that is our being in every remembering. To inherit is to forget.

This brief excursion has taken us in the name of Plato and his heirs from Anaximander to Heidegger and Derrida. This journey, from ancient Greece to contemporary European philosophy, is a journey many believe to be the right one, as if it were better than some others. It is a wonderful journey, but perhaps it is not better, perhaps one cannot choose philosophic journeys as if some had a

monopoly on truth, as if some better knew or remembered or understood a truth that comes to be, to appear, as if it were remembering more than forgetting. Perhaps the many peoples of the
earth have told many different stories, each a remembering and a
forgetting, different stories of remembering and forgetting. Here it
becomes important to listen and to remember how forgotten have
been many of these stories and the peoples who narrated them,
forgotten now in the sense of suppression and repression.

Australian aboriginal peoples speak of dreaming as if it were
remembering, all the while forgetting, images covering over while
repeating, masking while revealing. The shining that is dreaming
recalls the creatures of the earth from an immemorial time, as if
the light that revealed them distorted and transfigured them.
Dreams and dreamings give us images as if they were something
to remember, yet what they reveal is forgetting, the things we
have forgotten and a time and place and events that exist as if in
forgetting—I mean of course in unforgetting. The return of the
image is its unforgetting, the unearthing of its exposition.

The light that brings the image back to memory transfigures
and distorts it, obscures it and reveals it. The image can never be
what it is without transfiguration, without dis-appearance. Remembering is re-membering, transformation, transsubstantiation,
re-presents the gifts of the earth in other modalities, other times and
places, keeps them on the move. The volatility of memory is its reality, its transformation its truth, its transsubstantiation its preservation. In other words, re-membering is for-getting—I mean, forgetting is remembering as its truth is untruth. And indeed, the
untruth of truth is the forgetting of memory, the betrayal of exposition. Nothing appears, nothing is recalled, revealed, except in
exposition—I mean as if in language, except as image: exposure as
expression, calling; as *aisthēsis, mimēsis, poiēsis, catachrēsis, technē*;
as image, aesthetics, beauty, art; calling as giving. The unearthing
of exposition takes place as the unforgetting of the image. The image proliferates, the exposition betrays, the recollection transfigures. Transcendence, transfiguration, transformation are the remembrances of memory—I mean its forgettings in the modalities
of *perhaps* and *as if*.

In the unforgetting of what is here to come,[3] we may think of
forgetting in at least three different ways: something is always
forgotten, we can never remember or know everything, time and
history are forgettings; we desire to know, to remember, with such
a will that we forget the fascination of unforgetting even as we are
fascinated by it; forgetting is constitutive of being always, every-

where, past, present, and future, here and elsewhere, and in this forgetting everything is unforgotten, returning differently. Forgetting proliferates everywhere as remembering and unforgetting.

In *Being and Time*, Heidegger speaks of forgetting as a positive, ecstatic mode of having been, with a character of its own.

> [W]hen one projects one-self inauthentically upon the possibilities drawn from what is taken care of in making it present, this is possible only because *Da-sein* has forgotten itself in its ownmost thrown potentiality-of-being. This forgetting is not nothing, nor is it just a failure to remember; it is rather a "positive," ecstatic mode of having-been; a mode with a character of its own. . . . It is the temporal meaning of the kind of being that I initially and for the most part am as having-been. And only on the basis of this forgetting can the making present that takes care of and awaits retain things, retain beings unlike *Da-sein* encountered in the surrounding world. (Heidegger, *BT(S)*, 311–2)

Everything about this passage, in the context of *Dasein*'s care for self, appears to turn on inauthenticity. Forgetting is a positive mode of inauthentic being. Forgottenness is inauthentic having been where the historicality of being is the primordial condition of authenticity. Even so, only on the basis of this forgetting can *Dasein* take care of and retain things. The retention, duration, preservation of things is on the basis of forgetting. The unforgetting of being is the exposition of being itself.

Only a few years later, in *On Time and Being*, Heidegger speaks of what is more primordial than *Dasein* and, perhaps, than Being.

> In the beginning of Western thinking, Being is thought, but not the "It gives" as such. The latter withdraws in favor of the gift which It gives. That gift is thought and conceptualized from then on exclusively as Being with regard to beings.
>
> A giving which gives only its gift, but in the giving holds itself back and withdraws, such a giving we call sending. (Heidegger, *TB*, 8)

The It that gives (*es gibt*) is conceptualized as being, as a giving that gives gifts, and in giving withdraws, holds back, conceals. The forgetting-withdrawing-withholding of being is giving beyond gifts. The gift of memory is given in a for-getting and for-giving beyond any gift.

Heidegger says this repeatedly, in different voices.

> We have yet to consider why the question about the destiny of Being was never asked and why it could never be thought. Or is . . . [this] a sign of the forgetfulness of Being? (Heidegger, *LH*, 208)

> Yet Being—what is Being? It is It itself. The thinking that is to come must learn to experience that and to say it. "Being"—that is not God and not a cosmic ground. Being is farther than all beings and is yet nearer to man than every being, be it a rock, a beast, a work of art, a machine, be it an angel or God. Being is the nearest. Yet the near remains farthest from man. (210–1)

> Forgetting the truth of Being in favor of the pressing throng of beings unthought in their essence. . . . (212)

> This "there is / it gives" rules as the destiny of Being. Its history comes to language in the words of essential thinkers. Therefore the thinking that thinks into the truth of Being is, as thinking, historical. (*BT*, 215)[4]

Thinking is historical—that is, temporality and remembrance. I mean that in the giving we inherit. We bear witness to being in (un)forgetting. Exposition is unearthing in the forgetting of being.[5]

These passages express something of remembering and forgetting in the memory of gifts and the forgetting of giving. Being is—as we for-get—re-membered in the giving, as if it were the it that gives. Yet this forgetting is not the for-getting of being, for that is farthest. The for-getting of being is beyond all accounting, beyond re-membering. It is being itself, being it self, being exposed in the open as it self, as for giving. Such a giving is near and far, is the nearest and the farthest. This near and far is for-getting. If you will it is re-membering. Giving is unforgetting—that is, forgetting forgetting itself. Letting presence, bringing to openness, emerges from forgetting as unforgetting. I would add that the destiny of being is to be forgotten, is never anything to be grasped, remembered, or had but for giving.

Here are some names that we may have forgotten, if we ever remembered them:

immemoriality
diachrony
archaism
eschatology
messianism
etc.

re-calling
re-collecting
re-membering
un-forgetting
etc.

giving
for-giving
for-getting
etc.

not as if calling, collecting, assembling again—
but as if un-un-calling, -collecting, etc.
as if inter-rupting collecting
as if dis-possessing
as if non-neutrality
as if for-giving
etc.
etc.

Here are some propositions perhaps to unforget:

Forgetting is constitutive of being.
Being withdraws.
It gives Being by withdrawing.
The earth is given in seclusion.
The forgotten is the law.
Unforgetting is exposition.
Exposition is unearthing.
Unearthing is betrayal.

Perhaps.

Each is a question, many questions, is questioning, a way or
many ways of questioning, without question marks.

Perhaps.

Here, then, are the questionings of this book, this meditation and
participation in forgetting—and, thereby, perhaps in exposition
and memory.

With and without question marks.
With and without questioning.
Questioning before the question.
In the *Zusage* of questioning.
In the caesura of *anamnēsis*.

To be is to cross the river of forgetfulness.
To inhabit the caesura of exposition.
To recall the injustice of all things.
To unforget the injustice in justice.
To bear witness to the forgotten.

Perhaps.

Truth conceals.
Revealing is concealing.
Concealing is constitutive of truth.

Perhaps.

Unrevealing is constitutive of unconcealing.
Untruth is constitutive of truth.
The truth of truth is untruth.
The truth of remembering is forgetting.
Exposition is truth's betrayal.

Perhaps.

Truth is nothing to have.
Forgetting is dispossession.
Remembering is unforgetting.
Re-membering is corporeal transfiguration.

Perhaps.

Truth is the gathering of being.
Language cannot be gathered.
The image is ungathering.
Meaning is always lost.
Always on the way.

Perhaps.

Living is forgetting.
Knowing is *anamnēsis*.
Truth is recollection.
Recollection is unforgetting.
In the modality of *perhaps* and *as if*.
In the proliferation of the image.

We can know, we can remember, as if without forgetting.
We can possess the truth.
We forget.
Forgetting is negation, lack of memory.
Error is negation, lack of truth.

Perhaps.

Forgetting is decay.
Endlessness.
Fascination.

Alterity.
Corporeality.
Wandering.
Phantasms, images, simulacra.

Perhaps.

We do not know what bodies can do.
We forget.
We do not know what forgetting is.
We have forgotten.
Tout autre est tout autre.

Forgetting is forgotten.
The forgotten is the law.
Justice is restitution.
For injustice.
For the ruin of justice.
For injustice in justice.
For lost time.

Being is the search for lost time.
Time is always (on the edge of being) lost.

Perhaps.

We return from death to life, from disaster to being.
As if through forgetting.
Do we remember, do we forget, disaster and death?
Do we bear witness?
As if there were something to remember.
As if there were everything to forget.
As if to forget the injustice in justice.

Perhaps.

The ordinance of time is restitution for its injustice.
For the loss of time.

We have a duty to remember, we must not forget.
We have a duty to forget, we must not remember.
Memory is knowledge, memory is truthful.
Forgetting is exposition, forgetting is proliferation.
We have a duty to the truth and must be truthful toward our
     duties.
There is more to forgetting than not remembering.
There is more on heaven and earth than can be remembered.
The poet re-members.

Perhaps.

Enlightenment is maturation, resisting the domination of
    greater powers.
Enlightenment is restitution for injustices against men,
    women, children, and animals.
Enlightenment is restitution for injustices against the earth.
Enlightenment is injustice in the name of justice.
Enlightenment is exposition.
Exposition is betrayal.
Enlightenment betrays.

Perhaps.

Lost time is always arriving.
We cannot escape the search for lost time.
The order of things.
The exposition of things.
Betrays.
Lost time is disaster.
Disaster is inhuman.

Perhaps.

Memory is death.
Forgetting is life.
Life is power.
We must die to live.
We must forget to live.
We must remember to forget.
We must lose to find.
We must find ourselves among the animals.

Perhaps.

We live by forgetting.
We dream by remembering.
Remembering is forgetting.
Saying what cannot be said.

Perhaps.

Being is historical.
History is genealogy.
Genealogy is inheritance.
Inheritance is exposition.
Exposition is betrayal.

Perhaps.

To live is to remember what cannot be forgotten.
To live is to forget what cannot be remembered.
There is nothing we cannot forget.
Truth is remembered.
Truth is forgotten.
Masks are the palimpsest, the forgetting and covering
    over.
Covering over is overcoming.

Perhaps.

Being, truth, remembering are present, here, without lack.
Being, truth, forgetting are unpresent here in masks.
Being, truth, forgetting are phantasmatic.

Perhaps.

Personal identity and being.
Social identity and being.
Human and animal being.
Are the search for lost time.
For lost injustice.
Never to be found.
Never to be regained.
As if by forgetting.

Archaeology is remembering.
Genealogy is (un)forgetting.
Genealogy is archaeology.
The (un)forgotten is (the return of the) disaster.

Perhaps.

Reason forgets itself.
History forgets lost time
Forgets its own forgetting.
Seeks a time without loss.
Time wears masks.
Power is productive.
Forgetting is production.

Perhaps.

History is repetition.
Repetition is difference.

Becoming is betraying.
Betraying is forgiving.

Perhaps.

Memory is composed of images.
The passage of time is the proliferation of images.
Forgetting is the multiplication of images.
Remembering is the return of images.
The image is the disaster.
The return is the forgotten.

Perhaps.

The other is always forgotten.
The other is the forgetting.
The other must be remembered.
As if by forgetting.

Perhaps.

Remembering is unforgetting.
Forgetting is forgiving.
Forgiving is exposition.
Exposition betrays.

Perhaps.

Every day we dream.
Every day we forget.
Every day we betray.
Every day we enjoy.
Every day we mourn.

Perhaps.

Responsibility is infinite.
Responsibility is excessive.
Before memory.
Beyond memory.
Forgetting is diachrony.
In the caesura of lost time.

Perhaps.

Mourning is forgetting.
And remembering.
Inheriting is remembering.
And forgetting.

Spirits, specters come and go.
As if to remind us of what we have forgotten.
As if to make us forget what we must remember.
As if we were what we inherit.
By remembering and forgetting.

We cannot choose between remembering and forgetting.
We cannot choose between life and death.
We cannot succumb to temptation.
We cannot refuse the inheritance.

Perhaps.

I am, I say I am, I say who and what I am—
American, European, human, etc. etc.
I forget who and what I am—
I forget when I say what and who I am.
To be is not to be.
To remember is to forget.
To live is to die.

Perhaps.

As if by history.
As if by diachrony.
As if by ungathering in the midst of gathering.

As if by drowning.
As if by surviving.
As if in pain.
As if in terror.
As if in trauma.
As if in disaster.

Perhaps.

Being is empty.
Being is emptiness.
Emptiness is empty.
Emptiness is full.

Remembering is empty.
As if it were forgetting.
Forgetting is empty.
As if there were nothing to remember.
As if nothing were to be remembered.

Perhaps.

Memory is disaster. Identity is forgetting.
Identity is at the border.
Between remembering and forgetting.
Between life and death.
Between disaster and fulfillment.
Between the one and the other.

Perhaps.

Memory is possession.
Possession is having.
Giving is constitutive of having.
Forgiving is constitutive of being.
As if beyond possessing.
As if forgetting.

Perhaps.
Perhaps.

CHAPTER 1

Re-calling

[T]here is that theory which you have often described to us—that what we call learning is really just recollection (*anamnēsis*). If that is true, then surely what we recollect now we must have learned at some time before, which is impossible unless our souls existed somewhere before they entered this human shape. So in that way too it seems likely that the soul is immortal. (Plato, *Phaedo*, 72e–73a)

Thus the soul, since it is immortal and has been born many times, and has seen all things both here and in the other world, has learned everything that is. So we need not be surprised if it can recall the knowledge of virtue or anything else which, as we see, it once possessed. (Plato, *Meno*, 81cd)

I would begin by recalling that the dialogues in which Plato's *doctrine of recollection* (as it is called) is explored at length are among his most dramatic. *Phaedo* takes place at Socrates' death, and I believe that everything that happens and is said must be understood in terms of solace before this unmitigatable disaster. Whatever else it may be, philosophy is comfort in memory of a wound that cannot be healed of what must not be forgotten.

Meno's drama takes place on another stage, as far from death as possible—if anything in life is far from death. The entire dialogue answers to Meno's opening question whether virtue (*aretē*) can be taught, one of the most critical questions it is possible for human beings to ask. How are they to become good?—if they can, if it is possible to lead them to it. One might imagine several prior questions: what virtue is and whether it is different from what can be taught, for example arithmetic and philosophy—if either of these can be taught, if anything can be taught, if we can learn to ask questions of them. These are familiar Platonic questions, no less vital for that. Can we learn from others or do we acquire knowledge as if from ourselves? Is philosophy something learned or a way of thinking from ourselves? Are we good, do we live good lives because we have learned to do so from others, in the experiences of life, or in some other ways? And indeed, is there something to this good, to a good life, that we might acquire, or is it perhaps an illusion to think so?

These are among the momentous and compelling questions of life. Responding to the urgency and the imperative, Derrida imagines the following:

> Someone, you or me, comes forward and says: *I would like to learn to live finally (enfin).*
> Finally but why?
> *To learn to live*: a strange watchword. Who would learn? From whom? To teach to live, but to whom? Will we ever know? Will we ever know how to live and first of all what "to learn to live" means? And why "finally?" ...
> But to learn to live, to learn it *from oneself and by oneself,* all alone, to teach *oneself* to live ..., is that not impossible for a living being? ...
> And yet nothing is more necessary than this wisdom. It is ethics itself, to learn to live—alone, from oneself, by oneself. ...
> If it—learning to live—remains to be done, it can happen only between life and death. Neither in life nor in death *alone.* ... [it] can only *maintain itself* with some ghost, can only *talk with or about* some ghost (s'entretenir *de quelque fantôme*). ...
> And this being-with specters would also be, not only but also, a *politics* of memory, of inheritance, and of generations. (Derrida, *SM*, xvii–xviii)

To learn to live—but how? To teach oneself or another to live—is that not impossible, is it not necessary? From the first, it seems that *Meno* is framed by both necessity and impossibility. And who is Meno to take on this Herculean task? Is he up to it? Who could imagine that he is? Who could imagine that you and I are?

One the one hand, then, to this impossible yet irresistible question, Socrates responds by asking Meno to tell him what virtue is because "The fact is that far from knowing whether it can be taught, I have no idea what virtue itself is" (Plato, *Meno*, 71b). And perhaps it is nothing to know. "I share the poverty of my fellow countrymen in this respect, and confess to my shame that I have no knowledge about virtue at all. And how can I know a property of something when I don't even know what it is?" (71b). Meno takes for granted that some know—Gorgias for example (71c)—and perhaps believes he knows it for himself. He appears to have prepared a performance on whether virtue can be taught but not on what virtue might be. He appears to be a sassy youth out to show disrespect to his elder, only to discover that the elder knows more tricks than he has ever imagined. In the appearances of knowledge and virtue are many specters.

> But is this true about yourself, Socrates, that you don't even know what virtue is? Is this the report that we are to take home about you?
>   Not only that, you may say also that, to the best of my belief, I have never yet met anyone who did know. (71bc)

I have never yet met anyone who knows—not Gorgias, not Meno, not Socrates or Plato themselves. Why should we disbelieve this? Why should we insist that Socrates knows what he claims not to know? Perhaps because he might have forgotten.

What Socrates does not know is what virtue is. I mean the good, that beauty beyond words, almost certainly something not to know.[1] Later in the dialogue he appears to know whether mathematics and geometry can be taught. This discussion of recollection as learning is recalled in response to Meno's most famous question,

> But how will you look for something when you don't in the least know what it is? How on earth are you going to set up something you don't know as the object of your search? To put it another way, even if you come right up against it, how will you know that what you have found is the thing you didn't know? (80de)

How indeed? you might say. A question not so much of virtue and goodness, of ethics, of how to live, but of knowledge, learning, truth. How can you tell that something is true? How can you know that what you think you remember you truly remember? What can we do to really tell, to really remember? If it is something to do.

This appears to be the question of remembering and forgetting at the heart of the entire discussion. Socrates casually dismisses it.

> Do you realize that what you are bringing up is the trick argument that a man cannot try to discover either what he knows or what he does not know? He would not seek what he knows, for since he knows it there is no need of the inquiry, nor what he

does not know, for in that case he does not even know what he is
to look for.

Well, do you think it a good argument? (80e–81a)

Perhaps he does so because he sees in Meno a brightness of youth
much closer to cleverness than to wisdom. Meno wants to learn a
good argument—something quite different, perhaps, from recalling the truth or envisioning the good. Meno wants to know something—quite different, perhaps, from seeking it. Impetuous youth
remembers, in wisdom age forgets: is this not life itself and
ghosts? Memory hopes to keep time young, forgetting is archaic,
immemorial.[2]

The doctrine of recollection is presented here as a digression—
a removal, a disremembering—from the question of how to live. It
is not even the question of how to learn, but how to answer to a
clever argument employed by those who make a living presenting
clever arguments. What is to be done with a bright young, impres-
sionable person who is not only impressed by such arguments but
wants nothing more than to be clever at them himself? The last
thing, surely, is to give him a better argument. That would only
make him more clever. The first thing is to respond to a trick with
a better trick.

The argument that Meno finds persuasive is preceded by the
following words:

> I see, Socrates. But what do you mean when you say that we
> don't learn anything, but that what we call learning is recollec-
> tion? Can you teach me that it is so?
>
> I have just said that you're a rascal, and now you ask me if I
> can teach you, when I say there is no such thing as teaching, only
> recollection. Evidently you want to catch me contradicting my-
> self straightaway.
>
> No, honestly, Socrates, I wasn't thinking of that. It was just
> habit. If you can in any way make clear to me that what you say
> is true, please do. (81e–82a)

What we see in this brief exchange is how Socrates moves Meno
from a desire for a clever dialectical maneuver to a desire for
truth. This is a remarkable achievement. It is accomplished not by
an argument but by a story, presented as a recollection—one
might say of priests and priestess, gods and goddesses, life and
death, all manners of infinity.

> I have heard from men and women who understand the truths of
> religion . . .

... All nature is akin, and the soul has learned everything, so that when a man has recalled a single piece of knowledge— learned it, in ordinary language—there is no reason why he should not find out all the rest, if he keeps a stout heart and does not grow weary of the search, for seeking and learning are in fact nothing but recollection (*anamnēsis*). (81ae)

Many readings of this passage emphasize that recollection, *anamnēsis*, is remembrance. I would emphasize that if it is anything it is unforgetting, as if the soul could not hold onto the image of what it knew but lost it, forgot it completely except for a trace. Recollection is dispossession. I mean by this that it is not having, as if remembering were grasping the truth in hand, but giving, as if to return what once was given and dispersed. All nature is akin, the soul has learned everything—these are astonishing things to say. All nature, everything. How imagine that any soul, no matter how infinite, might find all of nature one, a single family (*suggenous*)? I mean to imagine that this kinship is not something to have, to know and possess, but to wonder at, as if it might be given. The modality of *anamnēsis* is *as if* and *perhaps*. It is the modality of forgetting.

Before I undertake this reading, I would add that I do not mean to overlook the other references to recollection in the dialogues, in *Phaedrus* and especially in *Philebus*, brief and passing references that seem to support the transcendent doctrine of recollection.[3] Here are two examples:

For only the soul that has beheld truth may enter into this our human form—seeing that man must needs understand the language of forms, passing from a plurality of perceptions to a unity gathered together by reasoning—and such understanding is a recollection of those things which our souls beheld aforetime as they journeyed with their god, looking down upon the things which now we suppose to be, and gazing up to that which truly is. (Plato, *Phaedrus*, 248e–249c)

Then by "recollection" we mean, do we not, something different from memory?

When that which has been experienced by the soul in common with the body is recaptured, so far as may be, by and in the soul itself apart from the body, then we speak of "recollecting" something. Is that not so?

And further, when the soul that has lost the memory of a sensation or what it has learned resumes that memory within itself and goes over the old ground, we regularly speak of these processes as "recollections." (Plato, *Philebus*, 34bc)

These passages intimate that souls once knew, possessed truth, and that discovery is the recapture, repossession of that truth. If you can believe it, it will be good to believe it. For the crucial thing this kind of story establishes—again if it can be believed—is that if you look for truth you will find it, because it is more like recollection than creation. It is so difficult to take invention, creation, inspiration for granted, it is better to tell stories that treat them as reversions.

Here, then, we see *anamnēsis* arrayed against the enemies of familiarity and fear. Unforgetting is a story—as if it were itself an unforgetting—of the greatest acts of mind and body and spirit as if they were a remembering. Not to mention as if mind and spirit were separable from the body. *Anamnēsis* takes place in the modality of unforgetting.

If so, then the knowledge and truth—and for that matter life itself, not to mention death—all appear here in the modalities of forgetting. This is the central theme of this book: life and death as forgetting. Here in *Meno* we can see three of these many modalities at work.[4]

1. Something is always forgotten. We can never remember everything. Remembering is an endless struggle to recover the image of what we have lost.

2. There is an irresistible will to remember what has been forgotten, an irresistible fascination with remembering—I mean unforgetting—beyond any possibility of a return.

3. Unforgetting is itself forgotten, and in the caesura of this second forgetting everything comes back as if it were remembered. Everything comes back beyond any remembering and forgetting, in the caesura of *as if* and *perhaps*.

Every one of these forgettings takes place in the modality of *as if*. Re-calling, re-collecting, re-membering all take place as images in the modality of *as if*. As if as unforgetting. I mean in exposition as for giving.

In Greek, then, memory is *mnēmē*; recollection is *anamnēsis*; remembrance is *mnēmosunē*; forgetfulness is *amnēmosunē*; *anamnēsis* is bringing back to memory from forgetting. And so we might ask, what is it to bring back, what is brought back from forgetting? The answer, perhaps, is *nothing, nothing in particular—as if it were everything, as if in the caesura*. Unforgetting is the exposition of things, images beyond themselves, always coming back in the caesura, in the modality of *as if*. Unforgetting is doubly, triply, multiply ambiguous, present and not present, here and there, now you see it now you don't. Unforgetting is beyond choice, yet in this beyond choice is all the freedom of the world, present as if disaster.

In case you may have forgotten, *Meno* begins with Meno's question whether virtue can be taught, or whether it comes by practice or in some other way (70a). This is Meno's question, side-stepped by Socrates, who sarcastically alludes to Gorgias as if he seems to know everything. Meno proposes a question with an answer he has learned from Gorgias. Learning here is memory. What does Meno remember, what does Socrates know? What have they forgotten? Socrates' answer is that here in Athens no one knows what virtue is (71b), and for that matter Socrates has never met anyone who knows (71c). It is something no one remembers. Perhaps they have forgotten, as if Socrates himself has forgotten.

> Didn't you meet Gorgias when he was here? ...
>
> I'm a forgetful sort of person, and I can't say just now what I thought at the time. Probably he did know, and I expect you know what he used to say about it. So remind me what it was, or tell me yourself if you will. No doubt you agree with him. (71cd)

Remind me, unforget me, I've forgotten. But don't remind me of what Gorgias said but of what you believe. Unforget yourself of yourself, not of others. We are all forgetful sorts of people. As we must be to know and to understand.

The subject is virtue, *aretē*, neither trivial nor minor. And perhaps it is something easily forgotten. Whatever it may be, Meno knows from Gorgias how to acquire it—though we never find out how. He remembers—and here indeed remembering is different from unforgetting. Unforgetting he must do by himself.

What is virtue? Many things indeed, "a whole swarm" (72a). What is its essential nature?

> [S]uppose I asked you what a bee is, what is its essential nature, and you replied that bees were of many different kinds. What would you say if I went on to ask, And is it in being bees that they are many and various and different from one another? Or would you agree that it is not in this respect that they differ, but in something else, some other quality like size or beauty? (72ab)

Perhaps we would not agree that virtue is like bees and honey, for we can remember seeing bees and tasting honey, but we cannot remember encountering virtue clearly. And for that matter, size and beauty might be different, too different to regard as qualities.

> I should say that in so far as they are bees, they don't differ from
> one another at all.
>   Suppose I then continued, Well, this is just what I want you
> to tell me. What is that character in respect of which they don't
> differ at all, but are all the same? (72bc)

Are you so sure, is it something you remember, might you
know without looking that while bees differ with respect to one
another (some are larger, some are smaller, some are queens, some
are workers), they do not differ as bees? Men and women do not
differ as human beings, then. Are you sure? Or do they differ all
the more as human beings, with the question of what that difference amounts to?
     Or as Meno puts it:

> I agree that health is the same in a man or in a woman. [but]
>   I somehow feel that this [virtue] is not on the same level as
> the other cases. (72d)

Socrates asks Meno to remember what Gorgias says of virtue,
that the virtue of human beings is "simply the capacity to govern
men" (73cd). Here the question turns to masters and slaves, then
to justice, reminding us of Aristotle:

> [H]e who is by nature not his own but another's man, is by na-
> ture a slave; and he may be said to be another's man who, being
> a human being, is also a possession. (Aristotle, *Politics*, 1254a)

> Where then there is such a difference as that between soul and
> body, or between men and animals... the lower sort are by na-
> ture slaves, and it is better for them as for all inferiors that they
> should be under the rule of a master. (1254b)

> A question may indeed be raised, whether there is any excellence
> at all in a slave beyond those of an instrument and of a serv-
> ant.... A similar question may be raised about women and chil-
> dren, whether they too have excellences;... excellence of charac-
> ter belongs to all of them; but the temperance of a man and of a
> woman, or the courage and justice of a man and of a woman, are
> not, as Socrates maintained, the same; the courage of a man is
> shown in commanding, of a woman in obeying. (1259b–1260b)

It appears here that human beings differ essentially in being human, and that different excellences entail different human lives,
vertically arranged.
     Meno says that he cannot find a single virtue—or essence of
virtue—among all the virtues. This remark is somewhere between
the banal—what do different things have in common?—and the

sublime—what is the One among the Many? What is the image in relation to its multiplicity? Here, in relation to virtue, it is closer to the latter, because it is by no means clear that the good is anything at all. When Meno says "I cannot yet grasp it as you want, a single virtue covering them all, as I do in other instances" (74ab), we might suppose that he has a point. Virtue is not like anything else. For example, "what is it that is common to roundness and straightness and the other things which you call shapes?" (75ab). Socrates' answer is that shape is "the only thing which always accompanies color" (75bc). He answers with an image.

Meno is dissatisfied—we might suppose for several reasons. Certainly a parent speaking to a child would not expect such a definition to be useful. In Meno's words, "if somebody says that he doesn't know what color is, but is no better off with it than he is with shape, what sort of answer have you given him, do you think?" (75c). Meno is no child, but a stubborn youth, and that is how Socrates answers him in what I consider to be the central image of the dialogue.

> A true one, and if my questioner were one of the clever, disputatious, and quarrelsome kind, I should say to him, "You have heard my answer. If it is wrong, it is for you to take up the argument and refute it." However, when friendly people, like you and me, want to converse with each other, one's reply must be milder and more conducive to discussion. By that I mean that it must not only be true, but must employ terms with which the questioner admits he is familiar. (75cd)

If you, Meno, are a quarrelsome sort, show me I'm wrong. If we're engaged in a friendly exchange, and want to learn from each other, then let's continue the discussion. And so they do, arriving at a definition acceptable to Meno.

> Color is an effluence from shapes commensurate with sight and perceptible by it.
> That seems to me an excellent answer. . . .
> Yes, it's a high-sounding answer, so you like it better than the one on shape. . . .
> Nevertheless, son of Alexidemus, I am convinced that the other is better, and I believe you would agree with me if you had not, as you told me yesterday, to leave before the Mysteries, but could stay and be initiated. (76d–77a)

What I imagine is happening here is that Socrates is bringing Meno around from being contentious to being receptive. If that is a good thing, if that is what a teacher wants, a student who listens and remembers. I would emphasize the mysteries.[5] In my view, two important pedagogical—perhaps philosophical—events are taking place, both deeply problematic. One is that Meno knows too much to learn, and must become open to learning something unfamiliar to learn anything at all. The problematic side of this important truth is that whatever his teacher does to open him up—cut him open, tear his heart, reach him where he lives, humiliate, even inspire him—is exactly what it sounds like, unobstructing him by force. Even inspiration runs the risk of imprinting. The other side of this truth, no matter how problematic and coercive it may also be, is that through time the imprinted images, the acts of intellectual control that cannot be avoided in teaching, dissipate into multiplicity. The temptation is to imagine that this is not so, that teaching takes hold. The truth is that teaching takes hold by reversion, that teaching passes through time and language and distance and proliferation into unteaching, unlearning, discernment, that we inherit to give away—finally, that what we may hope to remember is by forgetting. Meno must forget what he has learned from Gorgias—as he will no matter how tightly he hopes to hold onto it—and he will forget what he has learned from Socrates. Only then will he have learned something for himself—in the forgetting.

The other pedagogical event here is that what it is to be open is unknown and unknowable and uncontrollable. Words like *insight, inspiration, intuition* mark the event of understanding as a blow: unanticipatable, unpredictable, unimaginable. And still we anticipate and predict and imagine. That is the mystery, those are the mysteries. Mind and soul and body work in mysterious ways. We imagine this not to be so even as our imagination works through body and soul and mind in strange and enigmatic ways and images. Here Meno's approach to Socrates is problematic not because he knows too much, is too closed minded, but that what he has learned is pat, routine, that it does not recall the mysteries in their initiations.

Meno likes the answer he has been given. And perhaps that is the problem, that the best answers are too strange to be liked, too unfamiliar to be accepted. Perhaps the problem with arguments is that they tell us what we already know and do not disturb us with their truths. They give us remembrance without unremembering. I imagine that many of my readers would like as perfect as memory as possible. I ask them to remember being tortured or raped, the pain of childbirth or mutilation. Women forget—and in that for-

getting give birth to the transformation of the world. In our forgetting is transgression.

The question for Meno is what virtue is whole and sound. His
answer is that it is desiring fine things and being able to acquire
them. There is something to that answer in the Greek terms *aretē*
and *ethos*, though it may not address the issues that come down to
us from the good—I mean from the forgotten, from the immemorial injustice of which Anaximander speaks, in the immemorial
amnesty of forgetting.[6]

Socrates insists that Meno must tell him what justice is so that
"I should recognize it even if you chop it up into bits" (79c). Meno
finds this difficult if not impossible. Perhaps it is impossible. Perhaps all of science and philosophy insist on this impossibility.
Nothing remains the same when it is chopped up into bits, analyzed or synthesized, given over to thought or matter. That is the
point of reflection, to chop and combine and to follow the trajecto-
ries and proliferations of the processes. That is where reflection
brings us, to a forgetting so deep and shattering as to destroy any
possibility of gathering. Unforgetting is ungathering.

As Meno famously says of Socrates:

> Socrates, even before I met you they told me that in plain
> truth you are a perplexed man yourself and reduce others to
> perplexity. At this moment I feel you are exercising magic and
> witchcraft upon me and positively laying me under your spell
> until I am just a mass of helplessness. If I may be flippant, I think
> that not only in outward appearance but in other respects as well
> you are exactly like the flat sting ray that one meets in the sea.
> Whenever anyone comes into contact with it, it numbs him, and
> that is the sort of thing that you seem to be doing to me now. My
> mind and my lips are literally numb, and I have nothing to reply
> to you. Yet I have spoken about virtue hundreds of times, held
> forth often on the subject in front of large audiences, and very
> well too, or so I thought. Now I can't even say what it is. In my
> opinion you are well advised not to leave Athens and live
> abroad. If you behaved like this as a foreigner in another coun-
> try, you would most likely be arrested as a wizard. (80ab)

Is this not a vivid image of forgetting, not to mention violence?
Meno has spoken of virtue before large audiences but now finds
his mind dumb and spirit numb. If this is what it takes to open
him to truths he does not know and cannot anticipate, then forgetting is the condition of remembering as untruth is the condition of
truth. Socrates responds:

It isn't that, knowing the answers myself, I perplex other people. The truth is rather that I infect them also with the perplexity I feel myself. So with virtue now. I don't know what it is. You may have known before you came into contact with me, but now you look as if you don't. Nevertheless I am ready to carry out, together with you, a joint investigation and inquiry into what it is. (80cd)

He has forgotten if he ever knew what virtue is, but they can seek it together. Meno's response is on the remembering and forgetting.

But how will you look for something when you don't in the least know what it is? How on earth are you going to set up something you don't know as the object of your search? To put it another way, even if you come right up against it, how will you know that what you have found is the thing you didn't know? (80de)

How will you remember what you have forgotten? How will you know what you have not forgotten? The soul has learned all things but has forgotten, and can recall them and can know them. This is surely a special kind of forgetting, which remembers what it has forgotten. But that is perhaps the point, that the forgetting is not oblivion, that crossing the river of forgetting is not the same as nothing. If anything is the same.

Skipping over Socrates' story again, I would like to close the frame of the dialogue by noting that his account does not satisfy Meno, who is satisfied only by an outrageous and fraudulent wizard trick, as if his slave might know more than himself. Closing an extended interrogation filled with leading questions, Socrates concludes by asking Meno, "What do you think, Meno? Has he answered with any opinions that were not his own?" (85bc), preceded by,

Observe, Meno, the stage he has reached on the path of recollection. At the beginning he did not know the side of the square of eight feet. Nor indeed does he know it now, but then he thought he knew it and answered boldly, as was appropriate—he felt no perplexity. Now however he does feel perplexed. Not only does he not know the answer; he doesn't even think he knows. (84ab)

Thinking that one does not know—one has forgotten?—is the condition of knowing. Forgetting is the condition of unforgetting. To think that one knows, as Meno does at the beginning of the dialogue, is not to know.

It is worth noting that slavery appears elsewhere in the dialogue, in particular:

> But does this virtue apply to a child or a slave? Should a slave be capable of governing his master, and if he does, is he still a slave? (73d)

> If you have one of his works untethered, it is not worth much; it gives you the slip like a runaway slave. But a tethered specimen is very valuable, for they are magnificent creations. And that, I may say, has a bearing on the matter of true opinions. True opinions are a fine thing and do all sorts of good so long as they stay in their place, but they will not stay long. They run away from a man's mind; so they are not worth much until you tether them by working out the reason. That process, my dear Meno, is recollection, as we agreed earlier. Once they are tied down, they become knowledge, and are stable. That is why knowledge is something more valuable than right opinion. What distinguishes one from the other is the tether. (97e–98a)

It's as if the issue is not the recollecting but the tethering. Remembering is tethering, having, grasping. Recollection must confront the reality that the mind forgets, that truth slips away, that forgetting is the truth of remembering, that we forget and then remember. In the language of possession, we must first lose in order to find, must forget in order to recall, must be wrong in order to be right. And this condition does not pass away, though it is ceaselessly forgotten.

We are on the verge of unforgetting the question of forgetting. In brief, before we leap, let's finish off the dialogue, remembering its conclusion. We began with the question of whether virtue can be taught, as if to give an answer without knowing what virtue is. But Socrates does not know, knows nothing himself and believes that no one knows. Perhaps everyone has forgotten. And how would we know what virtue is if we could not learn it? Meno does not know what virtue is and does not want to know it as Socrates asks him to. He responds in frustration that no one can know, that no one can learn. Socrates responds with the doctrine of recollection. We can learn because we always knew. As if this were an answer to how we can tell. We can tell. That's the truth, the truth of truth. We can tell as if it were unforgotten. Meno is satisfied by that answer, and so the discussion resumes, not without some telling comments:

Then if he did not acquire them in this life, isn't it immediately clear that he possessed and had learned them during some other period?...

If then there are going to exist in him, both while he is and while he is not a man, true opinions which can be aroused by questioning and turned into knowledge, may we say that his soul has been forever in a state of knowledge?...

And if the truth about reality is always in our soul, the soul must be immortal, and one must take courage and try to discover—that is, to recollect—what one doesn't happen to know, or, more correctly, remember, at the moment....

I shouldn't like to take my oath on the whole story, but one thing I am ready to fight for as long as I can, in word and act—that is, that we shall be better, braver, and more active men if we believe it right to look for what we don't know than if we believe there is no point in looking because what we don't know we can never discover....

If I were your master as well as my own, Meno, we should not have inquired whether or not virtue can be taught until we had first asked the main question—what it is. But not only do you make no attempt to govern your own actions—you prize your freedom, I suppose—but you attempt to govern mine. And you succeed too, so I shall let you have your way. There's nothing else for it, and it seems we must inquire into a single property of something about whose essential nature we are still in the dark. (85e–97b)

The soul is forever in a state of knowledge. Why then, how then inquire? And why does Socrates repeatedly insist that he does not know? Perhaps we should not take an oath on this story, in whole or part, but take an oath instead to fight for truth and seek it, resisting all who would deny it. Finally, then, this is a question not just of truth but of freedom. It is the highest and most urgent of all concerns. It is unfortunate that it is cast in terms of mastery and slavery. Perhaps we should recall the tethering. Recall it as if to forget it, not as if to remember.

The discussion resumes on the question posed at the beginning, whether virtue can be taught. We must assume, if it is teachable, that it is knowledge.

Well, in the first place, if it is anything else but knowledge, is there a possibility of anyone teaching it—or, in the language we used just now, reminding someone of it? We needn't worry about which name we are to give to the process, but simply ask, Will it be teachable? Isn't it plain to everyone that a man is not taught anything except knowledge? (87c)

I would say that it is anything but plain. As Socrates himself suggests, with a striking allusion.

> Since then goodness does not come by nature, is it got by learning?
> I don't see how we can escape the conclusion. Indeed it is obvious on our assumption that, if virtue is knowledge, it is teachable.
> I suppose so. But I wonder if we were right to bind ourselves to that.
> Well, it seemed all right just now.
> Yes, but to be sound it has got to seem all right not only "just now" but at this moment and in the future. . . .
> I don't withdraw from the position that if it is knowledge, it must be teachable, but as for its being knowledge, see whether you think my doubts on this point are well founded. If anything—not virtue only—is a possible subject of instruction, must there not be teachers and students of it? . . .
> I have often looked to see if there are any, and in spite of all my efforts I cannot find them, though I have had plenty of fellow searchers, the kind of men especially whom I believe to have most experience in such matters. (89c–90b)

The kind of searcher Socrates claims ironically to have in mind is Anytus, who sits down beside them at this point in the famous scene in which he is shown to be opinionated unto death without experience or knowledge.[7] I'm concerned with whether it is plain that what is taught and learned is knowledge, and that it must be right not only "just now" but at this moment and in the future. Perhaps I mean that it is as unplain as remembering without forgetting. I mean as if it were tethering. Perhaps I mean that if it is true it is not plainly true, now and later, but that whatever can be taught or learned must be mobile, on the move, not yet settled, that we learn and thereby transform and transfigure knowledge. All as if they were virtue, which also then is something mobile, on the move, never settled—and thereby in this way is knowledge, in this way is acquired. Virtue is acquired as if it could not be acquired. Remembering is unforgetting as if it were forgotten—I mean remembered, always known (in some unfamiliar way). That is the only way to think of unknown truths. As truly unknown and yet knowable, as if they were truly forgotten and yet unforgettable—I mean as if they might be unforgotten. As if they were forgotten and might be forgotten again and yet might always be brought back from disaster.

The dead are dead, and yet we remember. We always hope to remember, to learn, to witness, to mourn. As if we could. As if inheritance were our selves, though nothing as such can be guaranteed to return.

Inheritance is not forgotten by Socrates and Meno.

> If then virtue is an attribute of the spirit, and one which cannot fail to be beneficial, it must be wisdom, for all spiritual qualities in and by themselves are neither advantageous nor harmful, but become advantageous or harmful by the presence with them of wisdom or folly. If we accept this argument, then virtue, to be something advantageous, must be a sort of wisdom. . . .
>
> To go back to the other class of things, wealth and the like, of which we said just now that they are sometimes good and sometimes harmful, isn't it the same with them? Just as wisdom when it governs our other psychological impulses turns them to advantage, and folly turns them to harm, so the mind by its right use and control of these material assets makes them profitable, and by wrong use renders them harmful. (88ce)

Inheritance of spiritual things—beauty, truth, the good, if they are things, if they can be inherited—is wisdom, and perhaps the question before us is how we acquire them, if we acquire them, if beauty, truth, and the good are things to be acquired. Perhaps they are not things, perhaps they are not to acquire but to give, perhaps we inherit them without possessing them, unlike the other class of things, wealth and the like, which we strive to possess.

It is as if the question of how to learn were of inheriting without having, of knowing without possessing, of forgetting as giving and of unforgetting as giving again. I mean of exposition, giving without having.

The conclusion of the dialogue is that virtue arrives from the gods, not perhaps so different from the belief that we always knew it even before we were human, or that it is given without having, as if it were calling and giving.

> On our present reasoning then, whoever has virtue gets it by divine dispensation. But we shall not understand the truth of the matter until, before asking how men get virtue, we try to discover what virtue is in and by itself. Now it is time for me to go, and my request to you is that you will allay the anger of your friend Anytus by convincing him that what you now believe is true. If you succeed, the Athenians may have cause to thank you. (100bc)

We must try to discover something extraordinarily difficult to discover. We must resist those who think they know and those who think it impossible to know. It is as if the good were nothing to know and yet we must endlessly pursue it as if we might know it.

This is the *as if* of exposition, of unforgetting. Let us recall at length the words of the dialogue that concern *anamnēsis*.

> I have heard from men and women who understand the truths of religion...
>
> Those who tell it are priests and priestesses of the sort who make it their business to be able to account for the functions which they perform. Pindar speaks of it too, and many another of the poets who are divinely inspired. What they say is this—see whether you think they are speaking the truth. They say that the soul of man is immortal. At one time it comes to an end—that which is called death—and at another is born again, but is never finally exterminated. On these grounds a man must live all his days as righteously as possible. For those from whom
>
>> Persephone receives requital for ancient doom,
>> In the ninth year she restores again
>> Their souls to the sun above.
>> From whom rise noble kings
>> And the swift in strength and greatest in wisdom,
>> And for the rest of time
>> They are called heroes and sanctified by men.
>
> Thus the soul, since it is immortal and has been born many times, and has seen all things both here and in the other world, has learned everything that is. So we need not be surprised if it can recall the knowledge of virtue or anything else which, as we see, it once possessed. All nature is akin, and the soul has learned everything, so that when a man has recalled a single piece of knowledge—learned it, in ordinary language—there is no reason why he should not find out all the rest, if he keeps a stout heart and does not grow weary of the search, for seeking and learning are in fact nothing but recollection (*anamnēsis*).
>
> We ought not then to be led astray by the contentious argument you quoted. It would make us lazy, and is music in the ears of weaklings. The other doctrine produces energetic seekers after knowledge, and being convinced of its truth, I am ready, with your help, to inquire into the nature of virtue. (81ae)

I have heard, I remember, I unforget. Socrates never claims to discover but as if to have heard, as if to unforget, as if the passing down of forgetting through time in the form of stories and storytelling were the form of knowledge.

Men and women who understand the truths of religion. Both men and women know and understand. All human beings, all souls, none is privileged in truth and knowledge and philosophy. And religion. The truths of religion—and perhaps of science and philosophy—are ancient stories told, and told again, by priests and priestesses of old.

Pindar speaks of it, and many of the poets who are divinely inspired.

> [T]his gift you have of speaking well on Homer is not an art; it is a power divine, impelling you like the power in the stone Euripides called the magnet, which most call "stone of Heraclea." ...For the poets tell us, don't they, that the melodies they bring us are gathered from rills that run with honey, out of glens and gardens of the Muses, and they bring them as the bees do honey, flying like the bees? And what they say is true, for a poet is a light and winged thing, and holy, and never able to compose until he has become inspired, and is beside himself, and reason [*nous*] is no longer in him. So long as he has this in his possession, no man is able to make poetry or to chant in prophecy. (Plato, *Ion*, 533d–4b)

Light and winged and holy. Perhaps we are looking for an unforgetting that is holy, winged, and light, always moving, giving, inspired and inspiring, not a memory or truth fixed in place, freezing our soul. Perhaps it is in poetry that we will find it. Perhaps in philosophy. Perhaps in neither and both. Here is an expression of it. Perhaps you remember, or unforget.

> Everything is such, not such, both such and not such, and neither such nor not such; this is the Buddha's admonition. (Nāgārjuna, *PMW*, 269)

Perhaps this is unforgetting, or exposition, all in the modality of *as if.* I mean that it is *as if* we might say or believe that *what* is forgotten, as a *what* or *being* or *something*, is *such*; that what is *forgotten* is in this way *not such*; that as recollected, known, brought to mind, it is *both such and not such*; and finally, that *as if* forgotten and remembered, *as if* from old, *as if* we always knew and never quite recalled, what is known or true is *neither such nor not such.* The Buddha knew and we recall as if it were always and everywhere known as if it were everywhere and always forgotten. This, perhaps, is unforgetting, *anamnēsis*. The Buddha recalled. Others call this *emptiness, śūnyatā.* Unforgetting is as if it were empty, everything remembered as forgotten.

They say—see whether you think they are speaking the truth. They *say*, Socrates *says*, they tell stories, Socrates tells stories, and in these stories they may speak the truth and we may understand it as truth. It is as if their stories are unforgettings for us and by us as if for them and by them. And *what they say is this*—something to recollect, something—perhaps nothing—in particular.

In particular, then, *the soul*, the animating spirit of each of us and of the earth everywhere, *is immortal*—that is, unforgetting and unforgotten. *It comes to an end—that which is called death—and at another is born again, but is never finally exterminated.* Death is not death. Coming to be is not coming to be. There is no final loss, no ultimate wound. Or else what we must learn—if it is something to learn—is how to live in remembrance—I mean unforgetting—of disaster. For *on these grounds a man must live all his days as right-eously as possible.* On these grounds indeed, if they are grounds. But the result, the imperative, is to live as well as possible. So we may conclude that unforgetting is the question, imperative, de-mand of justice, the call from the good. If that is anything in par-ticular.

Pindar's poem is explicit: Persephone—goddess of life in the midst of death, of joy in the midst of sorrow, of goodness in the midst of disaster—*receives requital for ancient doom.* Requital and restitution in Anaximander's words for a doom so archaic as to have been forgotten. Still demanding requital, restoration, unfor-getting. From and in this ancient doom, noble kings and heroes of strength and wisdom come forth. One might imagine this to be a tale of immemorial disaster from which the good emerges, shining and ringing, as if it were nothing, unforgotten as nothing in par-ticular. Here the nothing is not not death, but neither is it death. The good is not something, but neither is it nothing. The Buddha's admonition is unforgetting of what—I mean of nothing that—is unforgotten. Still it is possible to live as well as possible, heroi-cally, in the nothing of unforgetting.

Leading us perhaps to ask, what is it to live as well as possi-ble, to live finally? and is that something to learn, something to know, something to teach? And if not, what then might we learn from it and how? What might we unearth of living in and on the earth?

The soul is immortal—has always been present. Yet it *has been born many times*, coming and going, and *has seen all things both here and in the other world*, and *has learned everything that is.* Born many times, seen all things, in this world and beyond, having learned every-thing that is: these are escalations from many to infinity. Why should we imagine these as possibilities for any present? I mean, how can we take this as a truth to be known and possessed rather than as if a story of a being as if it might be present though it were impossible for it to be so, always becoming, on the move? Perhaps this is the modality of unforgetting—I mean exposition: to know or believe or express what is impossible as if it were necessary. As if we were all to be, as Irigaray says, "a political militant for the impossible, which is not to say a utopian. Rather, what I want is yet to be as the only possibility of a future" (Irigaray, *ILTY*, 10). As yet to be as if the only possibility in the midst of countless others.

When a person has recalled one thing he can *know anything*. This is the article of faith for anyone who hopes to know—philosopher, scientist, or ordinary person. All the forms and ways of knowledge, no matter how glorious or restricted, are there for seeking. That is, for unearthing. This is the article of faith of questioning— overstated to be sure. To question we must be able to go from what we know to what we do not—but not perhaps from just anywhere to anything, not perhaps to infinity, to everything, and never perhaps to know anything as if grasped in hand. Questioning demands not grasping but giving, moving, pursuing. Questioning demands *a stout heart* and *never growing weary of the search*. *Anamnēsis* is an expression of the call of questioning to which exposition is the answering—all as if unforgetting, where nothing in particular is forgotten. To inquire—that is, to question—is to unforget as if in a way that knowing is not—or perhaps I mean that unforgetting is (before) questioning. Unforgetting is the exposition of the question before the question, questioning before there is any question or knowledge or anything in particular to know. Derrida, after Heidegger, recalls it as *Zusage*:

> "Before" the question (which always presupposes language) there is a kind of consent to language, which belongs to it without truly belonging to it. And this he calls *Zusage*. *Zusage* is a manner of consenting, of saying "yes," to language, to the call. There is a "yes" there (which is a kind of consent, of *Gelassenheit*) more originary even than the questioning. (Derrida, *N*, 40)

What—if anything, nothing—is unforgotten is this exposition of what is before the question, before questioning, the call from the good to language—I would say to exposition. It is the affirmation of a call to life, to being, to truth, to unearthing, that appears to be anything and everything but affirmative. In this way it is forgotten, in its immemoriality and its wounds. And in this way as well it is affirmed in unforgetting, as unforgetting.

We ought not then to be led astray; we should not be lazy, we should be energetic seekers after knowledge; we should be convinced of this truth. This, perhaps, is the truth of truth, that it is something to be sought even if it can never be had. This, perhaps, is the truth of remembering that we forget, that we are to seek to remember as we forget. This, perhaps, is the forgotten, the *as if* that questions us constantly of what we forget when we seek to remember.

What is forgotten, what is forgetting, what are the questioning and call from the good that exceed every answer? What is forgetting, what is forgotten, is the call to answer and the responsiveness by which we answer. What we answer we forget. In another register:

> it is—
> as if we cannot know,
> as if Socrates does not know,
> we must inquire as if we can know,
> must live as if we can live well,
> the good is living as if in a story recalled from long ago,

as if from before and long ago:

> 1. Something is always forgotten. We can never remember everything. Remembering is an endless struggle to unearth the image of what we have lost.
> 2. There is an irresistible will to remember what has been forgotten, an irresistible fascination with remembering—I mean unforgetting—beyond any possibility of a return.
> 3. Unforgetting is itself forgotten, and in the caesura of this second forgetting everything comes back as if it were remembered. Everything comes back beyond any remembering and forgetting. In the caesura of *as if*. And *perhaps*.

Every one of these forgettings takes place in the modality of *as if*. The modality of *as if* is unforgetting.

CHAPTER 2

Re-membering

> Memory is, therefore, neither perception nor conception, but a state or affection of one of these, conditioned by lapse of time. As already observed, there is no such thing as memory of the present while present; for the present is object only of perception, and the future, of expectation, but the object of memory is the past. All memory, therefore, implies a time elapsed; consequently only those animals which perceive time remember, and the organ whereby they perceive time is also that whereby they remember. (Aristotle, *OM*, 449b24–30)

*T*o unforget is to return from forgetting, to re-member nothing as if it were anything, to interrupt oblivion with exposition, to re-call the sound of silence and unearth the depths of loss. Memory is another matter, perhaps. Memory appears as if it were something, fixed by the past, elusive but fully present once retained. If anything can be fully present. Unforgetting passes through the caesura of absence on the way to an other presence.

Aristotle speaks of the object of memory as defined by time, as if time might be definite and defining although it is always on the way to being lost. Perception, conception, imagination, expectation, and memory all have definite objects differing by time. We remember an object perceived in an elapsed time but we cannot remember the present or future. One might imagine this as one place where unforgetting appears. We may not remember the future, but we may unforget it in the mode of *as if*. It is not simply and irrevocably not present. It is present in the present and in the past as they are unforgotten. It is present as if on the way to being lost.

Aristotle appears to recall the modality of *as if* in the context of memory.

> Accordingly, if asked, of which among the parts of the soul memory is a function, we reply: manifestly of that part to which imagination also appertains; and all objects of which there is imagination are in themselves objects of memory, while those which do not exist without imagination are objects of memory incidentally. (450a21–450a25)

> It is clear that we must conceive that which is generated through sense-perception in the soul, and in the part of the body which is its seat,—viz. that affection the state whereof we call memory— to be some such thing as a picture. The process of movement stamps in, as it were, a sort of impression of the percept, just as persons do who make an impression with a seal. This explains why, in those who are strongly moved owing to passion, or time of life, no memory is formed; just as no impression would be formed if the movement of the seal were to impinge on running water; while there are others in whom, owing to the receiving surface being frayed, as happens to old walls, or owing to the hardness of the receiving surface, the requisite impression is not implanted at all. Hence both very young and very old persons are defective in memory; they are in a state of flux, the former because of their growth, the latter, owing to their decay. Similarly, both those who are too quick and those who are too slow have bad memories. The former are too moist, the latter too hard, so that in the case of the former the image does not remain in the soul, while on the latter it is not imprinted at all. (450a26–450b10)

Some such thing as a picture—as if it were an image, as if imprinted and stamped in, as if that stamp were not always ambiguous, too imaginative, too mechanical and more than mechanical, too moist or too hard or too something else. As if it were a printing press and as if printing were a perfected form of memory instead of decay. If we understand imprinting as decay, not only for the old and infirm, who are themselves decayed, if we understand moist and hard as figures of decay, we can understand memory as image differently from Aristotle.

> As regards the question, therefore, what memory or remembering is, it has now been shown that it is the having of an image, related as a likeness to that of which it is an image; and as to the question of which of the faculties within us memory is a function, it has been shown that it is a function of the primary

faculty of sense-perception, i.e., of that faculty whereby we perceive time. (451a15–451a17)

> The image, at first sight, does not resemble the cadaver, but it is possible that the rotting, decaying, cadaverous strangeness might also be from the image. (Blanchot, *el*, 344 (*TVI*) [my translation])

The image or picture—I mean the memory, perhaps the unforgetting—does not resemble the cadaver, but proliferates and decays on three levels of ambiguity.[1]

> On the worldly plane it is the possibility of give and take: meaning always escapes into another meaning; . . . we never come to an understanding once and for all. . . .
> . . . Here [the second level] it is no longer a question of perpetual double meanings—of misunderstandings aiding or impeding agreement. Here what speaks in the name of the image "sometimes" [*tantôt*: presently, soon, in a little while, yet to come, maybe someday, ever; deferring, postponing—all *as if, perhaps*] still speaks of the world, and "sometimes" [perhaps someday] introduces us into the undetermined milieu of fascination. . . . However, what we distinguish by saying "sometimes, sometimes," [« *tantôt, tantôt* »: presently, presently, later, later, soon, soon] ambiguity introduces by "always," [*toujour*, without the quotation marks] at least to a certain extent, saying both one and the other. . . . Here *meaning* does not escape into another meaning, but into the *other* of all meaning. Because of ambiguity nothing has meaning, but everything *seems* infinitely meaningful. Meaning is no longer anything but semblance; semblance makes meaning become infinitely rich. It makes this infinitude of meaning have no need of development—makes meaning immediate, which is also to say incapable of being developed, only immediately void [*vide*: empty]. (263)

What is immediately empty is forgotten; the image is this unforgetting in the mode of semblance, *as if*. The image or picture appears as if it were something present, and as if it were something else, proliferating and decaying.

> A picture painted on a panel is at once a picture and a likeness: that is, while one and the same, it is both of these, although the being of both is not the same, and one may contemplate it either as a picture, or as a likeness. Just in the same way we have to conceive that the image within us is both something in itself and relative to something else. In so far as it is regarded in itself, it is only an object of contemplation, or an image; but when consid-

ered as relative to something else, e.g., as its likeness, it is also a reminder. (Aristotle, *OM*, 450b11–451a2)

If it is a picture it may not be a likeness. If it is a memory it may be nothing to remember. As image it proliferates and decays as if to transfigure any likeness. Picture, likeness, repetition fix nothing in memory, are always on the move.

Aristotle distinguishes recollection from memory, where the latter is the implantation and the former its reinstatement. Even here, however, recollection is different from learning.

> But even the assertion that recollection is the reinstatement of something which was there before requires qualification—it is right in one way, wrong in another. For the same person may twice learn, or twice discover the same fact. Accordingly, the act of recollecting ought to be distinguished from these acts; i.e., recollecting must imply in those who recollect the presence of some source over and above that from which they originally learn. (451b6–451b10)

> If this order be necessary, whenever a subject experiences the former of two movements thus connected, it will experience the latter; if, however, the order be not necessary, but customary, only for the most part will the subject experience the latter of the two movements. But it is a fact that there are some movements, by a single experience of which persons take the impress of custom more deeply than they do by experiencing others many times; hence upon seeing some things but once we remember them better than others which we may have seen frequently. (451b12–451b16)

Right in one way, wrong in another, as perhaps are any truth and any memory, as if they were re-collection. We may twice or more learn or understand or grasp the truth that then departs in its multiplicity. We may twice or more by necessity understand that the image is never necessary.

One way to read this account is as if it were a mechanics of remembering. Another is as an account of unforgetting, by which I mean that the movements that are connected in a customary way are always more than mechanical. This is true as well in Spinoza: the mechanical operations of perception and memory open up materially and infinitely.

> P17: If the human Body is affected with a mode that involves the nature of an external body, the human Mind will regard the same external body as actually existing, or as present to it, until

the Body is affected by an affect that excludes the existence or presence of that body. (Spinoza, *E*, Pt. 2)

While external bodies so determine the fluid parts of the human body that they often thrust against the softer parts, they change (by Post. 5) their surfaces with the result (see A2 after L3) that they are reflected from it in another way than they used to be before, and still later, when the fluid parts, by their spontaneous motion, encounter those new surfaces, they are reflected in the same way as when they were driven against those surfaces by the external bodies. Consequently, while, thus reflected, they continue to move, they will affect the human Body with the same mode, concerning which the Mind (by P12) will think again, i.e., (by P17), the Mind will again regard the external body as present; this will happen as often as the fluid parts of the human body encounter the same surfaces by their spontaneous motion. So although the external bodies by which the human Body has once been affected do not exist, the Mind will still regard them as present, as often as this action of the body is repeated, q.e.d. (Cor. Dem.)

P18: If the human Body has once been affected by two or more bodies at the same time, then when the Mind subsequently imagines one of them, it will immediately recollect the others also. . . .

Schol.: From this we clearly understand what Memory is. For it is nothing other than a certain connection of ideas involving the nature of things which are outside the human Body—a connection that is in the Mind according to the order and connection of the affections of the human Body.

[83] What, then, will memory be? Nothing but a sensation of impressions on the brain, together with the thought of a determinate duration of the sensation, which recollection also shows. For there the soul thinks of that sensation, but not under a continuous duration. And so the idea of that sensation is not the duration itself of the sensation, i.e., the memory itself. (Spinoza, *TEI*, 36)

The fluid parts of the body move, touch other body surfaces—a mechanical account of imagination and memory. Memory is nothing but a connection of material sensations. The mind is affected by external bodies. Yet this affectation is infinite, and infinitely infinite, in the caesura of *as if*.

[N]o one has yet determined what the Body can do. . . . the Body . . . can do many things which its Mind wonders at. (Spinoza, *E*, Pt. 3, P2, Sch).

P14: The human Mind is capable of perceiving a great many things, and is the more capable, the more its body can be disposed in a great many ways. (Pt. 2)

P39: He who has a Body capable of a great many things has a Mind whose greatest part is eternal. (Pt. 5)

Here the mechanics of memory, by necessity, promote a infinite multiplicity. In this way remembering is re-membering, recollection is re-collection, and the image proliferates and decays. The mind passes from one idea and thing to another beyond limit. We do not know what the body or mind or memory can do, and remembering is the wonder of unforgetting.

> The decay of sense in men waking, is not the decay of the motion made in sense; but an obscuring of it, ... This *decaying sense*, when we would express the thing it self, (I mean *fancy* it selfe,) we call *imagination*, as I said before: but when we would express the *decay*, and signify that the sense is fading, old, and past, it is called *memory*. So that *imagination* and *memory* are but one thing, which for divers considerations with a hath divers names. (Hobbes, *L*, 88–9)

> Much memory, or memory of many things, is called *experience*. Again, imagination being only of those things which have been formerly perceived by sense, either all at once, or by parts at several times; the former, (which is the imagining the whole object, as it was presented to the sense) is *simple imagination*; as when one imagineth a man, or horse, which he hath seen before. The other is *compounded*; as when from the sight of a man at one time, and of a horse at another, we conceive in our mind a Centaur. So when a man compoundeth the image of his own person, with the image of the actions of another man; as when a man imagines himself a *Hercules* or an *Alexander*, (which happeneth often to them that are much taken with reading of romances) it is a compound imagination, and properly but a fiction of the mind. (89)

Imagination and memory are but one thing, which in a diverse world has many diverse names. Memory is a multifarious, imaginary thing filled with decaying and proliferating images beyond containment. The decay of sense is as it were fiction, fancy, imagination, memory, as if forgetting constituted memory, as if we desired to have forever what cannot be had. At least that is what Hobbes says of desire.

[T]he object of man's desire, is not to enjoy once only, and for one instant of time; but to assure for ever, the way of his future desire. . . .

. . . I put for a general inclination of all mankind, a perpetual and restless desire of power after power, that ceaseth only in death. (Hobbes, *L*, 161)

We desire to possess for ever, not only things but truths, images, memories, our selves, and other people. And yet we find ourselves in a perpetual restlessness of power and desire, perpetual proliferation and decay, forgetting and unforgetting. Hobbes takes for granted that this is something we do not desire, and many read him as sacrificing too much to the desire to grasp securely. Yet it is possible to enjoy the proliferation: power after power, desire after desire, risk after risk, image after image, as exposition. The names Hobbes gives to exposition are imagination, memory, and fiction. Though he appears to desire veracity he dwells among the phantasms.

The perpetual arising of phantasms, both in sense and imagination, is that which we commonly call discourse of the mind, and is common to men with other living creatures. For he that thinketh, compareth the phantasms that pass, that is, taketh notice of their likeness or unlikeness to one another. . . . Now this observation of differences is not perception made by a common organ of sense, distinct from sense or perception properly so called, but is memory of the differences of particular phantasms remaining for some time; as the distinction between hot and lucid, is nothing else but the memory both of a heating, and of an enlightening object. (Hobbes, *EOP*, 399)

But it happens sometimes, that words although they have a certain and defined signification by constitution, yet by vulgar use either to adorn or deceive, they are so wrested from their own significations, that to remember the conceptions for which they were first imposed on things, is very hard, and not to be mastered but by a sharp judgment and very great diligence. It happens too that there are many words, which have no proper, determined, and everywhere the same signification; and are understood not by their own, but by virtue of other signs used together with them. Thirdly, there are some words of things unconceivable. Of those things, therefore, whereof they are the words, there is no conception; and therefore in vain do we seek for the truth of those propositions, which they make out of the words themselves. (Hobbes, *DC*, 302)

To know truth is to remember it in relation to words—I mean language, semblance, exposition—something that is very hard, as if words were understood as if by unforgetting. There are many words that cannot be remembered, many propositions that cannot be recalled as true. Perhaps they can be re-membered and re-called, that is, called up again in the mode of questioning.

In British empiricism, memory is stationed in the mind beyond any questioning. This is true from the first in Locke and Hume, with Hobbes a more phantasmatic example. Like Hobbes, Locke employs memory to define what is present to the mind as if it were held in memory. This doubling of memory can be understood as a certain reading of *anamnēsis*. To know is to remember.

> If there be any innate ideas, any ideas in the mind, which the mind does not actually think on, they must be lodged in the memory, and from thence must be brought into view by remembrance; i.e., must be known, when they are remembered, to have been perceptions in the mind before, unless remembrance can be without remembrance. (Locke, *E*, 109)

> The use I make of this, is, that whatever idea, being not actually in view, is in the mind, is there only by being in the memory; and if it be not in the memory, it is not in the mind; and if it be in the memory, it cannot by the memory be brought into actual view, without a perception that it comes out of the memory; which is this, that it had been known before, and is now remembered. (111)

> Thus a man that remembers certainly that he once perceived the demonstration, that the three angles of a triangle are equal to two right ones, is certain that he knows it, because he cannot doubt the truth of it.... But he knows it in a different way from what he did before. The agreement of the two ideas joined in that proposition is perceived, but it is by the intervention of other ideas than those which at first produced that perception. He remembers, i.e., he knows (for remembrance is but the reviving of some past knowledge) that he was once certain of the truth of this proposition, that the three angles of a triangle are equal to two right ones. The immutability of the same relations between the same immutable things, is now the idea that shows him, that if the three angles of a triangle were once equal to two right ones, they will always be equal to two right ones. And hence he comes to be certain, that what was once true in the case, is always true; what ideas once agreed, will always agree; and consequently what he once knew to be true, he will always know to be true; as long as he can remember that he once knew it.... But because the memory is not always so clear as actual perception,

and does in all men more or less decay in length of time, this amongst other differences is one, which shows that demonstrative knowledge is much more imperfect than intuitive, ... (173–5)

11. As when our senses are actually employed about any object, we do know that it does exist; so by our memory we may be assured, that heretofore things that affected our senses have existed. And thus we have knowledge of the past existence of several things, whereof our senses having informed us, our memories still retain the ideas; and of this we are past all doubt, so long as we remember well. But this knowledge also reaches no farther than our senses have formerly assured us. (336)

It is tempting to emphasize the skeptical side of this view, that memory is no more reliable than sensory experience, that demonstrative knowledge and logical truths are similarly unreliable. It is a wonderful insight that all the truths we hold dear rely on memory and on the preservation of time. A similar note is sounded in Descartes, who insists that God preserves the existence of my self and the world against the possibility that it might end at any moment.

For a lifespan can be divided into countless parts, each completely independent of the others, so that it does not follow from the fact that I existed a little while ago that I must exist now, unless there is some cause which as it were creates me afresh at this moment—that is, which preserves me. For it is quite clear to anyone who attentively considers the nature of time that the same power and action are needed to preserve anything at each individual moment of its duration as would be required to create that thing anew if it were not yet in existence. Hence the distinction between preservation and creation is only a conceptual one, and this is one of the things that are evident by the natural light. (Descartes, M, 3, 33)

The note is similar in Descartes but for his purposes entirely subordinated to proof. There must be necessity and proof in every moment, in every preservation and creation. The distinction between creation and preservation is conceptual—that is, they are inseparable but irreducible. And so, perhaps, with remembering and forgetting. They are not opposites but inseparable and irreducible, beyond interweaving, so that forgetting is not subsumed under remembering. Nothing can prove existence; nothing can guarantee remembering. Preservation is creation, forgetting is remembering, memory is loss and decay. These are all they can be and do without proof and guarantees. Descartes insists on proof. For Locke, time and memory are the glue that holds the world together—world and being and identity and truth. But it is a glue that cannot hold, it works by failing to hold. It exposes the caesura, the wound, between remembering and forgetting, the wound of loss and time, of one and the other. Heterogeneity is this wound, what is forgotten is heterogeneous.

The caesura between one moment and another, one thing and another, one time and space and thing and person and another, the caesura in myself that is my self, is heterogeneous. The caesura in forgetting is the re-appearance of the other, and nothing—call it god—can make it whole. Nothing can prove that the other is myself, that the past is the present, that the present appearance is the past again, that what is here is again what was there. Time and space and materiality are riven by alterity. *Tout autre est tout autre*, as Derrida says. Every other is wholly other, every other is lost and forgotten in the caesura of here and there, now and then, the one and the other, the always more than one of heterogeneity and multiplicity.

This is a wonderful insight, but it remains within the modern ontological and epistemological project to show and reveal and prove what cannot be proven. By this I mean not so much to emphasize the proving or unproving but the solidity and continuity that time and memory provide—or fail to provide. Against this providing of memory, forgetting fails to provide, not as if it were a lack of memory, failing memory's task, but as if that were not forgetting's task. Similarly, perhaps, it is not the task of philosophy to provide proof but, again perhaps, another knowledge without proof, as if the world might be present without solidity and continuity, in the mode of forgetting—I mean in the mode of *as if*.

Here, then, working backward, where Locke insists that memory assures us of the existence of objects, but not after all so far, no further than our senses take us, we may imagine that forgetting assures us of nothing, not even of the nonexistence of objects, nor their existence, but their appearing and disappearing, no matter how fleeting or evanescent. Our memories retain ideas as if they were present when not, as if they were not present when they are, as if they were simulacra. We forget forgetting in the remembrance of memory.

What kind of knowledge might be provided by a forgotten memory? Certainly not the assurance of presence, certainly not retention as if ready to hand. Perhaps the inassurance of presence,

or the assurance of absence as well as presence, perhaps a retention that is always on the edge of loss. Perhaps the subject of
memory in Locke is not of time as held and fixed but as always
being lost, as always disappearing, of forgetting as this losing. Not
as if losing what might be retained, as the disappearance of what
has appeared or might reappear, but loss and disappearance as the
constitution of being and truth.

What kind of knowledge would this be? What kind of truth or
recollection? Not a knowledge that we can be certain can be
known again, but almost certainly one that is on the verge of disappearance, transformation, creation, transfiguration, interruption. Not a recollection of an earlier presence, but the invention of
a disparity in the disparition of the collection.

In a way the issue is of the wholly new, the other. In a way it is
of the wholly recalled, the same. In a way it is the dialectic of same
and other. Yet the relation of forgetting to memory is not a dialectic and knows nothing of same and other. Forgetting is wholly
other—if there be anything whole, anything other, if everything is
not other. *Tout autre est tout autre.* That is the motto of forgetting.
We forget the *tout* and the *autre*, the all and the other—I mean the
others. No matter how hard we try to remember we forget ourselves and the others, and still others. This is as true scientifically
and epistemologically—perhaps I mean especially true—as ethically and politically. No matter how hard we try to agree we differ; no matter how hard we try to differ we agree, repeat, recollect.
These are not opposites or alternatives but the very truth of being,
truth, and forgetting. Forgetting is the being of truth and of being
and remembering. Without empirical memory, experienced and
sensory repetition, there can be no truth, no logic, demonstration,
or philosophy—indeed, no life itself. Time—I mean space and
world and all the modalities of loss—is the mystery of being, and
to nonbeing. The key is unforgetting, unearthing.

In case you may have forgotten, memory is a critical faculty in
Hume. I mean the condition that constitutes experience.

> We find, by experience, that when any impression has been
> present with the mind, it again makes its appearance there as an
> idea; and this it may do after two different ways: either when, in
> its new appearance, it retains a considerable degree of its first
> vivacity, and is somewhat intermediate betwixt an impression
> and an idea; or when it entirely loses that vivacity, and is a per-
> fect idea. The faculty by which we repeat our impressions in the
> first manner, is called the memory, and the other the imagina-
> tion. It is evident, at first sight, that the ideas of the memory are

much more lively and strong than those of the imagination, and that the former faculty paints its objects in more distinct colours than any which are employed by the latter. When we remember any past event, the idea of it flows in upon the mind in a forcible manner; whereas, in the imagination, the perception is faint and languid, and cannot, without difficulty, be preserved by the mind steady and uniform for any considerable time. (Hume, *T*, Pt. 1, Bk. 1, Sec. 3, 8–9)

No one can take seriously the force and vivacity on which Hume places such emphasis. More or less seriously, one may ascribe it to his own vivacity and force—I mean the desire and will that pervade his philosophy, the will to know the difference between memory and imagination. This will to knowledge and truth is what drives the epistemological project. I would emphasize the forgetting essential to giving up that project.

For we imagine that we know the difference between memory and imagination most of the time. And if this knowledge and this difference do not guarantee certainty and accommodate error, we may imagine that through controlled methods of writing and organization we may authenticate our knowledge even as it remains corrigible and contingent.[2] These are methods of remembering, of course, not of imagination, which is allowed free play. But we can make ourselves remember and remember that we remember. Perhaps.

If we give up or minimize the epistemological project, then it is not so much memory's assurance that we may find emphasized in Hume, nor its force, but the central role that memory—I mean unforgetting—plays in his view of experience. We indeed imagine, we construct ideas from the pieces provided by experience, but experience itself is constituted by memory. The nature of impressions is to impress, to leave imprints on the mind and experience, to give themselves over to memory as ideas.

It is therefore by experience only that we can infer the existence of one object from that of another. The nature of experience is this. We remember to have had frequent instances of the existence of one species of objects; and also remember, that the individuals of another species of objects have always attended them, and have existed in a regular order of contiguity and succession with regard to them. Thus we remember to have seen that species of object we call flame, and to have felt that species of sensation we call heat. We likewise call to mind their constant conjunction in all past instances. Without any further ceremony, we call the one cause, and the other effect, and infer the existence of the one from that of the other. In all those instances from which we learn the conjunction of particular causes and effects, both the causes and effects have been perceived by the senses, and are remembered: but in all cases, wherein we reason concerning them, there is only one perceived or remembered, and the other is supplied in conformity to our past experience. (Pt. 3, Sec. 6, 87)

Ideas are the remembered traces of impressions that come and go, and these traces compose the continuity and reality and gravity of experience. Experience is the repetition of impressions as ideas, preserved as memories. Put another way, consciousness is memory, and memory is preservation and separation. More to the point, memory constitutes existence, what we remember is inseparable from conceiving it as existent. In this way, being and existence are divided and connected through forgetting and remembering.

There is no impression nor idea of any kind, of which we have any consciousness or memory, that is not conceived as existent; and it is evident that, from this consciousness, the most perfect idea and assurance of being is derived. . . .

. . . Though certain sensations may at one time be united, we quickly find they admit of a separation, and may be presented apart. And thus, though every impression and idea we remember be considered as existent, the idea of existence is not derived from any particular impression. (Sec. 6, 66)

Preservation (memory) and creation (imagination) are distinguished in the mind but are not different. This remarkable insight is but a marginal thought in the epistemological project. Of course we must be able to tell the difference between the past and the future, between what we remember and what we forget, between imagination and recollection. Of course we must and of course we do. Yet from the standpoint of forgetting, memory is not preservation but the past regained after it has been lost. A caesura opens between preservation and creation, remembering and forgetting, a caesura that belongs to forgetting and if to memory by way of forgetting, a caesura that haunts the durability and continuity of existence itself.

This is clear in Hume, from beginning to end. And perhaps that is what is so compelling to some of his readers and so repellent to others. Force and vivacity mark remembering over forgetting. Except that imagination is sometimes intense, vivacious, and forceful and memory is sometimes faint. We can and do tell the difference, but not perhaps as assurance and certitude, but as the grip of loss upon remembering—lost time, lost images, lost impressions. I mean, of course, the grip of forgetting—forgotten time, forgotten images, forgotten experiences, the forgetting of being and experience themselves, the forgetting of myself.

If you believe, as Hume appears to, that existence and being are present for us as causes and effects, then arguments concerning them are the stuff of being, remembered and forgotten.

> [W]e may choose any point of history, and consider for what reason we either believe or reject it. . . . It is obvious all this chain of argument or connexion of causes and effects, is at first founded on those characters or letters, which are seen or remembered, and that without the authority either of the memory or senses, our whole reasoning would be chimerical and without foundation. Every link of the chain would in that case hang upon another; but there would not be any thing fixed to one end of it, capable of sustaining the whole; and consequently there would be no belief nor evidence. And this actually is the case with all hypothetical arguments, or reasonings upon a supposition; there being in them neither any present impression, nor belief of a real existence. (Sec. 4, 83)

Real existence rests on cause and effect, cause and effect twice rest on memory, as what is remembered and as what connects causes with their effects. The link of the chain of the world is memory, and it is inseparable from the link of the arguments establishing the chain. In this way, existence is hypothetical, contingent, always on the verge of loss.

Indeed, although the chain is the same in argument as in being, and cause and effect are the same as memory, the caesura reappears between image and proof.

> It frequently happens, that when two men have been engaged in any scene of action, the one shall remember it much better than the other, and shall have all the difficulty in the world to make his companion recollect it. He runs over several circumstances in vain; mentions the time, the place, the company, what was said, what was done on all sides; till at last he hits on some lucky circumstance, that revives the whole, and gives his friend a perfect memory of every thing. Here the person that forgets, receives at first all the ideas from the discourse of the other, with the same circumstances of time and place; though he considers them as mere fictions of the imagination. But as soon as the circumstance is mentioned that touches the memory, the very same ideas now appear in a new light, and have, in a manner, a different feeling from what they had before.

Without any other alteration, beside that of the feeling, they become immediately ideas of the memory, and are assented to. (Bk.
3, Pt. 3, App. 627–8)

Read from the side of memory, this passage addresses the difficulty and unreliability of helping someone remember. Read from
the side of forgetting, it calls our attention to factors and elements
that are typically obscured: disparities in remembering and forgetting, the elusiveness of an impression or idea, the heterogeneity of
effective examples, the fictiveness of imagination, finally, the dependence of memory on affect and feeling. Here these disparate
elements become or produce a perfect memory, or give the sense
of perfect memory—as if such a memory could be perfect. The perfection is an affect, as is every other component. Indeed, the other
way to put this is that from the standpoint of forgetting, every
component of memory is altogether other. Every memory is altogether other to perfection, argument, and proof. Nothing but memory—I mean forgetting—can justify a memory. Clearly this means
anything but that memory justifies itself.

If we turn from the affect to the image, the scene plays itself
out again, full of decay. In memory Hume anticipates Blanchot
and the decay of the image.

> A painter, who intended to represent a passion or emotion of
> any kind, would endeavour to get a sight of a person actuated by
> a like emotion, in order to enliven his ideas, and give them a
> force and vivacity superior to what is found in those, which are
> mere fictions of the imagination. The more recent this memory is,
> the clearer is the idea; and when, after a long interval, he would
> return to the contemplation of his object, he always finds its idea
> to be much decayed, if not wholly obliterated. . . .
>
> And as an idea of the memory, by losing its force and vivac-
> ity, may degenerate to such a degree, as to be taken for an idea of
> the imagination; so, on the other hand, an idea of the imagina-
> tion may acquire such a force and vivacity, as to pass for an idea
> of the memory, and counterfeit its effects on the belief and
> judgment. (Bk. 1, Pt. 1, Sec. 5, 85)

From the standpoint of memory—I mean of knowledge and
truth—the issue is the passing of an idea for an impression, taking
on the appearance of truth. Degeneration and decay are a falling
away from truth. From the standpoint of the image—associated
here with forgetting—the key terms are passion, affect, emotion,
fiction, imagination, counterfeit, and decay. The image is fictive
and counterfeit, in the productive mode of imagination and *as if*.

Memory is never just memory but appears as if in the form of an image. The truth is never just truth but appears as if in the form of a counterfeit. The key to the image is its proliferation—that is, its appearance again in alteration. Proliferation and forgetting are the same.

That is almost what Hume says. I mean he says that the world is nothing but memory. All we need to do is to add forgetting, to understand remembering from the standpoint of forgetting, to understand and mean in the modalities of *perhaps* and *as if*.

> It is evident, that whatever is present to the memory, striking upon the mind with a vivacity which resembles an immediate impression, must become of considerable moment in all the operations of the mind, and must easily distinguish itself above the mere fictions of the imagination. Of these impressions or ideas of the memory we form a kind of system, comprehending whatever we remember to have been present, either to our internal perception or senses; and every particular of that system, joined to the present impressions, we are pleased to call a reality. But the mind stops not here. For finding, that with this system of perceptions there is another connected by custom, or, if you will, by the relation of cause or effect, it proceeds to the consideration of their ideas; and as it feels that it is in a manner necessarily determined to view these particular ideas, and that the custom or relation, by which it is determined, admits not of the least change, it forms them into a new system, which it likewise dignifies with the title of realities. The first of these systems is the object of the memory and senses; the second of the judgment.
>
> It is this latter principle which peoples the world, and brings us acquainted with such existences as, by their removal in time and place, lie beyond the reach of the senses and memory. By means of it I paint the universe in my imagination, and fix my attention on any part of it I please. I form an idea of Rome, which I neither see nor remember, but which is connected with such impressions as I remember to have received from the conversation and books of travellers and historians. This idea of Rome I place in a certain situation on the idea of an object which I call the globe. I join to it the conception of a particular government, and religion, and manners. I look backward and consider its first foundation, its several revolutions, successes, and misfortunes. All this, and every thing else which I believe, are nothing but ideas, though, by their force and settled order, arising from custom and the relation of cause and effect, they distinguish themselves from the other ideas, which are merely the offspring of the imagination. (Pt. 3, Sec. 9, 107)

From the standpoint of the epistemological project, memory must establish a standard of proof superior to fiction and imagination. We have seen that it cannot do so. And we may then despair of fulfilling the project of knowledge. Yet from the standpoint of forgetting, the standard of proof is not a standard but another fiction, the key mode of forgetting is *as if*. Thus, memory appears as if it were superior and more truthful than imagination. We form a kind of system—as if it were a system, as if every part belonged to that system, as if it were a reality. We are pleased to call it such. And then by custom—another fictive mode of forgetting—we produce other systems, other realities. The first of these systems is the world of memory and sensation, the second of the aesthetic judgment.

It is by this that we people the world, relate to others, cross between one and the other, overcome or overshadow or overpaint what is otherwise removed in time and place, lies beyond memory and sense. The world for us in its alterities and caesuras lies in the fictions and images that we can produce. Force and order replace the chaos and disorder of the unruly imagination. Forgetting haunts both as the condition of their possibility. In truth.

The being of the world proceeds by forgetting in the loss of time and the caesuras of images.

CHAPTER 3

Unremembering

Into those things from which existing things have their coming into being, their passing away, too, takes place, according to what must be; for they make reparation to one another for their injustice according to the ordinance of time....(Anaximander fragment; Simplicius *Phys.*, 24, 18 [DK 12 B 1]; trans. Robinson, *EGP*, 34)

[T]o remember and to bear witness to something that is constitutively *forgotten*, not only in each individual mind, but in the very thought of the West. (Lyotard, "*HJ*," 141)

To bear witness to the differend. (Lyotard, *DPD*, xiii)

[I]n witnessing, one also exterminates. (*I*, 204)

Reality is composed of the *différend*.[1]

*T*o bear witness...to what? What is it to bear witness? To re-member, to write, to speak, perhaps to unforget? To bear witness to what is forgotten in constituting the west, or east, perhaps in kin and kind? In witness to what is constitutively forgotten, as if witnessing were disconstitutively unforgetting, as if perhaps by unremembering?

As if unremembering were...what? Perhaps we cannot say. Perhaps we can know it in relation to kin and kind, in relation to injustice and disaster. What we are to remember, I mean perhaps to unforget, is the trauma that constitutes our kin and kind. As if we could forget.

Reality, existence, being are composed of the *différend*, of alterity, difference, caesuras, betweens; of forgettings, where what is

forgotten is unremembered as if it were an irreparable wound—
the disaster of being something or someone. Being takes place as if
in the trauma of coming to be, the injustice in justice, witnessing,
recalling, remembering, unforgetting what is forgotten in coming
to be. The wound is coming to be as if a member of kin or kind,
the disaster of assembling and the dissembling of forgetting.

Ah, the dissembling of forgetting—and unforgetting! The exposition and betrayal of being. To bear witness is to expose the
injustice of being as if to answer to its betrayal—and to give another. Peace is won in the betrayal of war; justice comes in the betrayal of injustice, in forgetting memories of wounds and suffering; witness is borne in sorrow and joy. "Are we obligated to
remember people and events from the past? If we are, what is the
nature of this obligation?...Who are the 'we' who may be obligated to remember...?" (Margalit, *EM*, 7).[2]

Who are we who must remember—if we must—and what are
we to remember? People and events from the past? *Who and what*?
And what, I have asked, are we to forget, what might not be
within our power to remember, what might we choose to forget?
With what injustice?

> The formative prison metaphor in philosophy...is Plato's
> parable of the cave....Plato leads us to conclude that, way back
> in the past, we knew what we were looking for but then some-
> how forgot it. The search for knowledge is therefore an exercise
> in reminiscence, that is, an effort to recall and recollect that
> which we once knew.
>
> In our own time, the formative metaphor is not Plato's cave
> but rather Freud's prison. In his prison ward of the unconscious,
> disturbing memories are locked up by a censor-jailer. They are
> removed from consciousness, but they are not destroyed; Freud's
> metaphor is the prison of repression, not the guillotine of forget-
> fulness. (1–2)

Margalit reads Plato as if knowledge were the recollection of
what we once knew. I do not deny that Plato's Socrates says this,
but I have suggested a different emphasis, upon the forgetting
rather than the remembering. The metaphors of prison and cave
that express our being in the world carry the sense, no matter how
ideal, of being released into air and sun. In other words, the forgotten is not constitutive of our being but peripheral even as if it
might be necessary. We live in a cave but the philosopher journeys
toward the light. We can escape the prison of repression. I am by
no means sure of either the prison or the escape.

And so perhaps the question changes, not whether or what we must remember but who we are who are to remember and is this remembering *who we are?* Even here, the question calls for amplification. Is this *who we are* generic, existential, given from being in general, or does it pertain to specific kin and kind—modern European for example? And again, must we choose, or does the existential disaster to which we must bear witness present itself as unforgotten in the constitution of who we are as human, as singular existents, as well as in kin and kind? What are the limits of unforgetting, and are they what we must unremember?

Nietzsche reads Greek tragedy, especially Aeschylus, from the standpoint of the great pairing of Dionysus and Apollo.

> Through Apollo and Dionysus, the two art deities of the Greeks, we come to recognize that in the Greek world there existed a tremendous opposition, in origin and aims, ... (Nietzsche, *BT*, #1)

> This joyous necessity of the dream experience has been embodied by the Greeks in their Apollo . . . the "shining one," the deity of light, ruler over the beautiful illusion of the inner world of fantasy. The higher truth, the perfection of these states in contrast to the incompletely intelligible, everyday world, this deep consciousness of nature, healing and helping in sleep and dreams, is at the same time the symbolical analogue of the soothsaying faculty and of the arts generally, which make life possible and worth living. But we must also include in our image of Apollo that delicate boundary which the dream image must not overstep . . . so in the midst of a world of torments the individual human being sits quietly, supported by and trusting in the *principium individuationis.* (#1)

> Under the charm of the Dionysian not only is the union between man and man reaffirmed, but nature which has become alienated, hostile, or subjugated, celebrates once more her reconciliation with her lost son, man. . . .

> In song and dance man expresses himself as a member of a higher community; he has forgotten how to walk and speak and is on the way toward flying into the air, dancing. His very gestures express enchantment. Just as the animals now talk, and the earth yields milk and honey, supernatural sounds emanate from him, too: he feels himself a god, he himself now walks about enchanted, in ecstasy, like the gods he saw walking in his dreams. He is no longer an artist, he has become a work of art: in these paroxysms of intoxication the artistic power of all nature reveals itself to the highest gratification of the primordial unity. (#1)

> From all quarters of the ancient world—to say nothing of the modern—...we can point to the existence of Dionysian festivals,....In nearly every case these festivals centered in extravagant sexual licentiousness, whose waves overwhelmed all family life and its venerable traditions; the most savage natural instincts were unleashed, including even that horrible mixture of sensuality and cruelty which has always seemed to me to be the real "witches' brew."...
>
> ...[Later] The two antagonists were reconciled; the boundary lines to be observed henceforth by each were sharply defined, and there was to be a periodical exchange of gifts of esteem....
>
> The horrible "witches' brew" of sensuality and cruelty becomes ineffective; only the curious blending and duality in the emotions of the Dionysian revelers remind us—as medicines remind us of deadly poisons—of the phenomenon that pain begets joy, that ecstasy may wring sounds of agony from us. At the very climax of joy there sounds a cry of horror or a yearning lamentation for an irretrievable loss. (#2)

Trust and dreams on the one side, sensuality and cruelty on the other. Each can take the world in its grip—and we do well to fear the witches' brew. Yet in the name of that fear another cruelty takes us in hand, and it does not purge us of terror. Trust and faith in reason is faith and trust in another dream—the one that Foucault calls "that other form of madness."[3]

I would read Aeschylus here (and Sophocles elsewhere) from the standpoint of another pair, remembering and forgetting, perhaps neither a duality nor an opposition, where each of Nietzsche's great forces is a forgetting and a remembering, and, moreover, is remembered and forgotten, but most important of all, looks back onto what constitutes it as a recollection of forgetting.

Think first of what Nietzsche says of *Prometheus*—perhaps of Aeschylus elsewhere, the *Oresteia* for example.

> [W]hat is most wonderful...is the profoundly Aeschylean demand for *justice*. The immeasurable suffering of the bold "individual" on the one hand and the divine predicament and intimation of a twilight of the gods of the other,...all this recalls in the strongest possible manner...the Aeschylean view of the world which envisages Moira enthroned above gods and men in eternal justice. (#9)
>
> Whoever understands this innermost kernel of the Prometheus story—namely the necessity of sacrilege imposed upon the titanically striving individual—must also immediately feel how un-

Apollinian this pessimistic notion is. For Apollo wants to grant repose to individual beings precisely by drawing boundaries between them and by again and again calling these to mind as the most sacred laws of the world, with his demands for self-knowledge and measure. . . .

In this respect, the Prometheus of Aeschylus is a Dionysian mask, while in the aforementioned profound demand for justice Aeschylus reveals to the thoughtful his paternal descent from Apollo, the god of individuation and of just boundaries. . . . "All that exists is just and unjust and equally justified in both."

That is your world! and world indeed!— (#9)

Joy and suffering, individuality and frenzy, that is your world, and it is justified, injustice as well as justice. Justice is Apollinian while the mask is Dionysian. Yet if injustice curls itself up inside justice, if injustice comes forth in justice, then both are masked, the one by the will to truth, the other by the will to power, two inseparable wills, living and acting in obscurity. *That is your world!* is the world forgotten—remembered in forgetting. Apollo and Dionysus are both forgotten and both forgetting. The Titans are the forgotten of Greek life. We can thereby see forgetting in action.

For the scene of Aeschylus's *Oresteia* was set a long time ago, in mythic, forgotten time, filled with events that are far too well remembered in their forgetting. For the wondrous story of the heroes of the Trojan war, those who won and those who were vanquished, is framed in memory of the most extreme desecrations and violences. Tantalus was beloved and honored of the gods, and he committed the most heinous crime imaginable, far too hateful for us to remember. And that is not all, for his son, Pelops, who was fed to the gods, himself had two sons, Atreus and Thyestes, who in their struggles were led to repeat Tantalus's crime in another register. Atreus fed Thyestes' children to him at a later banquet, and for that crime all of Atreus's children paid with one crime after another—called retribution—all the way down to Orestes, where the memories and forgettings came to an end.

Here are the generations forward: from Tantalus to Pelops to Atreus to Agamemnon to Orestes, with Niobe and Thyestes and Clytemnestra and Electra in the wings. And here are the generations backward: Orestes pays off Clytemnestra for her crime against Agamemnon, she pays him off for his crime against his daughter Iphigenia, Agamemnon is made to perform this crime by the gods in memory of his father Atreus and his father Pelops and Pelops's father Tantalus. It is not enough that Tantalus forever suffer torments to his body and soul, he must suffer in his children and their children, forever.

This is Anaximander's fragment on the register of vengeance. All things pay retribution for the injustices and crimes that brought them into existence by further infractions in the name of vengeance. Crimes and violations elicit further violations and crimes in the name of vengeance—called goodness—and in the consequences of cruelty visited upon innocent and guilty alike. Here no one is innocent, all are guilty, not only in the restitutions demanded by the crimes but in their dissemination.

And yet, or because, the first crime in this series—if there was a first—was not of human to human but of human to god. Tantalus's banquet, his desecration beyond all desecrations, was the offering of his son as food to the gods. This unthinkable, unrememberable crime is so far beyond the horror of Thyestes' feast upon his sons that we might well imagine saying that human crimes must be remembered so that we may learn something from them and from their punishments, but that crimes against the gods are something to forget. Tantalus's crime is too much to remember and yet we must not forget it—and indeed, who could possibly do so?

Forgetting and remembering here take place in desecration and violation. It is not things, events, and deeds that are to be remembered or forgotten, but the evil and terror of the world, profane and sacred. Terror and evil beyond any remembering.

What are we to do with this crime beyond all crimes? Remember it for what? Remember it as what? Perhaps attempt to forget it? This is not a crime of human against human, Greek against barbarian, Turk against Armenian. It is more than that. And other. How then think of it except as something to be forgotten, and to be remembered as forgotten? This is the thought of remembering and forgetting I would hope to recover, that what we remember is a forgetting, and that what we forget is not to be remembered as if something to remember but as something to forget. That is the positivity of the forgotten, the disaster beyond all disasters—and perhaps the joy beyond all joys. Something we cannot remember, cannot hope to remember, yet must not forget.

The story of Atreus is recalled by Aeschylus as one crime of vengeance after another, all interventions by the gods. It ends with another intervention, to end the series, to forget the horrors, to put vengeful memory to rest. So the story of Atreus, Aeschylus's *Oresteia*, begins and ends with forgetting, perhaps with different forgettings and different forgottens, as if what and how we remember is by forgetting. And more, it is as if the very possibility of life and being, of society and culture, is given in this remembered forgetting.

The *Oresteia* takes place in the midst of this forgetting as a remembering. All writing inhabits this space in which the writing is a remembrance and a reiteration of what cannot be remembered or repeated. I mean of course that even when recalled the events that transpire and their participants disappear in their appearance. It is the nature of writing to make things appear in this disappearance, to appear to remember what is forgotten.

The trilogy begins with *Agamemnon*, whose very first words mark the house of Atreus, which we may take for granted every Greek knew of by heart.

> WATCHMAN. I ask the gods for release from this misery, the year-long watch I lie awake keeping on the roof of the Atreidae, up above here like a dog; .... Whenever I find myself shifting my bed about at night, wet with dew, unvisited by dreams ... I weep in lament for this house's misfortune; it is not managed for the best as it was before. Now I wish for a happy release from misery when so the fire in the dark has appeared with its good news. (Aeschylus, *A*, ll. 1–21)

The misery and misfortune of this house is expressed and accomplished in the murder of its children, one after another. Orestes must suffer for his mother's murder—and who could deny it?—after her own crime against her husband for the murder of their daughter. Some might call it sacrifice, but what sacrifice of a daughter is honorable in a history of crimes against children? Indeed, one might imagine this as the ongoing story of war, the murder of children by children at the behest of their elders, who pursue their gains and goals by crimes against their own as well as others' children.

And where did it begin? Where does the violence begin? It always appears anew as a crime to be avenged, yet the lesson of time is that it never began, always took place before it could have begun. The crime is never the first crime, the joy and happiness are never first, time and history have no beginning and no end, and this immemoriality is both remembered and forgotten.

Of course Agamemnon remembers Atreus's feast, and Atreus remembered Tantalus, and Tantalus remembered—what we do not know and perhaps he forgot. The point is that the events are forgotten as what they are and remembered as they are forgotten. The principle that those who refuse to learn from history are doomed to repeat it appears to imagine that we might so learn, might so remember, even as the repetition is the recollection and the unlearning is remembered as forgotten.

Perhaps the learning is instead the following, that we are both doomed and promised to forget and to remember that we forget, even what we forget, that even in remembering we forget; and this is not a bad thing. Nor is repetition. Remembering and forgetting are both repetition. We will repeat even if we remember, and we will repeat what we forget. Forgetting is this (un)repetition.

I mean it is in justice. For what we forget and repeat are acts of justice in response to injustices in time and space that remain in justice. Justice and injustice are not the same, yet we cannot remember the one except as if it were the other. The law of the forgotten is that justice is injustice, that memory is forgetting.

> The senior lord spoke, declaring
> "Fate will be heavy if I do not obey, heavy as well
> if I hew my child, my house's own darling,
> polluting her father's hands
> with slaughter streaming from a maiden
> at the altar what is there without evil here?
> How can I desert the fleet
> and fail the alliance?
> Why, this sacrifice to stop the wind,
> a maiden's blood,
> is their most passionate desire;
> but Right forbids it. So may all be well!"
>
> When he put on the yoke-strap of compulsion, his mind's wind
> veering round to the unholy,
> the impious, the impure, from then
> his purpose changed to hard audacity;
> for men get overbold from the cruel derangement and its ugly
> schemes that begin their affliction.
> So he was hard enough to sacrifice
> his daughter, in aid of a war to punish a woman
> and as first-rites for the fleet to sail. (205–27)

It is not that what is forgotten—one crime after another—is a crime, only a crime. It is good and right and joyous to punish a criminal. Vengeance against Helen requires the sacrifice of a daughter, one woman for another, as Atreus's punishment of Thyestes—after it no longer mattered—required the murder and desecration of his children, one child for another, and Tantalus's sense of goodness required the desecration of the gods. The gods repay, and because they are gods their retribution is not a crime, not unjust. Yet their justice is indistinguishable from injustice, as the latter is the joy and fulfillment of justice. So Agamemnon's triumph remains a triumph after his death, his murder does not diminish the splendid achievement of the war, the murder of his daughter ends in glory.

I mean to say that as forgetting pertains to the good, what is forgotten is injustice yet in forgetting is justice. The injustice for which all things pay restitution is the being of all things, the restitution is their being. We cannot remember past crimes as crimes alone, cannot remember injustice except as someone's or something's justice, cannot recall the misery of the house of Atreus except as its renown.

And so the remembering travels down the generations from murder to murder, crime to crime, all recalled as justice. And the forgetting travels down the generations from crime to crime, all forgotten as injustice. Only Cassandra remembers, and she fails to remember how to forget. Her curse is that she cannot forget.

> Oh! Oh, this misery! Deep down again the fearsome work of truthful prophecy agitates and whirls me round with its stormy prelude. You see these young ones seated by the house, resembling dream-shapes? They are children killed, as if by people outside their family! Their hands are full of their own flesh for meat, clearly visible, holding their entrails and the vitals with them; most pitiable burden, which their father tasted. For that, I say that someone is planning retribution, a cowardly lion who roams free in the marriage-bed and has stayed at home—alas, it is against the master on his return. The ships' commander and overturner of Troy will meet with underhand destruction, through evil fortune; he does not know the kind of bite behind the hateful bitch's tongue when it brightly laid back its ears and licked. Such is the male's female murderer in her audacity. What loathsome monster should I be accurate in calling her—an amphisbaena, or a Scylla living in the rocks, destruction for sailors, a hellish mother raging and breathing war without truce on her dearest? How she cried in triumph, in her total audacity, just as at a battle's turn! Yet she appears to rejoice at the safe homecoming.
>
> And it's all the same if nothing of mine persuades you, of course: the future will come; and you will soon be at my side to pity and call me too true a prophet. (1214–41)

> There is one speech more I wish to make—or my own dirge: I pray to my last daylight from the sun, that my master's avengers requite my murder too on our enemies; mine is a slave's death, an easy victory.

> Oh! Mortal men and their dealings! When they succeed, a shadow may turn them round; if they fail, the wipe of a wet sponge destroys the picture. I pity the second much more than the first. (1322–31)

The clarity of her vision does not protect her from her fate, does not remove her from the crimes of history; moreover, she wills what Clytemnestra and Orestes will: vengeance and retribution. The libation bearers, those who mark the wounds and grieve, cannot separate their grief from vengeance.

> This house is now razed to the ground!
> Sunless and loathsome to men,
> blackness covers the house
> through the death of its master....
>
> For one who assaults a bridal bower
> no cure whatever exists; and all ways which converge
> in one road, to purify
> blood on polluted hands,
> go straight onward in vain.
> And for myself—because the gods brought
> my city its fate by siege, and from my father's house led me into
> the lot of a slave—,
> right or wrong, it is proper I accept a rule over my life in vio-
>   lence to my heart,
> and conquer my bitter loathing;
> yet these garments hide my weeping for my masters' helpless
>   fortunes, in secret, curdling grief. (*LB*, 50–83)

What can end this chain of wounds? And why should anything do so? Justice—I will not say *civilization*—demands it, all the while insisting on vengeance. Justice demands retribution for injustice yet knows that retribution is injustice again. Justice is in justice. This is what we must remember and in order to do so we must forget. Indeed, the forgetting is the remembering: we must forget the crime in order to forgive it, or else we forget the injustice of our own crime in order to commit it.

How else understand the will to put to death those who have put others to death except the selective recollection of the crime of murder? I mean the forgetting. So we may say that justice is forgetting, and that its injustice is another forgetting.

Aeschylus famously resolves this question by appeal to the gods, knowing that the transformation of the Furies—who never forget—into the Eumenides—for whom every crime is to be forgiven—is arbitrary and indefensible, though it is not another crime. Or perhaps I mean is to be remembered as if it were forgotten.

The Furies pursue Orestes for his crime of matricide. His mother has murdered her husband and taken his enemy for her lover: she deserves to die. It is tempting to imagine that all this is done in defiance of the gods, yet the Furies know that it cannot be so.

> CHORUS [Furies]. Lord Apollo, hear me in my turn. You are yourself no mere accomplice in these things, but you have been the single agent completely, as taking the whole responsibility. . . .
> Was it your oracle's injunction for the stranger to kill his mother?
> APOLLO. It was my oracle's injunction to bring vengeance for his father. Of course!
> CHORUS. And then did you promise to give refuge to the murderer with the blood still fresh on him?
> APOLLO. It was also my order to turn to this temple in supplication. . . .
> CHORUS. I will never leave this man alone! . . .
> APOLLO. And I will aid and protect the suppliant; the anger over one seeking refuge is terrible among both men and gods if he is willingly betrayed. (E, 198–233)

> CHORUS. Not Apollo, I tell you, nor mighty Athena could save you from wandering exile and neglect, with happiness unknown anywhere in your heart, a shadow drained of blood to feed divine powers. . . . Do you not even speak in reply, but spit my words back at me, when you have been nurtured and consecrated for me? Even while living you shall be my feast, not even slaughtered at an altar; and you shall hear this song to bind you. (299–306)

In a world of injustice—and what world is not?—injustice breeds injustice, justice turns itself into injustice, and memory demands retribution. Crimes demand punishment, and punishment is another crime. The myth that the state can harm and kill with impunity is a fiction of the state. To remember the crime is to remember it with both justice and injustice, that is, as unable to escape the injustice that insists on further harm. The task of the Furies is to remember and to make sure that we remember that Orestes killed his mother. What we must remember is the crime.

Perhaps we should forget. And yet we know that would be another crime. We are poised between crime and crime, between one injustice and another. As Anaximander says. And perhaps that is the best we can do. We can remember, we can forget, we must remember, we must forget.

And yet, crime, injustice, *adikia* are not the world. To pay restitution is not to remain enmired in guilt. Joy pairs with sorrow, forgetting with remembering, justice with injustice. Yet joy and sorrow—in life, of life—are not reciprocal, as if having one is lacking the other. That is far too simple. There is joy in justice, joy in responsibility, even driven by the Furies. Hatred, anger, whatever drives Orestes comes with a joy in life that, as hateful as it may be, is not just the sorrow of blood. If the impossibility of ethics is the condition of its possibility, that must be the condition of joy as well as sorrow, of justice as well as injustice.

There is a forgetting that would not recall the crimes of Atreus, and there is a forgetting that transcends those crimes, that would recall them in order then to forget them—in joy instead of bitterness. It is the joy of being responsible, ethical, good in the midst of the demand to kill in the name of ethics, refusing that demand again in the name of ethics, forgetting the justice of that demand. We do not forget injustice but bring goodness in justice by forgetting—I mean refusing—another crime. The Furies must become Eumenides by forgetting their fury.

This is not a simple task. There is no justification within memory for this task except that it must be done in the name of the ethics that would not forget. Aeschylus expresses this as the vote that ties, where Athena casts the deciding vote, in a way supplanting Apollo, in a way insisting that Athens can come into existence only in this breaking of the tie. The tie is between two systems of justice, where the older must give way to the newer, and vengeance gives way to mercy.

> CHORUS [Furies again]. You younger gods! The ancient laws—
> you have ridden them down! You have taken them out of
>   my hands for yourselves!
> I am dishonoured, wretch that I am; my heavy rancour
> releases on this land—woe to it!—
> a poison, a poison from my heart to requite my grief, dripping
> from below the earth, intolerable. From this
> a canker destroying leaves, destroying offspring—O Justice
>   [Justice]!
> will sweep over and strike the land with a blight killing men.
> I am groaning—what am I to do?
> I am laughed at; what I suffer
> from the citizens is hard to bear.
> Oh, your ruin is great,

you ill-fated daughters of Night
grieving for your dishonour!

ATHENA (using speech still). Let me persuade you to bear it
without heavy groaning! You have not been defeated, but the
verdict came out with the votes truly equal, with no dishonour
for you. On the contrary, there was bright and clear testimony to
hand from Zeus, and the giver of the oracle himself was himself
the giver of the evidence, that Orestes was to take no harm for
doing these things. And you should neither launch your rancour
heavily upon this land—do not stay angry—nor make its crops
sterile with droplets released from your lungs, ungentle spears
which devour the seed. I here give you my promise, in all right,
that you shall have an abode, a hidden place, in a land that is
righteous, seated on gleaming thrones by your altar-hearths,
richly in honour from these citizens. . . .
CHORUS. That I should suffer this, alas—
I the ancient in wisdom—[and] live on earth
[where] pollution goes, alas, without punishment!
All my force is in my breath,
and all my rancour.
(violently) Oh no! The shame! The hurt!
What is the pain going deep in my side?
Listen, mother Night!
I am taken from my age-old prerogatives
by the gods' irresistible trickery, I am made into nothing! . . .

ATHENA. I will not tire in telling you the good things, so you
may never say you are dismissed from this land without honour
or hospitality, an ancient goddess rejected by a younger one, myself, and by the mortal men who hold the city. . . . You may have
a settled holding in this land and be rightly held in honour for
ever. . . .
CHORUS. I shall accept a home with Pallas,
and I shall not dishonour
this city which Zeus the almighty and Ares
hold as a gods' outpost;
they delight in its guarding the altars of Greek deities.
For this city I make my prayer,
and prophesy with kind intent
good fortune in profusion to benefit its life,
burgeoning up from the earth
in sunshine's bright gleam. . . .
CHORUS. I wish no breath of harm blighting trees—
I speak now of my favour
to blow the flaming heat that robs plants of their buds
over the land's borders;

and may no persistent disease invade, destroying the crops.
I wish Pan to foster the sheep,
to thrive in carrying twin young;
and may the produce growing from richness in the soil
drink at the appointed time
the gods' gift of rain.
ATHENA (to the jurors). Do you hear this, you guardians of the
city—the nature of these undertakings?
The sovereign Furies have great power
among both immortals and those under the earth;
and in the case of men it is clear that they work their will to fulfilment,
giving some cause for singing, but others
a life with eyes dimmed by tears. (807–955)

What is mercy to vengeance but a justice of forgetting? The
Furies would remember the old ways and the demands of justice.
The Eumenides would forget the old ways and bring goodness
and joy again in the name of justice. Justice and injustice come together as forgetting and remembering, where neither is superior to
the other nor in opposition. Forgetting and mercy are not alternatives to punishment and vengeance. The Erinyes, Furies, must become benevolent Eumenides without relinquishing their archaic
task of justice. Vengeance must become goodness and sorrow
must become joy. This is impossible without remembering becoming forgetting. But it is not a forgetting of injustice and crime, but
the way in which justice itself is forgetting. The Furies must forget
their fury while remembering who and what they are, as forgiveness must forget the wound and rage that drives it while remembering the origin.

The origin is disaster, transfigured by forgetting into joy. The
origin is joy of life, haunted by forgotten specters of injustice.

In a book entitled *The Ethics of Memory*—as if ethics were anything without memory, as if forgetting were anything but ethical—
Margalit asks if we have a duty to remember.

> Are we obligated to remember people and events from the past?
> If we are, what is the nature of this obligation? Are remembering
> and forgetting proper subjects of moral praise or blame? Who are
> the "we" who may be obligated to remember: the collective
> "we," or some distributive sense of "we" that puts the obligation
> to remember on each and every member of the collective? (*EM*,
> 7)

Who are we, what is our obligation, what and how shall we remember? And for that matter, perhaps another we, have we a re-

sponsibility to forget, what and how shall we forget even as we remember? Once we pose these questions in these ways, do we not betray that the how and what of remembering is always a what and how of forgetting? We never remember everything of anything, never remember anything just as it was. So in order to remember we must forget. And it is as if the forgetting comes first.

That is not how Margalit understands it:

> An ethics of memory is as much an ethics of forgetting as it is an ethics of memory. The crucial question, Are there things that we ought to remember? has its parallel, Are there things that we ought to forget? (17)

Forgetting and remembering here are positive acts toward which we bear ethical responsibility. I continue to wonder if forgetting is the condition of responsibility itself.

Moreover, it is not just a question of our duty to remember and to forget, but whether it is good to remember, good to forget, perhaps good sometimes to remember and sometimes to forget, good sometimes for some and not for others.

Margalit begins his book as if to remember his parents, whose differences on memory frame the questions he would answer:

> As I reconstruct my parents' debate, it went like this:
> MOTHER: The Jews were irretrievably destroyed. What is left is just a pitiful remnant of the great Jewish people [which for her meant European Jewry]. The only honorable role for the Jews that remain is to form communities of memory—to serve as "soul candles" like the candles that are ritually kindled in memory of the dead.
> FATHER: We, the remaining Jews, are people, not candles. It is a horrible prospect for anyone to live just for the sake of retaining the memory of the dead. That is what the Armenians opted to do. And they made a terrible mistake. We should avoid it at all cost. Better to create a community that thinks predominantly about the future and reacts to the present, not a community that is governed from mass graves. (viii)

Margalit remembers his parents and remembers their debate—but of course he reconstructs it: takes it apart, rebuilds it, casts out what is of little use. Does he reconstruct his parents, does he take them apart, does he forget them as he would remember them?

Of course he does and of course he must. That is an inescapable forgetting. But it is by no means the most crucial. Here is a perhaps more telling example:

> In one of my own daily prayers I came across a report concerning the speedy and problematic career of a certain army colonel. The colonel was interviewed about a publicly known incident in his past, when he was the commander of a small unit. One of the soldiers under his command had been killed by so-called friendly fire. It turned out that the colonel did not remember the soldier's name. There followed a flood of outrage directed at the officer who did not remember. Why wasn't the name of this fallen soldier "scorched in iron letters" on his commander's heart?
>
> ...Is it really of special importance that the officer did not remember his dead soldier's name? Are there special obligations to remember people's names, or at least some names in certain situations? (18–9)

Are there special obligations to remember dead and living people, to remember them as themselves? If there is no such duty, what can duty mean? What but this is our responsibility to the past?

> The idea that the essence of a person is referred to and expressed by a personal name gives the name a particular role in memory. And I believe that the quasi-magical thought of the survival of the name, as the survival of the essence, is what lies behind the doctrine of the double killing: killing the body and killing the name. (23)

> The source of the wish for an immortal name is not mere vanity. Nor is it merely the desire to "make a name for yourself" in the sense of achieving glory. It is rather a horror of extinction and utter oblivion. The human project of memory, i.e., commemoration, is basically a religious project to secure some form of immortality. (25)

Yet Margalit does not rest memory with the name, but with the self:

> It seems that the least the officer could, and should, remember is the soldier's name. But had the officer recalled some definite description of the soldier, he would have done just as well— he would have shown that he actually remembered the young man himself. So on the face of it, remembering the name is remembering the soldier, but the obligation, if it is an obligation, is to remember the soldier and not necessarily to remember his name. (19–20)

Against the horror of extinction we hope against death that we will be remembered. We hope against death that those who follow will preserve us. And of course, following after is already forgetting. And what is to be remembered is death. So remembering is remembering loss, death, extinction, disaster. And of course I mean forgetting. The passing away, the death of death, is forgetting.

Here we may understand the name as a name, that is, a writing or speaking or thinking. I mean that the name is remembered as said, that it takes saying to recall, to remember: saying or writing, exposition. The name is to be written or said. The colonel did not have the name to say when called upon to say it. Even if he remembered the name, then or later, the crime was not to say it, not to orate it, not to make it public.

So we are speaking of a public, historical remembering and an historical, public forgetting. Both take place in the realm of language, expression, inscription, exposition. The as if of exposition, the transfiguration and mobilization of expression, is the remembering and forgetting of memory. This means that we are exposed in memory and forgetting, exposed in time, through the exposition of saying, speaking, writing. We hope to be remembered as if we were once present—not as if we were present now.

Margalit's recollection of memory turns around three pairs of distinctions, between ethics and morality, between thick and thin relationships, between myth and history, where the latter is perhaps closer to the distinction between the sacred and secular, the premodern and modern, and bears the force of exposition in the enchantment and disenchantment of the world.

> Thick relations are grounded in attributes such as parent, friend, lover, fellow-countryman. Thick relations are anchored in a shared past or moored in shared memory.... Thick relations are in general our relations to the near and dear. Thin relations are in general our relations to the stranger and the remote....
>
> Ethics, in the way I use the term, tells us how we should regulate our thick relations; morality tells us how we should regulate our thin relations. (7–8)

> Shared memory is torn between two worldviews, which are manifested, in their pure forms, by science on the one hand and by myth on the other.... between viewing the world as an enchanted place (myth) and viewing the world as a disenchanted place (critical history). (63–4)

> When history is contrasted with memory, history is habitually labeled as cold, even lifeless, whereas memory can be vital, vivid, and alive. What this contrast means is that stories about the past that are shared by a community are as a rule more vivid,

more concrete, and better connected with live experiences than is
critical history.... I am not talking of traditional societies, in
which the notions of shared memory and of collective sacred stories, or myths, go hand in hand. I am talking about communities
of memory that are supposed to have undergone the Gestalt
switch from an enchanted worldview to a disenchanted one. In
particular, I have in mind, secular modern nation-states. (67)

It may well be that forgetting is associated with enchantment
against the disenchantment of memory in a modern world; that
what is forgotten is archaic, mythic, enchanted, magical, where
what is remembered in caring and ethical ways is to be grasped in
the here and now of disenchantment. I mean to pose forgetting in
this context as an infinite absence rather than another presence,
infinite and absent in the virtual modalities of *as if*: magical, enchanted, charming, disastrous. In other words, I mean to call into
question the task of an enchanted worldview to promote community, as if that were something to accomplish, and of a secular
world view to promote disenchantment. I have in mind something
of Nancy's refusal of that accomplishment in relation to community:

> This is why community cannot arise from the domain of
> *work*. One does not produce it, one experiences or one is consti-
> tuted by it as the experience of finitude. Community understood
> as a work or through its works would presuppose that the com-
> mon being, as such, be objectifiable and producible (in sites, per-
> sons, buildings, discourses, institutions, symbols: in short, in
> subjects)....
> Community necessarily takes place in what Blanchot has
> called "unworking," referring to that which, before or beyond
> the work, withdraws from the work, and which, no longer hav-
> ing to do either with production or with completion, encounters
> interruption, fragmentation, suspension. Community is made of
> the interruption of singularities, or of the suspension that singu-
> lar beings *are*. (*IC*, 31)

Community is not something to be accomplished, not by
shared memory or myth or enchantment, but something to be interrupted, fragmented, unworked and unaccomplished—forgotten. We live as singular beings in the forgetting and unworking of
community. Forgetting is resistance, and what it resists is the notion of live memory and vivification through myth—all frequently
terrible in the deeds to which they give rise. I'm alluding to
Dachau and Hiroshima and Bosnia and Rwanda in my time, also

to many other memories of community that cement themselves around destruction and violence.

Perhaps nation states are the prime example of a cementing that seems to me to be based on cruelty and domination in the best of cases. Secular modern nation states impose far too many rules of bondage.

> Against the background of the question, Who will re-member the murdered Kulaks and who should remember them? I wish to raise two further questions: First, why cannot the ku-laks be remembered by humanity at large? That is, why cannot humanity be shaped into a community of memory and why can-not it be formed into an ethical community, based on the thick relation of caring? And second, should not the kulaks be remem-bered by humanity even if humanity is regarded, in my terms, as a moral community? Ought not this moral community to have some minimal sense of memory for, say, the Gulags, the kulaks, Majdanek and Treblinka, Hiroshima and Nanking, as warning signposts in human moral history?
>
> The first question I shall view from the perspective of two religious projects which, for lack of better labels, I shall call the Christian project and the Jewish project. The Christian project is an effort to establish, in historical time, an ethical community based on love. This community, ideally, should include all of humanity, ... [W]ith a little helping of grace, humanity can and should be established as an ethical community of love.
>
> The Jewish project retains the double tier of ethics and mo-rality at least for historical times, and postpones the idea of a universal ethical community to the messianic era. Jews are obli-gated to establish themselves as an ethical community of caring. The force of the obligation is gratitude to God for having deliv-ered their ancestors from the "house of slaves" in Egypt. . . .
>
> The two projects have a common feature. They both base their obligation on a debt of gratitude that should be kept in memory. The memories for which we ought to be grateful are positive memories: creation, the sacrifice on the cross, Exodus. These are memories of divine gifts to humanity, or, in the case of Exodus, to the Jews. In contrast, the candidates for memory in the case of humanity as a moral community are negative ones, mostly of terrible acts of cruelty. Such memories do not inspire gratitude. Instead, they ignite an appetite for revenge.
>
> Caring, is, I believe, at the center of our ethical relations, not gratitude. We owe each other two different kinds of things in ethics and morality: in morality, human respect; in ethics, caring and loyalty. (Margalit, *EM*, 71–3)

The distinction here between ethics and morality takes on a great, and perhaps incongruous weight in carrying the distinction between thick and thin relationships and gratitude and revenge. Gratitude and revenge haunt the memory of historical memories, as they do life itself. The question of the kulaks and other extinctions is what to do about them—of course whether to remember, but also what else? Shall we punish? Shall we build other ethical communities, open other ethical possibilities? Can we, and should we?

> Two questions emerge with regard to the project of establishing a universal ethical community. (1) Is it feasible? (2) Is it desirable? . . .
>
> Why is it so difficult to shape humanity into an ethical community? . . .
>
> In short, we may care for people and for communities we have not encountered nor are likely to encounter in our lifetime. So why should not humanity constitute such a community based on caring? The attitude of caring, after all, is based on belonging, not on achievement. So belonging to the "family of man" should be enough. What do we imagine when we imagine a community with whom we are supposed to have thick relations? My answer is that we imagine an extension of family relations that would include relatives we have not met. So why not imagine "the family of man" to be such an extended family?
>
> . . . A nation has famously been defined as a society that nourishes a common delusion about its ancestry and shares a common hatred for its neighbors. Thus, the bond of caring in a nation hinges on false memory (delusion) and hatred of those who do not belong. (74–6)

Margalit insists on an intimate relation between ethics and shared memory. Yet every one of these terms—*intimate, relation, ethics, sharing,* and *memory,* not to mention *between*—expresses a determinate condition, something to be grasped and held. From the standpoint of forgetting, each expresses dispossession and ungrasping, from love and intimacy to fragmentation and transgression to an ethics of loss and of what cannot be shared. An ethics of memory seeks memories to share. An ethics of forgetting seeks nothing but insists on giving everything as the condition of life and ethics. Caring and love are nothing to have, nothing to achieve, nor are community and humanity. They are to give and to give away. I mean of course in the mode of enchantment and *as if,* in the interstices of meaning and exposition, where there is nothing to grasp.

Margalit gives us a concrete example of memory and community, speaking of the Holocaust memorial monument in Berlin that
is to contain the commandment "thou shalt not kill":

> The way I see it, this suggestion makes two blunders. One,
> the standing of the Germans as a community of memory con-
> nected to the perpetrators does not leave them the option of act-
> ing on behalf of humanity at large. They are a side to this mem-
> ory. Moreover, there is something wrong in depicting the victims
> under the mere label of "human beings," when it is clear that
> many of them, especially the East Europeans, would have identi-
> fied themselves as Jews. So even if one strongly advocates the
> project of constructing a monument of shared memory for all of
> mankind, it is wrong for the Germans to do it, all the more so in
> Berlin.
>
> The monument in Berlin, as I view it, should be an effort by
> the German people to reestablish themselves as an ethical com-
> munity, encumbered with painful shared memories. The way for
> the Germans to reestablish themselves as an ethical community
> is to turn their cruelty, which was what tied them to the Jews,
> into repentance. (80–1)

Repentance is sometimes well and good, and there is much I
would agree with in the first paragraph. The second, however,
claims to know what the German people—and perhaps Jewish and
other people—must do to establish themselves as an ethical community. This runs against most understandings of the complexity
of post-traumatic disorders, individual or collective, where no one
possesses a solution to the wounding or the forgetting.

Perhaps it is wrong for Germans to take the high road and
speak for humanity. Perhaps it is wrong for any, including Jews.
Will it ever be possible and right for Germans and for Jews—or
any subgroup—to speak for humanity? Why should we imagine
that it will? To the contrary, the production of shared memories
concerning concentration camps, exterminations, genocides,
slaughters, and extinctions appears to be an ongoing project. One
can insist on forgetting—but perhaps that is impossible. One can
insist on remembering—but how? How remember without forgetting, and what and how shall one remember and forget, as if one
might do so finally?

> I still believe that the most promising projects of shared
> memory are those that go through natural communities of mem-
> ory, so to speak, and the issue is how to engage painful trau-
> matic memories from the past. . . .

> The source of the obligation to remember, I maintain, comes from the effort of radical evil forces to undermine morality itself by, among other means, rewriting the past and controlling collective memory. (82–3)

Rewritten in terms of forgetting, this would become the need for natural communities to engage traumatic memories and forgettings in resistance to forces of evil who would control collective memory. The point perhaps is that collective memory is not something to be controlled, but to be lived through as if in the mode of forgetting. So the forces that would make us forget must perhaps be responded to not by remembering but in our own forgetting. That is nothing to know or to grasp. As Margalit himself acknowledges.

> Now, what is the difference between living an emotion for a long time, say living in humiliation, and reliving it? There is, I believe, no clear-cut distinction, as there are no clear-cut identity conditions for an emotion, through time. That is, there are no conditions that determine whether it is the same emotion all over again or a new emotion that was rekindled by the old objects from the past....
> ...Humiliation, I believe, is not just another experience in our life, like, say, an embarrassment. It is a formative experience. It forms the way we view ourselves as humiliated persons very much the way a serious failure in a project that matters to us greatly brings us to view ourselves as failures. Humiliation, in the strong sense, in being a fundamental assault on us as human beings, becomes constitutive of one sense of who we are. (129–30)

Among other angles of this reading, especially that affective memory constitute who we are, is that there are no clear cut conditions for an emotion, therefore of a memory, that remembering an affect is not the same as having that affect. I would say that the affect itself, the original event, is not the same as itself. Margalit puts it this way, "what we are interested in is not the mood affecting memory but the memory of moods" (136). The memory of moods is not the same as the moods, but nothing can distinguish them finally. The moods as felt and the moods as remembered are both remembered and felt. I mean of course forgotten as felt. The having of a mood exists in the mode of forgetting. Memory does not return to the living mood but is another mood, a memory of a mood, a forgetting of whatever constitutes the mood and its reconstitution. Humiliation remembered reconstitutes me as humiliated as if I would seek to forget it.

If we believe that memory is a means to collective identity—as if that too were something to have—what is the purpose of forgetting—if such a purpose were something to have? And indeed, Margalit understands both memory and forgetting as having, underlying his sense of forgiving. Forgive and forget—I mean, forget and forgive. I would reiterate that forgiving and forgetting both allude to dispossession—extreme giving and extreme loss—in that way tied intimately to each other, as if the same. For just a moment forgetting the act of will embodied in forgiving—if there is one—forgiveness does not require but is forgetting—I mean something close to releasement from grasping. Holding onto memory is the condition of vengeance. Giving up memories is a crime, whether of trauma or of joy. Giving beyond holding, beyond possessing, forgetting loss without another loss, is much closer to the forgetting that is forgiving. I mean giving beyond gifts and forgetting beyond memories.

> What is the relation between forgiving and forgetting? ... I believe that the notion of forgiveness is deeply rooted in religion, and I believe that uncovering these roots is a necessary preliminary step before we can tackle their conceptual analysis. Still, my ethics and morality are humanistic, not religious. This means that the sources of their justification lie in humans, and not in any "higher" beings. (183)

This is a humanism that insists on something specific and determining about human beings—that they can be sources of ethics and morality. The alternative Margalit mentions is that the sources are not human but superhuman or divine. Both of these are positive conditions of memory: remember the gods, draw your strength from other human beings. And what if we forgot, not in the sense of denying or refusing the gods but in the play of remembrances, forgettings, unearthings, transformations, and transfigurations—endless expositions? Even at the point at which this play of exposition emerges, Margalit rejects it, though in at least one crucial respect he celebrates it.

> Our concepts of sin, forgiveness, and forgetting are rooted in religious picture. By picture I mean a collection of familiar objects that can provide a metaphorical model for the problematical concept. The expressions that describe a picture are "dead" metaphors whose metaphorical quality escapes their users. Users are in the grip of the picture if they are not aware of its metaphorical nature and cannot think of any alternative way of say-

ing what the picture expresses. The protest, "But how else could it be?" is the hallmark of being in such a grip. (184–5)

One might say that the *as if* of forgetting as compared with the inescapability of memory and of what is to be remembered emerges here in relation to another death, indeed two deaths: the death of metaphor and metaphors of death. A metaphor is dead, Margalit insists—surely another metaphor, is it a dead one? hasn't it been dead for a long, long time?—if we cannot think of any alternative, if it settles in our grasp, as if there is no other possibility, no other promise, as if necessity superseded *perhaps*. Yet a metaphor is always in the mode of perhaps, as is forgetting. So perhaps we should think not of dead metaphors but of metaphors of forgetting and the forgetting of metaphors as the *perhaps* and *as if* of exposition.

Margalit presents two metaphors—live or dead—of forgiveness, beginning with another figure: "the idea of sin as a bloodstain and of purification and atonement as the removal of the stain... 'There is blood on your hands; wash yourselves and be clean. Put away the evil of your deeds' (Isaiah 1:15–16)" (*EM*, 185). The first metaphor of forgiveness—perhaps more of forgetting—is that of the scapegoat. "The goat shall carry all their iniquities upon itself into some barren waste (Leviticus 16:22)" (*EM*, 186). Margalit comments:

> A goat is not an appropriate model for the forgiveness of sin because it is not a creature that we see as expressing innocence, even if it actually is an innocent creature. The "servant of God" of whom Isaiah says "The Lord laid upon him the guilt of us all" is compared not to a goat but to a lamb or a ewe. These are animals that, unlike the goat, are seen as representing innocence. One must separate the sheep from the goats. The scapegoat has entered Western culture as a creature that people blame and punish for sins it did not commit—sins that were actually committed by those doing the blaming and the punishing. But the scapegoat, even if totally blameless, is not a symbol of innocence. It generally represents radical otherness—the different, the totally strange and threatening. This is why it is so easy to place blame and sin on it. This change in the picture of the scapegoat upon entering Western culture is not a coincidence. It shows that the goat was always a bad model for the idea of forgiveness and carrying sins. (187–8)

I might imagine that Margalit's metaphor, separating the sheep from the goats, repeats the figure of having, as if we can know the difference between sheep and goat, innocent and guilty, and divide them in pens. Perhaps that is the picture of ethics he would insist on, and a similar picture of memory. I would insist on the disruptions of forgetting, even in the context of forgiving.

> Two religious models of sin and forgiveness still permeate the concept of forgiveness in present-day humanistic morality: forgiveness as blotting out the sin, and forgiveness as covering it up. Blotting out a sin means forgetting it absolutely. Covering it up means disregarding it without forgetting it. (188–9)

These two figures of forgiveness return us explicitly to memory and forgetting. Blotting and covering over are figures of forgetting as forcefully as of forgiving. One might say that in the context of remembering, forgiving is forgetting. One might say more strongly that forgiving is identical with forgetting, but that forgetting is as little blotting out or covering over as remembering is the thing or stain again.

One way to understand the role of forgetting is right here in Margalit's words. Blotting out a sin means forgetting it absolutely. Covering it up means disregarding it without forgetting it. Who is to say? Who can blot or cover over, with what measures and techniques? How can any blotting, smudging, obscuring, or smearing be absolute? What could be absolute forgetting?

I believe in loss, in contingent, total loss. I'm sure that some past events have vanished without recovery. Yet I'm also sure that the absoluteness of this loss calls for recovery, repetition. If it is lost absolutely, then we must be able to say it and reaffirm it. Loss requires repetition, and its absoluteness is more repetitions. The absoluteness of a loss is its trace, its repetition and recovery. Otherwise it is lost contingently.

Indeed, contingency is the absolute of loss. And contingency is forgetting. Anything can be forgotten, and indeed, anything and everything is forgotten somehow, to some extent, contingently, blotted out, covered over, smeared, smudged, blurred, obscured, hidden, etc. We cannot say what it means to forget, what it is to be forgotten, because what we say requires that we say it again, because saying it again is forgetting, because what is forgotten includes the forgetting.

It is the sense of memory as absolute—not perhaps what we can insist on remembering but what we may hope to recover—to which forgetting responds. Forgetting is the absolute contingency of memory, of history and time, absolute here in the sense that nothing can annul its contingency. There is forgetting in the most memorable of memories, in the most truthful of truths. Errancy and untruth, as Heidegger says, belong to the essence of truth. The meaning of truth is error and untruth. The meaning of memory is forgetting. The meaning of necessity is contingency. And the meaning of ethics is forgiveness.

Yet this very meaning in its contingency is nothing to have. We cannot hold onto a wound without forgetting, without dispossession. So we have a choice, of holding onto a wound so that it increases in its trauma, of grasping it more tightly even as we endeavor to cast it away, in both cases transforming it, modifying it, making it much more real, much more wounding, much more traumatic—losing and forgetting its very nature in claiming and holding onto it as tightly as possible.

Let it go. To forgive means to let it go—let us say here, as contingently as possible in the imperative of forgiveness. Let us say as truthfully as possible in the obscurity of forgetting. Let us say that the it itself takes on the contingency of memory and forgetting as we try to remember and as we try to forget. We do not know how to do these things, but we cannot avoid doing them and we always fail.

Forgetting is the contingency of memory, absolute in that it cannot be evaded, yet what and how is forgotten is never grasped, is contingent beyond any contingency. The imperative of trauma is that we must remember, that we must forget, that we cannot do either, and that we cannot escape.

This is the buddhist formula again: you must remember, you must forget, you must remember and forget, you must neither remember nor forget. That is the nature of remembering and forgetting. And the nature of retribution and forgiveness. They are imperatives to come, whose coming is always on the way. Forgetting and forgiving are never here, never present, yet they never disappear.

> There are thus four different pictures of forgiveness in the Bible: as carrying a burden, as covering up, as blotting out, and as canceling a debt.... The fourth picture, of forgiveness as canceling a debt, can be interpreted on any one of these levels: bearing part of the debt, ignoring the debt even though it still exists, or wiping it out completely. It seems to me that there is an opposition between forgiveness as covering up and as blotting out the sin. This opposition is the difference between the ideas of forgiving and forgetting. (191)

Picture, burden, covering up, blotting out, canceling a debt: these are pictures of pictures, images of images. What do we cancel, cover up, but another picture, another image? What do we mean by canceling except something never to be determined? Wiping, bearing, ignoring: these are figures of ethics on the one side and of forgetting on the other. Note how completely we may leave punishment aside in addressing these issues on a fundamental level!

I have repeatedly understood forgiving as related to giving and forgetting as related to forgiving—not, however, to gifts or sin. And certainly not to restoration.

> The idea I want to propose here is that the duties involved in forgiveness, both those of the one who asks for it and those of the one who bestows it, are similar to the duties involved in exchanging gifts. The purpose in both cases has to do with the nature of the personal relationship that existed before the offense occurred. But there remains a difference. Forgiveness, unlike ordinary gifts, is not intended to form or strengthen a relationship but rather to restore it to its previous state. (195)

> The central metaphor is not erasure but, rather, returning. (198)

Forgiveness that would restore a relationship to a previous state is memory without forgetting. The previous state—if there be such—is an event or relation to be recaptured. The contingency of forgetting and forgiving marks the recapture with the modality of *perhaps* and *as if*: as if we returned to the previous state, as if that were possible, perhaps we may or might. Contingency here is not lack of necessity, any more than forgetting is lack of remembering. It is exposition, multiplication, transformation, transgression. It is the becoming of the always other that is the simulacrum of the previous relation and state.

In other words, the impossibility of return marks the infinite possibility of return. The impossibility of remembering marks the infinite certainty of memory—in the mode of forgetting. Forgetting is the condition of remembering, even where we cannot remember and there is nothing to remember. Forgetting can make up, invent, perform remembering in the absence of anything to recall. Forgiveness also. For a forgiveness that insists on the sin reinstates it endlessly in the name of forgetting. So there must be the possibility that the forgiven sin was never a sin, never occurred, is nothing to remember. Forgive and forget what never took place, but perhaps might have, and might have been a terrible wounding. Forgiveness and forgetting take place in the modality of *perhaps* and *as if*. That is why literature, art, and language are the bearers of forgotten forgiveness.

Perhaps we might recall here the eternal return, anything and everything but restoration, repetition, the same again, yet nothing other. Forgiving and forgetting take place on the plane of the eternal return, which is nowhere and nothing and everywhere.

> The eternal return is a force of affirmation, but it affirms everything of the multiple, everything of the different, everything of chance *except* what subordinates them to the One, to the Same, to necessity, everything *except* the One, the Same and the Necessary. . . . If there is an essential relation between eternal return and death, it is because it promises and implies "once and for all" the death of that which is one.[4] (Deleuze, *DR*, 115)

It is worth repeating that forgetting is this force of affirmation, affirming everything of the multiple but a return to the same. The return of giving, forgiving, and forgetting is to endless becoming.

What does this mean in practical terms? Or is that the question before us, whether there is a practical meaning to forgiving and forgetting?

> There is no general duty to forget, not even in the truncated sense of duty to ourselves, since who we are depends on our not forgetting things that happened and that are important in our lives. But the role of memory in constituting who we are and what agents we are is in tension with the ideal of successful forgiveness as that which ends in forgetting the wrong done to us.
>
> I maintain that what is needed for successful forgiveness is not forgetting the wrong done but rather overcoming the resentment that accompanies it. (Margalit, *EM*, 208)

Yet if we are constituted by memory and forgetting, are we also constituted by resentment? That is an incredible hypothesis. So let us imagine that we are constituted by memory and forgetting in the context of love and care, understanding these as taking place contingently in the modality of *perhaps* and *as if*. Both the wrong and the resentment then also exist contingently in the modality of *as if* and *perhaps*, where forgetting reinscribes the contingency in the play of exposition. Here it is the *how* of forgiving and forgetting, the *how* and multiplicity of remembering and inscribing. It is in the stories that we weave of our past and future, who we and others were and hope to become, that we institute our own becomings through forgetting and forgiving.

Finally, then, let us conclude this discussion of our own be-coming—whoever we may be—in another practical vein.

> I believe that the Committee for Truth and Reconciliation in South Africa rightly sensed that there is more to the apartheid experience than just telling the facts. They felt, I believe, the need for elucidation, but they used the wrong terms for it "social truth," "narrative truth," "healing truth." These made truth, real truth, look like a very soft notion. (170)

I want to say that the Truth and Reconciliation Commission in South Africa (TRC)—and other such committees in other places—exist by forgetting, not of course everything, and not anything in particular, but forgetting in general. And it is by forgetting that they are able to remember, and if possible to mend. It is not by remembering facts that they reconcile and heal—memories are in-constant and varying. It is by forgetting, and in that way getting closer to traumatic wounds than any memory. There are no real hard truths—and for that matter, no soft ones—that reconciliation calls for. We must somehow get over a wound that cannot and for that matter should not be forgotten, that we must not get over. We must somehow move on ethically in memory of violent, destruc-tive, evil acts. Ethics asks us to judge and to remember and to care, both for those irreparably harmed by evil and for those who com-mitted the violence. Different carings, no doubt. But retribution alone cannot serve justice.

Only a god can save us, perhaps, in this case Athena. Some salvation must be forged in witness to evil that knows its evil as forgotten. Which is in some sense to say that it is no longer evil, or if it still is, then tomorrow it may no longer be. The children may not be presumed to be guilty, that is one of the forgettings. An-other is to forget that the crime is a crime, to pretend that evil is not evil. Yet if we are to draw good from evil, is that not to make it good? For example, if we learn from it to avoid future crimes, if we find new ways to build social institutions. More than forget-ting to give is to remember to discover. Here forgetting is the act of transformation that is memory, not the same again but a repeti-tion that transfigures, where in effect neither truth nor reconcilia-tion can remain stable.

It is time for an African perspective on reconciliation if not truth.

> The crimes that the African continent commits against her kind are of a dimension and, unfortunately, of a nature that ap-pears to constantly provoke memories of the historic wrongs in-

flicted on that continent by others.... Faced with such a balancing imposition—the weight of memory against the violations of the present—it is sometimes useful to invoke the voices of the griots, the ancestral shades and their latter-day interpreters, the poets....

The black poet—both within the continent and the diaspora—has been thrust into the heart of this hunger for closure, and has responded in a diversity of ways that testify to the poet's unique formation in colonialism and displacement (or alienation) and self-restoration through a humanistic ethos that sometimes appears to be a deliberate act of faith, more a quest than a cultural given.... Unlike the theologian, who takes his voice from the realms of deities, the poet appropriates the voice of the people and the full burden of their memory.... *To err is human, to atone, humane*, declares one: *to err is human, to forgive, African*, responds the other. Is a continent's humanity of such bottomless reserves that it can truly accommodate the latter?

The poets have confronted, in advance of the event, the great humanistic dilemma of South Africa, and it would appear, in the main, that the poet sometimes anticipates or vindicates the vision of the statesman. (Soyinka, *BMMF*, 19–22)

Soyinka—perhaps Africa—confronts Margalit's assumption that caring and forgiveness require social relationships beyond the human by recalling the voices of poets—griots, muses—who are both African and human, and where being African is more exacting. The dilemmas of life and ethics—for African humans—appear in exposition, where two different strategies of witness are in a sense the same no matter how conflicted they may seem.

> From within the same continent, two strategies of confrontation with one's history. They are offsprings of the same age, sprung from minds of a shared identity, and they appear to complement yet contradict each other.... How on earth does one reconcile reparations, or recompense, with reconciliation or remission of wrongs? Dare we presume that both, in their differing ways, are committed to ensuring the righting of wrongs and the triumph of justice? (23–4)

Reconciliation requires restoration to humanity so that the victims and the victimizers share a common world. Reconciliation requires that the victims receive restitution from the victimizers in recognition of their humanity in the production of a new system of relationships. The punitive model fails to serve inasmuch as it remains within the sphere of the crime.

> Just to let one's fantasy roam a little—what really would be preposterous or ethically inadmissible in imposing a general levy on South Africa's white population? This is not intended as a concrete proposal, but as an exercise in pure speculation.... A collective levy need not be regarded as a punitive measure; indeed—since the purpose is reconciliation, such an offer could originate from the beneficiaries of Apartheid themselves, in a voluntary gesture of atonement—it need not be a project of the state. (24–5)

Let us adopt this assumption that reparations need not be punitive as the cornerstone of witness. Some will find it punitive, some will insist on holding onto their privilege by every means. If we are to help the victims by harming the privileged, is that not by acts of punishment?

From the standpoint of memory and truth, the reparations re-instate the crimes. From the standpoint of forgetting, the reparations transform the crimes, transfigure the past, create another future than one that would hold onto the past. This is not without its own injustices—I mean betrayals—of the truths and conciliations of the TRC.

> We know that strategies for the transformation of society often demand a measure of pragmatism or, to put it crudely, deals. Secret, sometimes unrecorded, but deals nevertheless, a guarantee between the lines, legible only to signatories to the public document. Indemnity is often granted to the undeserving in order to minimize damage to the structure of society and even preserve lives ... [In South Africa] there remains a sense that the adopted formula for the harmonization of that society erodes, in some way, one of the pillars on which a durable society must be founded—Responsibility. And ultimately—Justice. (26–7)

> We recognize that the application of what, in effect, is an attribution of mitigation before the proof has, in this case, only one end in view, and that is to encourage revelation, to establish truth. Could it be then that, underlying it all, is the working out of that christian theological precept: "The Truth shall make you free?" Or do we seek answers, for this unusual lesson of our time, in a humanism that our own poets and philosophers have ascribed, ... as being uniquely African? Poets and statesmen of the temperament of Leopold Sedar Senghor would, I am certain, endorse this largeness of black generosity. (31–2)

A black generosity that leaves victims unrequited or a reconciliation beyond conciliation? Leading to the question of truth and memory that would somehow promote reconciliation.

But will the South African doctrine work, ultimately? Will society be truly purified as a result of this open articulating of what is known?... Nothing, in reality, is new. The difference is that knowledge is being shared, collectively, and entered formally into the archives of that nation. So, back to the question, this procedural articulating of the known, will it truly heal society? Will it achieve the reconciliation that is the goal of the initiators of this heroic process? For it is heroic—let that value be frankly attributed.... forgiveness is a value that is far more humanly exacting than vengeance. And so—will this undertaking truly "reconcile" the warring tribes of that community? My inclination is very much toward a negative prognosis. An ingredient is missing in this crucible of harmonization and that ingredient is both material and moral. (33–4)

Forgiveness is far more exacting than vengeance. This is an amazing thing to say. Not because human beings crave vengeance and find forgiveness too demanding if possible at all. It is that "more exacting" is given moral force in a context in which it cannot bear it. Soyinka is explicit, we do not know and cannot know what we need to know. We know there were crimes, we know that we can commit crimes in return, we know then what, where we will be? Impossible to know. He says it twice.

The moral element is glaring enough, though it is much too nebulous to assess—that element being remorse and, thus, repentance. Nebulous because one can only observe that an expression of remorse has been made. Is it genuine? Impossible to tell. (34)

The essential is to establish the principle: that some measure of restitution is always essential after dispossession. (36)

For whom, for what? For Africa as a continent? From whom in Africa as a continent?

What remains yet unsettled (not that it is hidden) is just who are the peoples who define themselves, within that same continental boundary, variously as Africans, as being *also* Africans or, as *something other than.*

... Where does that Africa begin and how far does it extend? Just how large and varied is this family of victims? Even if we find it near impossible to decide to whom reparations should actually be made, we can tackle the easier task, it being largely theoretical—identify on whose behalf reparations are being claimed. Is it for an entire continent? Is it for portions of it? Do we have, on that same continent—if indeed we decide that reparations are essential for the enthronement of a new, harmonized order of relationships—do we have on that same landmass called

Africa those from whom reparations should also be demanded? (43–4)

It may be that this question of something other—African, communal, collective, shared—is the exacting question of shared memory. Who or what shares what and to what end, for whom? Soyinka puts this question to Margalit of memory and sharing. Yet the question I am more interested in here is how—I mean of poetry and poets, of muses and arts. In the African context, in memory of African poets, Soyinka reminds us of the relation between memory and poets and their role in truth and reconciliation. I would keep Africa in mind to remind us of the relation between exposition and forgetting.

What of the black African poet in the history of crimes against Africa? What of the African black poet in the shared memories of tribal life? Soyinka speaks of the poet's unique formation in colonialism and self-restoration.[5] *Unique formation* as well as *colonialism* and *displacement*, probably including a *humanistic ethos*, all appear as determinate forms of being. Yet the transformation of the past into the future, truth and reconciliation (without capital letters), speak of becomings and forgettings. And indeed, the relation between becoming and forgetting is the question. Both the truth and the reconciliation must belong to becoming in the mode of remembering and forgetting. They cannot belong wholly to the past. They belong to the past in relation to a singularity of an experience that bears the weight of a memory that cannot be shared and yet must be preserved in its uniqueness for the future.

> A people who do not preserve their memory are a people who have forfeited their history.... It is quite fitting therefore that UNESCO has committed itself to the preservation of the Slave Route, establishing a scientific committee to document, preserve, and open up the landmarks of the Slave Route for posterity. That, in itself, constitutes an act of reparation, will it or not—reparation is still reparation by any other name!... But is that all it can be? Should be? An evocation of trauma several centuries removed, an immersion in accusatory and guilt-ridden history? (58)

Can a poet evoke traumas several centuries removed? Of course, more powerfully and poignantly in poetic language. Can poetry immerse us in accusatory and guilt-ridden history? I'm not so sure, though some poems have been laid down as the basis for violent retributions and agonizing self denials.

Which of these memories, then, least deserves the peace of amnesia? How come that a five-centuries-old "crime against humanity" committed against the Jewish race[6] has not been rele-
gated to the archives of lapsed injustices? Is it nothing but idle
compulsion that drives humanity to exhume and atone for past
crimes against its kind? And is the African world then, yet again,
of another kind, one that is beneath the justice of atonement and
restitution? Justice must be made manifest either for all, or not at
all.

*   *   *

[W]e say of the blindfolded beauty that is Justice: "Age cannot
wither her. Nor custom / Stale her infinite variety" Within that
infinite variety, we may seek pragmatic answers for the modalities of a marriage of the two contending tendencies that will
produce a healing millennial trilogy: Truth, Reparations, and
Reconciliation. (91–2)

We come then to three themes linked around memory and forgetting. One is humanity: our humanness lies in shared remembering, even if we do not truly share our humanity—not because we
are not all human but because we do not and may never know if
humanness is something to share. The second is our group identity, Jewish, South African, black, etc. Here it is not so clear that
the group requires shared memories, though many groups identify
themselves around certain memories—frequently terrible ones—
that constitute who they are. In both these cases it appears that if
we are human, if we are African, we are obliged to remember. Yet
even as Soyinka speaks of preserving memory he opens up the
recognition that to remember is to forget, that what Africa needs is
reparation. Memory is reparation, a way of answering to a past
that cries out for answers.

To which I would respond that pasts do cry out, and what
they cry for is to be forgotten, to be overcome, to be transformed,
to become something new and better. The ethical demand to remember is an ethical demand for an alternative, not to repeat, to
make different. The documentation and preservation of landmarks
of a slave route for posterity is for those who will never have to
take that route for themselves.

We might say that it is to remember and to repay in a certain
way, a certain modality. We might say that it is to forget, escape,
go elsewhere, again in a certain modality. So we come to the third
theme, that of the poet. For poetry is remembering and forgetting
in a certain modality of forgetting and remembering. And among
the forgettings is forgetting itself. This time I mean to speak of the

joined memory of forgetting in the exposition, the *as if*, of denial
that is the condition of slavery.

> Jean Genet, invited to write a play for black actors—a challenge
> that resulted in *The Blacks*, responded with the question, "But
> what is black? And to begin with, what colour is it?" I believe
> that on the mound of slaughtered slaves, pulled downward into
> their resting place and suffused in their ancestral exhalations, an
> allied question must have raised itself in my mind: "But what is
> slave? And to begin with, what humanity is it?"
>
> ... I refer to the condition—slave, the answer to the question:
> "to begin with, what is its humanity?" The answer to that ques-
> tion is: denial.
>
> Now what is a denial of humanity? ... The condition of
> "slave" is a denial of the freedom of action, of the freedom of
> choice. Bondage, be it of the body or of the human will. ...
>
> Nevertheless, there are house slaves and field slaves, and
> there are slaves in gilded cages and the world knows of others
> dangling on the gibbet, rotting on the magnolia tree. There are
> slaves as studs and slaves as victims of castration. There are
> married slaves and merely breeding slaves. And there are
> trusted slaves, keepers of their masters' purse, commercial rep-
> resentatives who travel long distances on their master's business
> and return to give dutiful account. ... But they have never been
> masters of their own existence, nor have they plotted their own
> destiny. To expel this incubus that makes hunchbacks of their
> invisible being, they must first seize and alter that des-
> tiny. ... Between pampered Ariel, with all his own magical pow-
> ers, and the boorish Caliban, there is only a difference of taste—
> both remain slaves of Prospero, and Africa remains trapped in
> the nightmarish illusions of a Tempest.
>
> With this recognition, can the project of reconciliation take
> root? (69–72)

Even for the privileged, who are themselves trapped in the
nightmarish illusions of their freedom, there is denial—forgetting—of their humanity. Let us remember that the questions are,
what color is black? and, what humanity is it? And perhaps we
might add the questions, what truth is it? and, what is speaking?—I mean remembering—in the context of reconciliation. What
reconciliation is it, what memory and forgetting, of the color of
black, the affirmation of humanity, and the truth that must be
spoken? If the condition of slavery is denial then the condition of
reconciliation is affirmation. Yet if slavery and mutilation are in
question, what is to be affirmed? Humanity, Soyinka suggests?

Let me change the question: what is affirmation? I suggest two answers: one the transformation of the world beyond denial, beyond mutilation and slavery—in other words, as if to forget. The other poetry, art, writing, exposition, in the caesura. No other modality of expression can affirm without lapsing into the simulacrum of what it recalls. Truth alone cannot reconcile—if there be such truth.

> Truth alone is never enough to guarantee reconciliation. It has little to do with crime and punishment but with inventiveness— devising a social formula that would minister to the wrongs of dispossession on the one hand, chasten those who deviate from the humane communal order on the other, serve as a criterion for the future conduct of that society, even in times of stress and only then, heal. Memory—of what has been, of acts of commission or omission, of a responsibility abdicated—affects the future conduct of power in any form. Failure to adopt some imaginative recognition of such a principle merely results in the enthronement of a political culture that appears to know no boundaries— the culture of impunity. (81–2)

Soyinka insists on restitution—on money. I would insist on transformations. And perhaps they require money. But they are poetic, beyond exchange. Something beyond exchange, beyond economic transactions even in words as well as funds, is a requisite for healing. Forgiveness as blotting or covering is beyond nothing. Forgiveness as giving beyond exposition is something otherwise.

Here is where Soyinka would take us, first Senghor's extreme forgiveness, inhuman perhaps in a sense still unremembered,[7] then something strangely different.

> No successful attempt can be made to gloss over the dilemma posed by Senghor, poet of peace and conciliator, so let us summarize it thus: articulating or celebrating memory, yet attempting to remain beyond its present impositions, is a feat that is possible only for a poet and priest, a contradiction that finds resolution in that elusive virtue that defines Senghor's "quality of mercy." It is of a different temper from that of Martin Luther King, whose quality of mercy is arbitrated with the rigor, not the catholicity of "love." Perverse though it seemed at the time—and is still thus regarded, to many of his critics and admirers—it is Senghor's, however, that now finds a prophetic resonance in the politics of post-Apartheid South Africa—a case of the poet yet again vindicating his role as one of the "unacknowledged legislators of the world?" (139)

Soyinka speaks in the voice of the name Senghor, poet of peace and conciliator. Yet perhaps it is not the man and poet who appears for us here, but the poem. And perhaps it is not poetry in words, but the appearance. For Soyinka turns from the literary classic—if that is what we have in mind as poetry—to something very small, a musical instrument that embodies poetry in itself.

It is not, however, the battle or the literary classic itself, or the feats of empire-building that constitutes our point of reference, but a little musical instrument called the Sosso-Bala. This instrument [the balafon] had been made by Soumare Kante himself toward the end of the twelfth century. Legend has it that its fabrication was inspired by genies, and is endowed with a supernatural, even sacred character....

Now what has the Sosso-Bala got to do with poetry, Negritude or anti-Negritude, with the Muse of remission, or the deities of rigorous equity? A lot, actually.... The poetry of Senghor is propelled—as has been perceptively remarked by analysts of his works—by the pulsating energy of the traditional griot, a leaping rhythm of self-surmounting ocean waves that is brought to the service of a variety of themes and subjects, even non-African ones. It was only fitting that this rare presence—the Sosso-Bala—should provide the climax, the *piece de résistance* of the three-day celebration....

Well, what was the crowning moment like? We had waited in great anticipation.... The wood appeared unpolished, revealed no suggestion of pedigree timber, the strikers were neither ebony nor ivory.

Yet there, right before us, lay eight centuries of history, poetry, of pride, inspiration, and sacred heritage. A simple, unassuming xylophone that was, however, born out of conflict, of a bloody struggle for power and the travails of nation-building, yet innocuous in its appearance, at once an embodiment of history, yet insulated from it, giving off its own statement of harmony and resolution that constitutes both its reality and innate contradiction....

And the sound? Well, again, an anti-climax. It was no Stradivarius of xylophones. A crisp, aged tonality, but nothing extraordinary, no mystic resonance such as the flute of Orpheus was reputed to have had, or the magic pipes of Akara-ogun in that Yoruba classic, The Forest of a Thousand Daemons. A few tentative notes, welling into a confident seam, then the voice of the female griot joined in, filling the auditorium with the plenum of history from which that instrument, the choir on stage, and we the black listeners had emerged, but the resultant harmony was one that enfolded the gathering in a mantle of humanity that excluded none, neither the colonizers nor the colonized, neither the slavers nor the enslaved, the disdainers or the disdained. . . . It was a dirge of ancestral severance, of loss too great to quantify, only benumbing, yet filled with evocation of a quiescent triumph that is an extract of human resilience, of a shedding of individuation into a tide of universal affirmation of a humane oneness.

Perhaps it is within this territory that lodges the impulse of forgiveness, since oneness eschews distinctions and makes war and peace, creativity and destruction, guilt and innocence, Negritude and Tigritude, Senghor and Depestre . . . all facets of an irreducible humanity and thus steers that dichotomized, even fragmented entity toward a resolution within an anterior harmony. I do not really know. . . . Within such a context, the Sosso-Bala becomes an unsolicited metaphor for the near intolerable burden of memory, a Muse for the poetry of identity and that elusive "leaven" in the dough of humanity—forgiveness, the remission of wrongs, and a recovery of lost innocence. (188–94)

A musical instrument, nothing special in itself and exceptional in its place and history; Soyinka's exposition of its exposition, again nothing special yet exceptional to infinity, touching Senghor's inhuman humanity. All take place, all appear in the caesura of exposition. Where else—in poem, music, dance, image—can forgiveness grow? How else but in unknown and unknowable ways?

What is forgiveness? With what forgetting? In what caesura?

Without the mind of a seer, I now maintain that I can predict (*vor-hersagen*) from the aspects and precursor—signs (*Vorzeichen*) of our times, the achievement (*Erreichung*) of this end, and with it, at the same time, the progressive improvement of mankind, a progress which henceforth cannot be totally reversible . . . a phenomenon of this kind in human history *can never be forgotten* (*vergisst sich nicht mehr*). (Kant, *CF*; quoted in Lyotard, *SH*, 408)[1]

*I*n a mode of extreme urgency Lyotard turns this unforgettable phenomenon toward its explicit subject, progress, under the names of *enthusiasm* and *the sublime.* "Under the somewhat enig-matic title, 'The sign of history,' I am going to suggest an introduc-tion to the reconsideration of the historico-political reality of our time" (Lyotard, *SH*, 393). What other than perhaps mortality might be more imperative than the historico-political reality of our time? Yet perhaps mortality—more than immortality—is more urgent. In-deed, the mortality of the phenomenon is the subject of the sign of history as what can never be forgotten. Even for a long, long time.

The theme of mortality and death as something other than the proper names and beings of those who live and die—and they are the phenomena that concern Lyotard—leads with some urgency of its own to beginning and ending and forgetting and remembering.

Anyone who tries to reflect on historico-political reality today (as always) comes up against names—proper names. . . . For we all of us have a sort of debt, or a sort of rivalry, with respect to names.

These proper names have the following remarkable property:
they place modern historical or political commentary in abeyance.
(393)

They call into question the relation of language and philosophy to
life and death, and they do so by questioning the relevance of any
claim to knowledge concerning life and death.

One could say that language fails us in relation to life and death.
Yet that is neither what I would say nor is it what I would want to
think about in relation to Kant's words. Not whether *there is progress*—the critical judgment that Lyotard questions, not whether humanity is constantly improving, but the losses marked by remembering and forgetting—and not just proper names. For Kant speaks
of the advance of history at the same moment that he speaks of the
end of art, another event for Lyotard. The sign of history marks the
end of art. Progress must abandon art.

> In science, then, the greatest discoverer only differs in degree
> from his laborious imitator and pupil, but he differs specifically
> from him whom nature has gifted for beautiful art. And in this
> there is no depreciation of those great men to whom the human
> race (*Geschlecht*) owes so much gratitude, as compared with na-
> ture's favorites in respect of the talent for beautiful art. For in the
> fact that the former talent is directed to the ever advancing perfec-
> tion of knowledge . . . in this it has a great superiority over those
> who deserve the honor of being called geniuses. For art stands
> still at a certain point; a boundary is set to it beyond which it can-
> not go, which presumably has been reached long ago and cannot
> be extended further. (Kant, *CJ*, §47, 152)

Life and death, beginning and ending, remembering and forgetting go together. The end of art is death, the loss and forgetting of
the meaning and vitality of art. Life forever then is also death, and a
perfect memory is a forgetting, a pretense that what is remembered
can be present again.

A phenomenon that can never be forgotten, an irreversible progress!—with the qualification that the reversal can never be total, as if
it might be reversible in part. Kant does not mean to insist that progress is unbroken, and indeed, some of those breaks may be reverses.
Two steps forward, one step back. Yet steps are strange on the bat-
tlefield of history, and one step back or even sideways might undo
hundreds of forward marches. It is this zigging and zagging that
marks the strangeness of claims to the ends of art. Art is never
straight enough to have an end, but always seems to circle and zag,
so that an end is always another beginning, another beginning is a
repetition, and we never know what meaning a work of art will have

for another future. It will have another meaning than any we can envisage today, including life and death. It is our temptation to forget this, thereby forgetting forgetting.

What would be a total reversal of the progress of history? Would the dead come back to life? Would it be to live another day, in another time and place, or would it be to repeat one life again and again, and how would this be different from death again and again? Once is enough for the same to hold us forever in its grip. Yet the same never holds us in that grip. We forget it enough to relax that hold.

Never to be forgotten appears before us as the death of death, the forgetting of forgetting. And in that reappearance it affirms forgetting and death. If there really is death, if there really is loss, then the dead will someday be gone, truly and irrevocably lost. And this will mark a new beginning, an end and an arrival. All of these losses are forgettings. Arriving is forgetting—what else could it be? The end of art, the end of science, the end of philosophy, and all their beginnings: all are forgettings and remembered as such. Which means that they are remembrances as well.

Let us review the words separated from the question of progress:

> I can predict the future.
> I can know what is to come.
> Without the help of prophecy.
> From the signs of our times.
> The achievement of the end.
> The improvement of humanity.
> That can never be reversed.
> A phenomenon that can never be forgotten.
>
> Science will never come to an end.
> Art stands still at a certain point.
> Knowledge is advancing toward perfection.

Let us imagine these as all entwined, and read them from the standpoint of enlightenment and forgetting. Let us then understand enlightenment as a certain kind of remembering, a certain kind of understanding, a certain possibility of *Mündigkeit*, maturity, with a certain forgetting—at least in English translation.[2]

> *Enlightenment is the human being's emancipation from its self-incurred immaturity.* Immaturity is the inability to make use of one's intellect without the direction of another. This immaturity is *self-incurred* when its cause does not lie in a lack of intellect, but rather in a lack of resolve and courage to make use of one's intel-

lect without the direction of another. *"Sapere aude!* Have the courage to make use of your own intellect!" is hence the motto of enlightenment. (Kant, *WE?*, 17)

Have courage to rely on your own memory! Have the audacity to know!—that is, to remember and to forget. And what of your forgetting and the forgetting of others? What of your immaturity and the immaturity of others? If there be such.

Something similar can be found in an author of a very different persuasion. For in supporting what he calls *the method of inquiry* for resolving doubt, Peirce contrasts it with the methods of *tenacity, authority*, and *a priority*, insisting that inquiry "is the only one of the four methods which presents any distinction of a right and a wrong way" (Peirce, *FB*, 19). By contrast, "the very essence of [the *a priori* method] is to think as one is inclined to think" (19). That is, to remember what one chooses to remember without fear of forgetting. Moreover,

> The *a priori* method is distinguished for its comfortable conclusions. . . . The method of authority will always govern the mass of mankind; and those who wield the various forms of organized force in the state will never be convinced that dangerous reasoning ought not to be suppressed in some way. (20)

The preferred method "must be such that the ultimate conclusion of every man shall be the same. Such is the method of science" (18).

One might choose to emphasize that the method of science is one that everyone can follow to the same result. One might choose to emphasize that because it is so critical and self-critical, the method of science is more *Mündigkeit*, worldly, mature—leading everyone to convergence rather than divergence. Yet these two terms express extreme forms of will present in what we may imagine is the quest for truth: some forms of this quest are not only better but more mature—that is, superior in all ways and not to be reversed; moreover, convergence is superior in all ways and more mature, even where the questions may call for divergence instead—in ethical and aesthetic affairs for example.

One of Kant's most striking views—it may be the definition of enlightenment itself—is that what is maturity and understanding for oneself converges to the universal for everyone. Freedom, individualized in self creation, in the realm of ethics promotes a universal law. It is in the realm of aesthetics alone that freedom—this time of the imagination—promotes diversity and variation, and even here it must be guarded by a hypothetical universal of taste. So the very form of the concept of enlightenment—that it reflects the worldliness of each person's reason, that knowledge is something we come to by ourselves, that once freed from the bonds of church and state authority, we will be free to know for ourselves, critically and individually—subordinates freedom to universality and consensus.

In the realm of art it frequently appears that the maturity and worldliness of each artist and spectator promote anything but consensus, and that only institutional practices promote agreement on artists and works. But that is perhaps why art can offer an alternative paradigm of freedom and understanding—filled one might say with forgetting, with divergence against all pressures toward convergence. Another refrain:

> I can predict the future—and everyone must agree.
> I can know what is to come—and can make you believe.
> Without the help of prophecy—which gives mysterious signs.
> From the signs of our times—which are clear enough to be read into the future's future.
> The achievement of the end—which will be agreed to by all.
> The progressive improvement of humanity—as if without disastrous loss.
> That can never be reversed—in any compelling respects.
> A phenomenon that can never be forgotten—as if that phenomenon were immortal.
>
> Science will never come to an end—but will live forever.
> Art stands still at a certain point—and has already died.
> Knowledge advances toward perfection—as if truth lent itself to perfection and consensus.

What if art has never stood still, and cannot? What if its mobility and volatility were not the fruits of youth and immaturity, but of a forgetting older than any age?

By now it may be clear that I would approach Kant's ideas of enlightenment and reason as ideas of remembering without forgetting, that the questions that might be turned back upon enlightenment from the standpoint of its inflated claims about itself may be of the form, what has it, what have I, forgotten, how can there be enlightenment and freedom without forgetting?

I would first return to Kant. We have seen that although Kant conceives of enlightenment as freedom, he chooses to express this freedom under the heading of *Mündigkeit*, worldliness, maturity, thereby organizing it in developmental terms. Enlightenment is a stage on the pathway from immaturity to maturity, from child to adult, from out of this world to within. This is a strange figure in the context of human freedom and self production. For those who are

still children, for those who think of human beings as children, maturity remains to come, and those who are mature—perhaps more
knowing, perhaps more forceful and more powerful—must impose
order on those who are not. In this way, one can pursue enlightenment at the same time and in the same way that one can refuse it to
the masses, or at least to any individual in particular. And one can
blame the individual rather than institutional powers.

Such a view remains within the precincts of memory, where maturity is, like memory, the possession of certain gifts. We must
know, we must be sure, we must have in our possession the
strengths and qualities of maturity, we must be enlightened and
must have enlightenment. With these we can pass out of childhood,
overcome our immaturity.

Forgetting intersects this picture at an odd angle. It presents to
maturity the question of what must be forgotten to be mature, what
forgetting maturity requires, what unworldliness is required to have
a world. We may wonder, as many have wondered—perhaps not
Kant—if there is something children know and feel that adults have
lost, if forgetting is more vital for maturity than remembering and
possessing truth. Lyotard speaks of this explicitly—indeed, he
speaks of two versions of unworldliness, as far apart and as close as
remembering and forgetting.

> What if human beings, in humanism's sense, were in the process
> of, constrained into, becoming inhuman (that's the first part)? And
> (the second part), what if what is "proper" to humankind were to
> be inhabited by the inhuman?
>
>   Which would make two sorts of inhuman. It is indispensable
> to keep them dissociated. The inhumanity of the system which is
> currently being consolidated under the name of development
> (among others) must not be confused with the infinitely secret one
> of which the soul is hostage.
>
> Shorn of speech, incapable of standing upright, hesitating over the
> objects of its interest, not able to calculate its advantages, not sen-
> sitive to common reason, the child is eminently the human be-
> cause its distress heralds and promises things possible. Its initial
> delay in humanity, which makes it the hostage of the adult com-
> munity, is also what manifests to this community the lack of hu-
> manity it is suffering from, and which calls on it to become more
> human. (Lyotard, *I*, 2–4)

I would read this as a direct response to Kant from within the
same assumptions—Lyotard calls them "humanist," speaks of "two
versions of humanism" (4). One insists that humanness presents a
promise of fulfillment, "That it always remains for the adult to free

himself or herself from the obscure savageness of childhood by bringing about its promise—that is precisely the condition of humankind" (4). One might say that this version of humanism assumes a promise to be remembered.

The other turns toward forgetting and unworldliness in the passage of time.

> Development imposes the saving of time. . . . But writing and reading which advance backwards in the direction of the unknown thing "within" are slow. One loses one's time seeking time lost. Anamnesis is the other pole—not even that, there is no common axis—the *other* of acceleration and abbreviation. (3)

The other of the promise of maturity, fulfillment, and progress is anamnesis, forgetting remembered. If there is a promise of humanization, it lies in turning backward in seeking lost time—never to be found, always in the finding. The image of maturity is of a development that succeeds in saving time toward fulfillment of a promise remembered. The image of lost time is of a forgetting that is a promise of arrival.

I would postpone forgetting and anamnesis here for a while in the context of Kant. For Kant is ambivalent on the nature and promise of immaturity. One the one hand, all the means for maturation have arrived, and it is individuals who are to blame for their lack of maturity.

> Idleness and cowardice are the reasons why such a large segment of humankind, even after nature has long since set it free from foreign direction (*naturaliter maiorennes*), is nonetheless content to remain immature for life; and these are also the reasons why it is so easy for others to set themselves up as their guardians. It is so comfortable to be immature. If I have a book that reasons for me, a pastor who acts as my conscience, a physician who determines my diet for me, etc., then I need not make any effort myself. It is not necessary that I think if I can just pay; others will take such irksome business upon themselves for me. (Kant, *WE?*, 17)

This is a humanistic account in another sense than the two Lyotard emphasizes. It takes for granted and presupposes that "men" (the quotation marks are important) choose to be immature as if that were a choice available to them, as if that determination were not already implicit in who and what they are. The "I" or "we" who gladly remain immature, who need not make any efforts at all, who need not think, are in this context *what* or *who*.

Kant goes on in what appears to be an entirely different direction:

> The guardians who have kindly assumed supervisory responsibility have ensured that the largest part of humanity (including the entirety of the fairer sex) understands progress toward maturity to be not only arduous, but also dangerous. After they have first made their domesticated animals dumb and carefully prevented their tame creatures from daring to take a single step without the walker to which they have been harnessed, they then show the danger that threatens them, should they attempt to walk alone. Yet this danger is not so great, for they would, after falling a few times, eventually learn to walk alone; but one such example makes them timid and generally deters them from all further attempts.
>
> It is thus difficult for any individual to work himself out of the immaturity that has almost become second nature to him. He has even become fond of it and is, for the time being, truly unable to make use of his own reason, because he has never been allowed to try it. (17–8)

The powers that be soon will see to it that most men and all women will regard maturity as highly dangerous. Does this mean risk of harm and death, of falling down upon the ground, or does it mean something more insidious, risking their humanity itself, falling down upon their virtue, what they are as human—girls and women, for example, treated like domesticated animals. When did it become acceptable to society that girls think for themselves? When was it acceptable to adults that children think for themselves? Especially in public.

This sense that the guardians exercise authority over immaturity, that they are guardians not only of the safety of individuals but of their individualities and subjectivities, leads directly to Lyotard and Foucault. Development is something done by some to others in the interests of saving time, of stocking up risks and chances against fulfillments and achievements. A promise always on the way can never be fulfilled.

Kant presents enlightenment as if it came from the free employment of reason without the impediments of dogma and rule, as if secular reason were without rules and dogmas, as if it did not itself present other impediments to truth, as if the guardians of church and state did not employ reason and maturity in the service of their rule. So we may imagine asking enlightenment a question from within its own claims to maturity, what it has forgotten, what obliterated in the service of its own rule, and whether that oblivion is not an infinite loss. Perhaps I mean the loss of faith that dogma counts on for security—something more, perhaps, than inconvenience. Perhaps I mean the depth of feeling that reason tends to ignore. Perhaps I mean the infinite wound that constitutes us as human, and that maturity obscures. The forgetting—anamnesis—of maturity in this way might be the loss of everything human in its name. Anamnesis then, as forgetting, is the restoration of everything human in the nothing, the emptiness, of a promise of maturity that can never be named or fulfilled.

> Statutes and formulae, those mechanical tools of a rational use, or rather misuse, of his natural endowments, are the shackles of a perpetual state of immaturity. And whoever would throw them off would nonetheless make only an uncertain leap over even the narrowest ditch, because he is not used to such freedom of movement. Hence there are only very few who have succeeded through their own intellectual toil in emerging from immaturity and who still walk confidently. (18)

Only a few have freed themselves from dogma—or have they found another dogma in the name of freedom? Only a few have gained maturity—or is the ongoing process without fulfillment or end? And finally, this process, is it toward anything, or away from anything, and must it be so in order to be truthful and free? What if enlightenment posed the question of forgetting as if it could not be overcome by any maturing or remembering? What if the question were always of forgetting and oblivion rather than of remembering and securing? What of a generosity of spirit that remained within the attraction of a promise always to come?

The way out to freedom is characterized by Kant in two ways. One is from the will to submit, as if the source of immaturity lay finally rather than proximately in each individual. Declare yourself free! You can overcome the greater powers. The second is public, the public not private use of reason, from barbarism to enlightenment.

> It is much more likely than an entire public should enlighten itself; indeed it is nearly unavoidable if one allows it the freedom to do so. For there will always be some independent thinkers even among the appointed guardians of the great masses who, after they themselves have thrown off the yoke of immaturity, will spread the spirit of rational appreciation of one's own worth and the calling of every human being to think for himself. . . .
>
> Yet nothing but freedom is required for this enlightenment. And indeed it is the most harmless sort of freedom that may be properly called freedom, namely: to make *public use* of one's reason in all matters. . . . the *public* use of one's reason must be free at all times, and this alone can bring about enlightenment among humans; the *private use* of one's reason may often, however, be

highly restricted without thereby especially impeding the progress of enlightenment. By the public use of one's reason I mean the kind of use that one makes thereof as a *scholar* before the *reading world*. I understand the private use of one's reason to be the use that one may make of it in a *civil* post or office with which one is entrusted. (18–9)

What is the public use of reason? Kant's answer does not overtly address reason, truth, or knowledge—that is, remembering and forgetting—but the public. The public use of reason addresses the entire public, perhaps everyone, perhaps all who think. Yet remembering and forgetting are present in the example: a man of learning, a man of knowledge, who reasons and remembers; the entire reading public, not singing, dancing, or storytelling, but a literate, reading public. And indeed, the difference between an oral and a written culture, an oral and a reading public, lies in remembering and forgetting.

The primary contrasts of public reason would appear to be with private reason and public unreason, in the extreme perhaps with private unreason. Kant appears to have another view in mind, that an official is bound by professional or institutional obligations not to openly voice his thoughts concerning his official duties. He may think for himself, and he may voice his views in public as a citizen or a member of a public, but not as a government official.

The issue here appears to be less of a concrete sense of reason, a determinate sense of how one reasons in public, and more of how and when one can make one's thoughts known to others. It appears that every institution imposes limits on what its members are permitted to say outside institutional boundaries. Perhaps every civic entity, including institutions and disciplines of learning, similarly defines what is permissible to say and do. As Foucault says, one must be "within the true." This, however, blurs the line between what one must say and what is to be presented as true: "a proposition must fulfill some onerous and complex conditions before it can be admitted within a discipline; before it can be pronounced true or false" (Foucault, *DL*, 224).

And it is a blurred line indeed. That one must think for oneself, must use one's own understanding against the control and guidance of others, becomes another form of guidance and control. This is true not only in relation to the implied question of whistle blowing—whether a member of a group is obligated not to divulge disagreements and divergences publicly—but also in relation to what counts as truth. The contrast might well be with liberty in Mill's sense, to think as one pleases. The contrast might well be with something quite different and perhaps more radical, to think and write and express and tell as one pleases—far beyond thinking and writing. What is at stake are liberty and freedom in the modality of thinking and expressing.

Put another way, enlightenment is either coming to share in public certain views and ways of arriving at them, or it is the acceptance of the views and fantasies of anyone against the claim that some knowledges are privileged. Maturity is either being led by one's own understanding to a shared public view or it is the pursuit and dissemination of one's own thoughts wherever they may lead. If the latter seems chaotic, it may well offer a demanding form of maturity, to accept what human beings think without insisting on collective authority. The authority of the mature becomes the nonauthority of each.

This means, of course, that there is no knowledge and truth that comes with maturity except the ability to pursue and to express them. There are no truths that deserve to be remembered except those that embody profound forgetting. What is forgotten, what is forgetting here is the insistence on authority, as if we may hope for some authority—our guardians: civil, liturgical, or disciplinary—to help us to repeat and remember what they tell us is true. Against this, we may refuse to remember, may instead endeavor to forget what they tell us except in the use of our own lives. I do not say *reason* because it carries with it a strong memory of guardianship. It is the very nature of reason to exclude from itself what is not reason, the very madness of reason. I mean the caesura.

> We have yet to write the history of that other form of madness, by which men, in an act of sovereign reason, confine their neighbors, and communicate and recognize each other through the merciless language of non-madness; to define the moment of this conspiracy before it was permanently established in the realm of truth, before it was revived by the lyricism of process. . . . What is originative is the caesura that establishes the distance between reason and nonreason; reason's subjugation of non-reason, wresting from it its truth as madness, crime, or disease, derives explicitly from this point. (Foucault, *Madness and Civilization*, ix–x)

What is originative is the caesura—what can this be but another name for forgetting? Between reason and nonreason lies not a knowledge, not a remembering, but a forgetting, an oblivion, a trace or caesura of what reason and truth are not, yet not as if there were another reason and another truth. Between reason and unreason lies an oblivion that is anything but maturity, that maturity cannot remember. Between one truth and another, one word and another, one saying and another, lies the forgotten caesura. In this context enlightenment begins by imagining that reason knows no caesura, that truth can be known without forgetting, that life's lessons can be remembered. It ends in the caesura of a forgetting that haunts every remembering.

It is time to pass from Kant to Foucault in memory of enlightenment with a brief pause at a passage from Hegel on remembering and forgetting:[3]

> The statues set up are now corpses in stone whence the animating soul has flown, while the hymns of praise are words from which all belief has gone. The tables of the gods are bereft of spiritual food and drink, and from his games and festivals man no more receives the joyful sense of his unity with the divine Being. . . . They are themselves now just what they are for us—beautiful fruit broken off the tree; a kindly fate has passed on these works to us, as a maiden might offer such fruit off a tree. Their actual life as they exist is no longer there, not the tree that bore them, not the earth, ... Our action, therefore, when we enjoy them . . . is external; it consists in wiping off some drop of rain or speck of dust from these fruits, . . . not in order to enter into their very life, but only to represent them ideally or pictorially (*vorstellen*) within ourselves. But just as the maiden who hands us the plucked fruits is more than the nature which presented them in the first instance . . . since in a higher way she gathers all this together into the light of her self-conscious eye, and her gesture in offering the gifts; so too the spirit of the fate, which presents us with those works of art, is more than the ethical life realized in that nation. For it is the *inwardizing* in *us*, in the form of conscious memory (*Er-Innerung*), of the spirit which in them was manifested in a still *external* way;—it is the spirit of the tragic fate which collects all those individual gods and attributes of the substance into the one Pantheon, into the spirit which is itself consciousness of itself as spirit. (Hegel, *PM*, 751–4)

In Hegel, the decayed image, fallen away from its animating spirit, engenders another image, the girl who gathers and offers fruits from the tree. The image is no longer alive, no longer filled with spirit, but remains in history as the promise of a future gathering.

In Nancy's words:

> this girl has no other existence than that of the fruits she presents. For this to occur, she cannot be the gathering together of their brilliance in the concentration of a gaze without being identically the multiplication of her inconsistent identity into the plurality which is alone consistent and preserved, of the works of the Muses. (Nancy, *M*, 54)

I have read these passages elsewhere in the light of the proliferation of the image into other images, the image of the girl as gathering other images as gifts from the Muses, the world as aesthetic phenomenon.[4] Here I wish to concentrate these images, and proliferate them, under the heading of memory and forgetting. Hegel's reading is that the animating spirit of past works is lost, forgotten, but they may be recollected in a later gathering, assembled into a single pantheon. So the forgetting is overcome—sublated—as if it were for the purpose of regathering and remembering.

And what of what has been truly lost, unrecoverably and ungatherably? What if memory failed the test of time, if life and truth were filled with loss? What if the future failed to gather, if it proliferated without gathering so that forgetting remained essential in the images to come, still forgetting, loss, and time? What if there were nothing to the image of maturity, no gathering or remembering, but lives to live and images to proliferate? What if the very meaning of remembering were to be on the outside edge of forgetting, on the verge of utter loss?

It is time for an interruption in the name of loss:

> And so it was that, for a long time afterwards, when I lay awake at night and revived old memories of Combray, I saw no more of it than this sort of luminous panel; sharply defined against a vague and shadowy background, like the panels which the glow of a Bengal light or a searchlight beam will cut out and illuminate in a building the other parts of which remain plunged in darkness: . . . in a word, seen always at the same evening hour, isolated from all its possible surroundings, detached and solitary against the dark background, the bare minimum of scenery necessary (like the decor one sees prescribed on the title-page of an old play, for its performance in the provinces) to the drama of my undressing; as though all Combray had consisted of but two floors joined by a slender staircase, and as though there had been no time there but seven o'clock at night. . . . To me it was in reality all dead.
>
> Permanently dead? Very possibly. (Proust, *ISLT*, I, 58–9)

This death of the past is Hegel's death. Proust is explicit.

> But when a belief vanishes, there survives it—more and more vigorously so as to cloak the absence of the power, now lost to us, of imparting reality to new things—a fetishistic attachment to the old things which it did once animate, as if it was in them and not in ourselves that the divine spark resided, and as if our present incredulity had a contingent cause—the death of the gods. (603)

Followed by:

The reality that I had known no longer existed. It sufficed that Mme Swann did not appear, in the same attire and at the same moment, for the whole avenue to be altered. The places we have known do not belong only to the world of space on which we map them for our own convenience. They were only a thin slice, held between the contiguous impressions that composed our life at that time; the memory of a particular image is but regret for a particular moment; and houses, roads, avenues are as fugitive, alas, as the years. (606)

Proust answers to Hegel's image of the death of the gods, and presents himself as perhaps the girl with fruits. His consolation is hers—her basket I mean, not her thoughts. And perhaps his consolation is not ours.

> I feel that there is much to be said for the Celtic belief that the souls of those whom we have lost are held captive in some inferior being, in an animal, in a plant, in some inanimate object, and thus effectively lost to us until the day (which to many never comes) when we happen to pass by the tree or to obtain possession of the object which forms their prison. Then they start and tremble, they call us by our name, and as soon as we have recognised them the spell is broken. Delivered by us, they have overcome death and return to share our life.
>
> And so it is with our own past. It is a labour in vain to attempt to recapture it: all the efforts of our intellect must prove futile. The past is hidden somewhere outside the realm, beyond the reach of intellect, in some material object (in the sensation which that material object will give us) of which we have no inkling. And it depends on chance whether or not we come upon this object before we ourselves must die. (59–60)

The most famous image of Proust's youth remains as vivid as ever, not without a struggle:

> Many years had elapsed during which nothing of Combray, except what lay in the theatre and the drama of my going to bed there, had any existence for me, when one day in winter, on my return home, my mother, seeing that I was cold, offered me some tea, a thing I did not ordinarily take. I declined at first, and then, for no particular reason, changed my mind. She sent for one of those squat, plump little cakes called "petites madeleines," which look as though they had been moulded in the fluted valve of a scallop shell. And soon, mechanically, dispirited after a dreary day with the prospect of a depressing morrow, I raised to my lips a spoonful of the tea in which I had soaked a morsel of the cake. No sooner had the warm liquid mixed with the crumbs touched my palate than a shiver ran through me and I stopped, intent

upon the extraordinary thing that was happening to me. An ex-
quisite pleasure had invaded my senses, something isolated, detached, with no suggestion of its origin. . . . Whence could it have
come to me, this all-powerful joy? I sensed that it was connected
with the taste of the tea and the cake, but that it infinitely transcended those savours, could not, indeed, be of the same nature.
Where did it come from? What did it mean? How could I seize and
apprehend it? . . .

And suddenly the memory revealed itself. The taste was that
of the little piece of madeleine which on Sunday mornings at
Combray . . . my aunt Leonie used to give me, dipping it first in
her own cup of tea or tisane. . . .

And as soon as I had recognised the taste of the piece of
madeleine soaked in her decoction of lime-blossom which my aunt
used to give me . . . so in that moment all the flowers in our garden
and in L. Swann's park, and the water lilies on the Vivonne and
the good folk of the village and their little dwellings and the par-
ish church and the whole of Combray and its surroundings, taking
shape and solidity, sprang into being, town and gardens alike,
from my cup of tea. (60–4)

In the vividness of what many regard as the greatest achievement of memory, Proust works in the shadow of death—not alone
Gilberte's death and his, nor his mother's and Swann's, but the
death of the gods, the animating spirit of time. The death of the gods
in Hegel, Nietzsche, and Proust is the death of time, the time of
death, remembered and forgotten, forgetting in remembering. People, places, and things all come back and are forgotten in the names
that we announce, the images that we face.

I need only, to make them reappear, pronounce the names Balbec,
Venice, Florence, within whose syllables had gradually accumu-
lated the longing inspired in me by the places for which they
stood. . . .

. . . Words present to us a little picture of things, clear and familiar, like the pictures hung on the walls of schoolrooms to give
children an illustration of what is meant by a carpenter's bench, a
bird, an anthill, things chosen as typical of everything else of the
same sort. But names present to us—of persons, and of towns
which they accustom us to regard as individual, as unique, like
persons—a confused picture, which draws from them, from the
brightness or darkness of their tone, the colour in which it is uni-
formly painted, like one of those posters, entirely blue or entirely
red, in which, on account of the limitations imposed by the process used in their reproduction or by a whim on the designer's
part, not only the sky and the sea are blue or red, but the ships
and the church and the people in the streets. (549–52)

What then is the project of memory but the death of the divine? As death, then, forgetting. As divine, forgiving. In this project, the girl does not insist on returning to have the past in remembering but on giving the fruits of memory in the form of their forgetting. I do not despair at this loss of time—indeed, I would affirm it. But it must be affirmed as the loss it is. For Proust it is affirmed as the death he lives it as being.

> At every moment of our lives we are surrounded by things and people which once were endowed with a rich emotional significance that they no longer possess. But let us cease to make use of them in an unconscious way, let us try to recall what they once were in our eyes, and how often do we not find that a thing later transformed into, as it were, mere raw material for our industrial use was once alive, and alive for us with a personal life of its own. (VI, 504–5)

> How much more worth living did it appear to me now, now that I seemed to see that this life that we live in half-darkness can be illumined, this life that at every moment we distort can be restored to its true pristine shape, that a life, in short, can be realised within the confines of a book! How happy would he be, I thought, the man who had the power to write such a book! What a task awaited him! ... to prepare his book with meticulous care, perpetually regrouping his forces like a general conducting an offensive, and he would have also to endure his book like a form of fatigue, to accept it like a discipline, build it up like a church, follow it like a medical regime, vanquish it like an obstacle, win it like a friendship, cosset it like a little child, create it like a new world without neglecting those mysteries whose explanation is to be found probably only in worlds other than our own and the presentiment of which is the thing that moves us most deeply in life and in art. (507–8)

And so we find that Proust remembers for his book, remembers his book as a monumental task, writes in search of lost time as if to bring about the future through images of the past, writes to save memory in the midst of forgetting—not for himself but for his work. The proliferation of images between death and life.

> This notion of Time embodied, of years past but not separated from us, it was now my intention to emphasise as strongly as possible in my work. And at this very moment, in the house of the Prince de Guermantes, as though to strengthen me in my resolve, the noise of my parents' footsteps as they accompanied M. Swann to the door and the peal—resilient, ferruginous, interminable, fresh and shrill—of the bell on the garden gate which in-formed me that at last he had gone and that Mamma would presently

come upstairs, these sounds rang again in my ears, yes, unmistakably I heard these very sounds, situated though they were in a remote past. . . . And this could only be because its peal had always been there, inside me, and not this sound only but also, between that distant moment and the present one, unrolled in all its vast length, the whole of that past which I was not aware that I carried about within me. . . .

. . . So, if I were given long enough to accomplish my work, I should not fail, even if the effect were to make them resemble monsters, to describe men as occupying so considerable a place, compared with the restricted place which is reserved for them in space, a place on the contrary prolonged past measure, for simultaneously, like giants plunged into the years, they touch the distant epochs through which they have lived, between which so many days have come to range themselves—in Time. (510–32)

In time, the search is exposition, the quarry monsters—I mean images. Proust's re-gathering of the past in a book as memory and time is the presentation of dead gods who are still gods in death. The living present and future of memory is the movement of forgetting. There is nothing here of maturity, nothing of a pantheon, there is beautiful fruit as there was beautiful fruit for the gods. What is dead is the verticality of the image and of those who insist on it repeatedly.

With this image I would return to enlightenment—I mean, of course, that there is nothing enlightened about the girl or her basket, but there is life in the caesura.

Foucault's reading of Kant's essay is remarkably faithful to it in the perhaps incredible sense that he (and Lyotard) both accept the terms or enlightenment Kant defines, of course in their own particular way. I have understood these as pertaining more to the individual subject and its formation than to the time of modernity. With respect to *the present* Foucault reads Kant on his own terms:

In itself and within the Christian tradition, Kant's text poses a new problem. . . .

. . . speaking schematically, we may say that this reflection had until then taken three main forms.

* The present may be represented as belonging to a certain era of the world, distinct from the others through some inherent characteristics, or separated from the others by some dramatic event. . . .

* The present may be interrogated in an attempt to decipher in it the heralding signs of a forthcoming event. . . .

* The present may also be analyzed as a point of transition toward the dawning of a new world. . . .

Now the way Kant poses the question of *Aufklärung* is entirely
different: it is neither a world era to which one belongs, nor an
event whose signs are perceived, nor the dawning of an accomplishment. Kant defines *Aufklärung* in an almost entirely negative
way, as an *Ausgang*, an "exit," a "way out." ... He is not seeking
to understand the present on the basis of a totality or of a future
achievement. He is looking for a difference: What difference does
today introduce with respect to yesterday? (Foucault, *WE?*, 44)

It is no minor matter that Kant writes within the Christian tradition—perhaps within the Greek-Judeo-Christian tradition, if there
be such. For indeed the question of remembering is a question of
tradition, and always raises questions of *perhaps, as if* and *if there be
such*. Is there a world, is there a distinct era of the world, what in
this have we forgotten? Are there signs in the present of a future
that will come as if without forgetting? In the dawning of a new
world, what will be left behind, forgotten, if anything, and for
whom? Do we remember, do we forget, within the boundaries of
identity and tradition—here, perhaps, Christianity again? Does the
secularization of enlightenment reason recall the name of European
Christianity, as if to forget the difference between reason and
dogma?

Finally, then, what difference, what forgetting, if any, marks the
difference between yesterday and today? Not to mention, whose and
which yesterdays and todays, in the plural?

Kant says that this Enlightenment has a *Wahlspruch*: ... that is, a
distinctive feature by which one can be recognized, and it is also a
motto, an instruction that one gives oneself and proposes to others. What, then, is this instruction? *Aude sapere*: "dare to know,"
"have the courage, the audacity, to know." Thus Enlightenment
must be considered both as a process in which men participate
collectively and as an act of courage to be accomplished person-
ally....

... Are we to understand that the entire human race is caught
up in the process of Enlightenment? In that case, we must imagine
Enlightenment as a historical change that affects the political and
social existence of all people on the face of the earth. Or are we to
understand that it involves a change affecting what constitutes the
humanity of human beings? But the question then arises of knowing what this change is.

Kant defines two essential conditions under which mankind
can escape from its immaturity (*minorité*). And these two conditions are at once spiritual and institutional, ethical and political.
(45–6)

Enlightenment takes place among human beings individually and collectively, affects the courage to know and institutions of knowledge, produces a historical change that affects the social and political existence of human beings and their humanity, and finally is both spiritual and institutional, ethical and political. I mean here to emphasize the *also* and the *both* that activate Foucault's reading. These may be interpreted as a conjunction without caesura, in the extreme that "There is Enlightenment when the universal, the free, and the public uses of reason are superimposed on one another" (47). That would appear to be without forgetting. They can be interpreted instead as the caesura that constitutes every one of these terms in itself as well as in their conjunction: universality, freedom, public, and reason. In this caesura, everything is ungathered into the forgotten space that reimposes the superimposition.

Foucault emphasizes the striking way in which Kant recognizes that enlightenment is, above all, a political problem, and the even more remarkable way in which he resolves it. For the public use of reason is accompanied by a private use, and the private use is defined by obedience instead of freedom of conscience. The passage above continues,

> The first of these conditions is that the realm of obedience and the realm of the use of reason be clearly distinguished. Briefly characterizing the immature status, Kant invokes the familiar expression: "Don't think, just follow orders"; such is, according to him, the form in which military discipline, political power, and religious authority are usually exercised. Humanity will reach maturity (*majeure*) when it is no longer required to obey, but when men are told: "Obey, and you will be able to reason as much as you like." ...
>
> We might think that there is nothing very different here from what has been meant, since the sixteenth century, by freedom of conscience: the right to think as one pleases so long as one obeys as one must. Yet ... he adds at once that reason must be free in its public use, and must be submissive in its private use. Which is, term for term, the opposite of what is ordinarily called freedom of conscience. (46)

Another caesura, if you will, between the employment of reason for itself—now become public as if in a general reversal of the public sphere—and submission in one's official roles, now become private as if that were the sphere of conscience. Reason, enlightenment, emerge from the caesura in which practical obedience is freedom.

Enlightenment, as we see, must not be conceived simply as a general process affecting all humanity; it must not be conceived only as an obligation prescribed to individuals: it now appears as a political problem. The question, in any event, is that of knowing how the use of reason can take the public form that it requires, how the audacity to know can be exercised in broad daylight, while individuals are obeying as scrupulously as possible. And Kant, in conclusion, proposes to Frederick II, in scarcely veiled terms, a sort of contract—what might be called the contract of rational despotism with free reason: the public and free use of autonomous reason will be the best guarantee of obedience, on condition, however, that the political principle that must be obeyed itself be in conformity with universal reason. (47)

A condition in which the caesura is a devil's contract—a more accurate description perhaps than madness.

Foucault turns from Kant's text to his historical role in equating modernity (and enlightenment) with critique: Kant's critiques, critique itself, critique as the employment of reason for itself.

Kant in fact describes Enlightenment as the moment when humanity is going to put its own reason to use, without subjecting itself to any authority; now it is precisely at this moment that the critique is necessary, since its role is that of defining the conditions under which the use of reason is legitimate in order to determine what can be known, what must be done, and what may be hoped. Illegitimate uses of reason are what give rise to dogmatism and heteronomy, along with illusion; on the other hand, it is when the legitimate use of reason has been clearly defined in its principles that its autonomy can be assured. The critique is, in a sense, the handbook of reason that has grown up in Enlightenment; and, conversely, the Enlightenment is the age of the critique. (47)

Here critique, understood to define enlightenment modernity, is inseparable from political legitimation. Critique is not the spirit of a modernity that is always in the process of passing beyond itself, but of one that would wrench a new legitimate authority from the vestiges of a dogmatic or illegitimate power. As a politics it takes for granted that critique is legitimation. And again, in the context of obedience and submission, it is a contract with the devil even in the name of Frederick II.

Modernity leads Foucault to the following characterizations as ascribed to Baudelaire:

I wonder whether we may not envisage modernity rather as an attitude than as a period of history. And by "attitude," I mean a mode of relating to contemporary reality; a voluntary choice made by certain people; in the end, a way of thinking and feeling; a way, too, of acting and behaving that at one and the same time marks a relation of belonging and presents itself as a task. . . .

1. Modernity is often characterized in terms of consciousness of the discontinuity of time: a break with tradition, a feeling of novelty, of vertigo in the face of the passing moment. . . . Modernity is not a phenomenon of sensitivity to the fleeting present; it is the will to "heroize" the present. . . .

2. This heroization is ironical, needless to say. The attitude of modernity does not treat the passing moment as sacred in order to try to maintain or perpetuate it. It certainly does not involve harvesting it as a fleeting and interesting curiosity. . . . Baudelairean modernity is an exercise in which extreme attention to what is real is confronted with the practice of a liberty that simultaneously respects this reality and violates it.

3. However, modernity for Baudelaire is not simply a form of relationship to the present; it is also a mode of relationship that has to be established with oneself. The deliberate attitude of modernity is tied to an indispensable asceticism. To be modern is not to accept oneself as one is in the flux of the passing moments; it is to take oneself as object of a complex and difficult elaboration: . . . . This modernity does not "liberate man in his own being"; it compels him to face the task of producing himself.

4. Let me add just one final word. This ironic heroization of the present, this transfiguring play of freedom with reality, this ascetic elaboration of the self—Baudelaire does not imagine that these have any place in society itself, or in the body politic. They can only be produced in another, a different place, which Baudelaire calls art. . . .

. . . I have been seeking to stress that the thread that may connect us with the Enlightenment is not faithfulness to doctrinal elements, but rather the permanent reactivation of an attitude—that is, of a philosophical ethos that could be described as a permanent critique of our historical era. (48–51)

I would emphasize two of these moments, the first the continuation of critique as a condition of modernity, now a permanent critique of our historical era, the second that this permanent reactivation of an attitude, an ethos, occurs in a different place called art.

In art, one might imagine that obedience and submission mean quite different things than they do in state institutions and for petty officials. They mean an obedience and submission to the art, the thing, the project, the work—perhaps in the caesura beyond any work. In art, one might imagine that the insistence on more critique, on a critique that is wary of itself, cannot become permanent. Permanence and art, critique and resistance, move in a shifting and volatile relation. Another way to put this is that we are speaking in the name of enlightenment and modernity of becoming, of trans-gression and transformation, that is, of and in the caesura. Critique legitimates, and even where it would criticize legitimation, it cannot become permanent as such in the caesura. The caesura is every-where and nowhere and anything but permanent. The proliferation of the image is endlessly forgotten. The permanence is impossible, and in being so promotes the endless unforgetting that is critique beyond critique.

And so we come back to anamnesis and forgetting to speak of critique. What comes after (and before) modernity in this sense of permanent critique? What came before—was it without critique? What will come after—will it remain critique? The answer calls for a positive response—this will come, this is critique, this is what we can know and remember. Yet the answer lies not here, in what we might remember, but in what we forget, in the interstice and the caesura, in the way in which critique fails itself as an ethos, a way of life, in what one cannot decide or know or remember or criticize, but must and will be and forget.

It is not critique and its critique that concerns me here, but the subject of forgetting, including time and history—if forgetting can have a subject. Foucault's reading of Kant is that this little text pre-sents philosophy's reason in the midst of time and history in a way that perhaps should not be forgotten.

> The hypothesis I should like to propose is that this little text is located in a sense at the crossroads of critical reflection and reflec-tion on history. It is a reflection by Kant on the contemporary status of his own enterprise. No doubt it is not the first time that a philosopher has given his reasons for undertaking his work at a particular moment. But it seems to me that it is the first time that a philosopher has connected in this way, closely and from the in-side, the significance of his work with respect to knowledge, a re-flection on history and a particular analysis of the specific moment at which he is writing and because of which he is writing. It is in the reflection on "today" as difference in history and as motive for a particular philosophical task that the novelty of this text appears to me to lie.
>
> And, by looking at it in this way, it seems to me we may rec-ognize a point of departure: the outline of what one might call the attitude of modernity. (48)

The key phrases for me here are Kant's reasons for undertaking his work at a particular moment, a reflection on *today* in history, and consequently as a point of departure. For to be at a particular mo-ment, let us imagine that moment as today, is to imagine a certain relation to time and history. It may be called modern, modernity,

and it may bear a certain attitude. But the key point is that it is impossible to be and to write at and for a particular moment. We have
understood this as iterability, and it presents a certain temptation—
to choose. Yet time does not permit us to choose in this way, insists
that we not choose when we choose, that we inhabit more than one
time at any particular moment, that we insist on inhabiting other
times when we inhabit any time, that there is always a point of departure in the attempt and desire to fix. In short, reflection on history and reason is always a reflection on another history and another reason, on forgotten knowledges and lost times and other
reflections. Modernity and history are always different and always
the same in the modalities of remembering and forgetting.

This realization and this temptation—which we may hope to refuse—define our subjectivities and our critical reflections, and they
put in question every meaning of permanence and every name,
proper or otherwise—every propriety, including the permanence of
immaturity—and perhaps maturity. They put in question the forgotten in the caesura between remembering and forgetting. What does
modernity forget, what must it forget to be modern—its past or its
future, its minority or its majority? What does it forget that it must
remember—perhaps in the name of critique? What lost times does
critique—including Kant's legitimizing critiques—remember, or for
that matter forget? What does enlightenment forget in its freedom
and in its submission—perhaps freedom itself? And finally, what do
we remember, and what might we forget, if we called this process of
reactivation of self in affect and performance, *art*?

Foucault concludes his discussion with a return to this permanence of critique.

> It seems to me that Kant's reflection is even a way of philoso-
> phizing that has not been without its importance or effectiveness
> during the last two centuries. The critical ontology of ourselves
> has to be considered not, certainly, as a theory, a doctrine, nor
> even as a permanent body of knowledge that is accumulating; it
> has to be conceived as an attitude, an ethos, a philosophical life in
> which the critique of what we are is at one and the same time the
> historical analysis of the limits that are imposed on us and an ex-
> periment with the possibility of going beyond them. (56)

Not a permanent doctrine or a body of knowledge, but an ongoing
attitude, ethos, life, in which critique is inseparable from the historical analysis of our limits and experimentation with going beyond
them. In the caesura. In resistance to grasping. Even here this permanence can become frozen in a critique and a transcendence that is
either another accumulation or one that promotes critique beyond

critique, an attitude and an ethos unrecognizable elsewhere, a reflective and critical—but not perhaps philosophical—life in which historical analysis is closer to forgetting than to remembering, so that we may experiment more radically and deeply with the possibility of becoming otherwise.

In other words, the framing of the critique, attitude, history, and beyond must all take place in the mode of forgetting—I mean in the provinces of what we call *art*, provided that what that name means is forgotten more than it is remembered. I mean that it takes place in the caesura between remembering and forgetting, between history and oblivion.

I have so far touched lightly on the differences between the German *Unmündigkeit*, the English *immaturity*, and the French *minorité*. Yet between the latter two, between these three and other languages, a caesura opens up between a stage of social development—if there be such—and social domination. An extreme caesura opens up between the derivative meaning in German of *Unmündigkeit*, unmouthing or unanswering, transported by sound and appearance to *immonde* in French, meaning out of this world, abominable and impure. Here is Cixous on this *immonde*, reading Lispector: birds, women, and writing are linked in memory of the men who wrote the Bible telling us what is abominable and what is unclean: *immondo* in French, *immundo* in Brazilian, *immundus* in Latin, impossible to say in English and German. The Bible here, for Cixous and Lispector, is not the anonymous, God-given Bible, but the he-bible written by those he-men. "So those He-Bible, it is they who tell us what is unclean and abominable" (Cixous, *BWW*, 113). G.H. almost kills a cockroach because it and she are *immund*, unclean, but the *imund* is the root.

> I was knowing that the Bible's impure animals are forbidden because the imund is the root. And the law commands that whoever partakes of the imund, must do so without knowing; for, he who partakes of the imund knowing that it is imund, must also come to know that the imund is not imund. Is that it?[5] (Cixous, *BWW*, 116; Lispector, *PGH*, 64, 65)

Is that it? An *imund* question. The law commands that we—birds and women, perhaps men—live in the propriety of the *mundus*, in the authority of the mouth. Those he-bible decide what is good and what is abominable to eat. G.H. imagines that if she can eat what oozes from the cockroach she will be saved. Eating is divine.

For redemption must be in the thing itself. And redemption in the thing itself would be my putting into my own mouth the white paste from the cockroach.

I knew that I would really have to eat the cockroach mass, and all of me eat it, even my very fear eat it. Only then would I have what suddenly seemed to me to be the anti-sin: to eat the cockroach mass is the anti-sin, sin that would kill myself.

The anti-sin. But at what a price.

At the price of my going through the sensation of death. (*PGH*, 157)

I dug my fingernails into the wall: now I tasted the bad taste in my mouth, and then I began to spit, to spit out furiously that taste of nothing at all, taste of a nothingness that nonetheless seemed to me almost sweetened with the taste of certain flower petals, taste of myself—I spit myself out, never reaching the point of feeling that I had finally spit out my whole soul.

I only stopped in my fury . . . when I realized that I was betraying myself. And that, poor me, I couldn't get beyond my own life. (160)

In the Christian tradition—perhaps not my tradition, if you will—eating is a passion. G.H.'s passion links body and blood with what is *imund* to eat, with what can be given in the mouth. G.H. comes to know, as we may know, by partaking of the *imund* that it is not *imund*.

to be "imund," to be unclean with joy. *Immonde*, that is, out of the *mundus* (the *world*). The monde, the world, that is so-called clean. The world that is on the good side of the law, that is "proper," the world of order.

Out there we shall be in the company of swans, storks, and griffons. (Cixous, *BWW*, 117)

What is unclean is expelled, thrown out of the world. By men. By masculine theological, divine law.[6] Law demands that *mund* be *mund*, that law be law, that reason be reason. But Cixous says, and G.H. knows, that what is impure is joy.

what was I afraid of? Being imund? With what?
Being imund with joy.[7] (Cixous, *BWW*, 117)

The purpose of the law is to forbid the root, to prohibit joy. Perhaps more than that, it is to make abominable—to abominate—the *imund*, the out-of-this-world, the improper. the deep, the *Unmündigkeit*, the inhuman.

The caesura that opens up between minority and majority, immaturity and maturity, unreason and reason opens up in French and

Brazilian into the passion of joy and the uncleanness of the root, opens up in German between *Unmündigkeit* and *Mündigkeit*, improper and proper, all in the mouth. The mouth—eating, language, asking, answering, exposition—is the caesura of the inhuman, animal and human mouths. All in the mode of forgetting, in the root. We forget the root. The root is our forgotten.

> All sudden understanding is in the last analysis the revelation of a clear nonunderstanding. Every moment of finding is the losing of oneself. . . . Only now, now I know of a secret. Which I am already forgetting; oh I feel that I am already forgetting . . .
> . . . I found out something I was unable to understand, my lips became sealed, and I retained only the incomprehensible fragments of a ritual. Although for the first time I feel that my forgetting is, in the last analysis, of a piece with the world. . . .
> Is my sacrifice for continuing to be human just forgetting? I shall now be able to recognize in the common faces of some people that . . . that they have forgotten. And that they no longer know that they have forgotten what they have forgotten. (Lispector, *PGH*, 8–9)

We forget the inhuman in what makes us human, the heterogeneity of the root.

In "The Sign of History," Lyotard turns toward the meeting ground Foucault describes between critical reflection and reflection on history as described by Kant in *The Conflict of the Faculties*, written nine years after "What is Enlightenment?" Lyotard's interest in this meeting ground follows Kant's direction: "The Conflict of the Philosophy Faculty with the Faculty of Law" is organized around the "Old Question Raised Again: Is the Human Race Constantly Progressing?" Kant's answer, "There is Progress," Lyotard directs toward the feeling of the sublime in its role as sign of history, with the following conclusion:

> But however negative the signs to which most of the proper names of our political history give rise, we should nevertheless have to judge them as if they proved that this history had moved on a step in its progress; i.e. in the culture of skill and of will. This step would consist in the fact that it is not only the Idea of a single purpose which would be pointed to in our feeling, but already the Idea that this purpose consists in the formation and free exploration of Ideas *in the plural*, the Idea that this end is the beginning of the *infinity of heterogeneous finalities*. (Lyotard, *SH*, 409)

This is cast by Lyotard as the "fission of the single purpose," framed in the light of the end of history. In other words, the single, the one and the same of history is fissioned, fractured by history itself. The end of history is one end only as its unity is dismembered and forgotten.

I would cast this discussion less toward the end, if that is possible, and more toward the sign. Nothing can make the proper names of the dead and wounded add up to a single end of history. In their burials, the proper names constitute heterogeneous histories, which means, as precisely as we can say it, that each régime is unable to include, has forgotten in its oblivions, something utterly profound and truthful in another. We bury the dead, and in so doing, even leaving a mark, we mark the impossibility of this constituting an end of history.

The signs, that is, mark oblivion. I certainly mean death, but I mean much more the losses and wounds, oblivions and caesuras, that constitute time and history and more than history and time. Time is lost, and cannot be saved; an end of history would hope to stock it up. That is Lyotard's language. Loss is loss, there is always oblivion, and though it can be recalled as oblivion, marks what cannot be brought back, what in every bringing back, cannot be. Proper names, Lyotard says, as if to indicate that it is not only time, not only lost time, but lost names, lost signs, lost meanings. *In the plural* expresses, takes place because of forgetting, and every plurality, every pluralism that does not know that it takes place in the midst of forgetting is a plurality without heterogeneity.

The Conflict of the Faculties follows the essay "What is Enlightenment?" and is followed in their own ways by Foucault's "What is Enlightenment?" and Lyotard's "The Sign of History." I put it this way to emphasize that the line that connects them is less one of progress—though that clearly returns—and more one of submission. What appears marginal in Kant's "What is Enlightenment?"— private reason—is reframed nine years later as the higher faculty:

> for a faculty is considered higher only if its teachings—both as to their content and the way they are expounded to the public— interest the government itself, while the faculty whose function is only to look after the interests of science is called lower because it may use its own judgment about what it teaches. Now the government is interested primarily in means for securing the strongest and most lasting influence on the people, and the subjects which the higher faculties teach are just such means. Accordingly, the government reserves the right itself to *sanction* the teachings of the higher faculties, but those of the lower faculty it leaves up to the scholar's reason. (Kant, *CF*, 26–7)

One may read this as a defense of the rights of the lower faculty, and in this way Kant defends a structure not unlike Foucault's emphasis on attitude and ethos, inherent in the faculties of reason it-self. The higher faculties—theology, law, and medicine—are official, and the state has interests in controlling them. But reason itself, in its public and unofficial use, must have a sphere it can call its own.

One may read this instead as a defense and support of govern-mentality. Kant does not question obedience and submission as pre-rogatives the state may claim and enforce upon its citizens. The poli-tics of an enlightened reason must always take second place to the political imperatives of the state. This does not mean that Kant does not argue for the rights of the lower faculty of reason properly within its sphere. As Mary Gregor puts it:

> "The Conflict of the Philosophy Faculty with the Theology Faculty," then, is essentially a vindication of the right of the phil-osophical faculty to freedom of expression, the right to have its ra-tional arguments answered by rational arguments rather than by force. (xxi)

Yet the argument, again in her own language, is that:

> Because it is in the government's interest to have a people it can rely upon, the government has the right to require that the facul-ties set forth their views on the doctrines it sanctions for the clergy to expound to the people, and the faculties have the corre-sponding duty to publish their views on the subject. (xix)

Perhaps the key point from the standpoint of governmentality is that on this reading Kant does not question the government's inter-est, does not concern himself with what would appear to be a view much closer to enlightenment, that if reason is universal and every-one seeks its maturation, then the government too, and other power-ful institutions, must be subservient to it. Governmentality may be qualified by reason, but its right is to sanction and control.

I do not mean to pursue this issue of governmentality beyond noting its role here. I am more concerned with the structure of sub-mission and obedience in the arena of separate faculties. If there are different faculties then, as Lyotard emphasizes, their relation is het-erogeneous. Judgment within each cannot include judgment be-tween. The relation between—this pertains to discourse and lan-guage, phrase regimens, and signs of history—is the caesura, judgment without criteria as Lyotard insists. My interest here is less in this absence of criteria than in the promulgation and transmission of the signs through history. In Mary Gregor's translation:

> Now I claim to be able to predict to the human race—even without prophetic insight—according to the aspects and omens of our day, the attainment of this goal. That is, I predict its progress

toward the better which, from now on, turns out to be no longer completely retrogressive. For such a phenomenon in human history *is not to be forgotten* (*vergisst nicht sich mehr*), because it has revealed a tendency and faculty in human nature for improvement ... which nature and freedom alone, ... could have promised. But so far as time is concerned, it can promise this only indefinitely and as a contingent event. (159)

The phenomenon in question is

of an evolution of a constitution in accordance with natural law which, to be sure, is still not won solely by desperate battles.... This evolution leads to striving after a constitution that cannot be bellicose, that is to say, a republican constitution. (157–9)

If we wished to pursue this question of constitutionality, we might emphasize the development and expansion of governmentality, understood as all the ways in which states and state institutions control the behavior of their citizens by regulation and normalization. We might include the more recent phenomenon of autocratic and tyrannical states that operate as if in the context of democratic constitutional structures, where voting rights in no way affect powerful spheres of control. Such phenomena undercut Kant's evolutionary claim on a purely political level—if there be such.

I remain more interested in what cannot be forgotten though it remain a promise only indefinitely and contingently. What can the words *promise, indefiniteness,* and *contingency* mean if they do not pertain to losses, wounds, and disappearances? What, if democracy remains a promise to come, is not to be forgotten? Surely the meaning of democracy, which must remain as much to come as any implementation. Surely a promise that remains indefinite and contingent remains open and undecided. The promise of the future exists in the modality of forgetting. The sign of the future—I would say also of the past—remains in the oblivion of the contingency of its promise, which means the oblivion of every sign, every mark, every trace, every promise, every meaning—past, present, and future. The modality of every prophecy, including Kant's, remains in the modality of an insight that is fully present only in its forgetting—its indefiniteness and contingency, the oblivion that surrounds its most penetrating truths.

The sign of history cannot be remembered except in the loss of time and meaning. Proper names are not what escape meaning but a different meaning that must and cannot be remembered. In this context, in this way, the promise of a future is the recollection—anamnesis—and unforgetting of a forgotten that will never be remembered. But it will come. In this way, the promise of a future is the enlightenment of a surpassing of the wounds and losses that must be forgotten. This surpassing is not an overcoming, is not a maturation, is not a passage from darkness into light. It is in one sense from darkness—the wounds forgotten—but never into light. Unforgetting is not light over darkness but the caesura between darkness and light, past and future, forgetting and remembering, the proliferation of meaning from the image beyond recall.

The anamnesis of the faculties takes for granted no faculties, higher or lower. It takes for granted that between one remembering and another, one truth and another, one practice and another, emerge the caesuras of forgetting, forgotten caesuras. The forgetting here is not anything forgotten, as if it might be remembered, but is forgetting as condition of remembering. If there is enlightenment— and that is doubtful—it has to lie in this condition and this forgetting, with no way out. It lies much closer to critique, understanding both the permanence and the critique as heterogeneous, that is, in their forgetting. The universal—permanence, totality, everywhere and everywhen—is the heterogeneous, infinitely forgotten. I might speak of a permanent anamnesis, where unforgetting, returning, recollection, and permanence all take place in the caesura of the forgotten.

CHAPTER 5

Counter-History

The fundamental faith of the metaphysicians is *the faith in opposite values.* . . .

For one may doubt, first, whether there are any opposites at all, and secondly whether these popular valuations and opposite values on which the metaphysicians put their seal, are not perhaps merely foreground estimates, only provisional perspectives, perhaps even from some nook, perhaps from below, frog perspectives, as it were, to borrow an expression painters use. For all the value that the true, the truthful, the selfless may deserve, it would still be possible that a higher and more fundamental value for life might have to be ascribed to deception, selfishness, and lust. . . . Maybe! (Nietzsche, *BGE*, #2)

A higher and more fundamental value for life, where philosophy, metaphysics, and Christianity are for death!—a recurrent theme of Nietzsche's writing. Socratism and Christianism are rooted in decay.[1]

Behind this mode of thought and valuation, which must be hostile to art if it is at all genuine, I never failed to sense a *hostility to life*—a furious, vengeful antipathy to life itself; for all of life is based on semblance, art, deception, points of view, and the necessity of perspectives and error. Christianity was from the beginning, essentially and fundamentally, life's nausea and disgust with life, merely concealed behind, masked by, dressed up as, faith in "another" or "better" life. Hatred of "the world," condemnations of the passions, fear of beauty and sensuality, a beyond invented the better to slander this life, at bottom a craving for the nothing, for the end, for respite, for "the sabbath of all sabbaths"—all this always struck me, no less than the unconditional will of Christianity to recognize *only* moral values, as the most dangerous and uncanny form of all possible forms of a "will to decline"—at the very least a sign of abysmal sickness, weariness, discouragement, exhaustion, and the impoverishment of life. (Nietzsche, *ASC*, 22–3)

Europe's will to truth is a will to death—joined with other figures of truth. For *Beyond Good and Evil* begins with the question, "Suppose truth is a woman—what then? Are there not grounds for the suspicion that all philosophers, insofar as they were dogmatists, have been very inexpert about women?" (*BGE*, Pref); and part one begins, just preceding the words on frog perspectives, "The will to truth which will still tempt us to many a venture, that famous truthfulness of which all philosophers so far have spoken with respect—what questions has this will to truth not laid before us! What strange, wicked, questionable questions!" (*BGE*, #1).

With the will to truth in hand for life and its questions for memory—semblance, art, deception—we may turn to history—perhaps for life, perhaps in truth (if there be such). Again, the question is not of history's truth, of remembering events as they happened, but of forgetting—for life, in deception, art, semblance, and error. What of forgetting as the image?

> To be sure, we need history; but our need for it is different from that of the pampered idler in the garden of knowledge. . . . That is, we need it for life and for action, not for the easy withdrawal from life and from action, let alone for white-washing a selfish life and cowardly, base actions. We only wish to serve history to the extent that it serves life, but there is a way of practicing history and a valorization of history in which life atrophies and degenerates: a phenomenon that it will likely be as painful as it is necessary to diagnose in the striking symptoms of our present age. (Nietzsche, *OULHL*, Foreword)

Forget for your life! Remember and study history at your peril! At the risk of atrophy and degeneration!

Some say that Nietzsche has academic history in mind, a science—*Wissenschaft*—of time. Memory, individual or collective, is another matter.

> Observe the herd as it grazes past you: it cannot distinguish yesterday from today, leaps about, eats, sleeps, digests, leaps some more, and carries on like this from morning to night and from day to day, tethered by the short leash of its pleasures and displeasures to the stake of the moment, and thus it is neither melancholy nor bored. It is hard on the human being to observe

this, because he boasts about the superiority of his humanity over animals and yet looks enviously upon their happiness—for the one and only thing that he desires is to live like an animal, neither bored nor in pain, and yet he desires this in vain, because he does not desire it in the same way as does the animal. The human being might ask the animal: "Why do you just look at me like that instead of telling me about your happiness?" The animal wanted to answer, "Because I always immediately forget what I wanted to say"—but it had already forgotten this answer and hence said nothing, so that the human being was left to wonder. (#1)

The animal, Nietzsche insists, does not remember, does not wonder, forgets that it forgets. In this way there is something in animals that human beings admire, not their reason or memory but their oblivion. There is something humans yearn for, not to remember. So perhaps forgetting is something humans might hope for as a means to a better life.

It is difficult to know how seriously to take these remarks on the animal and forgetting. Do animals forget, or do they remember too much? Do human beings yearn to be more like they imagine animals to be? Or do they fear it as they desire it? Are all animals alike, including human animals? Nietzsche places human beings among the animals—with what forgetting?

We no longer derive man from "the spirit" or "the deity"; we have placed him back among the animals. We consider him the strongest animal because he is the most cunning: his spirituality is a consequence of this. On the other hand, we oppose the vanity that would raise its head again here too—as if man had been the great hidden purpose of the evolution of the animals. Man is by no means the crown of creation: every living being stands beside him on the same level of perfection. And even this is saying too much: relatively speaking, man is the most bungled of all the animals, the sickliest, and not one has strayed more dangerously from its instincts. But for all that, he is of course the most *interesting*. (A, 580)

Even here it is not clear that human beings are more interesting— *more bungled* sounds more like Nietzsche—especially when we do not have a measure of a hidden purpose.

Forgetting is the issue, and again it is not clear how to take Nietzsche seriously. Perhaps to laugh.

Imagine the most extreme example, a human being who does not possess the power to forget, who is damned to see becoming everywhere; such a human being would no longer believe in his own being, would no longer believe in himself, would see everything

flow apart in turbulent particles, and would lose himself in this
stream of becoming; like the true student of Heraclitus, in the end
he would hardly even dare to lift a finger. All action requires forgetting, just as the existence of all organic things requires not only
light, but darkness as well. A human being who wanted to experience things in a thoroughly historical manner would be like someone forced to go without sleep, or like an animal supposed to exist
solely by rumination and ever repeated rumination. In other
words, it is possible to live almost without memory, indeed, to
live happily, as the animals show us; but without forgetting, it is
utterly impossible to live at all. Or, to express my theme even
more simply: *There is a degree of sleeplessness, of rumination, of historical sensibility, that injures and ultimately destroys all living things,
whether a human being, a people, or a culture.* (OULHL, #1)

It is tempting to link memory, sleeplessness, rumination (or reflection), and historical sensibility as sharing a destructiveness toward life. I mean the temptation as the link, as if these were the
same, or at least inseparable. Historical sensibility is the same as
reflection. This is not as plausible as Nietzsche suggests, and perhaps there are some forms of historical sensibility and rumination
that benefit human beings and contribute to life. Sleeplessness is
another matter, for it is not only claimed for rumination but it is associated with Heraclitus and becoming. It is as if true becoming and
true experience take place in a detail overwhelming in its multiplicity and intensity. We can live and act only in the midst of an oblivion to the plethora of becoming. We can imagine only in the caesura
of being.

This image of a plethora beyond the goodness of life cannot be
sustained in the context of Nietzsche. It is as if the excess of becoming must be held in check and pushed away, where we know that
Nietzsche dwells in the plethora.

In order to determine this degree and thereby establish the
limit beyond which the past must be forgotten if it is not to become the grave digger of the present, we would have to know exactly how great the shaping power of a human being, a people, a
culture is; by shaping power I mean that power to develop its own
singular character out of itself, to shape and assimilate what is
past and alien, to heal wounds, to replace what has been lost, to
recreate broken forms out of itself alone. . . . Cheerfulness, good
conscience, joyous deeds, faith in what is to come—all this depends, both in the instance of the individual as well as in that of a
people, on whether there is a line that segregates what is discerni-
ble and bright from what is unilluminable and obscure; on
whether one knows how to forget things at the proper time just as

well as one knows how remember at the proper time; on whether one senses with a powerful instinct which occasions should be experienced historically, and which ahistorically. This is the proposition the reader is invited to consider: the ahistorical and the historical are equally necessary for the health of an individual, a people, and a culture. (#1)

Forgetting and remembering are equally necessary—perhaps inseparable. Together they multiply the plethora.

The plethora is the issue, and I'd like to pursue it in the context of becoming. I mean to consider the thought—not unknown to philosophy nor forgotten—in which being is a becoming in which nothing is forgotten, nothing passes away except in the living present.

Not to forget, without loss, Nietzsche suggests, is to be doomed to a plethora of becoming, indeed, to be caught up the flux and flow and turbulence of particles. Yet are we not so caught up, do we not live in a turbulence of becoming, whether we grasp it or not?[2] It is by forgetting that we are able to be who and what we are, by an oblivion to some of what takes place in the turbulence. Being something determinate, living and being and acting as a human being, depends on exclusion and selection—and it is these that Nietzsche describes as forgetting. We cannot be what and who we are except by exclusion.

And the animal? Or the stone? How can they be what and who they are—if anything—except by selection and exclusion? An animal moves and acts, it kicks the stone, flicks the air, and eats the grass. Each of these acts marks a selection, forward and backward, future and past oriented. In choosing to act in this way it chooses not to act in that. In this choosing, or selecting, or simply determining, it marks the future and past with specification. That is surely the word we need: to be is *specification, identification, separation*, and specification is loss, oblivion, disaster, forgetting. Even so this requires more specification itself, not so much with respect to kinds of specification but with respect to forgetting.

What is selection, what exclusion? Are they forgetting, oblivion, loss? Is what Nietzsche calls *ahistorical* what might also be called *forgotten*?

[W]e saw the animal, which is wholly ahistorical and dwells within a horizon almost no larger than a mere point, yet still lives in a certain kind of happiness, at the very least without boredom and dissimulation. We will therefore have to consider the capacity to live to a certain degree ahistorically to be more significant and more originary, insofar as it lays the foundation upon which something just, healthy, and great, something that is truly human, is able to grow at all. . . . It is true: only when the human being, by thinking, reflecting, comparing, analyzing, and synthesizing, limits that ahistorical element, only when a bright, flashing, iridescent light is generated within that enveloping cloud of mist—that is, only by means of the power to utilize the past for life and to reshape past events into history once more—does the human being become a human being; but in an excess of history the human being ceases once again, and without that mantle of the ahistorical he would never have begun and would never have dared to begin. What deeds could a human being possibly accomplish without first entering that misty region of the ahistorical? (#1)

From this passage we can extract two forgettings, one the selection, exclusion, separation that historical being requires. In order to be and act and imagine human beings must be historical in such a way that they do not carry the entire weight of the past upon them, either reflectively in its minutiae or practically in despair. We must be able to set aside the weight of history, the grip of the past, in order to set ourselves toward the future, to escape sickliness of soul.

The second is not this kind of forgetting but is the forgotten itself, something that cannot be remembered because it does not belong to history. Ahistoricality is not located in history, a forgetting of something past that might be remembered, but something— perhaps nothing—that exceeds history, memory, and time. The image, perhaps, beyond imagining.

Here questions of animals and animality return, for it is uncertain whether we or Nietzsche might want to claim that animals live ahistorically in this second sense, whether nonreflective creatures— if that is what animals are: I am again unsure—forget because they do not remember. An excess of ahistoricality is incompatible with humanity—is this humanism? In an excess of history the human being disappears as well.

One might ask what it means for a human being in the flesh to disappear. Is this another oblivion, forgetting? Can we, can such human beings forget that they are human? If being human is anything to remember. Why not imagine instead that being human is something to forget? I mean this less in the mode of oblivion or obliviousness and more in the mode of *perhaps* and *as if*. These cannot mean or be, there can be no promise, except in the perhaps of forgetting. Forgetting here is the condition of alterity that haunts every present memory.

Not to mention endless love. Nietzsche gives us an example of such a love, yet the language in which he gives it opens it up to oblivion. If that were possible.

It is the most unjust condition in the world, narrow, ungrateful to the past, blind to dangers, deaf to warnings; a tiny whirlpool of life in a dead sea of night and oblivion; and yet this condition—ahistorical, antihistorical through and through—is not only the womb of the unjust deed, but of every just deed as well; and no artist will create a picture, no general win a victory, and no people gain its freedom without their having previously desired and striven to accomplish these deeds in just such an ahistorical condition. Just as anyone who acts, in Goethe's words, is always without conscience, so is he also without knowledge: he forgets most things in order to do one thing, he is unjust to whatever lies behind him and recognizes only one right, the right of what is to be. Thus, everyone who acts loves his action infinitely more than it deserves to be loved, and the best deeds occur in such an exuberance of love that, no matter what, they must be unworthy of this love, even if their worth were otherwise incalculably great. (#1)

One may love one's actions, and one's possessions, yet what is crucial is an exuberance of love that cannot be historical, that requires forgetting. Worthiness and unworthiness of action and of love take place in a forgetting of all measures of worth.

We shall call them historical human beings; a glance into the past drives them on toward the future, inflames their courage to go on living, kindles their hope that justice will come, that happiness is waiting just the other side of the mountain they are approaching. These historical human beings believe that the meaning of existence will come ever more to light in the course of a process; they look backward only to understand the present by observation of the prior process and to learn to desire the future even more keenly; they have no idea how ahistorically they think and act despite all their history, nor that their concern with history stands in the service, not of pure knowledge, but of life. (#1)

Suprahistorical human beings have never agreed whether the substance of this doctrine is happiness or resignation, virtue or atonement; but, contrary to all historical modes of viewing the past, they do arrive at unanimity with regard to the statement: the past and the present are one and the same. That is, in all their diversity, they are identical in type, and as the omnipresence of imperishable types they make up a stationary formation of unalterable worth and eternally identical meaning. (#1)

Historical beings derive their future from their past, yet they think and act ahistorically—forgetfully. Their concern for history is for life, for action, and in this way must occupy the caesura between past and present, present and future, ahistorically. Suprahistorical beings give themselves over to eternity as if the present had no meaning without it. Ahistorical beings occupy the present in its present meaning, which is all the meaning there is—not outcomes, fulfillments, ends. This does not mean that there is no becoming, no past, present, and future, no loss of time, but that the loss of time belongs to it intrinsically, that meaning takes place not in the fulfillment of the future but in the caesura of the forgotten.

What is suprahistorical or ahistorical? What can take place out of time and history? Clearly nothing, especially not for one who emphasizes becoming. We must understand ahistoricality and suprahistoricality not as nonhistoricality, atemporality—even here other possibilities offer themselves—but in relation to history, becoming, and time. Nietzsche describes this relation as the identity of past and present. Yet surely he does not mean this as an insistence on the sameness but as a refusal of historical difference. The past determines the present, the present determines the future. What the future will be is an outgrowth of its reception from the past. And indeed this must be so, and indeed it cannot be so. For between the past and future opens up a caesura, between past and future and between determination (by the past) and becoming. Suprahistoricality is pure becoming, yet there is no becoming that is not in time. So pure becoming has to include the loss of time, either by a memory that is so overwhelming as to constitute the present and future by something other than its presence and determination, or by an inheritance and genealogy that does not settle.

What forgetting brings to memory and history is resistance to gathering. The historical person, the person who thinks through history, gathers time into being. What being is—my being, our being— is the becoming of the future in time, gathered up in time. Nietzsche, Whitehead, and Bergson are as historical as they can be, yet they emphasize becoming as ungathering in time. So again, forgetting is not loss, is not lack of remembering, but is positively ungathering. Ungathering is not lack of gathering, as if unity were the primordial condition, as if chaos were lack of order, but is difference beyond gathering and assembling, alterity beyond similarity, caesura beyond binarity, disorder beyond any relation to order.

The ahistorical person dwells in difference, alterity, caesura, disorder without insistence—especially not an historical insistence— that these are subordinate to order and unity.

The One does violence to itself and guards itself against its other.

Being forgets its violence and forgets the forgetting of the forgotten.

Ahistoricality is Nietzsche's word for forgetting, one might say in the flux of becoming. *Suprahistoricality* is Nietzsche's memory of

Schopenhauer—too much Schopenhauer, perhaps—with too little forgetting. But Nietzsche supplements his remembering with a dose of poison—another image of forgetting.

> The excess of history has attacked the shaping power of life, it no longer understands how to utilize the past as a powerful nourishment. This illness is horrible, but nevertheless! If youth did not possess the prophetic gift of nature, then no one would even know that it is an illness and that a paradise of health has been lost. However, this same youth divines with the healing instinct of this same nature how paradise is to be regained; it is acquainted with the balms and remedies effective against the historical sickness, against the excess of history. What are the names of these remedies?
>
> Well, don't be surprised to find out that they are the names of poisons: the antidotes to the historical are—*the ahistorical and the suprahistorical*....
>
> With the term "the ahistorical" I designate the art and power to be able to forget and to enclose oneself in a limited horizon; I term "suprahistorical" those powers that divert one's gaze from what is in the process of becoming to what lends existence the character of something eternal and stable in meaning, to art and religion. Science—for it is science that here would speak of "poisons"—views in this strength, in these powers, antagonistic powers and strengths, ... (#10)

As is the eternal return, here in the spirit of striving, under the image of monuments.

> Of what utility to the contemporary human being, then, is the monumental view of the past, the occupation with the classical and rare accomplishments of earlier times? From it he concludes that the greatness that once existed was at least possible at one time, and that it therefore will probably be possible once again; . . . .
>
> And yet—so that we might immediately learn something new from the same example—how fluid and tentative, how imprecise that comparison would be! . . . Only if the earth always began its drama all over again after the conclusion of the fifth act, only if it were certain that the same entanglement of motives, the same *deus ex machina*, the same catastrophe would recur at fixed intervals, could the powerful human being possibly desire monumental history in its absolute iconic *veracity*, that is, with every fact depicted in all its peculiarity and uniqueness. This is unlikely to happen until astronomers have once again become astrologers. (#2)

Everything of the monumental depends on this worthiness of emulation, in which the past serves as model instead of impetus. Repetition as infinite return disrupts every emulation, every model. There is no model in repetition, only the event again in its differences. This is where Nietzsche and Blanchot differ from Hegel, for whom the monuments of the past perish so that the present may gather another spirit from them. Their decay is the future's vitality. The vitality history gives us is rooted in death and decay. The point of knowledge of the past—memory or history—is to control the differences becoming makes. The point of history is to control the caesuras of becoming. So it is the point of nonhistory, counterhistory, and forgetting—let us call them *archaeology* and *genealogy*—to release the differences and to give the caesuras back to becoming, to search endlessly, again and again, for lost time from within the unavoidability of loss. The unavoidability of loss is the adventure of becoming. The proliferation of images is the wonder and abundance of the image.

With this adventure I leave history aside in its becomings, turning toward the caesuras of genealogy, archaeology, and countermemory. The question for us now may be restated: What shall we remember of the forgetting of history?

CHAPTER 6

Counter-Memory

there is something else to which we are witness, and which we might describe as an *insurrection of subjugated knowledges*. (Foucault, *2L*, 81)

a whole set of knowledges that have been disqualified as inadequate to their task or insufficiently elaborated: naive knowledges, ... (82)

What emerges out of this is something one might call a genealogy, or rather a multiplicity of genealogical researches, a painstaking rediscovery of struggles together with the rude memory of their conflicts. (83)

Let us give the term *genealogy* to the union of erudite knowledge and local memories which allows us to establish a historical knowledge of struggles and to make use of this knowledge tactically today. (83)

If we were to characterise it in two terms, then "archaeology" would be the appropriate methodology of this analysis of local discursivities, and "genealogy" would be the tactics whereby, on the basis of the descriptions of these local discursivities, the subjected knowledges which were thus released would be brought into play. (85)

*A*fter Nietzsche, genealogy becomes something other than the tracing of family and kin through history and time. I suggest the connecting link is oblivion, forgetting, caesura. Nietzsche traces the genealogy of morals to expose the forgotten traces of the becoming of ethics—almost always Christian ethics—as another story, another ethics. What we take as good for all is good for some. What we take as powerful is weak. What we take as good for life is death.

Genealogy is not just hidden traces but movement and becoming. In this way it doubles itself as memory and forgetting. It reworks the movement of remembering and forgetting as it retraces the forgotten memories that constitute the present. It repeats forgetting as it retraces memory. In this way it avoids too simple and rigid a revelation of domination and subjugation.

In this set of passages describing genealogy, one forgetting appears after another, one lost truth upon another: subjugation—not just political and social domination, but the subjection of knowledge, making truth appear; disqualification—together with impropriety, unacceptability, inadequacy, all the ways in which knowledges are banished; the rediscovery of struggles, buried in the triumphant march of the victors; local discursivities—knowledges, truths, and enunciations that remain hidden in a regional terrain never to appear in public.

One crucial meaning of the locality, subjugation, and loss of knowledges remains hidden as a caesura in the collapse of the distinction between public and private that Foucault is famous for bringing to our attention. In the same way in which what is private—sexuality, madness, subjectivity, one's body—has been overtaken and overseen by governmentality, rendered an object for public institutions and economies, other knowledges of sexualities, madnesses, subjectivities, and bodies remain present as traces, local discourses and performances, energize human practices through local forgettings. In the most rational and public places, people practice local knowledges.[1] This is one of the vital truths of social life, the forgettings that animate the possibility of life itself.

In this context, forgetting is the lifeblood of socialization on both sides of subjugation: the forgetting that society demands to institute itself, to normalize itself; the forgetting that remains in full view, those disqualified subjugated knowledges that remain invisible in the face of those who practice them. They do not vanish in the sense that no one engages in them, believes and practices them, but in that no one authorizes them. Similarly, dark and allegedly primitive people do not vanish even as they have no standing, remain forgotten in public institutional spaces.

In this way, archaeology and genealogy reveal what is already revealed though forgotten, disqualified and subjugated. The forgotten is not entirely forgotten, the invisible is not altogether invisible, subjugation is always joined together productively with resistance. As Foucault says of power:

—Power is not something that is acquired, seized, or shared, something that one holds on to or allows to slip away; power is exercised from innumerable points, in the interplay of nonegalitarian and mobile relations.
—Relations of power are not in a position of exteriority with respect to other types of relationships . . . but are immanent in the latter; . . . .
—Power comes from below; that is, there is no binary and all-encompassing opposition between rulers and ruled at the root of power relations, and serving as a general matrix. . . .
—Power relations are both intentional and nonsubjective. . . .
—Where there is power, there is resistance, and yet, or rather consequently, this resistance is never in a position of exteriority with respect to power. . . . These points of resistance are present everywhere in the power network. Hence there is no single locus of great Refusal, no soul of revolt, source of all rebellions, or pure law of the revolutionary. Instead there is a plurality of resistances, each of them a special case: resistances that are possible, necessary, improbable; others that are spontaneous, savage, solitary, concerted, rampant, or violent; still others that are quick to compromise, interested, or sacrificial; by definition, they can only exist in the strategic field of power relations. (Foucault, *HS*, pp. 94–96)

It is tempting to imagine that a subjugated knowledge might be reinstated. I would insist that it could not return as if it had never been forgotten, but as unforgotten, returning as a ghost. It is therefore tempting to imagine in return—and I would succumb to this temptation—that this ghostliness surrounds memory as memory, so that remembering is always imbued with trauma, loss, disaster, and forgetting. But there is another forgetting—many other forgettings—present in these passages. Resistance does not appear as such, nor for that matter does power. Power is productive out of sight, and its invisibility and oblivion is inherent in its productivity. This is true in Foucault's understanding of disciplinary power:

Traditionally, power was what was seen, what was shown and what was manifested and, paradoxically, found the principle of its force in the movement by which it deployed that force. . . . Disciplinary power, on the other hand, is exercised through its invisibility; at the same time it imposes on those whom it subjects a principle of compulsory visibility. (Foucault, *DP*, 184)

It is true as well in the ways in which resistance haunts power, as the invisible, unnoticed, vanished, omnipresent other face of power. When Foucault speaks of resistance everywhere, he means it in very practical terms.

And if I don't ever say what must be done, it isn't because I believe that there's nothing to be done; on the contrary, it is because
i think that there are a thousand things to do, to invent, to forge,
on the part of those who, recognizing the relations of power in
which they're implicated, have decided to resist or escape them.
From this point of view all of my investigations rest on a postulate
of absolute optimism. I do not conduct my analyses in order to
say: this is how things are, look how trapped you are. I say certain
things only to the extent to which I see them as capable of permit-
ting the transformation of reality. (Foucault, RM, 174)

Yet these thousand things to do, to invent, to forge, must present
resistances as something forgotten, invisible, difficult to make present, even as they are everywhere all the time. In other words, Foucault's absolute optimism is the affirmation of forgotten practices in
the present that can transform reality and ourselves in being redis-
covered, unearthed, brought to light. In the relations of power that
dominate and control are relations of freedom in the mode of forgetting. Here imagining and forgetting are inseparable. Perhaps I mean
exposition. In our exposure to the dominations and productions of
the world are the transfigurations of exposition—always in the
mode of *as if* and *perhaps*.

Finally, then, to conclude this discussion—but by no means to
have presented a complete list—there are the extraordinary passages on the archive that mark the possibility of being and thinking
as forgotten that present who we are and what is possible for us, in
this way far from nothing: a history and a remembering that consists
in withdrawing and forgetting.

The analysis of the archive, then, involves a privileged region: at
once close to us, and different from our present existence, it is the
border of time that surrounds our presence, which overhangs it,
and which indicates it in its otherness; it is that which outside
ourselves, delimits us. . . . In this sense, it . . . establishes that we are
difference, that our reason is the difference of discourses, our history the difference of times, our selves the difference of masks.
That difference, far from being the forgotten and recovered origin,
is the dispersion that we are and make. (Foucault, *AK*, 130–1)

Calling for an affirmative discourse of forgetting.

do you think that I would keep so persistently to my task, if I were
not preparing . . . a labyrinth into which I can venture, in which I
can move my discourse, opening up underground passages, forcing it to go far from itself, finding overhangs that reduce and de-
form its itinerary, in which I can lose myself and appear to eyes

that I will never have to meet again. . . . Do not ask who I am and
do not ask me to remain the same. (17)

my discourse, far from determining the locus in which it speaks, is
avoiding the ground on which it could find support. . . . It is trying
to deploy a dispersion that can never be reduced to a single system of differences, a scattering that is not related to absolute axes
of reference; it is trying to operate a decentring that leaves no
privilege to any center. . . . On the contrary, its task is to *make* difference,: to constitute them as objects, to analyse them and to define their concept. (205)

In *The Archaeology of Knowledge* and "Nietzsche, Genealogy, and
History," Foucault contrasts genealogy and archaeology with history. Another contrast with history, not to be too easily forgotten, is
between history and memory, where those who do not know history—in this case because it has been taken away from them—
remember too little but more than enough to lend themselves to political manipulation. Speaking of Yugoslavia and Croatia, Slavenka
Drakulić says the following: "It is easy for political leaders to use
images like the ones that I remember [of war, atrocities, annihila-
tion], to use people's emotional memory and build hatred upon it.
Because in totalitarian societies, where there is no true history, each
person has in his own memory a collection of such images, and it
becomes dangerous if he has nothing more than that" (Drakulić,
WPC, B7). People who do not know their histories of crimes, violences, destructions lend themselves to manipulation in the name of
memories. Perhaps.

The issue is of the truth of history—I mean the truths of histories. Perhaps this is a place where we can remember forgetting in
the caesuras between memory and history, history and time, between one history and another, one truth and another. Perhaps forgetting relates to lost time in a way that answers to the loss, but
does not give the answer as if it were to be refound. Drakulić recognizes that truth and history can be taken away but believes that
memories remain, so that the issue of history and truth is of what
has been made forgotten by state powers and official policies. The
issue is that such powers always make something forgotten, insist
on remembering history in a certain mode that requires forgetting
and obliterating for its construction.

Yet Drakulić is surely wrong to think that some other history
will not make something else forgotten, that there is a truth of history that overrides the forgetting of memory. To the contrary, I
would say, it is the traces of remembered losses, of violences and
wounds, remembered and forgotten, from which any recovered his-

tory of state power may be rebuilt. The academic history that constructs a certain narrative of Croatian injustice may be replaced by another academic or institutional history. Both will engage in obliteration of some memories of wounds and traumas.

That is where Foucault's reading of archaeology and genealogy enters, right in the midst of the caesura between one history and another, one memory and another, one truth and another. The question of truth is the question of the caesura—that is of forgetting and obliteration. As he sums it up, "The political question, to sum up, is not error, illusion, alienated consciousness or ideology; it is truth itself. Hence the importance of Nietzsche" (Foucault, *TP*, 133). The political question is truth itself, and is not settled by the truth but puts it into question. The issue of Croatian history is the question of régimes of truth.

That is how Foucault reads history—as a *régime* of truth, as the production of institutions of truth. In this way, history is instituted as its own truth. Archaeology and genealogy resist this institution, the first as a mode of analysis, the second as a mode of practice—if this distinction can be defended. But that is less important here than the recognition that both insist on the locality of discursivity, knowledge, and truth. Both insist on the local forgettings and the questionings that emerge from them of history and memory. The analysis of a local truth remains local. The insurrection proceeds as much by subjugation as the knowledges it would bring into play. In relation to Nietzsche and genealogy, Foucault describes this as follows:

> Humanity does not progress from combat to combat until it arrives at universal reciprocity, where the rule of law finally replaces warfare; humanity installs each of its violences in a system of rules and thus proceeds from domination to domination.
>
> The nature of these rules allows violence to be inflicted on violence and the resurgence of new forces that are sufficiently strong to dominate those in power. (Foucault, *NGH*, 150–51)

Here, as in his later discussions of power, domination and power contain their own disruptions, not by controlling them but in that power and domination can never be total; history and truth can never be complete. Domination releases forces that dominate the dominators—less the individuals and more the forces and institutions. Wherever there is power there is resistance, wherever there is domination there is counter-domination. wherever there is history there is counter-history, wherever there is truth there is another truth. Archaeology and genealogy are these other truths and other practices. That is, questions and still other questions, practices and alternative practices. Archaeology and genealogy take place in

Heidegger's opening of the questioning of questioning.[2] What is questioning, where does it begin and end, what is life (and philosophy) but this questioning of questioning? And what is this questioning but forgetting? What is forgetting, where does it begin and end, and what is life (and truth) but the caesura between remembering and forgetting, the question of (the question) of truth itself?

The affirmative side of genealogy seems buried, suffocated in the succession of dominations. Even where domination turns back on domination, it remains domination. Even where resistance accompanies power, it appears that power is domination. Yet power becomes production rather than control, productive power, and one of its productions is resistance. And it does so entirely visibly, in the light, and entirely invisibly as well. Visibility and invisibility are not opposites or complements but express the boundaries and transgressions of each. Power and resistance, remembering and forgetting, are not opposites or complements but express the transgressions and boundaries of each. Most important of all, forgetting is aligned with resistance and invisibility in the coming of the event.

For the key to the affirmation lies not in the domination of domination but in the space in which it takes place. On the one hand, genealogy takes place in the smallest crevices, detailed minutiae, interstices and caesuras:

> Genealogy is gray, meticulous, and patiently documentary. It operates on a field of entangled and confused parchments, on documents that have been scratched over and copied many times. (Foucault, *NGH*, 139)

> Genealogy, consequently, requires patience and a knowledge of details and it depends on a vast accumulation of source material. . . . In short, genealogy demands relentless erudition. (140)

> Genealogies are therefore not positivistic returns to a more careful or exact form of science. They are precisely anti-sciences. (Foucault, *2L*, 83)

This raises the question of how something so drab and scholarly—gray, meticulous, and patient—can be an insurrection except as one of the unexpected ways in which resistance arises. The answer has to be that history and domination fail to exhaust totality, that they include emergences and transformations—singulars, deviations, accidents, contingencies.

> to follow the complex course of descent . . . is to identify the accidents, the minute deviations—or conversely, the complete reversals—the errors, the false appraisals, the faulty calculations that gave birth to those things that continue to exist and have value for

us; it is to discover that truth or being do not lie at the root of what we know and what we are, but the exteriority of accidents. (Foucault, *NGH*, 146)

> *Entstehung* designates *emergence*, the moment of arising. It stands as the principle and the singular law of an apparition. As it is wrong to search for descent in uninterrupted continuity, we should avoid thinking of emergence as the final term of an historical development; . . . . (148)

Emergence and interruption belong to history as forgetting belongs to memory, the apparition of singularities, of what does not belong. To the question that follows—Nietzsche's question—"How can we define the relationship between genealogy and history," Foucault responds in terms of rupture and discontinuity, as he does in *The Archaeology of Knowledge* and *The Discourse on Language*:

> in our time history aspires to the condition of archaeology, to the intrinsic description of the monument.
>
> This has several consequences. First of all, . . . the proliferation of discontinuities in the history of ideas, ...
>
> Second consequence: the notion of discontinuity assumes a major role in the historical disciplines. . . .
>
> Third consequence: the theme and the possibility of a *total history* begins to disappear, and we see the emergence of something very different that might be called a *general history*. (Foucault, *AK*, 7–9)

> I believe we must resolve ourselves . . . : to question our will to truth, to restore to discourse its character as an event; to abolish the sovereignty of the signifier.
>
> [Demanding]
>
> A principle of *reversal*, first of all. Where, according to tradition, we think we recognise the source of discourse, . . . we must rather recognise the negative activity of the cutting-out and rarefaction of discourse. . . .
>
> Next, then, the principle of *discontinuity*. . . . Discourse must be treated as a discontinuous activity, its different manifestations sometimes coming together, but just as easily unaware of, or excluding each other.
>
> The principle of *specificity* declares that a particular discourse cannot be resolved by a prior system of significations. . . . We must conceive discourse as a violence that we do to things, or, at all events, as a practice we impose upon them. . . .
>
> The fourth principle, that of *exteriority*, holds that we are not to burrow to the hidden core of discourse, . . . ; instead, taking the discourse itself, its appearance and its regularity, that we should look for its external conditions of existence, for that which gives

rise to the chance series of these events and fixes its limits. (Foucault, *DL*, 229)

From the standpoint of knowledge, rupture and discontinuity represent breaks in unity and accountability. We might call that forgetting. But rupture and discontinuity pertain to practice—even the practices of history, archaeology, and genealogy—as well as knowledge and science. Foucault spells out resistance as interruption.

> The historical sense gives rise to three uses that oppose and correspond to the three Platonic modalities of history. The first is parodic, directed against reality, and opposes the theme of history as reminiscence or recognition; the second is dissociative, directed against identity, and opposes history as knowledge. They imply a use of history that severs its connection to memory, its metaphysical and anthropological model, and constructs a counter-memory—a transformation of history into a totally different form of time.
>
> First, the parodic and farcical use. The historian offers this confused and anonymous European, who no longer knows himself or what name he should adopt, the possibility of alternate identities, more individualized and substantial than his own. . . . Taking up these masks, revitalizing the buffoonery of history, we adopt an identity whose unreality surpasses that of God who started the charade. . . .
>
> The second use of history is the systematic dissociation of identity. . . . If genealogy in its own right gives rise to questions concerning our native land, native language, or the laws that govern us, its intention is to reveal the heterogeneous systems which, masked by the self, inhibit the formation of any form of identity.
>
> The third use of history is the sacrifice of the subject of knowledge. . . . The historical analysis of this rancorous will to knowledge reveals that all knowledge rests upon injustice (that there is no right, not even in the act of knowing, to truth or a foundation for truth) and that the instinct for knowledge is malicious (something murderous, opposed to the happiness of mankind). (*NGH*, 160–3)

The systematic dissociation of identity, the sacrifice of the subject, are violences toward history, justified perhaps by the murderousness of knowledge. One might understand the issue, in terms of forgetting, as the realization that remembering, having the past again, is malicious, murderous, and destructive of happiness. We have seen this before in Nietzsche's forgetting of history, so Foucault's genealogy here bears at least two signs of forgetting in the midst of historical memory: the destruction of knowledge as the condition of memory and history, and the interruption of history as the *Entstehung* of genealogy. Genealogy is meticulous and gray but it takes place in the disruptions of the continuity of time that we associate with history and memory. The claim to know the past, to possess knowledge of history, is a domination that calls for resistance as withdrawal, insurrection, and forgetting.

Nevertheless, the first resistance calls for a closer look. Parody is a different interruption, one that carries itself through history and memory at the heart of their activity. What we remember, what we know as history, what we insist that we recognize and know as the past always appears as its own parody, which we repeat in counter-memory. Counter-memory then is a memory and a remembering that dissociates itself—let us say both inevitably and resistantly—in the act of recognition—I mean mimicry—itself. Parody is aesthetic, a resource we associate with literature and art, but its activity is the forgetting in remembering, the dissembling in assembling, the production of a different form of time.

What could be a different form of time, a different time? The appearance, manifestation, realization of such a time is in parody— let us say it is aesthetic, appears as if it were in art—as forgetting. The different time is the forgotten, which here means that whose existence is invisible and inaudible, forgotten traces of what is present as time. Genealogy here is the forgetting in the traces, meticulously tracing traces that are never remembered but present as forgotten.

This brings us to a different meaning and understanding of *exteriority*, not as the outside of an inside but the heterogeneity of the inside-outside, remembered-forgotten that is not only memory but history, genealogy, life itself. Counter-memory is the other time whose existence takes place in the first time, in the lost or forgotten first time, where the counter is forgetting on top of forgetting—the return of the forgotten—and where the "-" is the caesura.

If we are to think of history from the standpoint of the forgotten—counter-memory, genealogy, and archaeology—we might wish to pass through the discussions in *The Order of Things* where history itself is foregrounded as if it were something to remember, as if it were something to know. History arrives in history as a form of knowledge, arises when

> [t]he last years of the eighteenth century are broken by a discontinuity similar to that which destroyed Renaissance thought at the beginning of the seventeenth; . . . a discontinuity as enigmatic in its principle, in its original rupture, as that which separates the Paracelsian circles from the Cartesian order. (*OT*, 217)

Rupture, discontinuity, breaks are history, in history and as history. This more than anything appears to be Foucault's message concerning history and time. History and time insist on continuity, demand and create a continuum of time. Yet their being—the being of history and of time—comes into existence at a moment, discontinuously, and continues in its continuum with breaks, ruptures, and further discontinuities.

Such a view cannot mean that history and time are *really* discontinuous, that *the truth* of time is ruptures and breaks. Ruptures, discontinuities, and breaks pertain to the succession and to its knowledge. Knowledge of history is itself ruptured, discontinuous, and broken, as is the experience and flow of the histories in which these knowledges emerge. That is the emergence of *Entstehung* and *Ereignis*. Put another way, emergence is not a fact; *Entstehung* and *Ereignis* are not facts of rupture that replace facts of juncture. They are time and history in the mode of forgetting the being of history and time themselves, displacement as time and history themselves.

The Order of Things is framed as a break in European history—by no means the history of the world if there be such—in which classical representation replaces the prose of the world. In the preface, Foucault alludes to Borges's Chinese encyclopaedia from "The Analytical Language of John Wilkens" as establishing "that the common ground on which such meetings are possible has itself been destroyed" (*OT*, xvi; Borges, *ALJW*). This common ground is one of meaning, as if we can understand, communicate, think, write only on such a ground, and as if creating a common ground were the task of representation and of history.

This gesture toward the nonexistence of a common ground is followed first by the chapter on *Las Meninas* in which that ground—no ground at all—is the subject-sovereign of representation (that cannot be represented),[3] then second by the chapter on the prose of the world in which there is no history, history cannot appear, the world is too full of resemblances for history as knowledge to make its appearance.

> *Convenientia, aemulatio, analogy*, and *sympathy* tell us how the world must fold in upon itself, duplicate itself, reflect itself, or form a chain with itself so that things can resemble one another. (Foucault, *OT*, 25–6)

> There is something in emulation of the reflection and the mirror: it is the means whereby things scattered through the universe can answer one another.... But which of these reflections coursing through space are the original images? Which is the reality and which the projection? It is often not possible to say, for emulation

is a sort of natural twinship existing in things; it arises from a fold in being, the two sides of which stand immediately opposite to one another. (19–20)

History disappears here in several ways. One is that the arrow of time is submerged and made to vanish in the endless play of similitudes, of signs of signs of signs. History's truth depends on a cut in this endless folding and refolding. A second is that this fold in being competes with history's folds, where the first is face to face and the second is spread out in time. A third is that no cut cuts away the ways in which things scattered answer to each other. History imposes a linear cut.

> The semantic web of resemblance in the sixteenth century is extremely rich: *Amicitia, Aequalitas (contractus, consensus, matrimonium, societas, pax, et similia), Consonantia, Concertus, Continuum, Paritas, Proportio, Similitudo, Conjunctio, Copula.* (OT, 17)

> There are no resemblances without signatures. The world of similarity can only be a world of signs. (26)

And so we may see that one of the marks of history is its refusal of the refolding of memory—which is another name for forgetting. History insists that what it knows it knows without withdrawal. The prose of the world is nothing but withdrawal, nothing but forgetting, in the great web of mirrors in which everything is present, everything is folded together in a way that means everything and nothing. History unfolds the folds and does not refold them. Memory and forgetting are a plethora of refoldings.

On this reading history emerges as a form of knowledge that unfolds the darkness of being and the plethora of signs. It appears in a chapter that again appears to deny it, under the heading of classifying. And it comes on stage through the doorway of history— what historians say about the sciences in the 17th and 18th centuries.

> Histories of ideas or of the sciences—by which is meant here an average cross-section of them—credit the seventeenth century, and especially the eighteenth, with a new curiosity: the curiosity that caused them, if not to discover the sciences of life, at least to give them a hitherto unsuspected scope and precision. (OT, 125)

The sciences of life—including history—are discovered, come into existence as if they were objects before the eye, not as if they were brought into existence by a prior history, curiosity, and questioning, and where history is not something to discover but to create. And the historians who discover—when did they come into existence, what is the value and truth of what they say, against what background can we measure history's truth, under what scheme of memory?

> Historians want to write histories of biology in the eighteenth century; but they do not realize that biology did not exist then, and that the pattern of knowledge that has been familiar to us for a hundred and fifty years is not valid for a previous period. And that, if biology was unknown, there was a very simple reason for it: that life itself did not exist. All that existed was living beings, which were viewed through a grid of knowledge constituted by *natural history*. (*OT*, 127–8)

History itself did not exist. All that existed were living beings who lived and died.

Foucault asks the question of the coming to be in time of such a thing as natural history:

> How was the Classical age able to define this realm of "natural history," . . . ? What is this field in which nature appeared sufficiently close to itself for the individual beings it contained to be classified, and yet so far from itself that they had to be so by the medium of analysis and reflection? (*OT*, 128)

So close and so far are figures of folding, unfolding, and refolding. Natural history—perhaps any history—must take the unbounded phenomena of nature on the one hand and the boundless forms of meaning—images, signs, words, appearances of all kinds—and create an image both of the natural world and of its analysis and its reflection. This reflection and analysis is history—in this case natural history, the history of the production of classifiable things. "For natural history to appear . . . it was necessary . . . for History to become Natural. In the sixteenth century, and right up to the middle of the seventeenth, all that existed was history" (128).

That is, stories of classification on the side of the classified and the classifiers: many different stories. Natural history insisted on an overarching History of Nature under the heading of the classification of inexhaustibly multiple things.

> Natural history finds its locus in the gap that is now opened up between things and words—a silent gap, pure of all verbal sedimentation, and yet articulated according to the elements of representation, those same elements that can now without let or hindrance be named. . . . Before this language of language, it is the thing itself that appears, in its own characters, but within the reality that has been patterned from the very outset by the name. . . .

> Thus the old word "history" changes its value, and perhaps rediscovers one of its archaic significations. In any case, though it is true that the historian, for the Greeks, was indeed the individual who *sees* and who recounts from the starting-point of his sight, it has not always been so in our culture. (129–30)

Not always so and perhaps not so today: a recounting that is indissociable from memory, not because of the validity or authenticity of the seeing but in the folds of memory and forgetting that constitute the story. The story is everything, told about everything, from within the caesura or fold of being.

Natural history is nature's history, being's temporality, in the mode of totality or infinity. The multiplicity and multiplication of each being and kind of being's story recedes or multiplies to infinity. The aggregate of beings has a story only under the heading of totality. Discontinuity, rupture, break do not speak of the truth of totality—that it is discontinuous—but break off the truth of totality, turning History into histories, inseparable from memory—which can never be Memory so long as there is forgetting.

In Foucault's words, closing the section on natural history:

> And it is in this classified time, in this squared and spatialized development, that the historians of the nineteenth century were to undertake the creation of a history that could at last be "true"—in other words, liberated from Classical rationality, from its ordering and theodicy: a history restored to the irruptive violence of time. (132)

It is as if the truth of time and history were this irruptive violence against the continuum of time. Yet it is also as if the name of history belonged to this square box of classification, as if history were not a story but an ordered totality. Irruptive violence fragments this order and its totality. And perhaps there is today no other choice. But forgetting—which must never be forgotten—offers another way, another possibility, if not another choice. It is important not to understand history as a choice, as if we might make another. Even as we understand ourselves to construct history as an assemblage of knowledges we live in it, remember and forget. We forget even as we choose an assemblage, forget in order to create the assemblage, but have already forgotten in living and remembering.

Natural History emerged as Natural and as History in the midst of histories. The Age of History emerged as History again in the midst of histories, detached and presented itself as history. In a pure act of forgetting.

> How is it that thought detaches itself from the squares it inhabited before—general grammar, natural history, wealth—and allows what less than twenty years before had been posited and affirmed in the luminous space of understanding to topple down into error, into the realm of fantasy, into non-knowledge? (217)

One might imagine that the older (view of) history was untrue, wrong, inadequate, replaced by a newer (understanding of) history. Yet if this were so, one might also imagine that the older view might coexist with the newer, coexist in history. For history, old or new, includes both the older and newer (views of) history.

Foucault insists that the newer does not follow Hegel, nor does it produce an inclusive history that includes the old. A transformation takes place in which the old is largely forgotten—and this despite the historians who struggle to recall those older views as predecessors and precursors of the newer. If there is such a thing as newer history, it can never be History even where it claims to be such.

From a very different perspective, Ferry makes a similar point concerning the transformation from the medieval to the modern world in relation to animals.

> 1587: The inhabitants of the village of Saint-Julien took legal action against a colony of weevils. . . .
>
> Forty or so years earlier, in 1545, an identical trial had taken place against the same creepers (or at least their ancestors). The affair ended in victory for the insects. . . . The [episcopal judge] had refused to excommunicate them, arguing that as creatures of God the animals possessed the same rights as men to consume plant life; . . . . (Ferry, *NEO*, ix)

> What kind of breach must have opened within humankind for the ritual performed in all seriousness in one era to turn to high comedy in another? (xvi)

Ferry's answer is given by modern, secular, humanist society in which only human beings have rights.[4] This means that such a society, and such a humanism, arises to constitute modernity in a monumental act of forgetting—and this is true whatever one's view of modernity. It is not that the past is forgotten, but that it is recalled in a modern mode, as if it were a precursor of the present. This means that history itself takes place as forgetting, in effect that there is no history as such, no truth of history as such, that the distinction between history and memory (and forgetting) is porous and insubstantial. The age of history is the age of a certain kind of history, a certain kind of construction, a certain relation to past and future.

Foucault describes this relation as follows:

> History in this sense is not to be understood as the compilation of factual successions or sequences as they may have occurred; it is the fundamental mode of being of empiricities, upon the basis of which they are affirmed, posited, arranged, and distributed for the use of such disciplines or sciences as may arise. . . . Since it is the mode of being of all that is given us in experience, History has become the unavoidable element in our thought: . . . . In the nineteenth century, philosophy was to reside in the gap between history and History, between events and the Origin, between evolution and the first rending open of the source, between oblivion and the Return. It will be Metaphysics, therefore, only in so far as it is Memory, and it will necessarily lead thought back to the question of knowing what it means for thought to have a history. (*OT*, 219–20)

This question of what it means for thought to have a history is perhaps not so different from the question of what it means for anything, human or natural, to have a history. The answer, no matter how different, is always the same: as philosophy resides in the gap between history and History, so does history (and so does History), a gap or caesura between one oblivion and another, the other and the same. Metaphysics is memory, but so is history, that is, the caesura between the same and the other beyond time.

The Order of Things is concerned with History as science, whether European (*Wissenschaft* or *Recherche*) or American. This science takes place in the field of empiricities, and takes that field for granted. This scientization of experience is the first emergence of knowledge as forgetting, in which the empirical replaces experience itself, and in which replacement is or touches oblivion as a certain kind of forgetting.

The emergence of the human sciences takes place around the figure of Man as a transcendental doublet:

> Man, in the analytic of finitude, is a strange empirico-transcendental doublet, since he is a being such that knowledge will be attained in him of what renders all knowledge possible. (318)

> Man is a mode of being which accommodates that dimension—always open, never finally delimited, yet constantly traversed—which extends from a part of himself not reflected in a *cogito* to the act of thought by which he apprehends that part; and which, in the inverse direction, extends from that pure apprehension to the empirical clutter, the chaotic accumulation of contents, the weight of experiences constantly eluding themselves, the

> whole silent horizon of what is posited in the sandy stretches of non-thought. (322–3)

> The question is no longer: How can experience of nature give rise to necessary judgments? But rather: How can man think what he does not think, inhabit as though by a mute occupation something that eludes him, animate with a kind of frozen movement that figure of himself that takes the form of a stubborn exteriority? (323)

How can human beings think, and remember, what they do not think, and have forgotten? The answer of modernity is that thought can be thought as if it were not forgotten. The answer we are considering here, with Foucault, is that the thought is of the forgotten as if not to remember it. The forgotten remains forgotten, forgetting is oblivion, yet we can think and remember the forgetting if not the forgotten.

The question is how this is possible. Or perhaps that is not the question, since it appears to repeat the insistence of the human sciences that we can know what do not know. I mean to question the *how*, not the possibility. Perhaps there is no way, no how, but a memory of forgetting that takes place in the interstices of language, thought, representation, and being.

The human sciences are to be understood here as occupying the space between remembering and forgetting, representing and its impossibility.

> man for the human sciences is not that living being with a very particular form (a somewhat special physiology and an almost unique autonomy); he is that living being who, from within the life to which he entirely belongs and by which he is traversed in his whole being, constitutes representations by means of which he lives, and on the basis of which he possesses that strange capacity of being able to represent to himself precisely that life. (352)

> The object of the human sciences is not language (though it is spoken by men alone); it is that being which, from the interior of the language by which he is surrounded, represents to himself, by speaking, the sense of the words or propositions he utters, and finally provides himself with a representation of language itself. (353)

History here is not a human science but much more enigmatic, together with psychoanalysis and ethnology.

> Psychoanalysis and ethnology occupy a privileged position in our knowledge—not because they have established the foundations of their positivity better than any other human science, . . . but rather because . . . they form an undoubted and inex-

haustible treasure-hoard of experiences and concepts, and above all a perpetual principle of dissatisfaction, of calling into question, of criticism and contestation of what may seem, in other respects, to be established. (373)

This contestation does not take place in the light, let us say as if we struggled to remember this or that, to remember this way or that way, but as if we struggled to think what we cannot think, to remember what we have forgotten.

The privilege of ethnology and psychoanalysis, the reason for their profound kinship and symmetry, must not be sought, therefore, in some common concern to pierce the profound enigma, the most secret part of human nature; in fact, what illuminates the space of their discourse is much more the historical *a priori* of all the sciences of man—those great caesuras, furrows, and dividing-lines which traced man's outline in the Western *episteme* and made him a possible area of knowledge ... they are directed towards that which, outside man, makes it possible to know, with a positive knowledge, that which is given to or eludes his consciousness. (378)

It is necessary to look more closely at the historical *a priori* and the archive—to remember what is of itself forgotten, I mean forgetting. The goal of ethnology and psychoanalysis is not to remember, not to bring to presence, not to answer the enigma, but to remain within the enigma itself in its furrows and caesuras. It may not be necessary to stay with Foucault's agenda, the positivities of the human sciences, to accept the importance of positive knowledge. It may be more relevant to emphasize that what is given is given elusively, that what eludes consciousness is the giving of knowledge and experience itself.

The positive figure of representation and the human sciences is man who, "as the archaeology of our thought easily shows ... is an invention of recent date. And one perhaps nearing its end" (387). That is, *The Order of Things* ends with another figure of forgetting, in which man—the empirico-transcendental doublet who defines both representation and anthropological humanism—is about to disappear and be forgotten. For he cannot be remembered as the subject of representation when representation is no longer the subject of language. "[O]ne can certainly wager that man would be erased, like a face drawn in sand at the edge of the sea" (387). One can certainly wager that any memory will be forgotten.

In *The Archaeology of Knowledge*, from the beginning history appears in contrast with histories, where in the disciplines that we call the history of ideas, the history of science, the history of philosophy, the history of thought, and the history of literature ... which ... evade very largely the work and methods of the historian, attention has been turned ... away from vast unities like "periods" or "centuries" to the phenomena of rupture, of discontinuity. (*AK*, 4)

Ruptures, discontinuities, interruptions are forgettings: they are not to be overcome or overlaid by more and more precise knowledge; they do not promise assembling but insist on remaining disassembled; "they suspend the continuous accumulation of knowledge, interrupt its slow development, and force it to enter a new time" (4). To enter a new time is to shatter the continuity of history, not only the accumulation of knowledge as history, but history itself as assembling and assembled. History is disassembled and dissembling—caesuras and forgottens, resisting the totality of the subject:

Continuous history is the indispensable correlative of the founding function of the subject: the guarantee that everything that has eluded him may be restored to him; the certainty that time will disperse nothing without restoring it in a reconstituted unity; the promise that one day the subject—in the form of historical consciousness—will once again be able to appropriate, to bring back under his sway, all those things that are kept at a distance by difference, and find in them what might be called his abode. (12)

The word *difference* is said here to be able to keep things at a distance. And both difference and distance are linked with forgetting: distance as that which depends from forgetting, which requires an oblivion that withholds the terms from each other; difference as something other than the multiplication of identities, other than the return of identity. *Separation* and *exteriority* are Levinas's terms for alterity, expressing the otherness of otherness. Alterity appears, if it does so, in the mode of forgetting. Not a forgetting that would remember, that takes place in the obscurity of memory, but a forgetting that separates and divides without a dream of unity, forgotten in the disparities of disparition.

Such a forgotten allows us to understand the archive differently, not as the imperceptible ground of an epoch, the hidden trace of history's historicality, the multiplicities of our histories, but as the counter-memory of disparition.

it is that which outside ourselves, delimits us. ... In this sense, we are difference, ... our reason is the difference of discourses, our history the difference of times, our selves the difference of masks. That difference, far from being the forgotten and recovered origin, is the dispersion that we are and make. (131)

We are a dispersion forgotten without recovery, a forgetting in disparition. And we are not alone. Whatever we remember is forgotten in the disparition of counter-memory without an origin, even where memory insists on the origin's return.

Archaeology and genealogy, then, are history in the mode of forgetting and counter-memory. Archaeology is the tracing of forgetting without a origin, genealogy is the insurrection of what has been forgotten. Memory and history take place in the disparition that is forgetting, the counter-memory of memories and histories.

CHAPTER 7

Body and Image

> The phenomenology of memory proposed here is structured around two questions: *Of what* are there memories? *Whose* memory is it? (Ricoeur, *MHF*, 3)
>
> in the margins of a critique of imagination, there has to be an uncoupling of imagination from memory . . . . (5–6)

*I*t is time—we may have forgotten—to reconsider questions of who or what is remembered, who or what is forgotten, who or what remembers and forgets. I mean to raise these questions not to decide who or what but to postpone deciding, to consider the possibility that we cannot decide, must not decide, must not imagine that we can securely recall the who or what of history and time.

Ricoeur insists that we can decide—who and what, with his aid; and, moreover, can decide to uncouple memory from the image and imagination—as if we could. Right here, in the words *as if*, we see the return of the image—as if it were the original, as if it were the truth, as if the imagination were fictive, semblance, while memory is as if it were the thing itself.

Yet the thing itself is the image, the appearance and proliferation of the thing. And the thing itself is material no matter how it may appear. This is where we may find ourselves returning to Spinoza and others for whom memory and forgetting are material, corporeal, not only human.

As material as the image and imagination may be, as if memory and forgetting may be, matter is not understood today to remember or to forget, but as if inert. Yet it is not unknown to think of it as memory, and if so, perhaps as forgetting.

Who or what remembers—and forgets? And what does it or who remember—and forget? What if the answer were that remembering and forgetting belonged to nature, being, thereby to beings, among them humans? What if the answer were that beings belong to being in the mode of remembering—thereby of forgetting? Here being and belonging are nature before the separation of mind and body, are as corporeal as they are mental, including memory and forgetting.

We have recalled the modern epistemological project as if to know and to remember what cannot be known and cannot be remembered. We have recalled the forgetting that undergirds this project, both in constructing the project itself—which must forget to know and remember—and in what is remembered and known. Ricoeur would know who and what in memory, as if that were not itself forgetting. He would have us know what we know we have forgotten.

In "The Origin of the Work of Art," and in many other works, Heidegger locates art in the struggle between world and earth as if all four, including the struggle, forgot what we imagined they might remember.

> To be a work means to set up a world. . . . *The world worlds*. (Heidegger, *OWA*, 44)
>
> That into which the work sets itself back and which it causes to come forth in this setting back of itself we called the earth. Earth is that which comes forth and shelters. . . . The work moves the earth itself into the Open of a world and keeps it there. *The earth lets the earth be an earth*. (46)
>
> The world is the self-disclosing openness of the broad paths of the simple and essential decisions in the destiny of an historical people. The earth is the spontaneous forthcoming of that which is continually self-secluding and to that extent sheltering and concealing. World and earth are essentially different from one another and yet are never separated. The world grounds itself on the earth, and earth juts through world. . . .
>
> The opposition of world and earth is a striving. . . . In essential striving, rather, the opponents raise each other into the self-assertion of their natures. (48–9)

The key words here on the side of *world* are *opening, setting up, lighting, self-disclosing, destiny, history*; on the side of *earth* are *coming forth, sheltering, abiding, spontaneity, self-seclusion, sheltering, concealing*. The struggle or striving is the coming into appearance of that which always withdraws.

The clearing in which beings stand is in itself at the same time concealment. . . .

Beings refuse themselves to us down to that one and seeming least feature which we touch upon most readily when we can say no more of beings than that they are. . . .

Concealment can be a refusal or merely a dissembling . . . the clearing happens only as this double concealment. The unconcealedness of beings—this is never a merely existent state, but a happening. . . .

We believe we are at home in the immediate circle of things. That which is, is familiar, reliable, ordinary. Nevertheless, the clearing is pervaded by a constant concealment in the double form of refusal and dissembling. . . . The nature of truth, that is, of unconcealedness, is dominated throughout by a denial. . . . *This denial, in the form of a double concealment, belongs to the nature of truth as unconcealedness.* (53–4)

Heidegger speaks the language of truth: the nature of truth is unconcealedness in the midst of a double concealment, refusal or dissembling. The coming into the open, the appearing of things, takes place as a refusal—things refuse to come fully into the open— or dissembling—things appear as other than they are. Yet if we understand that things are other, that truth and memory relate to others in their otherness, then when things appear as other than they are this is the way they are. Truth is dissembling; unconcealment is concealment; there is no oppositional relation between them; each is the other again in its transformations.

Moreover, if we understand refusal and dissembling as forgetting—the being of beings is forgotten, beings are forgettings—then this double denial and concealment returns us to remembering and forgetting. We can never remember things as they are because they are always other than they are, thereby forgotten in their being. The being of beings is what we strive to remember; the return of things is remembering; remembering is forgetting. Moreover, this forgetting is constitutive, meaning that it is infinitely more than forgetting something—indeed, it is infinity itself as infinitely more.

What is infinity itself? What is forgotten, who forgets? Infinity as forgetting, forgetting to infinity, refuse an answer, dissemble every answer, including Ricoeur's. We forget forgetting, we forget the forgotten. In relation to the image, this means that the dissembling of the image betrays every chance of uncoupling memory from imagination. The image returns and intercedes, as we remember we forget. Moreover, the refusal of which Heidegger speaks—the refusal of the things of the earth to give themselves over to us to know and to recall—takes place as error, in errancy, thereby dissembling. The image dissembles as if into other images. The image proliferates, and in this proliferation are infinite images of finity and infinity, memories and images as forgettings.

The purpose of this chapter is not to return to the image in proliferation but to proliferate the materiality of the image as the forgotten. The question here is how to think of matter as remembering and forgetting. One answer is Heidegger's, as refusal and dissembling. The dissembling and withdrawing of bodies and things is the forgetting of time and the image in proliferation. It is important that dissembling and withdrawing take on different meanings here, that the withdrawal of being as forgetting is more than the opacity and resistance of beings, much closer to semblance as dissembling. The refusal of things is not just their obdurateness, their impenetrability, but is closer to an act of forgetting in the modality of appearing. Dissembling and refusal are both modes of appearing as concealment and dissembling, of the image in proliferation. Appearing is unconcealing, and remembering is unforgetting.

How shall we think of bodies, material things, corporeality as forgetting as if inert things might forget or at least might demand and impose and call for forgetting from us? The answer is surely that they are not inert—if anything can be inert. So the issue of forgetting pertains to the vitality of bodies—to their exposition. The refusal of things in the mode of forgetting is a withdrawal in the mode of expression, not an inert inexpressiveness. Dissembling is not inert but expressive. Forgetting takes for granted that things express, that beings are expressive, and that where their expression is mute, this inexpressiveness is expression, a forgetting of expression, a dissembling of appearing. What is forgotten is the exposition of things, the exposition in things. Things are exposed to each other expressively. Otherness—more than one—is exposition.

To think of the juxtaposition of expression with the vitality of bodies is to return to Spinoza and to those who have been profoundly affected by him.

> For indeed, no one has yet determined what the Body can do, i.e., experience has not yet taught anyone what the Body can do from the laws of nature alone, insofar as nature is only considered to be corporeal, and what the body can do only if it is determined by the Mind. For no one has yet come to know the structure of the Body so accurately that he could explain all its functions—not to mention that many things are observed in the lower Animals that far surpass human ingenuity, and that sleepwalkers do a great many things in their sleep that they would not dare to awake. This

shows well enough that the Body itself, simply from the laws of its own nature, can do many things which its Mind wonders at. (Spinoza, *E*, 3, P2, Sch)

P6: Each thing, as far as it can by its own power, strives to persevere in its being.

P7: The striving by which each thing strives to persevere in its being is nothing but the actual essence of the thing.

P8: The striving by which each thing strives to persevere in its being involves no finite time, but an indefinite time.

No one knows, perhaps no one will ever know what bodies can do, and this lack of knowledge is forgetting. We do not know because we forget what bodies can do, and this doing and forgetting take place in the laws of bodies themselves. This is in part what infinity means, and Spinoza shares with Levinas the insight that the body, any body, is other in its bodyness, so that corporeality is forgetting. This does not mean it is not lawful, but the presence of infinite numbers of infinite natural laws is something that can be present and appear only as absence, in a forgetting. Here excess and forgetting are inseparable.

Each thing is entirely lawful, belongs to determinate causal succession, yet its being is so abundant as to transcend any knowing, any finite determination. Each thing is powerful and desirous, strives to exist, strives in its being to persevere beyond any finite time. Bodies are affective, intensive, powerful, expressive, striving, and these exceed any finite knowledge, any complete presence. The famous proposition in which bodies and ideas are joined—"The order and connection of ideas is the same as the order and connection of things" (2, P7)—is an expression of bodies' expressiveness. Ideas are the expressions of bodies, and bodies, things, God, the world are expressive.

D6: By God I understand a being absolutely infinite, i.e., a substance consisting of an infinity of attributes, of which each one expresses (*exprimit*) an eternal and infinite essence.
    Exp.: I say absolutely infinite, not infinite in its own kind; for if something is only infinite in its own kind, we can deny infinite attributes of it; but if something is absolutely infinite, whatever expresses essence and involves no negation pertains to its essence. (*E*, 1)

The essence of God is God's expression, God or substance expresses itself as attributes and modes, bodies express themselves as ideas, the world expresses and is expressed, to infinity.

Among these expressions are images. Ricoeur notes one famous side of Spinoza, that memories are images and images are inadequate (*HMF*, 5).

> [II.] I begin, therefore, by warning my Readers, first, to distinguish accurately between an idea, or concept, of the Mind, and the images of things that we imagine. And then it is necessary to distinguish between ideas and the words by which we signify things...many people either completely confuse these three—ideas, images, and words—or do not distinguish them accurately enough, or carefully enough, ...
>
> . . . But these prejudices can easily be put aside by anyone who attends to the nature of thought, which does not at all involve the concept of extension. He will then understand clearly that an idea (since it is a mode of thinking) consists neither in the image of anything, nor in words. For the essence of words and of images is constituted only by corporeal motions, which do not at all involve the concept of thought. (Spinoza, *E*, 2, P49, Sch)

This side is extensive, though I would emphasize another dimension. First, however, is the way in which imagination and memory are inadequate—and this of itself is a response to Ricoeur.

> P19: The human Mind does not know the human Body itself, nor does it know that it exists, except through ideas of affections by which the Body is affected.
>
> P24: The human Mind does not involve adequate knowledge of the parts composing the human Body.
>
> P25: The idea of any affection of the human Body does not involve adequate knowledge of an external body.
>
> P28: The ideas of the affections of the human Body, insofar as they are related only to the human Mind, are not clear and distinct, but confused.
>
> P31: We can have only an entirely inadequate knowledge of the duration of the singular things which are outside us.

On one side bodies are affected by other bodies *ad infinitum*, and this affecting composes memory and imagination. The proposition that is key to this understanding defines the succession of finite bodies.

> P28: Every singular thing, or any thing which is finite and has a determinate existence, can neither exist nor be determined to produce an effect unless it is determined to exist and produce an effect by another cause, which is also finite and has a determinate

existence; and again, this cause also can neither exist nor be determined to produce an effect unless it is determined to exist and produce an effect by another, which is also finite and has a determinate existence, and so on, to infinity. (*E*, 1)

On this side again, finite bodies affect each other—imagine and remember each other—and all such knowledge, all such relations are inadequate. Inadequacy here is to infinity.

Even here, then, one might imagine that such an inadequacy is not a lack—Spinoza calls it *privation*—but a positivity: too much and too many finite relations, too many finite causal influences, too great a dependence on finite and contingent relations. What we know comes from and depends on infinite numbers of relations, infinite numbers of other finite bodies. There is nothing in bodies as such that is of itself erroneous, suggesting that it is in other bodies that knowledge is forgotten and becomes error.

P17: . . . I should like you to note that the imaginations of the Mind, considered in themselves contain no error, or that the Mind does not err from the fact that it imagines, but only insofar as it is considered to lack an idea that excludes the existence of those things that it imagines to be present to it. (*E*, 2)

In parts 3 and 4 this line of thought is unfolded in terms of the affects, pertaining especially to the emotions of joy and sorrow, love and hatred.

P12: The Mind, as far as it can, strives to imagine those things that increase or aid the Body's power of acting. (*E*, 3)

P16: From the mere fact that we imagine a thing to have some likeness to an object that usually affects the Mind with Joy or Sadness, we love it or hate it, even though that in which the thing is like the object is not the efficient cause of these affects.

P17: If we imagine that a thing which usually affects us with an affect of Sadness is like another which usually affects us with an equally great affect of Joy, we shall hate it and at the same time love it.

P22: If we imagine someone to affect with Joy a thing we love, we shall be affected with Love toward him. If, on the other hand, we imagine him to affect the same thing with Sadness, we shall also be affected with Hate toward him.

P27: If we imagine a thing like us, toward which we have had no affect, to be affected with some affect, we are thereby affected with a like affect.

P28: We strive to further the occurrence of whatever we imagine will lead to Joy, and to avert or destroy what we imagine is contrary to it, or will lead to Sadness.

P9: An affect whose cause we imagine to be with us in the present is stronger than if we did not imagine it to be with us. (*E*, 4)

In other words, the material world is made up of infinite numbers of finite bodies in infinite numbers of relations, too large and excessive to be known, where each body is affected by emotions and imaginations it is unable to control. Infinity here for finite things is inadequacy, contingency, and dependence. One might say that infinity here is the forgetting by finite things of their infinite nature.

For the other side of Spinoza turns infinity in a different direction. Immediately following proposition 28, part 1, which expresses the infinite successiveness of finite things, he expresses another infinite.

P29: In nature there is nothing contingent, but all things have been determined from the necessity of the divine nature to exist and produce an effect in a certain way.
. . .
    Schol.: Before I proceed further, I wish to explain here—or rather to advise [the reader] what we must understand by *Natura naturans* and *Natura naturata*. For from the preceding I think it is already established that by *Natura naturans* we must understand what is in itself and is conceived through itself, or such attributes of substance as express an eternal and infinite essence, i.e., (by P14C1 and P17C2), God, insofar as he is considered as a free cause.
    But by *Natura naturata* I understand whatever follows from the necessity of God's nature, or from any of God's attributes, i.e., all the modes of God's attributes insofar as they are considered as things which are in God, and can neither be nor be conceived without God. (*E*, 1)

Nature is composed of finite and of infinite things, and these sides cannot be separated. The finite and inadequate knowledge of finite things contains within itself infinite powers. Inadequate knowledge is as infinite as is adequate knowledge. "Inadequate and confused ideas follow with the same necessity as adequate, or clear and distinct ideas" (*E*, 2, P36). Moreover, this conjunction expresses one of the most striking and enigmatic sides of Spinoza.

P38: Whatever so disposes the human Body that it can be affected in a great many ways, or renders it capable of affecting external Bodies in a great many ways, is useful to man; the more it renders the Body capable of being affected in a great many ways, or of affecting other bodies, the more useful it is; on the other hand, what renders the Body less capable of these things is harmful. (*E*, 4)

P39: He who has a Body capable of a great many things has a Mind whose greatest part is eternal. (*E*, 5)

Spinoza's image here is that finite adaptation bears a direct relation to eternity. The inadequacy of images and imagination, the inadequacy of finite knowledge, is infinite. The inadequacy of finite memory is an infinite expression of the infinite, creative powers of nature. Contingent and inadequate memories are traces of infinity in the form of remembering and forgetting. The adequate idea of a finite body exists in the pairing of remembering and forgetting, presence and absence, that is, as semblance.

Schol.: I say expressly that the Mind has, not an adequate, but only a confused [NS: and mutilated] knowledge, of itself, of its own Body, and of external bodies, so long as it perceives things from the common order of nature, i.e., so long as it is determined externally, from fortuitous encounters with things, to regard this or that, and not so long as it is determined internally, from the fact that it regards a number of things at once, to understand their agreements, differences, and oppositions. For so often as it is disposed internally, in this or another way, then it regards things clearly and distinctly, as I shall show below. (Spinoza, *E*, 2, P29)

Every body here is forgotten in the excesses of its strivings, in the infinities of its expressions. Bodies are expressive, expressions of God, expressive in their attributes and modifications, in relation to other bodies and in their strivings. The being of this world is expressive, including bodies, finite and infinite, human and natural. Lower animals and ordinary natural things do many things that minds wonder at and forget. The world of wonder is a world of un-forgetting.

Such a wonder can be found in others. The divinity and soul in each finite thing marks the infinite expression of its finitude, an expressiveness present in each drop of matter, in each corporeal thing, present in a forgetting. Leibniz is an example, presenting two figures that express forgetting as semblance and refusal, though closer to the former:

66. Whence we see that there is a world of creatures, of living beings, of animals, of entelechies, of souls, in the smallest particle of matter.

67. Each portion of matter may be conceived of as a garden full of plants, and as a pond full of fishes. (Leibniz, *M*)

Each thing contains a world of creatures, of living things—animals, entelechies, plants, gardens. Each drop of matter teems with vitality and expression. Yet we can never know this abundance in detail, it withdraws from us in the confusion of its teeming. Moreover, the very small and very large represent dissemblance: the smallest creatures are unknown and unknowable to us. The world teems with abundance, echoes with expression, glows with wonder, all confused traces present in forgetting, dissembled in their appearances. The ungraspable abundance is never graspable, never something to be possessed, never recapturable in memory. Dispossession is forgetting and abundance is forgotten.

Even the totality is more than a totality, does not reduce itself even before God into something that can be grasped.

> 51. But in simple substances the influence of one monad upon another is purely *ideal* and it can have its effect only through the intervention of God, ...

> 56. Now this *connection*, or this adaptation, of all created things to each and of each to all, brings it about that each simple substance has relations which express all the others, and that, consequently, it is a perpetual living mirror of the universe.

> 83. . . . souls in general are the living mirrors or images of the universe of creatures, but minds or spirits are in addition images of the Divinity itself, or of the author of nature, able to know the system of the universe. . . .

> 60. . . . Because God, in regulating all, has had regard to each part, and particularly to each monad, whose nature being representative, nothing can limit it to representing only a part of things; although it may be true that this representation is but confused as regards the detail of the whole universe, and can be distinct only in the case of a small part of things, that is to say, in the case of those which are nearest or greatest in relations to each of the monads; otherwise each monad would be a divinity. . . . They all tend confusedly toward the infinite, toward the whole; but they are limited and differentiated by the degrees of their distinct perfections.

Leibniz says that all things are adapted to each other, each to each and to all. Each is a living mirror of the others and of the universe as a whole, including divinity itself. Yet mirror after mirror—each expressive, each a semblance, each dissembling: images after images after images—is an image of an uncontainable abundance. Leaving God aside—who is another infinity, whose divine infinity may not be graspable even by itself, who therefore is present and remembered only in a withdrawal and a forgetting— mirrors of mirrors of mirrors, each a finite expression and confused imitation, augment and multiply the abundance. In other words, on the side of semblance, forgetting is multiplication, is exposition.

Let us follow Plato, Descartes, Leibniz, and Spinoza here to imagine that wonder is unforgetting, that the gasp of wonder is the strike of *anamnēsis*, that the philosophy that is born in wonder lives in an unforgetting that can never be recalled, that the world is full of wonder in being full of forgetting. Forgetting is not a void but much closer to *Śūnyatā*, whose emptiness is codependent origination, an abundance in which all things are so entwined that none can be separated from the others, each augmenting the others. We do not and cannot know what bodies can do because those bodies are so infinitely entwined with each other as to exceed any determination. This is true in a world in which there is nothing but determination. Causal determination exceeds all determinations into what appears as if it were indetermination. Remembering things as they are present exceeds all presence and presentations.

It is perhaps not so clear in Bergson that matter is excessive. Even so, he approaches memory in the context of the unbounded expressiveness of things. There is nothing but images, things are images, expressive as images.

> Here I am in the presence of images, in the vaguest sense of the word, images perceived when my senses are open to them, unperceived when they are closed. All these images act and react upon one another in all their elementary parts according to constant laws which I call laws of nature, and, as a perfect knowledge of these laws would probably allow us to calculate and to foresee what will happen in each of these images, the future of the images must be contained in their present and will add to them nothing new. (Bergson, *MM*, 1)

This is a picture akin to Spinoza's and Leibniz's, the world of corporeal things—including I myself and we ourselves—is composed of images—vibrant, glowing, expressive images; yet also determined, calculative, lawful images. In this picture, right from the start we see the appearance of a forgetting that belongs to the most deterministic totality of material things. In their determination, in the condition that the endless future of the images is contained in the present and can add nothing new, is an abundance that can be grasped at no time and in no place. What then is the presence of this future in the present except as traces of what can exist only as forgotten?

These images are material, corporeal, bodies.

> Yet there is *one* of them which is distinct from all the others, in that I do not know it only from without by perceptions, but from within by affections: it is my body.... *All seems to take place as if, in this aggregate of images which I call the universe, nothing really new could happen except through the medium of certain particular images, the type of which is furnished me by my body.* (1–3)

The body is an image and produces images, and these images are bodies. Moreover, these bodies and these images exist in the modality of *as if*, one that is as if it were the modality of forgetting. The modality of *as if* here is of semblance and dissembling, not of refusal as withdrawing, lacking presence, but of excess, multiplication: more and other presences. The image proliferates, and this proliferation is forgetting. What is forgotten is not, then, an original against which the proliferation comes up short, but an original that traces a line of flight of multiple becomings of other images, other semblances. Forgetting here is multiplication. The proliferation of bodies, lawfully and deterministically, is the production of images in proliferation, all in the modality of *as if*, all appearing as if by way of forgetting.

Memory here in Bergson is productive and additive, again in the modalities of as if and forgetting:

> We assert, at the outset, that if there be memory, that is, the survival of past images, these images must constantly mingle with our perception of the present, and may even take its place. For if they have survived it is with a view to utility; at every moment they complete our present experience, enriching it with experience already acquired; and, as the latter is ever increasing, it must end by covering up and submerging the former. It is indisputable that the basis of real, and so to speak instantaneous, intuition, on which our perception of the external world is developed, is a small matter compared with all that memory adds to it. (69–70)

> Our perceptions are undoubtedly interlaced with memories, and inversely, a memory, as we shall show later, only becomes actual by borrowing the body of some perception into which it slips. These two acts, perception and recollection, always interpenetrate each other, are always exchanging something of their substance as by a process of endosmosis. (71–2)

Here is another response to Ricoeur's question. Memory borrows the body for its perception and imagination. Bodies remember, memories are bodily, the inseparable relations between memory and perception, memories and imagination, are the productivities of bodies, productivities that exist in the modalities of *as if*, thereby made possibly only in the multiplication of further modalities of forgetting.

Here then are the difficult thoughts to which we have been led: bodies are productive, productions of production; production is exposition; and exposition is forgetting. What is forgotten is the wonder of exposition. The forgotten is in abundance.

> Now, if every concrete perception, however short we suppose it, is already a synthesis, made by memory, of an infinity of "pure perceptions" which succeed each other, must we not think that the heterogeneity of sensible qualities is due to their being contracted in our memory, and the relative homogeneity of objective changes to the slackness of their natural tension? And might not the interval between quantity and quality be lessened by considerations of tension, as the distance between the extended and the unextended is lessened by considerations of extension? (237–8)

The difference between the heterogeneous and the homogeneous in matter is a synthesis in memory, a contraction in which heterogeneity is forgotten and homogeneity is produced. I mean of course remembered. Memory requires homogeneity yet its nature requires heterogeneity. Heterogeneity, then, far beyond the subtle differences among bodies—let us call it heterogeneity itself: otherness, alterity, disparition, abundance—is the forgotten. Memory takes place as if in the modality of homogeneity by way of forgetting heterogeneity.

With this understanding, that matter exposes disparition and that disparition is forgotten, we may turn from Bergson—still within the epistemological project—to the space he shares with Deleuze and Guattari, of intensity and intensification, and with Spinoza and Whitehead on their reading—though he appears to reject it.

> Difference is not diversity. Diversity is given, but difference is that by which the given is given as diverse. Everything which happens and everything which appears is correlated with orders of differences: differences of level, temperature, pressure, tensions, potential, *difference of intensity*.... Intensity is the form of difference in so far as this is the reason of the sensible. Every intensity is differential, by itself a difference. The reason of the sensible, the condition of that which appears, is not space and time but the Unequal in itself, *disparateness* as it is determined and comprised in difference of intensity, in intensity as difference. (Deleuze, *DR*, 222–3)

> the Earth—the Deterritorialized, the Glacial, the giant Molecule—is a BwO [body without organs]. This BwO is permeated by unformed, unstable matters, by flows in all directions, by free inten-

sities or nomadic singularities, by made or transitory particles. . . . There simultaneously occurs upon the earth a very important, inevitable phenomenon, that is beneficial in many respects
and unfortunate in many others: stratification. Strata are Layers,
Belts. They consist of giving form to matters, of imprisoning intensities or locking singularities into systems of resonance and re-
dundancy, of producing upon the body of the earth molecules
large and small and organizing them into molar aggregates.
(Deleuze and Guattari, *TP*, 40)

After all, is not Spinoza's *Ethics* the great book of the BwO?
The attributes are types or genuses of BwO's, substances, powers,
zero intensities as matrices of production. The modes are everything that come to pass: waves and vibrations, migrations, thresh-
olds and gradients, intensities produced in a given type of substance starting from a given matrix. (153)

Spinoza asks: what can a body do? We call the *latitude* of a
body the affects of which it is capable at a given degree of
power, . . . *Latitude is made up of intensive parts falling under a capacity, and longitude of extensive parts falling under a relation.* (256–7)

Intensity is difference, disparition, disparateness as the condition of diversity and multiplicity, understanding these as given in
experience as relations, as relative. Every intensity is a difference, is
disparition itself—if difference, intensity, and disparition can be
themselves. This takes us right up to forgetting because we may say
that what is given can be remembered but that disparition is forgotten. Deleuze explains this as the subordination of intensity to extensity, of disparition to qualities and quantities, to form. We know intensity—or intensity for us is—only as developed with extensity, as
covered over by qualities. This covering over is forgetting. Difference, disparition, intensity are experienced as forgotten, covered
over. Experience is disparity covered over or forgotten by identity.
Identification is the construction and forgetting of the intensities
beneath. Heterogeneity is the forgotten; homogeneity is forgetting.
Singularities appear by means of forgetting.

One might wish to query how Deleuze can name what has been
forgotten as singularities, disparitions, differences, heterogeneities.
This may be offered as a skeptical query: how can one remember
what has been forgotten, and what if it has been forgotten completely? The answers are that remembering is unforgetting and that
forgetting leaves a trace. This answer is incomplete: it leaves open
the possibility that nothing will ever be completely forgotten, where
that possibility is the threat of forgetting and the forgotten. This returns us to the question of the name, this time not skeptically but

affirmatively. What do we affirm as the forgotten, and with what affirmation? Is it difference, disparition, intensification? Can we know or experience these to the point where we can avow them?

This is the question of this chapter, in the modality of materiality. How can we think of matter in the modality of forgetting? The answers we are exploring are as exposition—exposure and expression—and intensification. We have only partly examined exposition under the heading of the expression of matter. Material things speak, sing, engage in the modality of expressivity and responsivity. Exposition is more than expression, however, but pairs it with exposure. Things touch each other, are exposed to each other—intimately, heterogeneously, expressively. Exposition is touch, touch then is forgotten, whether in heterogeneity, singularity, and disparity or in homogeneity, collectivity, and similarity. Exposition exposes things to each other, and in this exposure—always as if in memory—is forgotten.

This understanding can be found more visibly present in Whitehead than in the others we have considered, perhaps too visibly. The "final realities" (Whitehead, *PR*, 22) of the world are actual occasions—atoms of creativity whose origination lies in memory.

> The first phase [of concrescence, the becoming of an actual occasion] is the phase of pure reception of the actual world. . . . In this phase there is the mere reception of the actual world as a multiplicity of private centres of feeling. (Whitehead, *PR*, 212)

Actual occasions feel (or prehend), and what they feel are other actual occasions' feelings (or prehensions). This prehension is an act of memory, the reproduction of past feelings, and of feelings of feelings.

> According to this account, the experience of the simplest grade of actual entity [or occasion] is to be conceived as the unoriginative response to the datum with its simple content of sense. . . . Occasions A, B, and C enter into the experience of occasion M as themselves experiencing sensa s_1 and s_2. . . . There is thus a transmission of sensation emotion from A, B, and C to M. (115)

Such a picture of material things is that they are nothing (in their first phase) but memories of past material things. Yet they are creative. "'Creativity' . . . is that ultimate principle by which the many, which are the universe disjunctively, become the one actual occasion, which is the universe conjunctively" (21). Each drop of being is a drop of creative experience, and there is no creativity without remembering and forgetting.

Nine categorial obligations define the process of becoming. The first three express what may be understood as memory without forgetting, though not without selection and exclusion:

> (i) *The Category of Subjective Unity.* The many feelings which belong to an incomplete phase in the process of an actual entity, ... are compatible. ...
>
> (ii) *The Category of Objective Identity.* There can be no duplication of any element in the objective datum of the "satisfaction" of an actual entity, ...
>
> (iii) *The Category of Objective Diversity.* There can be no "coalescence" of diverse elements in the objective datum of an actual entity, ... (26)

Each element here plays one and only one role in the becoming and identity of each entity. In this way, we can imagine a memory of this becoming and this identity as achieved by ordering every composition of elements into the constitution of what is remembered.

Yet again, this is a creative becoming. There is valuation, reversion, and transmutation, all transformations and mutations of elements.

> (iv) *The Category of Conceptual Valuation.* From each physical feeling there is the derivation of a purely conceptual feeling whose datum is the eternal object determinant of the definiteness of the actual entity ... physically felt.
>
> (v) *The Category of Conceptual Reversion.* There is secondary origination of conceptual feelings with data which are partially identical with, and partially diverse from, the eternal objects forming the data in the first phase of the mental pole. ... The diversity is a relevant diversity determined by the subjective aim.
>
> (vi) *The Category of Transmutation.* ... the prehending subject may transmit the *datum* of [a physically derived] conceptual feeling into a characteristic of some *nexus*. ... In this way the nexus (or its part), thus characterized, is the objective datum of a feeling. ...

We may understand creativity here as intensification following Blanchot's three levels of ambiguity—three levels or meanings of intensity:

> 1. Matter is creative, intense, and transformative; we can never know or remember any material thing once and for all.
>
> 2. Matter is filled with desire; intensity composes the undetermined milieu of fascination of material becomings.
>
> 3. Intensity expresses the other of all meaning, all matter, all being and becoming. Intensity empties out the becoming of things into something beyond all meaning. Meaning is no longer

anything but semblance; semblance makes meaning become infinitely rich. It makes this infinitude of bodies have no need of
development—makes the material world immediate, which is
also to say incapable of being developed, only immediately
empty.[1]

When he speaks directly of intensity, Whitehead emphasizes
origination and feeling.

> (vii) *The Category of Subjective Harmony*. The valuations of con-
> ceptual feelings are mutually determined by the adaptation of
> those feelings to be contrasted elements congruent with the sub-
> jective aim.
> (viii) *The Category of Subjective Intensity*. The subjective aim,
> whereby there is origination of conceptual feeling, is at intensity
> of feeling. . . .
> (ix) *The Category of Freedom and Determination* . . . that in each
> concrescence whatever is determinable is determined, but that
> there is always a remainder for the decision of the subject-
> superject of that concrescence. (27–8)

What is determinable is determined—in memory. We can remember
what is determined and determinate. But there is always a remain-
der in the self-determined becoming of each actual occasion, a re-
mainder that cannot be remembered because it is always in process
of becoming, empty from the standpoint of memory. Here forgetting
is not the absence of determined remembrance but the presence of
determinate freedom. And that is perhaps the point of forgetting
here. The forgotten is not indeterminate. It is empty in the sense that
it is immediately present as the material world in the disparition of
its exposition.

Matter here is the forgotten, not as the inert, passive, substratum
underlying activity and agency, but as the agency and activity
themselves. The difficulty is that if something is active, then it appears that something else is passive and inert. Matter here is always
and everywhere creativity, power, desire, and fascination, and we
are creative and fascinated in the intensities of material becomings.
Matter is remembered as what it is, but in terms of a forgetting that
is the constituting of its being.

The category of subjective intensity is a category of *as if*, the infinite modality of a future that truly awaits becoming, so that every
present and future glows with the radiance that only semblance can
provide, the infinite possibilities of the *perhaps* and *as if* of exposition. Matter as such is intense, intensity, intensifications: affective,
full of feeling, exposition. To be exposed to others—other singulari-

ties, other possibilities, other futures—is an exposure filled with intensities—affects and multiplicities.

Another way to put this, in the language of semblance, is that the appearance and reality of material things are as images, on the one side images of other images in the modality of memory, on the other side images in proliferation, giving birth to and creating other images. The difference between images is nothing, empty, mere intensities. Yet these intensities express more materialities and meanings than any something can provide. What we remember is but the tiniest portion of what there is and what we forget; and the being of what we forget is not the same as the being of what we remember—that is but the first level or modality of intensity. It is in the modality of forgetting as if it were forgotten. The being of the forgotten is the inescapability of *perhaps* and *as if*.

CHAPTER 8

Past and Future

> By submitting to the primacy of the question "What?" the phenomenology of memory finds itself at the outset confronting a formidable aporia present in ordinary language: the presence in which the representation of the past seems to consist does indeed appear to be that of an image. We say interchangeably that we represent a past event to ourselves or that we have an image of it, an image that can be either quasi visual or auditory. . . . Memory, reduced to recall, thus operates in the wake of the imagination. . . .
>
> As a countercurrent to this tradition of devaluing memory, in the margins of a critique of imagination, there has to be an uncoupling of imagination from memory as far as this operation can be extended. (Ricoeur, *MHF*, 5–6)

*T*wo lines of becoming open for us here—and we must not forget the possibility Nietzsche offers, that becoming demands forgetting. It goes without saying that it requires remembering, that becoming after is remembering before—and perhaps is also remembering after, recalling what is to come. That is another story. The two for us here are the becoming in time recalled as genealogy and the becoming for life that is forgetting.

Ricoeur's subject is, like Margalit's, the ethics of memory—not the ethics, the goodness, of forgetting, though he does not neglect it. He draws his subject from a familiar view of ethics, that it pertains to action not to knowledge, to practice not to truth.

> So how is it possible to speak of an ethics of memory? It is possible because memory has two kinds of relation to the past, the first of which, as I have already mentioned, is a relation of *knowledge*, while the second is a relation of action. This is so because remembering is a way of doing things, not only with words, but

with our minds; in remembering or recollecting we are exercising
our memory, which is a kind of action. It is because memory is an
exercise that we can talk of the use of memory, which in turn
permits us to speak of the abuses of memory. The ethical problems
will arise once we begin to reflect on this connection between *use*
and *abuse* of memory. (Ricoeur, *MF*, 5)

It is apparent that Ricoeur has Nietzsche in mind: the use and
abuse of history, the use and abuse of memory. If history and memory—not to overlook forgetting—can be used and abused. If use and
abuse are ethical conditions.

[A]t the end of this tradition of treating memory as an art stands
Nietzsche in . . . "On the Advantage and Disadvantage of History
for Life." This is interesting because the title itself is about "use,"
not the use of memory itself, but of the philosophy of history in
the Hegelian sense of treating the practice of history as a science.
(5)

Yet is Ricoeur sure that Nietzsche does not regard memory and history themselves as abusive, that without forgetting, history as a discipline and memory as restoration are themselves abusive? Is it philosophy alone that abuses, that makes of history and memory and
time abusive, or is there something of life itself in the abuses—still
as if history and forgetting and memory might be used and abused?

Here is perhaps a certain way in which philosophy—now
Ricoeur's philosophy, not Hegel's—can insist on its abusiveness:

So it is through this approach to memory as a kind of action
that we can best broach the problem of the ethics of memory. Before doing that, however, I wish to construe a framework of
thought which will permit me to place ethics within a broader
context. I will consider three levels in this practical approach:
first, the *pathological-therapeutic* level; second, the *pragmatic* level;
and finally, the properly *ethical-political* approach to the act of
memory. (6)

Propriety appears here doubled, and perhaps that is always how it
must appear. Memory and history can be properly used or abused,
and there is a form of philosophy—here ethical-political—that properly approaches memory in its uses and abuses.

It is not, then, history itself, perhaps remembering and forgetting also, in themselves, that may be proper or improper. There is
another propriety, having to do with what Ricoeur has already re-
minded us concerns truth—the truth of history, remembering, and
forgetting. In the question of truth itself are many proprieties and
improprieties. In the question of action itself are many uses and

abuses. It appears that truth itself is a question of practice if it can be said to be abusive. If there is a properly ethical-political approach to memory—that is, to truth—it defines—or knows—what is proper and improper, useful and abusive.

Even so, and with many questions concerning these levels— which are higher, which more useful?—these technical categories mask fundamental questions about remembering and forgetting.

> The first level demands close attention, because it is here that abuses are rooted in something that we could call the wounds and scars of memory. We have a good example in the present state of Europe: in some places we could say that there is too much memory, but in other places not enough. Likewise, there is sometimes not enough forgetting, and at other times too much forgetting. How is it possible to graft these misuses upon the capacity to memorise? (6)

We could sometimes say that there is too much memory, sometimes and somewhere not enough, at other times and place too much forgetting. Even with the wounds and scars of memory, how can memory and forgetting be too much or too little, improper and abusive? Is it not better to remember—and to forget? Might an ethics of remembering and forgetting be something other than propriety and rule?

Ricoeur opens his imposing work *Memory, History, Forgetting* with a phenomenology of memory, one of "three clearly defined parts" (Ricoeur, *MHF*, xv).

> The first part, devoted to memory and to mnemonic phenomena, is placed under the aegis of phenomenology in the Husserlian sense of the term. The second part, dedicated to history, comes under the scope of an epistemology of the social sciences. The third part, culminating in a meditation on forgetting, is framed within a hermeneutics of the historical condition of the human beings that we are. (xv–xvi)

One might imagine many human beings who would say that memory and history constitute the temporal conditions of the human beings that we are, so it is by no means trivial or irrelevant that what frames the historical condition of humanity is forgetting rather than remembering. Even so, the question of memory for Ricoeur is a question of reliability. That is what presents the aporia of memory and history to us as we frequently understand them. If memory is tied to images and imagination, then the degrading of the image—if you will, its proliferation and multiplication—appears to put truth to the test—if you will, a certain view of truth if not the very truth of truth.

> I do not want to conclude on this note of perplexity, but instead with the provisional response that can be given to the question of trust that the theory of memory passes on to the theory of history. This is the question of the reliability of memory and, in this sense, of its truth. . . . This search for truth determines memory as a cognitive issue. . . . Let us call this search for truth, faithfulness. From now on, we will speak of the faithfulness of memories, of memories being true to . . . , in order to express this search, this demand, this claim, ... The study that follows will have the task of showing how the epistemic, veridical dimension of memory is united with the practical dimension tied to the idea of the exercise of memory. (54–5)

Everything that pertains to forgetting arises in this insistence on faithfulness as the chalice of memory, in place of an other truth, a truth betrayed rather than a truth in trust. I mean, of course, truth as unconcealment, a truth that is anything but faithfulness, but is the happening of truth through work, secluding and setting back.

> Truth happens only by establishing itself in the conflict and sphere opened up by truth itself. (Heidegger, OWA, 61)

> The earth is essentially self-secluding. To set forth the earth means to bring it into the Open as the self-secluding.
> This setting forth of the earth is achieved by the work as it sets itself back into the earth.[1] (47)

Indeed, what might it mean to think of memory's truth as setting forth and setting up? Might this be the truth of forgetting if not the forgetting of truth? I mean the unfaithfulness of faithfulness, the impossibility of making time into a epistemological object.

For us here, however, Heidegger has something to say on reliability, speaking of the equipmental character of equipment, where the example is a peasant woman's shoes, far again from the faithfulness of truth.

> The equipmental quality of the equipment consists indeed in its usefulness. But this usefulness itself rests in the abundance of an essential being of the equipment. We call it reliability. By virtue of this reliability the peasant woman is made privy to the silent call of the earth; by virtue of the reliability of the equipment she is sure of her world. World and earth exist for her, and for those who are with her in her mode of being, only thus—in the equipment. . . . the reliability of the equipment first gives to the simple

world its security and assures to the earth the freedom of its steady thrust. (34–5)

Indeed, though abundance of reliability is distant from faithfulness and adequacy, we may learn from Heidegger how to think of faithfulness of memory in relation to forgetting. At the end of the essay he returns to abundance and, perhaps, to reliability, in the context of giving and gifts.

> Bestowing and grounding have in themselves the unmediated character of what we call a beginning. . . .
>   A beginning, on the contrary, always contains the undisclosed abundance of the unfamiliar and extraordinary, which means that it also contains strife with the familiar and ordinary. (76)

Let us take this strife with the familiar and ordinary as a mark of reliability—one might say the opposite of everyday consistency. Let us keep in mind Derrida's suggestion that *The Origin of the Work of Art* is an extended meditation on giving and the gift.[2] Reliability is typically linked with familiarity. And perhaps that is what we expect of memory, to return to us what is familiar and ordinary. For Heidegger, reliability is linked with strangeness and unfamiliarity, with extraordinary giving. This is another view of memory in which forgetting (what is familiar) is the key to remembering.

It is important to emphasize at this point that to insist that memory is filled with forgetting, that the knowledge and truth they give are related more closely to abundance and extraordinariness than to familiarity and ordinariness, is not to deny memory's truth, but to insist on its abundance as its reliability and truth. Reliability is abundance, which means that we do not and cannot expect what is reliable to return in exactly the same way, to be recalled in exactly the same way, but to dispossess memory as forgetting in the nature of what is reliable and what is true.

Another way to put this is that the hallucinatory nature of memory and of images in no way invalidates their truth. To the contrary, it opens up the phantasmagoria that are given truth, the abundance that is reliability.

Still another way to approach this is through the following questions, first of reliability, then of memory. Which is better, more reliable, which is reliability itself, to have a very accurate test for one disease and no test for others, or to have a less accurate test for all diseases? To have a vaccination for one disease that almost entirely prevents it, or to have a vaccination for hundreds of diseases that works successfully part of the time? Is it more reliable to have a small amount of highly accurate information, or to have a great deal of somewhat inaccurate information? Finally, is it more reliable to have a test for one condition that gives few false positives and few false negatives, but is useless for all other conditions, or to have a test for many conditions that gives many false positives and many false negatives?

I ask which is better, more reliable? The answer may be both and neither. The answer may be, it depends. Or, put another way, in Derrida's terms, there may be no such choice. Not only because sometimes it is better to have more accurate information and sometimes to have more information, however inaccurate, about more things, but because each is reliable, each reflects reliability, and reliability is nothing to choose because its conditions are constantly changing.

I have neglected issues of fruitfulness, productiveness, and generativity of other tests and other truths. We may hope that a reliable truth will multiply other truths.

Turning to memory—I mean forgetting. Which is better, more reliable, to accurately remember a small number of events and facts or to inaccurately remember a large number of facts and events? Which is more reliable memory, one that recalls very little, highly accurately, or one that has forgotten a great deal, but remembers a great deal as well? Which is more truthful memory, one that remembers because it has forgotten, or one that has forgotten many if not all things, and in that forgetting remembers? And multiplies in remembering.

Is this not the hallucinatory nature of memory and forgetting? Of images, their production and their proliferation? Is this not the phantasmagoria of truth, that it appears and must appear to be truth, and in that appearing presents itself differently at different times, to different people, in different contexts, betrays itself in its appearing? The point to emphasize is that it does appear, does present itself, is remembered. So if the question is, do we remember, the answer is that we remember too much, remember forgetting and unforgetting, and in this too much we do remember. Remembering too much is unforgetting.

The question for us in the shadow of Ricoeur is how to participate in the epistemology of time as memory, history, and forgetting without defining the object as if it were only too familiar. Memory appears to insist on recalling what is familiar. Forgetting appears to insist on losing what is taken for granted. The alternative is that with forgetting taken as primary, with memory as unforgetting, the strangeness and abundance of things is what is apparent in forgetting. We must forget what is familiar in order to encounter and re-member what is unfamiliar.

My concern here is not with this *what* but with the strangeness of history from the vantagepoint of forgetting. This is how we may un-derstand Ricoeur's treatment of forgetting. For he understands for-getting to arise in the place of history, and history to arise in the place of memory. This *in the place of* would not be as dangerous as it is if it were not caught up in the epistemological project over which the philosopher-historian presides. I do not mean that the philoso-pher is a historian or the historian a philosopher, but that both take charge of the claims to knowledge.

The claim to knowledge, the epistemological project, defines his-tory for Ricoeur, the insistence that history is a social science and that it provides historical knowledge. Whatever the phenomenology of memory may provide, if it is a knowledge it is not that of history. As Ricoeur says, we have settled, ended, the phenomenology of memory (135). Surely we cannot have settled the question of mem-ory, which is as old and as young as the question of time, haunted and riddled by forgetting. So the object of historical knowledge, whatever that may be, must be haunted by ghosts of memory, time, and forgetting.

Let us think polemically, in our time, of historical knowledge as the ghost of the forgotten, as if such a knowledge forgot nothing, knew nothing of the forgotten, even as certain times and places may have vanished into oblivion. The forgotten is constitutively forgot-ten; lost historical knowledge is misplaced. So the question of such a history is why and how it is not constitutively haunted by ghosts of oblivion that are not misplaced but here before us in historical claims to knowledge. What has been lost, misplaced, what has van-ished and been forgotten in the production of history as knowledge?

One answer is memory, with its phenomenology. Another an-swer is time, as if history were a timeless knowledge of time. This does not mean that history does not change, or that historians and history do not express change, but that the knowledge itself, though it may change, is of a truth that does not constitutively change.

A third answer is forgetting. And here Ricoeur's approach to time and memory returns again in history as aporia, as

> the resurgence of the aporias of memory in their cognitive and practical aspects, principally the aporia of the representation of an absent something that once happened, along with that of the use and abuse to which memory lends itself as actively exercised and practiced. Yet this obstinate return of the aporias of memory at the heart of historical knowledge cannot take the place of a solution of

> the problem of the relations between knowledge and the practice
> of history and the experience of lived memory, even if this solu-
> tion were to present ultimately indecisive features. . . .
>
> It remains the case that the autonomy of historical knowledge
> in relation to the mnemonic phenomenon remains the major pre-
> supposition of a coherent epistemology of history both as a scien-
> tific discipline and a literary one: At least this is the presupposi-
> tion assumed in this middle part of this work. (135–6)

The aporia constitutive of memory and its phenomenology cannot
be allowed to interrupt the coherence of the epistemology of history
as a scientific discipline and as a literary practice. Literary history,
history as storytelling, oral and mythic history, all appear to be constituted by the aporia of the absent forgotten that appears, by no
means fully present, in the telling. If so, then history is founded as a
discipline in the forgetting of the forgotten of this telling.

This is aporia indeed. Yet it is followed in Ricoeur's account by
citation of Certeau:

> I have adopted the expression the "historical"—or better "his-
> toriographical"—operation to define the field traversed by the fol-
> lowing epistemological analysis. I owe it to Michel de Certeau in
> his contribution to the large-scale project edited by Jacques Le
> Goff and Pierre Nora under the title *Faire de l'histoire*. Beyond this,
> I have also adopted the broader lines of the triadic structure of
> Certeau's essay, although I give them different contents on some
> important points. (136)

These different contents lead toward what Certeau calls elsewhere
(not in *The Writing of History* but *The Practice of Everyday Life*) the
marginalization of life and history.[3]

> Marginality is today no longer limited to minority groups, but
> is rather massive and pervasive; this cultural activity of the non-
> producers of culture, an activity that is unsigned, unreadable, and
> unsymbolized, remains the only one possible for all those who
> nevertheless buy and pay for the showy products through which a
> productivist economy articulates itself. Marginality is becoming
> universal. A marginal group has now become a silent majority.
>
> This does not mean the group is homogeneous. The proce-
> dures allowing the re-use of products are linked together in a kind
> of obligatory language, and their functioning is related to social
> situations and power relationships. (xvii)

Marginality and marginalization are ways in which groups are
forgotten, decentered and disempowered in global networks of
power. History is in this way about the powerful—let us call them,
in the spirit of this work, the *unmarginal*. Certeau's movement is re-

ciprocal: the marginalized are forgotten, yet they engage in practices that displace—and in this way recall—the forgetting that is their marginalization. Perhaps that description is not felicitous. The point is that everyday life consists of bringing to appearance practices that resist marginalization—that forget forgetting—without becoming empowerments themselves—without being present enough to be remembered as history. Marginality—universal and everywhere—resists history.

Ricoeur begins his account of history as representation and historiography with the myth of writing in *Phaedrus*, on the one hand fully acknowledging its duplicity, on the other—this is Ricoeur's own striking aporia—insisting on the disciplinariness of history. It is as if the aporia and the forgetting do not undermine the historiography but remain marginal, as if the opposition between false and true memory, duplicity and authenticity, never becomes an apposition.

> I shall speak in the manner of Plato's *Phaedrus* of the mythic birth of the writing of history. That this extension of the myth of the origin of writing may sound like a myth of the origin of history, thanks to rewriting, is, if I may put it this way, authorized by the myth itself, inasmuch as what is at stake is the fate of memory, ... And does not Plato indirectly include his own writing, he who wrote down and published his dialogues? But it is to true memory, genuine memory, that the invention of writing and its related drugs is opposed as a threat. How then can the debate between memory and history not be affected by this myth?
>
> To get quickly to the point, what fascinates me, as it does Jacques Derrida, is the insurmountable ambiguity attached to the *pharmakon* that the god offers the king. My question: must we not ask whether the writing of history too, is remedy or poison? (275a). (141)

The inherent duplicity of the *pharmakon* is the duplicity and forgetfulness of memory. It is not quite the remembering of forgetting—I mean unforgetting—not on Ricoeur's reading of Plato. "Again it is memory by default (which I am proposing to call memorization) that is at issue here" (142). If there be such a distinction between memory and memorization, if remembering can ever be taken for granted, if forgetting does not haunt and interrupt remembering—and, indeed, interrupt and haunt writing. "The narrative continues: writing is compared with painting (*zōgraphia*), whose works present themselves 'as if they are alive [*hōs zōnta*]'" (142).

As if they are alive but are dead; as if images were not, as everything is, somewhere between the living and the dead, the past and the future, the original and the proliferation, the one and the other.

In effect, we have passed from the metaphor of imprinting to that of writing, another variety of inscription. Therefore it is really inscription in the generality of its signification that is at issue. But it remains that the kinship with painting is perceived as disturbing (*deinon*; "strange") (275d). . . . the picture makes one believe in the reality through what Roland Barthes calls a "reality effect," which, as is well known, condemns the critic to silence. This is certainly the case with "written discourse": "it continues to signify just that very same thing forever" (275d). Yet, where is the repetitive side more clearly indicated in a nonproblematic way if not in memorized writings, learned by heart? The case turns out to be even more damning: written down once and for all, the discourse is in quest of some interlocutor, whoever it may be—one does not know to whom it is addressed. This is also the case for the historical narrative that gets written and published: it is tossed to the winds, it is addressed . . . to whomever knows how to read. There is a parallel vice: questioned, "it can neither defend itself nor come to its own support" (275e). This is certainly the case for a history book, as for any book. It has cut its ties to its speaker. (142–3)

In the name of true and genuine memory and discourse, this image of critique seems to say it well: writing, thinking, images wander, and this wandering is not just a bad thing—or for that matter good. Wandering is the condition of the discourse being a discourse, from me to you, from today to tomorrow, from one city to another, from one time to another. The loss of time is its gain. And forgetting is another name for wandering.

But then, what quality does that other kind of discourse—"a legitimate brother of this one" (276a)—that of true memory, offer? "It is a discourse that is written down, with knowledge, in the soul of the listener, it can defend itself, and it knows for whom it should speak and for whom it should remain silent" (276a). This discourse that can defend itself before the one to whom it is well fitted is the discourse of true, happy memory, assured of being "timely" and of being capable of being shared. . . . It is this underlying kinship that allows us to say that "the written one can be fairly called an image [*eidōlon*]" (276a) of what is "living," "breathing" in memory. The metaphor of life introduced above, with the painting of living beings, can thus be shifted to the fields of the sensible farmer who knows how to plant, grow, and harvest. For true memory, inscription is a kind of sowing, its true words are "seeds" (*spermata*). Thus we are authorized to speak of "living" writing, for this writing in the soul and for these "gardens of letters" (276d). Here, despite the kinship among these *logoi*, lies the gap between a living memory and a dead deposit.

This remnant of writing at the very heart of memory authorizes our envisaging writing as a risk to run: "When he [the farmer] writes, it's likely he will sow gardens of letters for the sake of amusing himself, storing up reminders for himself 'when he reaches forgetful old age' and for everyone who wants to follow in his footsteps and will enjoy seeing them sweetly blooming" (276d). (143)

Ricoeur reads Plato as perhaps Plato intended himself to be read, that life takes place in the soul as if it were tended by a farmer in the field, sowing truth and goodness. Living memory is mobile, growing, flourishing. Yet these are terms of time, memory is doubled twice, each time returning forgetting as the transformation and transfiguration of life. In other words, sowing and growing are augmenting and creating against the inert silence of death. Only death—and perhaps not even death—can hold onto a memory as if it did not wander, as if it might be held secure against forgetting, as if amusement and play were not endowed by forgetting against the death of remembrance.

Forgetfulness is named for a second time. Above it was entailed by the alleged gift of writing. Now it is something undergone as a consequence of old age. But it does not lack the promise of amusement. Do we not have then a struggle against forgetfulness that preserves the kinship between "the abusive and the legitimate brother?" And, faced with forgetfulness, playfulness? Playfulness that will be welcomed by those old graybeards Nietzsche will condemn in his second *Unfashionable Observation*. But how serious is the game that animates those discourses that have as their object justice and as their method, dialectic? A game in which one takes pleasure, but equally a game where one is as happy as a human being can be: the just person, in effect, finds himself crowned with beauty (277a)! (143–4)

Beauty—I mean exposition—is the fruit and condition of a wandering and forgetful memory. The farmer is happy—if that is the word—in the passage and movement of time, the growing and enrichment of crops, the wealth and abundance and playfulness of life, all given by a forgetting that is the very meaning of abundance. Fixed memories—there are none!—freeze the abundance—that is impossible! Forgetting and the forgotten abound the abundance.

All this is present on Ricoeur's and Derrida's reading (Derrida, *PP*) in the ambiguity of the *pharmakon*, which is given as a figure of abundance and forgetting. The ambiguity and abundance and wandering of the *pharmakon* surpass any memory, any certainty; the living uncertainty of the *pharmakon* is given in the irresistibility of forgetting. This applies to writing, to poetry, and remains ambiguous for philosophy—throughout the dialogues I would insist, here in *Phaedrus* and in *Sophist* and *Timaeus* as well.

> Is this farewell also addressed to the pharmakon of the myth? We are not told. We do not learn whether philosophical discourse is capable of conjuring up the equivalent of a potion concerning which we never know whether it is healing or poisonous.
>
> What would be the equivalent of this indecisive situation for our attempt to transpose the myth from the *Phaedrus* to the plane of the relations between living memory and written history? . . . In order to be fulfilled, the suspicion would have to be exorcized that history remains a hindrance to memory, just like the *pharmakon* of the myth, where in the end we do not know whether it is a remedy or a poison, or both at once. We shall have to allow this unavoidable suspicion to express itself again more than one time. (144–5)

If such a suspicion might be exorcised without a *pharmakon*. And indeed, this *unavoidable suspicion* is more than a suspicion if we understand forgetting as constitutive of the unforgetting that is remembering—I mean the exposition of life and truth themselves.

If we listen to Certeau this exposition of life and truth today is marginal, as if it were ever anything but. Here would appear to be another reading of writing in *Phaedrus*, that if human beings are marginal, not to mention everything else, then their products— writing, memory, knowledge, truth, goodness—are also marginal. This is so in a double sense, Certeau's double. One is that they, like human individuals, are marginal, which means first that they are never empowered—authorized—to tell the truth, to remember the past, to foretell the future—as such. Not as such, but as if. And second, they are means and ways in which marginality is resisted— again as if and perhaps. There may be an educated, living memory, written on the soul. But it is no less marginal for that, and is a story written and told in the unforgetting of its marginalization.

The thesis of this book on unforgetting and especially this chapter is that forgetting is this double gesture. The exposition of the margins is by way of forgetting, and in these margins, by way of exposition—images in proliferation, pictures and writings as if—is a resistance to the authority of memory as if by way of forgetting. Forgetting here is not the absence of memory, a lack of veracity, but another truth in the margins of memory's truth. Forgetting does not undermine history but is both what history countermands and what makes it possible. History does not overcome the marginalization of forgetting—let us temporarily say of the past—but repeats it, insists on it, re-presents it, transforms it, undermines its authority. It is by undermined authority that memory and history accomplish their task, in the margins.

In the margins is the condition that answers to what Ricoeur calls the problematic of forgetting in both memory and history. He calls it problematic even as he insists that forgetting constitutes the condition of his entire investigation into memory and history. Let us say in time. Forgetting joined with forgiveness is the condition of being in time.

> Forgetting and forgiveness, separately and together, designate the horizon of our entire investigation. Separately, inasmuch as they each belong to a distinct problematic: for forgetting, the problematic of memory and faithfulness to the past; for forgiveness, guilt and reconciliation with the past. Together, inasmuch as their respective itineraries intersect at a place that is not a place and which is best indicated by the term "horizon": Horizon of a memory appeased, even of a happy forgetting. (412–3)

One might say that everything turns on this doubled theme of happy memory and forgetting. Why happy? Why, in order to be happy—to live—must memory and forgetting themselves be happy, as against the exposition of learning to live? To live is to struggle to live. To live happily is no less of a struggle. To live is to remember and to forget, but far more important, is to live in the margins constituted by forgetting.

What, however, of forgiveness, linked by Ricoeur with forgetting as the horizon of his entire investigation, linked here perhaps with the margins of time and being, of earth and world? Do world and earth have margins, are they marginal, has everything become marginal—or were they always? That is what forgetting and forgiving ask of us in their own right, decoupled from memory and vengeance, the one the voids, gaps, interruptions, caesuras of things in and beyond time, the earth in wonder, the other the giving beyond gifts that is the earth in abundance. In the margins and the caesuras, forget before you remember! In the caesuras and the margins, forgive beyond any gifts! Forgiveness is amnesty, before forgetting.

Faithfulness and *pathology* are key words for Ricoeur in relation to memory, even as he marks his work and life itself with forgiving and forgetting. Memory—here by no means in the margins—hopes not to forget and despairs of forgetting. Forgiving them becomes pathological if it is tied to forgetting. In order to forgive we must forget. And what if in order to forgive we must not forget? What if the forgotten were the condition of forgiveness?

> In the first instance and on the whole, forgetting is experienced as an attack on the reliability of memory. An attack, a weakness, a

lacuna. In this regard memory defines itself, at least in the first instance, as a struggle against forgetting. . . . But at the same time
and in the same fell swoop, we shun the specter of a memory that
would never forget anything: We even consider it to be monstrous. . . . Could forgetting then no longer be in every respect an
enemy of memory, and could memory have to negotiate with forgetting, groping to find the right measure in its balance with forgetting? And could this appropriate memory have something in
common with the renunciation of total reflection? Could a memory lacking forgetting be the ultimate phantasm, the ultimate figure of this total reflection that we have been combatting in all of
the ranges of the hermeneutics of the human condition? (413)

Even here, the frame of the question is of a memory lacking forgetting—possessing or not possessing it. It is not of a forgetting that
might or might not be remembered, that might or might not be
memory. The idea of a faithful memory guards the oblivion of forgetting, though we know that forgetting is anything but oblivion
and that the forgotten is anything but nothing. I mean that it exceeds everything. Forgetting and the forgotten are the conditions of
remaining in the margins, the surpluses and excesses against which
memory as such would hold fast. It is impossible to hold fast, it is
impossible to avoid death, and they are inseparable. This impossibility, however, gives the truth of forgetting and forgiveness. We cannot hold fast against forgetting and we cannot hold fast against forgiveness. That does not mean that either is easy. But *difficult* is a
difficult word.

Not, however, as difficult as the word *trace*. For if we are to remember forgetting, we must do so in relation to its traces. Ricoeur
describes three such traces, about which the project of forgetting is
organized:

I proposed distinguishing three sorts of traces; the written trace,
which has become the documentary trace on the plane of the his-
toriographical operation; the psychical trace, which can be termed
impression rather than imprint, impression in the sense of an affection left in us by a marking—or as we say, striking—event; finally, the cerebral, cortical trace which the neurosciences deal
with. (415)

It is at this critical point that the grand bifurcation that will
command the last two sections of this study is proposed—namely,
the polarity between two great figures of profound forgetting,
which I shall name forgetting through the erasing of traces and a
backup forgetting, a sort of forgetting kept in reserve (*oubli de
réserve*), ... Our entire problematic of the trace, from antiquity to
today, is truly the inheritor of this ancient notion of imprint,

which, far from solving the enigma of the presence of absence that
encumbers the problematic of the representation of the past, adds
to it its own enigma. (414–5)

In this return of the image of the imprint with its traces, forgetting reappears at the forefront of the stage, supplanting memory's
imprinting and faithfulness. The erasure of traces is not the negation
of memories nor the smoothing out of imprints but the semblance of
the caesura, the proliferation of the image. The return and reappearance and repetition of (the same) image is a proliferation, thereby—
we cannot choose—repetition and difference, restitution and betrayal. This is forgetting as such, because the memory is proliferation and dispossession, has nothing to keep hold of or to possess.
The dispossession of forgetting is the proliferation of the image is
the multiplication of traces is the abundance of giving beyond any
wounds.

This is to say that forgiveness is not the forgetting of anything in
particular, not the setting aside of this trace of injustice or that, but
the forgotten itself, in the caesuras and in the margins, that is, the
proliferation of the image that is the wonder and abundance of the
earth. Forgiveness exceeds every memory in the wonder of giving in
abundance.

On the plane of traces, Ricoeur sketches the distinction he has
established between the psychical and the cerebral traces, this time
in the name of the mnestic trace. It remains a question for science,
this time not of history but of neuroscience. Another way to put this
is in terms of the relation between scientist and philosopher, taking
for granted, without forgetfulness, the disciplinary distinctions that
Ricoeur's entire discussion accepts and that mine here calls into
question.

(1) We will first ask, what is the position in principle of the philosopher who I am in contrast to scientists who speak in general
terms of mnestic or nonmnestic traces? (2) What can be said more
specifically about mnestic traces? What mutual instruction can the
phenomenologist and the neurologist provide to one another? It is
at this stage of questioning that the major interrogation will be
carried to its highest problematic level. (3) Finally, what place
does the question of forgetting occupy in the table of dysfunctions
of memory? Is forgetting itself a dysfunction? It is with this third
segment of questioning that forgetting through the effacement of
traces will best be determined. (416)

Is forgetting a dysfunction? It appears a question in the midst of
the relation between the phenomenologist philosopher and the neu-
roscientist. What is this relation, one to be remembered and sus-

tained or one to be forgotten and overcome? The answer for us here, as it has been throughout, is that there is no such choice but there is a temptation. So let us affirm the temptation: it lies in the nature of a disciplinary and linguistic distinction, once established, that it can never be erased, can never be forgotten without traces, but these traces cannot be established once and for all so as to re-mark the distinction that founds them. The most immediate practical implication of this is that the taxonomy of traces is an act of violence that must be erased even as it is impossible to do so. Forgetting takes place in this caesura, the impossibility of de-tracing and re-tracing the traces that are forgotten in time and being.

In this context, what is the contribution of neuropsychology to issues of forgetting, not to overlook forgiving? On the side of the memories we may be desperate to possess, neuroscience reveals the depth of loss in its own duplicity.

> The neurosciences that target memory can provide instruction, in the first instance, about the conduct of life on the level of reflective knowledge in which a hermeneutics of life would consist. Beyond this direct utility, there is our curiosity about the things of nature, and among these the brain is doubtless the most marvelous product. . . . This instruction helps to warn us about the pretentious hubris that would make us the masters and possessors of nature. Our entire being-in-the-world is shaken by this. (422–3)

Let's take this shaking at its face value: our entire being-in-the-world, not to mention the world itself, is shaken by the activities of forgetting and their traces. Let's then imagine that the neurosciences themselves bear this shaking at their heart. We posit function where dysfunction is the reality, so that the curiosity that moves reflection enables human life and practice, pursues remembering as if it were unforgetting—and in the same way pursues possession as if it were for giving. Abundance and wonder, in their marginalities, multiplicities, and heterogeneities, are the caesuras of exposition. That is our shaken being in the world.

Ricoeur questions the possibility of such a being but hesitates at the answer:

> But is forgetting a dysfunction, a distortion? In certain respects, yes. In the matter of definitive forgetting, indicating an effacement of traces, it is experienced as a threat: it is against this forgetting that we conduct the work of memory (*oeuvre de memoire*) in order to slow its course, even to hold it at bay. The extraordinary exploits of the *ars memoriae* were designed to ward off the misfortune of forgetting by a kind of exaggerated memorization brought to the assistance of remembering. . . . In brief, forgetting is lamented

in the same way as aging and death: it is one of the figures of the
inevitable, the irremediable. And yet forgetting is bound up with
memory, . . . : its strategies and, under certain conditions, its culti-
vation worthy of a genuine *ars oblivionis* result in the fact that we
cannot simply classify forgetting through the effacement of traces
among the dysfunctions of memory alongside amnesia, nor among
the distortions of memory affecting its reliability. (426)

Forgetting is not to be classified among the dysfunctions and distortions of memory, but is the object of its own art. If that is so, if there
can be an *ars* in the margins. If forgetting is not already present in
the arts themselves, in the margins. If forgetting can be classified
without being remembered.

Learn to laugh! Zarathustra says. Learn to forget! or learn to
love forgetting because that love is life itself.

I will pass over Ricoeur's argument concerning the persistence
of traces, taking us back to the mechanics of memory:

the passive persistence of first impressions: an event has struck us,
touched us, affected us, and the affective mark remains in our
mind. (427)

An image comes back to me; and I say in my heart: that's really
him, that's really her. I recognize him, I recognize her. This recognition can take different forms. It takes place already in the course
of perception: a being was presented once; it went away; it came
back. Appearing, disappearing, reappearing. (429)

The enigma of the presence of absence is resolved, we have
just said, in the effective reality of the mnemonic act and in the
certainty that crowns this reality. (430)

As if appearing, disappearing, reappearing were not interruptions,
marginalia, caesuras. *Fort/Da*. Now you see it, now you don't. Recognition is everything, and traces persist. Really, but perhaps not
with certainty. To the contrary, the embellishments, transformations,
enrichments of the returning image carry all the more assurance.
Putting aside the epistemology of true and false memories, the truth
of memory is always as if far beyond the limits of the return. The
image proliferates in both true and false memory, and it is by proliferation—forgetting—that recognition is assured. I can build an edifice on what I remember, on the building, embellishing, ornament-
ing that is memory. I mean forgetting.

All this is to explain why the arts bear a special relation to forgetting—perhaps I mean why they seem to bear such a relation, because semblance is this embellishment that constitutes forgetting as
being, the exposition of reality itself. Reality is composed of forget-

ting—that is its wonder and abundance. Reality is composed of pro-liferations, margins, caesuras, interruptions. I don't mean reality as against unreality, real truth as against apparent truth, but the appearing and becoming in which reality and unreality are composed.

Recognition here is the sudden grasp—and grasp it is—of an elusive trace, and its appearance is at once the thing again and its transfiguration. Reappearance, appearance again, is never the first appearance, and must not be. The interval of time is both absolute loss—which is in no way incompatible with memory and return—and gain. More to the point, the interval undercuts the rule of reappearance, the certainty of recognition. We can remember but we can't be sure. More memorably, we can be sure and yet be wrong. But that is the epistemological version, supported by neuropsy-chological evidence on false memories. The affirmative version is that we must embellish and transform to be sure, and must do so in such a way as to augment any recognition and recollection. The world is full of augmentation in the midst of endless loss. That is the story of forgetting.

Ricoeur classifies amnesty under commanded forgetting, an abuse and paradox he considers analogous to commanded remem-bering. Yet there is a relation between amnesty and amnesia that is deeper and more primordial, though it must first pass through for-giveness.

> The question now posed concerns an enigma different from that of the present representation of an absent thing bearing the seal of the anterior. It is twofold: on the one hand, it is the enigma of a fault held to paralyze the power to act of the "capable being" that we are; and it is, in reply, the enigma of the possible lifting of this existential incapacity, designated by the term "forgiveness."
> ... Forgiveness—if it has a sense, and if it exists—constitutes the horizon common to memory, history, and forgetting. (457)

Ricoeur insists that forgiveness must pass through a fault, that its trajectory remains caught within the poles of fault and forgive-ness. I repeat that forgetting is more and other—utterly other—than is embodied in the pair remembering and forgetting, and forgiving is more and other—utterly other—than is caught between the poles of fault and forgiveness. One indication that this is so is the dispro-portion Ricoeur names. There is no measure, no proportion between blame and forgiveness. The sin is a sin, the fault is a fault. Forgive-ness—giving beyond gifts—is tied to fault and sin.

Let us instead think of a wound. Let us extend this wound from blame and fault to loss and death. Let us introduce forgiveness not into the Christian world of moral judgment but into Anaximander's world in which time and being are unjust, an injustice that demands amnesty beyond measure. Forgiveness enters the world at the point at which there is no measure, together with the forgetting of measure.

In this way forgiving is giving beyond measure in the abundance and wonder of the earth. Wounds and suffering are in the abundance, which does not make them less wounding. Death is death, loss is loss, disastrous in the risk of being forgotten. Yet the forgetting of what was, no matter how wounding, does not replace the forgetting of the abundance, does not replace it and does not make it better. The proliferation of the image, the arrival of the stranger, the appearance and disappearance of alterity and heterogeneity are neither good nor bad, but are conditions of goodness and evil. We live in the abundance, full of pain and wounds, joy and love. We live and we die, and in the wonder and abundance of each the other looms and glows.

It is no part of memory and forgetting to make a loss a fault, nor does forgiving resolve that fault into a wound. Forgiveness takes on the burden of the wound of forgetting, but it is more than that, in and from and toward the abundance. Wonder and abundance do not cease in wounds and faults, but are enriched by them in their pain. One might think of writing and giving and being from and of and beyond the disaster. Just an insinuation in advance:[4]

> The disaster ruins everything, all the while leaving everything intact. It does not touch anyone in particular; . . . . We are on the edge of disaster without being able to situate it in the future: it is rather always already past, ...
> *The disaster takes care of everything.*
> The disaster is related to forgetfulness—forgetfulness without memory, ...
> The disaster is the gift; it gives disaster: as if it took no account of being or not-being. (Blanchot, *WD*, 1–5)

Does Ricoeur know of (this) disaster?

Forgiveness is extreme giving in abundance beyond good and bad, life and death. The abundance of disaster. Forgiveness is extreme giving from the good—I mean the forgotten. The disaster of abundance. Nothing can make disaster whole, but the earth continues in abundance and wonder. For giving is the affirmation of giving and abundance in the midst of shatterings that are never to be made whole. There is no beautiful death, but there is beauty in death as there is in life, and abundance in the midst of disaster. For giving is the dispossession that relinquishes the grip of death upon us without imagining that there is no death or that death is not disaster. We live, we write, we dream, we go on, we create after the disaster, in the midst of forgotten disasters. Amnesty is more than we will ever know. Forgiveness is more than we will ever lose.

This is not what Ricoeur says. He ties forgiveness to a fault as he ties amnesty to memory, knowing all the while that it is the tie that binds them irrevocably. And he rejects the giving in forgiving as belonging to a system of exchange, setting aside all ways of giving beyond gifts. We come to the thought that forgiving is beyond gifts and forgetting is beyond memory. Forgetting and forgiving are beyond grasp.

> we take note of a remarkable relation which, for a time, places the request for forgiveness and the offering of forgiveness on a plane of equality and reciprocity, as if there existed a genuine relation of exchange between these two speech acts. Our exploration of this track is encouraged by the kinship found in numerous languages between forgiving and giving. In this regard, the correlation between the gift and the counter-gift (the gift in return) in certain archaic forms of exchange tends to reinforce the hypothesis that the request for and the offer of forgiveness are held to balance one another in a horizontal relation. (458–9)

> A final effort of clarification resting once again on a horizontal correlation will therefore be proposed with the pair, forgiveness and promise. In order to be bound by a promise, the subject of an action must also be able to be released from it through forgiveness. The temporal structure of action, namely, the irreversibility and unpredictability of time, calls for the response of a twofold mastery exerted over the carrying out of any action. My thesis here is that a significant asymmetry exists between being able to forgive and being able to promise, as is attested by the impossibility of genuine political institutions of forgiveness. Thus, at the heart of selfhood and at the core of imputability, the paradox of forgiveness is laid bare, sharpened by the dialectic of repentance in the great Abrahamic tradition. What is at issue here is nothing less than the power of the spirit of forgiveness to unbind the agent from his act. (458–9)

Every key term here is presented as broken by the caesura of time and the wounds of being, insisting on mastery—the twofold mastery exercised over action in time. Every reading of Ricoeur's turns on an insistence on this mastery and its impossibility beyond the ability of time and being to fulfill. Together with the binding of a promise there is the impossibility of holding one to it through time and space. The promise of the future and the promise of another place are a different promise, a promise for different people and different places. This is not paradox but exposition, exposure to alterity

and its expression, the promise and call of the other, which cannot
be fulfilled in any recognizable way within the other's otherness.

Indeed, it is the otherness, alterity, deviance, transportation,
transgression of exposition that promises forgetting and forgiving,
as well as any linking they may provide. It is this alterity that undercuts the fault that Ricoeur insists on as constituting forgiveness—
as if anything might not be taken as a fault, as if any fault might not
promise something else in time. Ricoeur's own placement is in relation to sin, where the forgotten is promised in relation to disaster—
wounds without sin, disasters beyond evil. That is the point of the
forgotten in forgiving, that disaster is beyond the wounds that make
it so—beyond as in the excessiveness of the wounds and the excesses of abundance beyond any wounds.

> the radical nature of the experience of fault requires us to confine
> ourselves within the limits of the self-ascription of fault, to sketch
> out at this level the conditions for a common recognition of a fun-
> damental guilt. The specific form taken by such attribution of fault
> to the self is avowal, admission, that speech act by which a subject
> takes up, assumes the accusation. This act assuredly has some-
> thing to do with remembering inasmuch as in remembering a
> power of connection capable of engendering history is confirmed.
> But remembering is, in principle, innocent. And it is as such that
> we have described it. (461)

If there is a fundamental guilt—Anaximander's injustice,
Adam's fall—then remembering is guilty. What and when and who
remembers is always a wound against who and when and what
might have been remembered. That is the promise that goes hand in
hand with guilt. I mean betrayal, in its the doubled meaning, in
which the guilt betrays abundance and innocence betrays guilt—
duplicity and revelation. Expression and revelation are everything
here: that is why simulation and semblance are shattering. Exposition is always beyond itself, innocent and guilty, present and absent,
all in the mode of *perhaps* and *as if*. The key to memory, history, and
forgetting is the simulation and proliferation, the *as if* that haunts
the promise of their future and any presence, that interrupts the
grasp of innocence and guilt by the undetermined promises in the
caesura.

But of course Ricoeur knows this:

> The "there is" of the voice of forgiveness says this in its own way.
> This is why I will speak of this voice as a voice from above. It is
> from above, in the way that the admission of fault proceeds from
> the unfathomable depths of selfhood. It is a silent voice but not a
> mute one. Silent, because there is no clamor of what rages; not

mute, because not deprived of speech. An appropriate discourse is in fact dedicated to it, the hymn. A discourse of praise and celebration. It says: *il y a, es gibt*, there is . . . forgiveness—the form of the universal designating *illéité*. For the hymn has no need to say who forgives and to whom forgiveness is directed. There is forgiveness as there is joy, as there is wisdom, extravagance, love. Love, precisely. Forgiveness belongs to the same family. (467)

There is forgiveness as (if) there is love, as (if) there are joy, wisdom, memory, forgetting. As if we knew finally what any of these were, as if we knew finally how to live or love or enjoy or forgive. As if we had not always forgotten—and always remembered.

But why from the height, rather than in the depths or right here before me? Why St. Paul's hymn to love,[5] rather than the lyrics of the adolescent lover, swooning in a crush? What is the proper form of forgiving, remembering, enjoying, or loving? What is the designated fulfillment of the promise to love or to forgive? Do we not violate it in every insistence upon it? And is this not testimony to what it is—nothing in particular?

I will rephrase the problem in these terms: if there is forgiveness, at least on the level of the hymn—of the Abrahamic hymn, if one likes—is there some forgiveness for us? Some forgiveness, in the sense of the French partitive [as in *du pardon*]. Or must one say, with Derrida: "Each time that forgiveness is in the service of a finality, be it noble and spiritual (repurchase or redemption, reconciliation, salvation), each time that it tends to reestablish a normalcy (social, national, political, psychological) through a work of mourning, through some therapy or ecology of memory, then 'forgiveness' is not pure—nor is its concept. Forgiveness is not, and it should not be, either normal, or normative, or normalizing. It should remain exceptional and extraordinary, standing the test of the impossible: as if it interrupted the ordinary course of historical temporality." This "test of the impossible" is what we must now confront. (469–70)

As if this impossibility of forgiveness undermined and negated the possibility of forgiveness, of escaping retribution. As if—as Derrida has said repeatedly—the condition of impossibility were not the very condition of possibility. This condition is indeed before us, no matter how difficult it may be to contemplate—or for that matter, to live. But I insist that we live it and practice it within its difficulty, and that this has to be true as well for its exposition. That is, we say it and reveal it no matter how difficult it may be to communicate it. I mean no matter how impossible it is to be understood as we hope to be understood. If we want to be understood on the subjects of giving and forgiving, as if they were not permeated by forgetting.

> In principle, there is no limit to forgiveness, no measure, no moderation, no "to what point?" . . .

> As enigmatic as the concept of forgiveness remains, it is the case that the scene, the figure, the language which one tries to adapt to it belong to a religious heritage (let's call it Abrahamic, in order to bring together Judaism, the Christianities, and the Islams). This tradition—complex and differentiated, even conflictual—is at once singular and on the way to universalisation through that which a certain theatre of forgiveness puts in place or brings to light. (Derrida, *CF*, 27)

> In principle, therefore, always in order to follow a vein of the Abrahamic tradition, forgiveness must engage two singularities: the guilty (the "perpetrator" as they say in South Africa) and the victim. As soon as a third party intervenes, one can again speak of amnesty, reconciliation, reparation, etc., but certainly not of pure forgiveness in the strict sense. . . . [O]ne day a black woman comes to testify before the [Truth and Reconciliation] Commission. Her husband had been assassinated by torturers who were police officers. She speaks in her language, . . . something like this: "A commission or a government cannot forgive. Only I, eventually, could do it. (And I am not ready to forgive.)"

> These are very difficult words to hear. This woman victim, this wife of the victim . . . surely wanted to recall that the anonymous body of the State or of a public institution cannot forgive. It has neither the right nor the power to do so, and besides, that would have no meaning. The representative of the State can judge, but forgiveness has precisely nothing to do with judgement. Or even with the public or political sphere. . . . This woman, perhaps, wanted to suggest something else again: if anyone has the right to forgive, it is only the victim, and not a tertiary institution. . . . [W]ho would have the right to forgive in the name of the disappeared victims? They are always absent, in a certain way. The disappeared, in essence, are themselves never absolutely present, at the moment when forgiveness is asked for, the same as they were at the moment of the crime, and they are sometimes absent in body, often dead.[6] (42–44)

The institutionalization of these questions—which appear to be beyond the grasp of any institution—takes the form in our time of prescription and imprescription, always questions of legitimation in the context of what cannot be legitimated—sovereign power and collective forgiveness.

The question of imprescriptibility arises because prescription exists in the law for all violations and crimes. On the one hand, the legislation of civil law itself includes a dual form, acquisitive and liberating. Under the first form, it provides that, after a certain period of time, a claim of ownership of property cannot be opposed to the one who has possession of it in fact; it thus becomes a means of acquiring definitive ownership of property. Under the second form, one is freed from an obligation, from a debt, through its liquidation. On the other hand, prescription is a provision of criminal law, where it consists in the termination of legal action. Once a certain period of time has passed, it forbids the plaintiff from bringing a suit before the competent court. . . . Under all its forms, prescription is an astonishing institution, which is reluctantly authorized by the presumed effect of time on obligations that are supposed to persist over time. . . . [I]t is refusing, after a lapse of arbitrarily defined years, to move back up the course of time to the act and to its illegal or irregular traces. The traces are not erased: it is the path back to them that is forbidden, and this is the meaning of the word "cessation" applied to debts and to the right of criminal prosecution. (Ricoeur, *MHF*, 471–2)

It is astonishing within the assumption that the past remains in memory, present, available, requiring prescription. If the crime was committed it remains a crime. If the crime deserves punishment, if the contract was written years ago, it deserves regard.[7] Ricoeur takes for granted that time means nothing of itself, so that it becomes necessary under law to implement it as something through prescription. He does not consider the possibility that the past is other as past, that the event is other as occurrence, that the right to prescribe comes to a halt before the other.

It is against this backdrop that we must place the legislation that declares the imprescriptibility of crimes against humanity, and among these the crime of genocide. . . . By suppressing the statute of limitations, the principle of imprescriptibility authorizes the indefinite pursuit of the authors of these immense crimes. In this sense, it restores to the law its force to persist despite the obstacles to carrying through the effects of the law. (472)

The obstacles do not vanish. The past is lost. The right and ability to bring to justice require documents and testimony that no longer exist. More to the point, perhaps, the individuals and their lives may no longer exist in fault and sin after many years have passed. How long does a crime remain a crime? Why suppose the answer is forever? Why should this be so? Why are we tied to the injustice of the past in particular crimes even after many years have passed? Might these years themselves be restitution?

Does it not depend on the crime? Why take it for granted, except for God, that a crime remains a crime, the same crime, the same injustice, forever? That is not what Anaximander says. The injustice, crime, for which we are charged is not any particular crime but being itself, and no particular restitution but restitution itself. If injustice and restitution are beyond exchange, immemorial, then nothing answers to them and there is no measure of them. Justice and forgiveness are beyond exchange. Altitude appears to be another matter.

> I want to consider the particular structure of the dilemmas of forgiveness along with the difficulties that result from extending the problematic of forgiveness to a model of exchange tied to the concept of the gift. The etymology and the semantics of numerous languages encourage this comparison: *don-pardon*, gift-forgiving, *dona-perdono, Geben-Vergeben*. Now the idea of gift has its own difficulties, which can be divided into two parts. It is important first to recover the reciprocal dimension of the gift in contrast to an initial characterization of it as unilateral. It is then a matter of restoring, at the heart of the relation of exchange, the difference in altitude that distinguishes forgiving from giving, following the essence of exchange. (479–80)

Yet parallel with the impossibility of giving and forgiving Derrida argues against the reciprocity of the gift. He has Levinas in mind, for whom the immeasurability of these and other, even everyday ideas is given from the face of the other. The face beyond haunts daily practices with immeasurability. Many societies regard gift giving as reciprocal, exchange gifts measured against each other. Many of the same societies understand that such reciprocities and such economies are not exchanges at all, but hint at immeasurable conditions of divinity, power, force, and goodness.[8] The gift that enhances the authority and status of the noble and wealthy reveals the limits of wealth. The gift that demands that other aristocrats reciprocate expresses the immeasurability of nobility and aristocracy. A gift must be impossible or it is no gift, even in the context of an exchange. Moreover, on the other side, that of betrayal, every gift that appears to be beyond reciprocity falls back into taking.

The point is that there is nothing to remember, nothing to fix, in giving or forgiving. These are impossible and immeasurable; and even so and because, they serve reciprocal social relations. They become taking in the very form and immeasure of giving. This is their betrayal, but it is not their cancellation or nullification. It is rather the nature of betrayal, to show and reveal more than can be revealed or shown. In other words, they are witness to forgetting.

giving obliges giving back (*do ut des*); giving secretly creates inequality by placing the givers in a position of condescending superiority; giving ties the beneficiary, placing him or her under obligation, the obligation to be grateful; giving crushes the beneficiary
under the weight of a debt he cannot repay....

I would like to suggest that not only is the market exchange
attacked by the critique, so too is a higher form of exchange extending all the way to the love of one's enemies.... The commandment to love one's enemies begins by breaking the rule of reciprocity and requiring the extraordinary. Faithful to the gospel
rhetoric of hyperbole, according to this commandment the only
gift that is justified is the one given to the enemy, from whom, by
hypothesis, one expects nothing in return. But, precisely, the hypothesis is false: what one expects from love is that it will convert
the enemy into a friend. (481–2)

Does one expect this from love, does one expect from forgiveness
that the enemy will become a friend, that the wound will cease to be
a wound, that the victim will be healed? I do not think so. I think
that love—it is indeed love according to some vernaculars—is most
compelling in the face of a wound. I am speaking of writing, in the
face of disaster.

Let me put it this way: The question Ricoeur poses is whether
certain crimes or faults are beyond forgiveness, or whether forgiveness is beyond crime. The institutionalization of punishment for
state crimes without a statute of limitations says nothing about forgiveness. Let me put it another way: I—historically a Jew—might
well not insist on punishing every German for the concentration
camps and gas chambers, yet I might never forgive. Certainly I
would never forget. This does not mean that I would disdain having
German friends, albeit perhaps with a certain queasiness. And I
might well insist on punishing some Germans—Eichmann for example—though I might well forgive Germans in general because in
general they cannot be blamed. Or if I do not forgive them I may
agree to treat them as ethical without qualification.

Forgiveness is the giving of this "without qualification" when
there is a profound qualification. And I believe it is inescapable for
any of us. We live in a profoundly qualified world, and every one of
us is imperfect in a deep and wounding sense. Certainly I have done
things I am ashamed of, and would hope to have made the best of.
What can this mean but that I and others will remember and that
they and I will accept me without qualification? Perhaps because we
are all guilty. Perhaps because we forgive and forget. But we should
not forget and yet we must forgive. And this forgiveness can never
become a prescription, either in the sense that one must forgive or

that one must act or feel in any particular way. This impossibility and yet the absolute necessity of forgiveness and forgetting is Anaximander's law. We are all unjust and in this injustice we pay endless restitution—who knows how or how much? Amnesty is the impossible of the human condition.

And indeed, we confront this impossibility in every condition of disaster.

> I would like to mention, in light of these puzzles, the specific difficulties courageously assumed by the initiators of the famous Truth and Reconciliation Commission, ... The mission of this commission, which met from January 1996 to July 1998 and presented its five-volume report in October 1998, was to "collect testimony, console the injured, indemnify the victims, and amnesty those who confessed to committing political crimes." "Understanding, not revenge." . . . Neither amnesty nor collective immunity. In this sense, it is indeed under the aegis of the model of exchange that this alternative experience of purging a violent past deserves to be mentioned. (483)

Did the commission accomplish its task? Did it bring about reconciliation? Did it heal the civil wounds of apartheid? How could it do so, and why imagine that it might do so? Was not South Africa in the same position as Europe after the Second World War? How to go on? With justice and forgiveness, some of this and some of the other. As for what going on might bring, is that a condition of the work of the commission or also of the formation of the new South African state?

> On the side of the victims, the benefits are undeniable in therapeutic, moral, and political terms, all together. Families who fought for years to know the facts were able to express their pain, vent their hatred in the presence of the offenders and before witnesses. At the price of long hearings, they had an opportunity to tell of tortures and to name the criminals. In this sense, the hearings truly permitted the public exercise of the work of memory and of mourning, guided by an appropriate process of cross-examination. . . .
>
> This being so, it is perhaps expecting too much from this unprecedented experience to ask to what extent the protagonists progressed along the path toward genuine forgiveness. It is difficult to say. (483–4)

It is difficult to say here, perhaps anywhere, whether forgiveness is genuine, whether there should be an institutionalized and rationalized forgiveness. Derrida denies it. What if forgiveness were always in the caesura between the genuine and ungenuine? What if pain and suffering held us in their grip no matter how genuine and deep the forgiveness? What if the impossibility of forgiving haunted the most profound exercise of reconciliation? And indeed, why imagine that reconciliation requires forgiveness—or that anything can require it?

We may recall that Soyinka separates indemnity from the history of trauma.[9] Indemnity, of course, if only to mark a threshold that cannot otherwise be surmounted. Reconciliation crosses a threshold, in the caesura: something material, tangible is required. Wounds and traumas are another matter, calling for poetry and images, for transformations and transfigurations. And there is the question whether the wounds should heal, and whether that is possible. Suppose the wounds cannot heal, still there must be reconciliation, or if not that, something that marks the beginning of a future as well as the disasters of the past. Life must go on if there is to be a future. Life will go on and there will be a future, and we are responsible for taking that step.

Forgiveness is not the only possibility, and may be no possibility at all. But it may offer a miracle of what cannot be rationally calculated, the passage from the past to a future that cannot be anticipated.

> Often, the commission exposed brutal truths that the agencies of political reconciliation between former enemies could not accept, as is shown by the rejection of the commission's report by many people. It is not a sign of despair to recognize the noncircumstantial, but more properly structural, limitations belonging to an enterprise of reconciliation which not only requires a great deal of time but also a work upon the self, in which it is not an exaggeration to see under the figure of a public exercise of political reconciliation something like an incognito of forgiveness. (485)

> The disproportion between the word of forgiveness and that of admission returns under the form of a single question: What force makes one capable of asking, of giving, of receiving the word of forgiveness? (485–6)

Why should there be such a force? Why should forgiveness answer to anything, even remembering and forgetting? Why should it have a task to perform? Ricoeur's answer turns (back) to the interiority of the self. He does so in terms of agency and the public sphere. "It is now to the heart of selfhood that our investigation must be directed. But to what power, to what courage can one appeal in order simply to ask for forgiveness?" (486). And he does so again in terms of unbinding the agent from the binding that is the relation of memory to the past. If that is what it is.

It is from our ability to master the course of time that the courage to ask for forgiveness seems able to be drawn. This is what Hannah Arendt attempts to show in *The Human Condition*. . . . Her argument rests on reestablishing a very ancient symbolism, that of *unbinding/binding*, then on pairing forgiving and promising under this dialectic, one of which would unbind and the other bind us. The virtue of these two capabilities is that they answer in a responsible manner to the temporal constraints on the "continuation of acting" on the plane of human affairs. (486)

The faculty of forgiveness and the faculty of promising rest on experiences that no one can have in isolation and which are based entirely on the presence of others. If the origin of these two faculties is inherent in plurality, their area of exercise is eminently political. (487)

Arendt's words emphasize the imperative of binding for human action, joined with the complementary imperative of unbinding. We must promise and we must keep our promises. We must intend and fulfill our intentions. We must act in reliable ways. All these are imperatives, individual and collective. What they are not are certainties and possessions.

We have seen that the *animal laborans* could be redeemed from its predicament of imprisonment in the ever-recurring cycle of the life process, . . . only through the mobilization of another human capacity, the capacity for making, fabricating, and producing of *homo faber*, who as a toolmaker not only eases the pain and trouble of laboring but also erects a world of durability. . . . We saw furthermore that *homo faber*, could be redeemed from his predicament of meaninglessness, . . . only through the interrelated faculties of action and speech, which produce meaningful stories as naturally as fabrication produces use objects. . . . From the viewpoint of the *animal laborans*, it is like a miracle that it is also a being which knows of and inhabits a world; from the viewpoint of *homo faber*, it is like a miracle, like the revelation of divinity, that meaning should have a place in this world.

The case of action and action's predicaments is altogether different. Here, the remedy against the irreversibility and unpredictability of the process started by action . . . is one of the potentialities of action itself. The possible redemption from the predicament of irreversibility—of being unable to undo what one has done though one did not, and could not, have known what he was doing—is the faculty of forgiving. The remedy for unpredictability, for the chaotic uncertainty of the future, is contained in the faculty to make and keep promises. The two faculties belong together in so far as one of them, forgiving, serves to undo the deeds of the past, whose "sins" hang like Damocles' sword over every new generation; and the other, binding oneself through promises, serves to set up in the ocean of uncertainty, which the future is by definition, islands of security without which not even continuity, let alone durability of any kind, would be possible in the relationships between men. (Arendt, *HC* [1998], 236–7)

Without being able to bind oneself in time, one would be at its mercy. Without being able to forgive, one would be bound irrevocably to the wounds of the past. Let us accept these claims as true— not, however, simply. Action takes place in time, binds it and unbinds it. That is in the nature of action, as it is in fabrication and thought. I do not share Arendt's recurrent Aristotelian distinctions between thinking, acting, and making or Kant's parallel view of distinct faculties. More exactly, I think that they exist to call themselves into question. Here, however, I am more interested in the binding in time by deeds, promises, stories, images—by labor, art, and action, that is, in exposition. All bind time in making something present, all unbind it in many ways, in the gestures of making present that make unpresent, or that make present in different ways.

This the role of forgetting, and it appears here immediately in the binding itself. Forgiveness unbinds us as if we were bound. Yet how did we become so bound? What bound Orestes to his deed, to be haunted and hunted down by the Furies? Anaximander speaks of the injustice of all things and their restitutions. But he does not say what is unjust, and does not calculate restitution. When Athena releases Orestes from his bondage as murderer of his mother, does she unbind him or does she transfigure him and his act into sovereignty as she transfigures the Furies into Eumenides? In other words, perhaps as Nietzsche intends, is the unbinding, forgetting, and forgiving not inherent in the very bonds that bind us, in that we must act again in binding, we must avenge, destroy, enact, compel, release?

Is there something distinctive in practice and time, in truth and memory, in knowledge and reality that binds us tightly unless we find means to release them, or are they all unbound by the ties that bind? Can we enact justice for a crime, with or without forgiveness, as if there were such a thing as given justice, mechanical rightness? Is this impossibility of which Derrida and Ricoeur speak present in the binding as well as in the unbinding?

Ricoeur shares Arendt's sense that promises bind us to the future. And so they do. But having said that, we can see that nothing particular answers to that binding. Binding is not bondage, we remain free not slaves, we fulfill our promises in all sorts of ways. I do not say in any way whatever, but deny that any particular way is the only way. To the contrary, through time and changing circumstances, promises open up infinite possibilities of fulfillment. I will tell you the truth, pay my loan back, give you what you need, come when called. Who could specify any of these, or for that matter deny in principle or general that any particular act failed? The point is that promising is an act and fulfilling the promise is an act—many acts—and the inherent displacement of acts in time, of memories in time, remains in the plurality where Arendt locates it.

> Because the remedies against the enormous strength and resiliency inherent in action processes can function only under the condition of plurality, it is very dangerous to use this faculty in any but a realm of human affairs. Modern natural science and technology, which no longer observe or take material from or imitate processes of nature but seem actually to act into it, seem, by the same token, to have carried irreversibility and human unpredictability into the natural realm, where no remedy can be found to undo what has been done. Similarly, it seems that one of the great dangers of acting in the mode of making and within its categorical framework of means and ends lies in the concomitant self-deprivation of the remedies inherent only in action, so that one is bound not only to do with the means of violence necessary for all fabrication, but also to undo what he has done as he undoes an unsuccessful object, by means of destruction. Nothing appears more manifest in these attempts than the greatness of human power, whose source lies in the capacity to act, and which without action's inherent remedies inevitably begins to overpower and destroy not man himself but the conditions under which life was given to him. (*HC* [1998], 238)

Yet this plurality with its powers is both the absolute condition of action and meaning, the absolute condition of appearing, and of all the remedies that would unbind it. Plurality it is and it is bound, and being bound as plurality it is always unbound. Binding is exposition, and in the saying and the appearing, in the stories and the other stories, between teller and audience, is exposition. We are exposed in action as exposition, exposure as expression, calling; as *aisthēsis, mimēsis, poiēsis, catachrēsis, technē*; as image, aesthetics, beauty, art; calling as giving. Calling as giving is forgetting, and forgetting is betrayal. Binding betrays the world; unbinding betrays binding, betrays betrayal, acting, thinking, and speaking—all the forms and images of being, being something, being in time and memory, take place in exposition, in proliferation. Unbinding is the proliferation of binding, not its abrogation. That is what plurality is and means.

> In this respect, forgiveness is the exact opposite of vengeance, which acts in the form of re-acting against an original trespassing, whereby far from putting an end to the consequences of the first misdeed, everybody remains bound to the process, permitting the chain reaction contained in every action to take its unhindered course. In contrast to revenge, which is the natural, automatic re-action to transgression and which because of the irreversibility of the action process can be expected and even calculated, the act of forgiving can never be predicted; it is the only reaction that is in an unexpected way and thus retains, though being a reaction, something of the original character of action. Forgiving, in other words, is the only reaction which does not merely re-act but acts anew and unexpectedly, unconditioned by the act which provoked it and therefore freeing from its consequences both the one who forgives and the one who is forgiven. . . .
>
> The alternative to forgiveness, but by no means its opposite, is punishment, and both have in common that they attempt to put an end to something that without interference could go on endlessly. (240–1)

Yet like it or not the processes go on endlessly. Punishment and vengeance are not alternatives or opposites but justice in action. The endless spiral of vengeance is not after all so different from the endless spiral of justice, law, and practice. Forgiveness is not so much within this spiral as the condition that it takes for granted—its impossibility again. Justice would be impossible without forgiveness, by which I mean neither letting justice and vengeance go nor releasing and unbinding the criminal from the crime—the Christian image of forgiveness to which Arendt and Ricoeur are both attached—but the recognition and reality that there is no binding that is not unbinding, that we are always unbound by variants, alternatives, transformations, transfigurations—and for that matter, no unbinding that is not also bound, inherited from and constituted by the past. Forgiveness is the abundance of reliability of action as forgetting is the abundance of reliability of memory.

Just a few years later, Arendt approached forgetting and unbinding in a different way, beginning with the context of testament and memory rather than of action.

> *Notre héritage n'est précédé d'aucun testament*—"our inheritance was left to us by no testament"—this is perhaps the strangest of the strangely abrupt aphorisms into which René Char, French poet and writer, compressed the gist of what four years in the resistance had come to mean to a whole generation of European writers and men of letters. (Arendt, *BPF*, 3)

They had lost their treasure.

What was this treasure? As they themselves understood it, it seems to have consisted, as it were, of two interconnected parts: they had discovered that he who "joined the Resistance, found himself," that he ceased to be "in quest of [himself] without mastery, in naked unsatisfaction," that he no longer suspected himself of "insincerity, of being a carping, suspicious actor of life," that he could afford "to go naked." . . . they had been visited for the first time in their lives by an apparition of freedom, . . .because they had become "challengers," had taken the initiative upon themselves and therefore, without knowing or even noticing it, had begun to create that public space between themselves where freedom could appear. "At every meal that we eat together, freedom is invited to sit down. The chair remains vacant, but the place is set." (4)

There is nothing in this situation that is altogether new. . . . Yet the only exact description of this predicament is to be found, as far as I know, in one of those parables of Franz Kafka which, unique perhaps in this respect in literature, are real *parabolai*. . . .
Kafka's parable reads as follows:

He has two antagonists: the first presses him from behind, from the origin. The second blocks the road ahead. He gives battle to both. To be sure, the first supports him in his fight with the second, for he wants to push him forward, and in the same way the second supports him in his fight with the first, since he drives him back. But it is only theoretically so. For it is not only the two antagonists who are there, but he himself as well, and who really knows his intentions? His dream, though, is that some time in an unguarded moment—and this would require a night darker than any night has ever been yet— he will jump out of the fighting line and be promoted, on account of his experience in fighting, to the position of umpire, over his antagonists in then fight with each other. (Arendt, *BPF*, 6–7)[10]

Here the stage of forgetting is set by revolutionary history and practice, which at its conclusion brings a loss of everything revolutionary. The halo that surrounds the present disappears when the present becomes past. Let us not take this halo to express divinity or purity, but that the living vitality of the past is forgotten in its becoming past. Forgetting is the pastness of the past: loss, transfiguration, multiplication; but also augmentation, addition, transformation.

What makes this parable, and perhaps all of Kafka's parables, so compelling is that they take place in the present, take place as if the lived reality of forgetting could somehow detach itself from memory and time. The battle takes place in the present. That is not the way Arendt reads the parable.

> The first thing to be noticed is that not only the future—"the wave of the future"—but also the past is seen as a force, and not, as in nearly all our metaphors, as a burden man has to shoulder and of whose dead weight the living can or even must get rid in their march into the future.... Seen from the viewpoint of man, who always lives in the interval between past and future, time is not a continuum, a flow of uninterrupted succession, it is broken in the middle, at the point where "he" stands, and "his" standpoint is not the present as we usually understand it but rather a gap in time which "his" constant fighting, "his" making a stand against past and future, keeps in existence. (10–1)

> Only insofar as he thinks, and that is insofar as he is ageless—a "he" as Kafka so rightly calls him, and not a "somebody"—does man in the full actuality of his concrete being live in this gap of time between past and future.... This small non-time-space in the very heart of time, unlike the world and the culture into which we are born, can only be indicated, but cannot be inherited and handed down from the past; each new generation, indeed every new human being as he inserts himself between an infinite past and an infinite future, must discover and ploddingly pave it anew. (13)

In this way the flow of testament, understanding, reconciliation—in Hegel all brought under development and time—occupies the field of the present. There is nothing past in the parable, and the understanding we may seek always appears in the imperative of the present. We seek now, remember and forget today, forgetting belongs to the present, lost time is now today, as is the search for it, today, the image, the past, memories of the past and future, proliferate right here today. Forgiveness is the extreme giving that defines the present as the forgotten. In the present we are in search of what is and has been and will be lost. We remember and forget the ekstases of time in the here and now.

Something of this appears in Certeau, this time in the context of history. For he understands the practice of historiography—written history, disciplined history in our time—as both writing and the construction of the past, let us say two spheres of dominance that remain marginal in the present.

> Amerigo Vespucci the voyager arrives from the sea. A crusader standing erect, his body in armor, he bears the European weapons of meaning. Behind him are the vessels that will bring

back to the European West the spoils of a paradise. Before him is the Indian "America," a nude woman reclining in her hammock, an unnamed presence of difference, a body which awakens within a space of exotic fauna and flora (see the frontispiece accompanying the title page).[11] An inaugural scene: after a moment of stupor, on this threshold dotted with colonnades of trees, the conqueror will write the body of the other and trace there his own history. From her he will make a historied body—a blazon—of his labors and phantasms. She will be "Latin" America. (Certeau, *WH*, xxv)

As he puts it based on the example: "*The Writing of History* is the study of writing as historical practice" (xxvi). As against a history that is not written, a writing that is not historical, and a certain view of truthful knowledge. The modality of written history is always that of *as if* and *perhaps*.

> Historiography (that is, "history" and "writing") bears within its own name the paradox—almost an oxymoron—of a relation established between two antinomic terms, between the real and discourse. Its task is one of connecting them and, at the point where this link cannot be imagined, of working *as if* the two were being joined. This book is born of the relation that discourse keeps with the real that is forever its object. What alliance is there between *writing* and *history*? (xxvii)

The writing of history is exposition, including the semblance of the real that is claimed by every science. And it is this semblance of discipline and science that is exposed in modern history. "Modern Western history essentially begins with differentiation between the *present* and the *past*" (2)—with a forgetting.

> In this way it is unlike tradition (religious tradition), though it never succeeds in being entirely dissociated from that archeology, maintaining with it a relation of indebtedness and rejection. This rupture also organizes the content of history within the relations between *labor* and *nature*; and finally, as its third form, it ubiquitously takes for granted a rift between *discourse* and the *body* (the social body). It forces the silent body to speak. It assumes a gap to exist between the silent opacity of the "reality" that it seeks to express and the place where it produces its own speech, protected by the distance established between itself and its object. The violence of the body reaches the written page only through absence, through the intermediary of documents that the historian has been able to see on the sands from which a presence has since been washed away, and through a murmur that lets us hear—but from afar—the unknown immensity that seduces and menaces our knowledge. (2–3)

Foucault's voice echoes through the themes of rupture, discourse and the body, forcing the body to speak, the violence of the body and the washing away of presence on the sands of history, but most of all, perhaps, in the understanding that history has a history, a discourse, and a writing, that histories come into existence and pass away in the modalities of *as if*. Modern history is one of these becomings and passings.

That, perhaps, is where Foucault and Certeau depart from Arendt and Ricoeur, in the rupture of time and the history that would know it and preserve it.

> Historiography tends to prove that the site of its production can encompass the past: it is an odd procedure that posits death, a breakage everywhere reiterated in discourse, and that yet denies loss by appropriating to the present the privilege of recapitulating the past as a form of knowledge. A labor of death and a labor against death.
>
> This paradoxical procedure is symbolized and performed in a gesture which has at once the value of myth and of ritual: *writing*. Indeed, writing replaces the traditional representations that gave authority to the present with a representative labor that places both absence and production in the same area. (Certeau, *WH*, 5)

One way to put this is that the writing that in its nature wanders and proliferates is put in service to preservation and authorization. Still another way turns this entire vision back onto the subject, reminiscent again of Foucault, and a point at which Ricoeur's understanding of forgiveness—it must heal the self—faces the caesura of that subject self.

> The subject appears within his own text: . . . in the manner of an unassailable lacuna that brings to light a lack within the text and ceaselessly moves and misleads him, or indeed *writes*.
>
> This lacuna, a mark of the place within the text and the questioning of the place through the text, ultimately refers to what archeology designates without being able to put in words: the relation of the *logos* to an *archē*, a "principle" or "beginning" which is its other. . . . The *archē* is *nothing* of what can be said. It is only insinuated into the text through the labor of division, or with the evocation of death.
>
> Thus historians can write only by combining within their practice the "other" that moves and misleads them and the real that they can represent only through fiction. They are historiographers. Indebted to the experience I have had of the field, I should like to render homage to the writing of history. (Certeau, *WH*, 14)

Homage, that is, to the aporias of written history, of history that puts itself in the forgotten caesuras of time through writing.

Expressed in quite a different way—the issue of Adolf Eichmann for Arendt—what became the slogan of the banality of evil—one that profoundly disturbed those who had lost loved ones to Eichmann's SS—is the presentness of evil. No matter how distant and past, evil is present here and now in the practices and decisions it calls forth. That is the wound of vengeance, why Arendt's account cannot be accepted, that vengeance is the natural response to a crime. Evil engenders evil. But there is nothing natural about this and it is not necessary. What is necessary is that the crime—if it is a crime, always as if—is here now again in the wound or vengeance or punishment or pardon. It is here now and will be here now no matter how completely forgotten. We are historical creatures who inherit, and we inherit whether we like it or not, inherit as heirs in ways we can determine and ways we cannot, in no particular ways. Particular ways come from present actions by institutional powers: the state punishes or decides not to punish, courts of law convict.

Forgiveness is not what institutions or individuals achieve, but is the opening in the present to the presentness of the unpresent— and for that matter, the absence of the present, the opening of choice that is more than any choice. Forgiveness is the excessive generosity that life and practice demand—with thought and art—as the impossible condition of abundance, especially in the form of unknown alternatives, alterities and arrivals. The unknown and forgotten are the conditions of abundance of and in the present. They exist in the mode of betrayal.

Although he explicitly denies it, Ricoeur pairs forgiveness off in exchanges that are not exchanges, not oppositional, not reciprocal: forgiveness and promise, forgiveness and repentance. The first seems to me just, provided that we understand the impossibility of the promise—to the people of Israel for example of having a land of their own. They are asked to live in the promise of a gift that will always be giving and never given. The second insists that the fault be a fault, that the sinner repent. Only then is forgiveness possible. In other words, forgiveness is tied to memory and not forgetting. Is tied to grasping and not to releasing. Is binding and not unbinding. In other words, in the name of grace it insists on an exchange. The agent must be unbound from what he has done, through repentance if necessary.

> Under the sign of forgiveness, the guilty person is to be considered capable of something other than his offenses and his faults. He is held to be restored to his capacity for acting, and ac-

> tion restored to its capacity for continuing. This capacity is sig-
> naled in the small acts of consideration in which we recognized
> the *incognito* of forgiveness played out on the public stage. And,
> finally, this restored capacity is enlisted by promising as it pro-
> jects action toward the future. The formula for this liberating
> word, reduced to the bareness of its utterance, would be: you are
> better than your actions. (Ricoeur, *MHF*, 493)

You are better, all of us are better—and worse—than our actions,
our feelings, our memories. All of us and everything else is more,
excessive, other. And the form of this excess is as if it were forgotten. It can certainly not be remembered, even in the midst of the
most detailed and intense memories. Nor can it be anticipated.

That is where we must imagine Ricoeur takes us, concluding
with the words that begin Levinas's *Totality and Infinity*. I am refer-
ring to the recognition that the immemoriality of the giving that is
bestowed as forgiveness is as if it were an eschatology, a future
promised without fulfillment, in the ruptures and caesuras of a coming that remains always to come.

> The discourse that suits this recapitulation is no longer that of
> phenomenology, nor of epistemology, nor of hermeneutics; it is
> the discourse of the exploration of the horizon of completion of
> the chain of operations constituting this vast memorial to time
> which includes memory, history, and forgetting. I venture to
> speak in this respect of eschatology to underscore the dimension
> of anticipation and of projection belonging to this ultimate hori-
> zon. The most appropriate grammatical mood is that of the opta-
> tive of desire, at equal distance from the indicative of description
> and the imperative of prescription. (493–4)

Indeed, one might tell the entire story of memory and forgetting
in the modalities of desire, whose ruptures and excesses haunt and
transfigure time and being with what is as if always remaining un-
done, always coming, joy beyond joy. Ricoeur chooses a famous
name. "What I do know, however, is that the object of the entire
quest merits the beautiful name of happiness" (49). A beautiful
name indeed, but perhaps as if it were without finality. Perhaps as if
together with the other beautiful name of *betrayal*—I mean exposition. There is always more to any self, any agent, any happiness, any
thing than appears in any moment, any condition, any promise. It
betrays itself, and betrays more than itself (and of course less, understood as a different more). Forgiveness becomes the reconciliation of a memory that hoped to be happy in its recognitions.

> I can say after the fact that the lodestar of the entire phe-
> nomenology of memory has been the idea of happy memory. It

was concealed in the definition of the cognitive intention of memory as faithful. Faithfulness to the past is not a given, but a wish. Like all wishes, it can be disappointed, even betrayed. . . . I consider recognition to be the small miracle of memory. And as a miracle, it can also fail to occur. But when it does take place, in thumbing through a photo album, or in the unexpected encounter with a familiar person, or in the silent evocation of a being who is absent or gone forever, the cry escapes: "That is her! That is him!" And the same greeting accompanies step by step, with less lively colors, an event recollected, a know-how retrieved, a state of affairs once again raised to the level of "recognition." (494)

Again, the question is why reconciliation is the goal more than transgression, why unification is the miracle more than differentiation, why juncture rather than disjuncture, heterogeneity, or alterity. Forgetting here is the refusal and the impossibility of reconciliation in alterity. It is instead the miraculous inescapability of alterity in reconciliation—the forgetting that is memory itself beyond itself, as if in exposition and betrayal.

This caesura that marks the betrayal of exposition is reserved by Ricoeur for forgetting against the conciliations of remembering.

Why can one not speak of happy forgetting in precisely the same way we were able to speak of happy memory?
An initial reason is that our relation with forgetting is not marked by events of thinking comparable to the event of recognition, which we have called the small miracle of memory—a memory is evoked, it arrives, it returns, we recognize in an instant the thing, the event, the person and we exclaim: "That's her! That's him!" The arrival of a memory is an event. Forgetting is not an event, something that happens or that someone causes to happen. (502)

Forgetting is not an event, but then perhaps in the betrayal of forgetting, remembering is not an event but a process, a becoming, an ongoing struggle and proliferation. Here memory is no more happy than forgetting, each is living as well as possible in the face of the caesuras of the meaning of death.

A second reason for setting aside the idea of a symmetry between memory and forgetting in terms of success or accomplishment is that, with respect to forgiveness, forgetting has its own dilemmas. They have to do with the fact that, if memory is concerned with events even in the exchanges that give rise to retribution, reparation, absolution, forgetting develops enduring situations, which in this sense can be said to be historical, inasmuch as they are constitutive of the tragic nature of action. In this way action is prevented from continuing by forgetting, either by the intertwining of roles that are impossible to untangle, or by insurmountable conflicts in which the dispute is unresolvable, insuperable, or yet again by irreparable wrongs often extending back to far-distant epochs. (502)

I have understood forgetting as the absolute condition of action, tragic or comedic. Life and action go on in the inescapability and the imperative of forgetting—which is the abundance of life and being. Action takes place in the belief and hope as if world and time were in abundance. Irreparable wrongs extending backward to infinity face forward to endless forgettings.

The most irreducible reason for the asymmetry between forgetting and memory with respect to forgiveness resides in the undecidable character of the polarity that divides the subterranean empire of forgetting against itself: the polarity between forgetting through effacement and forgetting kept in reserve. It is with the admission of this irreducible equivocalness that the most precious and the most secret mark of forgiveness can come to be registered. (503)

For reasons that remain obscure to me, Ricoeur denies that effacement haunts memory as its promise and achievement. Memory remains undecidable along with and in virtue of forgetting. Indeed, forgetting is the name of the undecidability and equivocalness of remembering—I mean the semblance and rupture and fascination and proliferation of images of memory.

What is then proposed in opposition to this ruinous competition between the strategies of memory and forgetting is the possibility of a work of forgetting, interweaving among all the fibers that connect us to time: memory of the past, expectation of the future, and attention to the present. This is the path chosen by Marc Augé in *Les Formes de l'oubli* [translated as *Oblivion*]. A subtle observer and interpreter of African rituals, he sketches three "figures" of forgetting that the rituals raise to the level of emblems. To return to the past, he says, one must forget the present, as in states of possession. To return to the present, one must suspend the ties with the past and the future, as in the games of role reversal. To embrace the future, one must forget the past in a gesture of inauguration, beginning, and rebeginning, as in rituals of initiation. And "it is always in the present, finally, that forgetting is conjugated" (Augé, *FO*, 78). (504)

Here forgetting is the inescapable condition of being in the present. Beyond Nietzsche's suprahistoricality, not in past as past or future, not in action or thought, the present as such in time is forgetting.

> Oblivion is a necessity both to society and to the individual. One must know how to forget in order to taste the full flavor of the present, of the moment, and of expectation, but memory itself needs forgetfulness: one must forget the recent past in order to find the ancient past again. That is the principal argument of this book, which therefore is presented as a small treatise on the use of time. (Augé, *O*, 3)

> Memory and oblivion stand together, both are necessary for the full use of time. . . .
> Oblivion brings us back to the present, even if it is conjugated in every tense: in the future, to live the beginning; in the present, to live the moment; in the past, to live the return; in every case, in order not to be repeated. We must forget in order to remain present, forget in order not to die, forget in order to remain faithful. (89)

This is as close as one might hope to get to forgetting as forgetting, the conjugation of the present as present, raising the specter— if it is a specter—of forgetting forgetting. "Must not forgetting, outsmarting its own vigilance, as it were, forget itself?" (Ricoeur, *MHF*, 504). And what would this be but the return of the forgotten, to which we must bear witness at the risk of our own betrayal?

> A third track is also offered for exploration: the path of a forgetting that would no longer be a strategy, nor a work, an idle forgetting. It would parallel memory, not as the remembrance of what has occurred, nor the memorization of know-how, not even as the commemoration of the founding events of our identity, but as a concerned disposition established in duration. . . . Would there not then be a supreme form of forgetting, as a disposition and a way of being in the world, which would be insouciance, carefreeness? . . . It would simply add a gracious note to the work of memory and the work of mourning. For it would not be work at all. (504–5)

Indeed, the work of forgetting—if it is work, if it might not be work at all—can be done only in the shadow of its own forgetting, a forgetting beyond idleness and work, beyond memory and memorization. Such a forgetting is something positive in its own right, still as if nothing at all. Similarly, memory and mourning are something positive in their own right, yet as if nothing at all, nothing in particular, always evoking other questions for the future and for elsewhere. It is always the question of the other, the other questions and things and memories, to which forgetting returns, if it returns. Like the prodigal, forgetting returns with nothing, yet everything in the world depends on it. It certainly does not return with the son alone.

It certainly returns with the son in the margins—let us say together with the daughter and the animals, marginal figures all.

CHAPTER 9

Everyday Life

> [T]he common character of the mildest, as well as the severest cases, to which the faulty and chance actions contribute, lies *in the ability to refer the phenomena to unwelcome, repressed, psychic material, which, though pushed away from consciousness, is nevertheless not robbed of all capacity to express itself.* (Freud, *PEL*, 146)

*F*reud's *Psychopathology of Everyday Life* is filled with examples of forgetting that answer to the description he so strikingly gives of repressed psychic material that is pushed away from consciousness without losing its capacity to express itself. This is the psychoanalytic account of the traces that belong to forgetting, with the recognition that these forgotten traces remain expressive, as if to say that expression is the prevailing condition of psychic life, perhaps of nature and reality themselves. This suggests the persuasive hypothesis that what psychoanalysis offers is something close to what Levinas calls *exposition*—exposure and expression—under the figures of loss and displacement. We—and everything else perhaps—are exposed to others expressively. Others are present in our exposure, in their bodies, in the signifyingness and expressiveness of faces and bodies. Exposure is expression, faces and bodies and things express in their presence and in their absence, in memory and in forgetting. The task of the psychoanalyst is to express the expressions—and inexpressions—that constitute being psychically in the world, including the displacements and repressions that are this being in the modality of forgetting.

Such a view produces the following effect: the absence and displacement—the forgettings and forgotten traces—express the attachments and detachments of the libido; the expressiveness of consciousness remains present in the unconscious, which is no less expressive than the former; the forgotten expresses no less than the remembered.

It is worth considering another image—itself an image of images—of this process of repression and return:

> The crudest conception of these systems is the one we shall find most convenient, a spatial one. The unconscious system may therefore be compared to a large ante-room, in which the various mental excitations are crowding upon one another, like individual beings. Adjoining this is a second, smaller apartment, a sort of reception-room, in which consciousness resides. But on the threshold between the two there stands a personage with the office of door-keeper, who examines the various mental excitations, censors them, and denies them admittance to the reception-room when he disapproves of them. (Freud, *GIP*, 306)

This is from *The General Introduction to Psychoanalysis*, well after Freud's discussion of dreams. Here one might emphasize the image—Freud was fascinated by images—as memory, and the proliferation and multiplication as forgetting. Images proliferate, I've argued that is what they do, what images are, they proliferate as exposition.[1] And exposition is betrayal—violation and revelation. Images in Freud are the ways in which excitations multiply, under an image of a threshold and a doorkeeper who examines, censors, and expels these images from consciousness, where all the while they are present as repressed. From the standpoint of the image, images proliferate obliquely, where the doorkeeper presents another image of the stream of images, images present even on the outside and kept in the dark.

Moreover, this play of images in Freud is augmented by his images of dreams, of images in dreams—dream images—that are present as images, that multiply as images, in a work of indirection and displacement. On the one hand, Freud insists that we can separate the meaningless from the meaningful, the forgetting from the remembering: "Dreams are often meaningless, confused, and absurd, yet there are some which are sensible, sober, and reasonable. Let us see whether these latter sensible dreams can help to elucidate those which are meaningless" (101). On the other hand, he knows that the disorderliness and obliviousness of dreams is the aspect of most interest to him, perhaps to us, perhaps in dreams themselves.

As he says himself, after describing "two prosaic dreams":

> there occur in them recollections of daily life or of matters connected with it. Even that would be something if it could be as-

serted of all dreams without exception. But that is out of the question, this characteristic too belongs only to a minority of dreams. In most dreams we find no connection with the day before, and no light is thrown from this quarter upon meaningless and absurd dreams. (102)

Here the absurdity and meaninglessness of dreams is their most compelling characteristic. Freud place himself between the meaningful and the meaningless, the remembered and the forgotten. On the side of the remembered—what we can remember if we do not now— we seek causality and connection. "Can these be explained by the stimuli? Is it really the stimulus that we experience? If so, why is the experience visual, when it can only be in the very rarest instance that any stimulus has operated upon our eyesight?" (101). On the other side—if these are sides, if there are sides to be taken between one image and the other—in most dreams, in most images, there is no connection. The image does not resemble.

That is not what Freud says, though it remains throughout everything he says. The image of order returns from the image of disorder. Can memory be explained? Can forgetting be explained by (our memory of) what caused it? And finally, if we revel in the absurdity and meaninglessness of dreams, insist on forgetting, do we present a demand for explanation, an insistence on memory, that we have already forgotten?

> if the dream is a somatic phenomenon it does not concern us; it can only be of interest to us on the hypothesis that it is a mental phenomenon....
>
> ... In that event, they are a performance and an utterance on the part of the dreamer, but of a kind that conveys nothing to us, and which we do not understand. Now supposing that I give utterance to something that you do not understand, what do you do? You ask me to explain, do you not? Why may not we do the same—*ask the dreamer the meaning of the dream*? (Freud, *GIP*, 105–6)

On the one hand, then, we remember dreams that mean nothing to us because we do not recall what would give them meaning. What then are we to do but seek and find an explanation? On the other hand, the question then becomes, of what good is this explanation? What would count as a good explanation—for the dreamer, the patient, especially, who "has said to himself something of this kind: 'This is all very pretty and very interesting. I should like to go on with it. I am sure it would do me a lot of good it if were true. But I don't believe it in the least, and as long as I don't believe it, it doesn't affect my illness'" (300). These are words famously if not notoriously said about *mere* images, *mere* art: fiction, *mimēsis*. If it were true it would be wonderful; it seems to be true and is certainly pretty, even beautiful, and very interesting and provocative. But it cannot truly or seriously be believed. Or for that matter remembered.

We have traversed a journey from the forgetting that is the condition of everyday life to a forgetting that inhabits every image in proliferation. It is a journey worth recapitulating, especially in relation to the depths of everyday life, taking those depths for granted.

Let's begin again—a gesture of forgetting—with dreams, that side of everyday life that is forgotten when awake. Dreams are forgotten by many in their daily lives, neglected and trivialized when remembered, yet are powerfully experienced both asleep and awake. It may well be that in the vernacular, Freud's fame lies in the work of dreams, that more than the techniques of psychoanalysis, his own personal work with dreams—narratively, interpretively, and recollectively—mark his gift to the future.

Let us begin with the hypothesis that guards and guides—and indeed, inaugurates—*The Interpretation of Dreams*:

> In the following pages, I shall demonstrate that there is a psychological technique which makes it possible to interpret dreams, and that on the application of this technique, every dream will reveal itself as a psychological structure, full of significance, and one which may be assigned to a specific place in the psychic activities of the waking state. (Freud, *ID*, 151)

In another interpretive technique, this opening may be carved up in small pieces, each of which reveals itself as a psychological structure full of significance:

In the following pages. The narrative gesture *par excellence* that tells us that we are about to recall, or to have recalled for us, in writing, something we are expected to remember and not forget. That is, Freud will tell us something that we can hold on to and grasp.

A psychological technique. That is, a technique for reading and understanding the psyche, but also a technique of and from the psyche, first Freud's, but then yours and mine and psychoanalysts', perhaps anyone who pays attention to dreams. There is a technique, a repeatable, memorable practice, that makes it—

Possible to interpret dreams. About which we may wonder if dreams were interpretable before, whether they were interpreted correctly or erroneously before, whether the effacements and misdirections and distortions of dreams misled earlier interpreters. Freud is dismissive. "In spite of thousands of years of endeavor, little progress has been made in the scientific understanding of dreams" (151). So the technique is a scientific technique, and the wealth of interpretations of dreams that precede the promulgation of this technique know nothing of dreams.

The *scientific understanding* of dreams is then a recent phenomenon, preceded by darkness concerning the dreams that light up nearly every night sky. Surely there were many wonderful interpretations, but they were not scientific. Narrative, poetic, medicinal interpretations; everyday, nightmarish, feverish dreams; all continue in darkness, waiting for the appearance of a scientific technique. This is as persuasive and insistent a figure of unforgetting as possible, especially if we include the tendency of dreams to be forgotten, either completely or in obscurity. Dreams wear masks, and it takes a Freud to strip off the mask to reveal the meaning of the dream. As it takes a Nietzsche to put another mask on top of masks, to deny the meaning and truth of what wears no masks.

Freud insists that *every dream* can be interpreted by this technique. None will resist. Every dream is a psychological structure, whose significance can be revealed, and *assigned to a specific place* in the waking psychic activities of the dreamer.

Perhaps the most useful phrase for us here, however, is that each dream, no matter how opaque and indirect, is *full of significance*. Such a claim suggests something far more sweeping, that every dream but also every psychic state, conscious and unconscious, every manifestation, psychic or corporeal, indeed, every thing in the world is full of significance, signifies more than we will ever know, signifies beyond remembering. Freud's technique, carried toward the realization that we dream about almost everything, dream obliquely and indirectly, carries everything in human life and without toward a significance that can be interpreted, is expressive in more ways than we will ever know.

I say *more than we will ever know* in the face of Freud's claim that his scientific technique opens up the significance of every dream to emphasize the indirectness and obliquity. Every thing enters human experience expressively and obliquely, and it is our task to interpret and understand it. I suggest that no matter how effective Freud's or any other technique may be, the figure he offers is of a dream and an expression that is full of significance by betrayal, that meaning and significance offer themselves in their traces and effacements far beyond any grasp.

Put another way, assigning a dream or a thing or a person or any everyday appearance or practice to a specific place does not exhaust that thing or dream, but augments its significance in the abundance.

There remain the traces and misdirections, which we may imagine—imagination is the key here—can themselves take any form. The key to Freud's understanding of dreams is the doubled gesture in which dreams—and everything else—offer themselves up to understanding by a scientific technique in a context in which they by necessity must exceed that understanding in the forms of appearance and gestures in which they offer themselves up.

Freud's first interpretation of the technique is that dreams are wish-fulfillments: *"When the work of interpretation has been completed the dream can be recognized as a wish-fulfilment"* (175). It is preceded by a disclaimer that offers itself in the caesura between remembering and forgetting. "I do not wish to assert that I have entirely revealed the meaning of the dream, or that my interpretation is flawless" (174). Still, it is scientific, objective and repeatable by others. Yet the flaws call attention to the obliquity and indirection of dreams. If they are wish-fulfilments they do not appear as if they were so. In other words, the key to dream interpretation lies in the modality of *as if* and *perhaps* that characterizes dreams, interpretations, and understandings.

> We find ourselves standing in the light of a sudden discovery. The dream is not comparable to the irregular sounds of a musical instrument, which, instead of being played by the hand of a musician, is struck by some external force; the dream is not meaningless, not absurd, does not presuppose that one part of our store of ideas is dormant while another part begins to awake. It is a perfectly valid psychic phenomenon, actually a wish-fulfilment; it may be enrolled in the continuity of the intelligible psychic activities of the waking state; it is built up by a highly complicated intellectual activity. But at the very moment when we are about to rejoice in this discovery a host of problems besets us. If the dream, as this theory defines it, represents a fulfilled wish, what is the cause of the striking and unfamiliar manner in which this fulfilment is expressed? What transformation has occurred in our dream-thoughts before the manifest dream, as we remember it on waking, shapes itself out of them? How has this transformation taken place? Whence comes the material that is worked up into the dream? What causes many of the peculiarities which are to be observed in our dream-thoughts; for example, how is it that they are able to contradict one another? (176)

Here again, Freud's words and images are worth attending to closely, not so much to call them into question, but to envisage the depth and range of the images he calls into play so as to present an interpretation of a dream and to characterize that interpretation. I would put it this way: there is almost nothing in Freud that appears to make things simpler than they are; and indeed, a close look at the figures that come into play suggests that figurality and obliquity are more the matter than the wish. How the wish-fulfilment is clothed, the sense that all figures of psychic life wear clothes—masks and palimpsests—comes one might say from Freud.

Thus, though the dream is not like a musical instrument, meaningless unless given meaning by the musician interpreter, neither for that matter is a musical instrument. Intentions and meanings in the instrument wait silently for the player. In the same way, perhaps, in other things, in their complexities and withdrawals, imperceptible expressions and revelations wait to be touched. One might go further with this figure to insist that it is by touching that the instrument expresses, and that it is in touching that all other things express themselves and are expressive. Touch is the forgotten expressiveness of all corporeal things.

At the other end of this figure is Freud's recognition and insistence that dreams—and perhaps everything else—reveal themselves obliquely—strangely and unfamiliarly, bearing transformations and transfigurations. What is striking and familiar about dreams is that there is something peculiar, strange, and contradictory about them. Following the figure of exposition we have been exposing, dreams and everything else bear meaning obliquely. Their expression is strange and unfamiliar, surprising and contradictory. World and earth express themselves to us indirectly and obliquely. Expression is in abundance. Finally, the appearance of things, in the abundance of their expressiveness, is by way of indirection and forgetting. It is in forgetting that things come to be expressive, allow themselves to be remembered.

The play of exposition permeates dreams. They are present and experienced in the ongoing play of *as if*. As wish-fulfillments they are present in a multiplicity.

> The first dream which we have considered was the fulfilment of a wish; another may turn out to be the realization of an apprehension; a third may have a reflection as its content; a fourth may simply reproduce a reminiscence. Are there, then, dreams other than wish-dreams; or are there none but wish-dreams? (Freud, *ID*, 177)

The final question appears to have already been answered many times over. Its reappearance suggests a certain displacement in relation to wish-dreams, let us say a doubled displacement inside and out. Perhaps what are almost certainly not wish-dreams may turn out to be wish-dreams. Perhaps there are other then wish-dreams though it appears not to be so. Appearance is deceiving. And even here—one might say throughout—Freud's relation to the play of appearance and reality is both pervasive and oblique. That may be another way to characterize his work, as the play of forgetting in the field of real memories. How this happens in Freud is always in wonder.

> It is easy to show that the wish-fulfilment in dreams is often undisguised and easy to recognize, so that one may wonder why the language of dreams has not long since been understood. There is, for example, a dream which I can evoke as often as I please, experimentally, as it were. If, in the evening, I eat anchovies, olives, or other strongly salted foods, I am thirsty at night, and therefore I wake. The waking, however, is preceded by a dream, which has always the same content, namely, that I am drinking. I am drinking long draughts of water; it tastes as delicious as only a cool drink can taste when one's throat is parched; and then I wake, and find that I have an actual desire to drink. The cause of this dream is thirst, which I perceive when I wake. From this sensation arises the wish to drink, and the dream shows me this wish as fulfilled. (177)

One may wonder at why the most evident of appearances has not been understood by everyone. If one is thirsty one will dream of drinking draughts of water. Well, maybe that was true of Freud and some others. But he and we know that many do not dream this way, that when they dream they forget their dreams, that even these simple dreams prompted by thirst are clothed in striking apparel in dreams. Misdirection—forgetting—is the constitutive condition of dreams

> A friend who was acquainted with my theory of dreams, and had explained it to his wife, said to me one day: "My wife asked me to tell you that she dreamt yesterday that she was having her menses. You will know what that means." Of course I know: if the young wife dreams that she is having her menses, the menses have stopped. I can well imagine that she would have liked to enjoy her freedom a little longer, before the discomforts of maternity began. It was a clever way of giving notice of her first pregnancy. (179)

If she dreams of having her menses she has become pregnant and her menses have stopped. Freud reads this as the wish to continue to be independent. It might also be the wish (but not as a fulfilment) to be pregnant, or the enjoyment of not having to think about menses.

The point, no matter what interpretation we offer, is that there is a misdirection between pregnancy and the dream. The dream hides the pregnancy, clothes and stains it.

The misdirection of dreams as their constitutive condition appears in the transition Freud offers between wish-fulfilment and distortion.

> If I now declare that wish-fulfilment is the meaning of every dream, so that there cannot be any dreams other than wish-dreams, I know beforehand that I shall meet with the most emphatic contradiction. My critics will object: "... Dreams which present the most painful content, and not the least trace of wish-fulfilment, occur frequently enough. . . . Besides those dreams that convey into our sleep the many painful emotions of life, there are also anxiety-dreams, in which this most terrible of all the painful emotions torments us until we wake. . . . "
>
> Nevertheless, it is not difficult to parry these apparently invincible objections. It is merely necessary to observe that our doctrine is not based upon the estimates of the obvious dream-content, but relates to the thought-content, which, in the course of interpretation, is found to lie behind the dream. Let us compare and contrast the manifest and the latent dream-content. It is true that there are dreams the manifest content of which is of the most painful nature. But has anyone ever tried to interpret these dreams—to discover their latent thought-content? If not, the two objections to our doctrine are no longer valid; for there is always the possibility that even our painful and terrifying dreams may, upon interpretation, prove to be wish-fulfilments. (185–6)

Let us compare and contrast the manifest and latent dream content; let us turn from the manifest to the underlying reality; more important, perhaps, let us turn to the forgetting that obliquely constitutes the significance of every dream.

> Why do not the dreams that show an indifferent content, and yet turn out to be wish-fulfilments, reveal their meaning without disguise? . . . Why does not the dream say directly what it means? . . . If we call this peculiarity of dreams—namely, that they need elucidation—the phenomenon of distortion in dreams, a second question then arises: What is the origin of this distortion in dreams? (186)

Freud presents two different conditions under a single heading: dreams are distorted, disguised; and they require elucidation. It is important not to conflate these, and it is important to pay attention to them. Dreams are distorted *and* cry out for interpretation. This is not the view that dreams are opaque, difficult to understand, because they are so strange and remote from the tools that would comprehend them. It is that dreams are both distorted and cry out. It is that dreams are forgotten so that they may, obliquely, be remembered—that is, unforgotten. Both of these conditions are imperative.

Freud's answer is a well-known, traditional answer: what is true lies hidden, under the surface.

> It is quite incredible with what obstinacy readers and critics have excluded this consideration and disregarded the fundamental differentiation between the manifest and the latent dream-content. (186n)

> If my little daughter does not like an apple which is offered her, she asserts that the apple is bitter, without even tasting it. If my patients behave thus, I know that we are dealing with an idea which they are trying to repress. The same thing applies to my dream. I do not want to interpret it because there is something in the interpretation to which I object. After the interpretation of the dream is completed, I discover what it was to which I objected; it was the assertion that R. is a simpleton. I can refer the affection which I feel for R. not to the latent dream-thoughts, but rather to this unwillingness of mine. If my dream, as compared with its latent content, is disguised at this point, and actually misrepresents things by producing their opposites, then the manifest affection in the dream serves the purpose of the misrepresentation; in other words, the distortion is here shown to be intentional—it is a means of disguise. (190)

The interpretation of the dream gives us the latent content, in this case a derogatory view of a friend. The mechanism of distortion is doubled: the latent content—the derogatory view—is masked by an extreme affection. The latent content is doubly repressed, that is, doubly forgotten.

This may be the most telling insight we might take from this example. The content itself is minor; the mechanism, the doubled forgetting, appears to be of such importance as to go far beyond dreams. Distortion in dreams is a mode of forgetting that is actually a form of remembering, tracing. And reciprocally, perhaps, if we take distortion for granted, the possibility of remembering, interpreting a dream, suggests that forgetting constitutes the possibility of having any dream, of remembering any thought, of consciousness and reality themselves. Reality appears to us, in dreams and elsewhere, distorted through what is forgotten in order that it appear as real.

If this is so, then we have another—no doubt distorted—interpretation of Lyotard's insistence that we must bear witness to the forgotten while the witness—every witness, witness itself—is a traitor, most of all, that reality is composed of forgettings, distortions, betrayals. Moreover, Freud does not suggest that this diminishes the value of dreams. To the contrary, their appearance as distorted tells us more, not less, than we would otherwise know. In presenting reality under the semblance of a distortion, Freud encounters, in the interpretation of his dream, both the latent content and the repression.

I've suggested that we imagine that the latent content appears only through the guise of repression, wearing a disguise—in other words, wearing masks. The mask obscures, but also presents and thereby reveals the face it covers. It does not and cannot blot out the face, but presents it masked. Reality presents itself, is remembered and recalled, as if it were forgotten. But being forgotten is not non-being but a mode of being—*as if*, forgotten.

The figure through which Freud explores this forgetting is not through repression but through the image of censorship, reminding us of Kant:[2]

> The political writer who has unpleasant truths to tell to those in power finds himself in a like position. If he tells everything without reserve, the Government will suppress them—retrospectively in the case of a verbal expression of opinion, preventively if they are to be published in the Press. The writer stands in fear of the censorship; he therefore moderates and disguises the expression of his opinions. He finds himself compelled, in accordance with the sensibilities of the censor, either to refrain altogether from certain forms of attack, or to express himself in allusions instead of by direct assertion; or he must conceal his objectionable statement in an apparently innocent disguise. (191)

This image presents three further figures: suppression, fear, and concealment. The truth is concealed for fear of suppression. Yet why be afraid of suppression if concealment is another form of repression? In Freud's dream example, his fear is not at the censorship but at the reality: he does not want to know that he has thought of a friend as a fool. I have suggested that there is a component of not wanting to know in every knowing, every appearance.[3] Indeed, this not wanting to know is the constitutive condition of knowing, wanting to forget is the constitutive condition of remembering, not so much emphasizing the wanting as the imperative and the demand that constitutes meaning and reality. I must not know now what I want to be know later. I must not recall now what I hope to recall later. I must forget it now, and I must forget something else later, if I am to know or to remember.

In other words, I am taking the interpretation of the dream as the constitutive condition of its having a meaning. The meaning does not lie in the dream, but in the process of its revelation. This revelation works by taking distortion and censorship for granted, obscuration and displacement. The meaning of the dream is not its latent content but its forgetting and displacement into manifest images. The latent image proliferates into other, manifest images.

I have passed over another latent image, that of the political writer and the state. The distortion of the dream image follows the trajectory of suppression by state power. Not only may we imagine that this takes place in a political arena framed by struggles over authority and power, but the greater forces of the state are put in play. In other words, the suppression and repression are exercises in power, they are coercive and exercise violence, they evoke fear and intimidate desire. Desire and fear permeate the entire practice of distortion and repression. This allows us to understand wish-fulfilment more profoundly.

> Dream-distortion, then, proves in reality to be an act of the cen-
> sorship. We shall have included everything which the analysis of
> disagreeable dreams has brought to light if we re-word our for-
> mula thus: *The dream is the (disguised) fulfilment of a (suppressed, re-
> pressed) wish.* (203)

Dreams are the manifestation of desires, which can only appear in disguised form.

Freud returns to the authority of the censor, reclaiming the image of political power. He returns to a figure we have seen before, the strange and uncanny doorkeeper who reappears in Kafka's parable.

> We should then assume that in every human being there exist, as
> the primary cause of dream-formation, two psychic forces (ten-
> dencies or systems), one of which forms the wish expressed by the
> dream, while the other exercises a censorship over this dream-
> wish, thereby enforcing on it a distortion. The question is, what is
> the nature of the authority of this second agency by virtue of
> which it is able to exercise its censorship? If we remember that the
> latent dream-thoughts are not conscious before analysis, but that
> the manifest dream-content emerging from them is consciously
> remembered, it is not a far-fetched assumption that admittance to
> the consciousness is the prerogative of the second agency. Nothing

can reach the consciousness from the first system which has not previously passed the second instance; and the second instance lets nothing pass without exercising its rights, and forcing such modifications as are pleasing to itself upon the candidates for admission to consciousness. . . . It may be shown that psychopathology simply cannot dispense with these fundamental assumptions. (191–2)

Psychopathology—we are speaking here of dreams, later in everyday life—requires the assumption of a doorkeeper to consciousness, in other words of a forgetfulness constitutive of memory, of presentations and identifications. Indeed, then, we should begin with the title Freud gives to *The Psychopathology of Everyday Life*, emphasizing *psychopathology* and *everyday life*—that is, life itself. He has been criticized for applying mechanisms that represented pathologies to ordinary experience. Yet it is clear that the spirit of his work is in reverse, that the mechanisms of everyday life are repression, censorship, and distortion—ways of forgetting—that go awry in exceptional cases. The term *psychopathology*, then, might be read not as expressing the diseases of everyday life but the mechanisms of desire and affect that work there obliquely.

And of course, the other term is *everyday life*, that is, life itself. Life is pervaded by forgetting. Freud's original exploration of the subject was under the heading *On the Psychic Mechanism of Forgetfulness*, expanded under its later title. The point perhaps is that it is forgetfulness that guides the investigation. We might well ask, what kind of psychopathology is one that concerns itself with forgetfulness? Why is this pathological, and what should we do about it? The answer has to be that the mechanisms and processes are interesting in their own right. Forgetting is far more interesting than it appears to be.

Let us then imagine that the psychopathology of everyday life, understood to emerge from and embody forgetfulness pervasively and at its core, is not the disease or abnormality of life but the forgetting that constitutes it. Calling it *psychopathology* suggests an absence of pathology, hypothetical if not actual. Calling dreams *distorted* suggests that there are undistorted dreams, again at least hypothetically. One might imagine that Freud takes for granted that what is forgotten and distorted is a reality in contrast with which its presentation is distorted, that there is a remembering of what really happened, what is really felt, and a distorting and a forgetting by way of contrast.

Yet the mechanism we have seen in dreams is that the presentation, the work of dreams, is by way of distortion. Similarly, the forgetfulness of everyday life is not the absence of reality but the way in which reality is present in everyday life. The mechanism of the doorkeeper suggests that outside the door reality goes on its way, and that those who enter consciousness must leave some truth at the door, must bend and twist themselves to enter. The reality of consciousness—dreams and life—is always twisted and bent, full of forgetting, full of unconscious processes. The reality principle is just as twisted in its appearance as any distortion. Reality, then, is intrinsically and constitutively forgotten; this is really and truly so in consciousness; consciousness is conscious by way of forgetting—that is, as if by way of exposition. Reality is a story told, and there is no reality that is not a telling—meaning a forgetting.

So that this insight does not pass over into something different, let me emphasize that in the case of dreams, Freud's example of what is forgotten is linked with a intense affect. Affects, feelings, emotions, desires permeate dreams and everyday life obliquely. They do so truly and really, and it is important that we know and understand this as well as feel it as we do. But the truth and reality of the feelings are oblique, by way of forgetfulness. Similarly, the key to mourning according to Freud—I will return to this presently—turns on the affective attachment of the libido to the lost object. The object is overwhelmed with feeling, coloring all its memories with forgettings. The very form of memory in mourning—perhaps always—is given in the shapes and colors of libidinal attachments. This is true in all cases, pathological and nonpathological—if there be such. I insist at this point that the nonpathological exists in Freud in the modality of *as if* and *perhaps*, that is, in exposition and forgetting.

Here then is Freud on everyday forgetting addressing the familiar example of proper names:

> I was led to examine exhaustively the phenomenon of temporary forgetfulness through the observation of certain peculiarities, which, although not general, can, nevertheless, be seen clearly in some cases. In these, there is not only forgetfulness, but also false recollection; he who strives for the escaped name brings to consciousness others—substitutive names—which, although immediately recognized as false, nevertheless obtrude themselves with great tenacity. The process which should lead to the reproduction of the lost name is, as it were, displaced, and thus brings one to an incorrect substitute.
>
> Now it is my assumption that the displacement is not left to psychic arbitrariness, but that it follows lawful and rational paths. In other words, I assume that the substitutive name (or names)

stands in direct relation to the lost name, and I hope, if I succeed
in demonstrating this connection, to throw light on the origin of
the forgetting of names. (Freud, *PEL*, 3)

The key here is displacement and substitution: these are not arbitrary but—what? The answer eludes us and has been the cause of
many controversies and disputes. Is it intentional, due to an underlying mechanism, has it a hidden origin? All of these, yet each is difficult to grasp because of the indirection. The displacement and substitution are more directly recognized as intrinsic and constitutive.
We remember by displacement, even when we remember correctly
and certainly when we fail to remember. Forgetfulness is intrinsic
and constitutive of memory and of consciousness itself, not only in
lost memories and distorted recollections.

Moreover, this displacement lends itself to interpretation; we
can seek and can find connections and origins. It is as if true memory asks no questions, but false memory, forgetting, presents us
with an endless play of questions and answers, in which remembering and forgetting appear and disappear. It is as if true memory is
just that, attenuated in its ramifications and investigations, while
false memory opens onto the abundance of mysteries of consciousness, unconsciousness, time, and memory.

Freud's initial example is of his substituting the name *Botticelli*
for *Signorelli*. He assumes that this is neither accidental nor a property of the name *Signorelli*.

> I can no longer conceive the forgetting of the name Signorelli as an
> accidental occurrence. I must recognize in this process the influ-
> ence of a motive. There were motives which actuated the interrup-
> tion in the communication of my thoughts . . . which later influ-
> enced me to exclude from my consciousness the thoughts
> connected with them . . . —that is, I wanted to forget something, I
> repressed something. To be sure, I wished to forget something
> other than the name of the master of Orvieto; but this other
> thought brought about an associative connection between itself
> and this name, so that my act of volition missed the aim, and *I for-
> got the one against my will*, while I *intentionally* wished to forget the
> other. . . . The substitutive names . . . show me that my object to for-
> get something was neither a perfect success nor a failure. (5)

When we recapitulate the conditions for forgetting a name
with faulty recollection we find: (1) a certain disposition to forget
the name; (2) a process of suppression which has taken place
shortly before; and (3) the possibility of establishing an outer association between the concerned name and the element previously
suppressed. . . . [O]n more thorough examination, one finds more

and more frequently that the two elements (the repressed and the new one) connected by an outer association, possess besides a connection in content, and this can also be demonstrated in the example, *Signorelli*. (7)

Freud is explicit here that he is proposing an underlying intention, indeed a motive, for forgetting one name and substituting another. The key is that the substitution is not accidental; moreover, it is nonaccidental repeatedly and in different ways. A certain disposition to forget, a process of suppression, an outer and an inner association and connection. These all exist in the modality of displacement. It is not enough that a memory be displaced, that a connection be disconnected, but it is disconnected and displaced and forgotten over and over and in different relations. Forgetting is pervasive and repetitive. And indeed, we may wonder if true memory, without visible substitution, can be any less displaced, or whether its displacements are not more hidden and oblique, indeed more displaced.

For reasons that I fail to understand, such a picture of memory is frequently read as diminishing the accuracy of memory. No memories are true as they stand. Yet the phrase *as they stand* can be read without the least skepticism—to the contrary. Truth is an endless process of burrowing, digging, turning over. The key here is to understand that forgetting is the condition of turning over and overturning. Not just its motive or intention, but the constitutive displacement that turning over requires.

Freud gives many other examples of forgetfulness in everyday life, several from his own experience. The key in every case is a double displacement, one at the level of repression—let us say where the forgetter has good reason not to recall something—the other at the level of the appearance, in the present case the name, which is displaced in virtue of the relation of the elements of the name to the object of repression. In other words, the elements of an exposition take on associative meanings that function at the level of composition: metonymically, metaphorically, synecdocally. One might well imagine that the appeal of Freud's analysis is that it blends almost seamlessly the dream of modernity to know by way of science with the prose of the world in which "the world must fold in upon itself, duplicate itself, reflect itself, or form a chain with itself so that things can resemble one another" (Foucault, *OT*, 25–6).[4]

The folding of the world upon itself, the reflection and the mirror, the answering of things to each other scattered through the universe: all this is in such abundance, is so excessive, that it cannot be remembered as such. The experience of distortions in dreams, displacements in everyday life, dispersions throughout the universe is an experience of forgetting not remembering. This is so even as what we do is to remember: we remember obliquely, dispersedly, indirectly; our recollections are transgressive and transfigurative. The multiplication and proliferation of the image is remembering by forgetting, exposition in the modality of *as if*.

The thesis, then, is that the associative exposition of everyday life is a resistance to the grasping of the modern epistemological project, not because the latter suggests that we will ever have all the knowledge to be had. Such a claim is frequently heard, but even the endless pursuit of knowledge under the headings of science and discipline take for granted the propriety and reality of such a knowledge, as well as the reality and propriety of tests and proofs.[5] The mirroring of all things scattered and dispersed scatters and disperses the knowledges and signs. The interpretation of distorted dreams is an adventure in displacement and transfiguration. Like all such interpretations, it is an adventure in exposition—imaginative, creative, originative, proliferative. Freud claims persuasiveness and conviction for his interpretations, but the method he employs engages in double and triple displacements, so that the conviction and persuasion are themselves interpretive displacements. I mean to praise this not to blame it. Even more I mean to emphasize the forgetting in the displacements that makes recollection possible.

Here, then, is my thesis linking emulation and psychoanalytic interpretation: realities with their signs appear obliquely, dispersed, and proliferate by misalignments and indirections. Moreover, these belong to realities and their signs: reality is composed of indirection and misalignment, of forgettings and forgottens. Dreams and everyday life are a record of such forgettings: the forgotten is not secreted away in some hidden place, in or outside the world. It is present in every appearance, small and large, and in every crumb and morsel of that appearance. Reality is composed of forgettings.

> The mechanism of forgetting, or rather of losing or temporary forgetting of a name, consists in the disturbance of the intended reproduction of the name through a strange stream of thought unconscious at the time. Between the disturbed name and the disturbing complex, there exists a connection either from the beginning or such a connection has been formed—perhaps by artificial means—through superficial (outer) associations. . . .
>
> In general, one may distinguish two principal cases of name-forgetting; when the name itself touches something unpleasant, or when it is brought into connection with other associations which

are influenced by such effects. Thus, names can be disturbed on their own account or on account of their nearer or more remote associative relations in the reproduction....

However, we are far from having described all the peculiarities of this phenomenon. I also wish to call attention to the fact that name-forgetting is extremely contagious. In a conversation between two persons, the mere mention of having forgotten this or that name by one often suffices to induce the same memory slip in the other. But wherever the forgetting is induced, the sought–for name easily comes to the surface.

There is also a continuous forgetting of names in which whole chains of names are withdrawn from memory. If, in the course of endeavoring to discover an escaped name, one finds others with which the latter is intimately connected, it often happens that these new names also escape. The forgetting thus jumps from one name to another, as if to demonstrate the existence of a hindrance not to be easily removed. (28–9)

The mechanism of forgetting—the way in which a name appears and disappears—is through a *disturbance* of the name *through a strange stream of thought*, not unlike a dream or story. This stream is *unconscious at the time*, but can be revealed by another story, which displays or forms a *connection through associations*. In other words, to avoid unpleasant, painful connections *in one series of thoughts* another series is instituted that *disturbs* the recollection. Moreover, such a phenomenon *is extremely contagious*. And *whole chains of names are withdrawn from memory* by further disturbances and displacements. Displacement fosters displacement, indirection promotes indirection, the play of signs proliferates into other plays and other signs.

I do not say this is art. I do not say this is literature or writing. That could be said but it is not my point here. I say that the disturbance and displacements of everyday life are everywhere as exposition. In everyday life we are exposed everywhere as if in exposition, where the mirrors and repetitions and images proliferate as if by misdirection and displacement. The one thing I would insist on adding is that disturbance, displacement, indirection are present in remembered names, in accurate memories, no less than in forgotten names. We remember and we forget by forgetting, in a play of signs that is abundance far beyond any present sign or given memory. The mechanism of forgetting is the mechanism of remembering. Remembering happens because *forgetting jumps from one name to another* around and through and over and under one hindrance after another. I say *hindrance* but I am speaking of the exposition of remembering.

Freud's examples continue to follow this trajectory.

> the earliest recollections of a person often seemed to preserve the unimportant and accidental, whereas (frequently though not universally!) not a trace is found in the adult memory of the weighty and affective impressions of this period. As it is known that the memory exercises a certain selection among the impressions at its disposal, it would seem logical to suppose that this selection follows entirely different principles in childhood than at the time of intellectual maturity. However, close investigation points to the fact that such an assumption is superfluous. The indifferent childhood memories owe their existence to a process of displacement. It may be shown by psychoanalysis that in the reproduction they represent the substitute for other really significant impressions, whose direct reproduction is hindered by some resistance. (30)

Memories owe their existence to *a process of displacement and substitution*, promoted *by some resistance*. It may be a question for some who read Freud here whether there are experiences and memories without resistance. Yet that is the point at issue: resistance, displacement, and substitution are not occasional, episodic human conditions but the constitutive conditions of consciousness (human and inhuman in Lyotard's sense).[6] Dreams, memories, images all exist in the mode of displacement, including distortions and supplementations.

> I particularly emphasized a peculiarity in the temporal relation between the concealing memory and the contents of the memory concealed by it. The content of the concealing memory in that example belonged to one of the first years of childhood, while the thoughts represented by it, which remained practically unconscious, belonged to a later period of the individual in question. I called this form of displacement a retro-active or *regressive* one. Perhaps more often, one finds the reversed relation—that is, an indifferent impression of the most remote period becomes a concealing memory in consciousness, which simply owes its existence to an association with an earlier experience, against whose direct reproduction there are resistances. We would call these *encroaching* or *interposing* concealing memories. What most concerns the memory lies here chronologically beyond the concealing memory. Finally, there may be a third possible case, namely, the concealing memory may be connected with the impression it conceals, not only through its contents, but also through contiguity of time; this is the *contemporaneous* or *contiguous* concealing memory. (30–1)

The question I am raising—no doubt in a manner foreign in some ways to Freud—is not shirked by him:

> How large a portion of the sum total of our memory belongs to the category of concealing memories, and what part it plays in various neurotic hidden processes, these are problems into the value of which I have neither inquired, nor shall I enter here. I am concerned only with emphasizing the sameness between the forgetting of proper names with faulty recollection and the formation of concealing memories. (31)

Are we all neurotic, are all these process pathological? That appears to be Freud's question, and is not mine. Mine is whether conscious processes are described here in their most pervasive and effective (not to say affective) practices. Is this not consciousness itself, to work by misdirection even when no such obliquity appears in consciousness? Is the effectiveness and transparency of consciousness not another working of the very same mechanisms? Is forgetting not the condition of memory, indirection the condition of connection, the impossibility of memory the constitutive condition of remembering? Is concealment not the condition of unconcealment? That is the question Freud evokes, though it sounds suspiciously like Heidegger.[7]

Yet of course Freud never says this. Reality intrudes as if it were the thing itself. To forget is not to remember something real, the truth. Yet this thing itself must appear; it is caught, as all images are, between the inside and outside of appearance, between what is said and what is unsaid, what is remembered and forgotten— manifest and latent in Freud's language. What is latent is not outside appearing, but both appears and can be made to appear differently. Reality is not appearance's other but exposed in proliferation, multiplies in realization, is recalled and known in forgetting and displacement.

All this is to say that the psychopathology of everyday life and the distortions of dreams are everyday life and dreaming themselves, that the most accurate recollections and the most faithful dreams are accurate and faithful in virtue of the displacements, indirections, and obliquities that compose their reality as the forgotten. To bear witness is to proliferate and multiply and to mirror and unmirror.

With this understanding, we may take a look at *The Psychopathology of Everyday Life* in a more comprehensive or serial way, considering the moments of pathology: *forgetting*—proper names, words, orders of words, impressions and resolutions; *concealing*—

childhood memories; *mistakes*—in speech, reading and writing, actions, combined acts; *errors*; concluding with *determinism, chance, and superstition*. These terms are presented by Freud as deviations, yet they are present in everyday life constantly and everywhere. Freud characterizes his understanding of these deviations in what he calls "the general result" of the preceding discussions:

> *Certain inadequacies of our psychic functions—whose common character will soon be more definitely determined—and certain performances which are apparently unintentional prove to be well motivated when subjected to psychoanalytic investigations, and are determined through the consciousness of unknown motives.* (118)

I am calling into question from the standpoint of the performances that appear accidental the insistence that they are inadequate. They, and perhaps all the others, psychic life and perhaps the world in general, are determined in unknown ways. On the one hand, there is the insistence on an unknown, underlying reality and its adequacy, against which deviations are inadequate; on the other hand, there is such a play of interpretations as to constitute a proliferation of meanings as the reality. The underlying reality, together with its manifest appearances, multiplies at both levels. The result of psychoanalytic investigation is that there is always much more going on under the surface and as it comes to the surface. Psychoanalysis gives us much much more.

Indeed, the principles Freud insists on, against the obscurantism of superstition, in practice do not lay to rest the activities of the psyche but multiply them. First the phenomena themselves:

> a faulty psychic action must satisfy the following conditions:
> (a) It must not exceed a certain measure, which is firmly established through our estimation, and is designated by the expression "within normal limits."
> (b) It must evince the character of the momentary and temporary disturbance. The same action must have been previously performed more correctly or we must always rely on ourselves to perform it more correctly; if we are corrected by others, we must immediately recognize the truth of the correction and the incorrectness of our psychic action.
> (c) If we at all perceive a faulty action, we must not perceive in ourselves any motivation of the same, but must attempt to explain it through "inattention" or attribute it to an "accident." (118)

In other words, it must appear ordinary, everyday; it must appear a deviation; it must appear accidental. I emphasize the repeated words *it must appear as*. The phenomenon must appear in both its arrival and its interpretation in the modality of *as if* and *perhaps*. Perhaps I would emphasize the latter.

Now the explanatory principles:

> I. By assuming that a part of our psychic function is unexplainable through purposive ideas, we ignore the realms of determinism in our mental life. Here, as in still other spheres, determinism reaches farther than we suppose. (118)

Perhaps determinism is in abundance, so that the refusal to explain is offset not by seeking an exclusive explanation, but as we have seen in Spinoza, opens up the multiplicity of expositions in the surpluses of determinism.

> III. Although conscious thought must be altogether ignorant of the motivation of the faulty actions described above, yet it would be desirable to discover a psychologic proof of its existence; indeed, reasons obtained through a deeper knowledge of the unconscious make it probable that such proofs are to be discovered somewhere. As a matter of fact, phenomena can be demonstrated in two spheres which seem to correspond to an unconscious and hence, to a displaced knowledge of these motives. (129–30)

One might suppose that the question is whether a deterministic account of an underlying cause might lay to rest our confusion about accidents and deviations. At the underlying level they are not accidental but intended. The question concerns what is intended as well as the nature and composition of the intention. Not, perhaps, so much the intentions and motives as the explanatory procedures; and not so much these as the displacements and transfigurations. Whether or not there are unconscious intentions, whether or not the unconscious is motivated, it works by displacement and forgetting. The world of the unconscious is abundant in meaning, really and truly meaningful in abundance.

Freud insists on this, albeit still in the context of pathology:

> (a) It is a striking and generally recognized feature in the behavior of paranoiacs, that they attach the greatest significance to trivial details in the behavior of others. Details which are usually overlooked by others they interpret and utilize as the basis of far-reaching conclusions. . . .
>
> The category of the accidental, requiring no motivation, which the normal person lets pass as a part of his own psychic functions and faulty actions, is thus rejected by the paranoiac in his application to the psychic manifestations of others. All that he observes in

others is full of meaning; all is explainable. But how does he come
to look at it in this manner?

    Probably here, as in so many other cases, he projects into the
mental life of others what exists in his own unconscious activity.... In a certain sense, the paranoiac behavior is justified; he
perceives something that escapes the normal person; he sees
clearer than one of normal intellectual capacity, but his knowledge
becomes worthless when he imputes to others the state of affairs
he thus recognizes. (130–1)

One might imagine this to be the issue in all of the accidents and
deviations, all the petty knowledges and connections, that constitute
the world of everyday life. It is true for me—said by the paranoiac
or the mistaken or the superstitious—is not false, and for that matter
not true only for them. Freud emphasizes that what paranoiacs perceive is frequently insightful and apt: only their conclusions are de-
lusional. We might go so far as to imagine a world of paranoiacs
taught not to ascribe their delusions to others, precisely because we
are all paranoiacs together. It would be a world of accidental meanings that proliferate, as if there were only accidents in meanings.

    The other category of such accidentalism is described as *supersti-
tion*, here another term for containment and exclusion.

    (b) The phenomena of superstition furnish another indication
of the unconscious motivation in chance and faulty actions.... [A
patient of mine] was over ninety years old; it was therefore perti-
nent to ask oneself at the beginning of each year how much longer
she was likely to live.

    ... This day, it happened that the driver did not stop in front
of her house, but before one of the same number in a nearby and
really similar-looking parallel street. I noticed the mistake and re-
proached the coachman, who apologized for it.

    Is it of any significance when I am taken to a house where the
old woman is not to be found? Certainly not to me; but were I *superstitious*, I should see an omen in this incident, a hint of fate that
this would be the last year for the old woman.... Of course, I explain the incident as an accident without further meaning. (131–2)

From the standpoint of forgetting, there are no accidents, no appearances without further meaning. Meaning proliferates. Freud
knows this too well, so he must block the proliferation.

    There are two differences between me and the superstitious per-
son: first, he projects the motive to the outside, while I look for it
in myself; second, he explains the accident by an event which I
trace to a thought. What he considers hidden corresponds to the

unconscious with me, and the compulsion not to let chance pass as chance, but to explain it as common to both of us.

...I believe that a large portion of the mythological conception of the world which reaches far into the most modern religions, is nothing but psychology projected to the outer world....

It is difficult to express it in other terms; the analogy to paranoia must here come to our aid. (131–2)

Is it not incredible that Freud would link, first superstition, then myth, and all modern religions with paranoia, that these are nothing but psychology projected to the outer world? *Nothing but*, indeed? Or perhaps all this and more. What religious and superstitious people do is what paranoiacs do, they project from their inner lives onto the world more than takes place in that world. The other world is orderly and real, we must not augment it improperly with our inner perceptions, feelings, and beliefs. Yet what if we all did that all the time? What if the outer world were not only the result of our projections, but always full of projection: exposition, affect, proliferation? Would that make it less truthful, or more? Perhaps in a different way: full of meaning after meaning, some of which might not produce effective bridges. But let's not be too quick to keep the paranoiacs off our bridges while building them! There might be room for a gifted paranoiac to bring his delusions to the building of monuments so that they might be guarded against unforeseen dangers.

Freud knows this as well. There is a truth to the most wonderful and remarkable delusions, fantastic and phantasmatic. Whether inner or outer—and who is finally to say?—such truths continue to circulate in wonder and abundance.

To the category of the wonderful and uncanny, we may also add that strange feeling we perceive in certain moments and situations when it seems as if we had already had exactly the same experience, or had previously found ourselves in the same situation....

I believe that it is wrong to designate the feeling of having experienced something before as an illusion. On the contrary, in such moments, something is really touched that we have already experienced, only we cannot consciously recall the latter because it never was conscious. In the latter, the feeling of *Déjà vu* corresponds to the memory of an unconscious phantasy. There are unconscious phantasies (or day-dreams) just as there are similar conscious creations, which everyone knows from personal experience. (137)

You can believe it if you will, but there is truth in it. It is a truth that crosses from the inner to the outer. So the question is how tightly we insist on holding on to the separation of inner from outer when all of psychoanalysis makes that impossible.

Freud concludes chapter and book with a return to displacements:

> VII. . . . The mechanism of the faulty and chance actions, as we have learned to know it through the application of analysis, shows in the most essential points an agreement with the mechanism of dream formation, . . . The incongruities, absurdities and errors in the dream content, by virtue of which the dream is scarcely recognized as a psychic function, originate in the same way—to be sure, through freer usage of the existing material—as the common error of our every-day life; *here, as there, the appearance of the incorrect function is explained through the peculiar interference of two or more correct functions. . . .*
>
> An important conclusion can be drawn from this combination: the peculiar mode of operation, whose most striking function we recognize in the dream content, should not be attributed only to the sleeping state of the psychic life, when we possess abundant proof of its activity during the waking state in faulty actions. The same connection also forbids us from assuming that these psychic processes which impress us as abnormal and strange, are determined by deep-seated decay of psychic activity or by morbid state of function.
>
> But the common character of the mildest, as well as the severest cases, to which the faulty and chance actions contribute, lies *in the ability to refer the phenomena to unwelcome, repressed, psychic material, which, though pushed away from consciousness, is nevertheless not robbed of all capacity to express itself.* (145–6)

In the mildest, the most ordinary, everyday practices, repression pushes material away from consciousness that remains expressive. The forgotten continues to be remembered—and perhaps, in not so mild an example, whatever we remember includes the work of forgetting as well as mourning. For we have always lost something, our lives are filled with grief and loss for broken attachments. Unattachment and disattachment leave traces in the most prolific and manifest gifts.

> Now in what consists the work which mourning performs? . . . The testing of reality, having shown that the loved object no longer exists, requires forthwith that all the libido shall be withdrawn from its attachments to this object. Against this demand a struggle of course arises—it may be universally observed that man never willingly abandons a libido position, not even when a substitute is already beckoning to him. This struggle can be so intense that a turning away from reality ensues, the object being clung to

through the medium of a hallucinatory wish-psychosis. The normal outcome is that deference for reality gains the day. . . .

Now let us apply to melancholia what we have learnt about grief. In one class of cases it is evident that melancholia too may be the reaction to the loss of a loved object; where this is not the exciting cause one can perceive that there is a loss of a more ideal kind. . . . This would suggest that melancholia is in some way related to an unconscious loss of a love object, in contradistinction to mourning, in which there is nothing unconscious about the loss. (Freud, *MM*, 155)

The depressed narcissist mourns not an Object but the Thing. Let me posit the "Thing" as the real that does not lend itself to signification, the center of attraction and repulsion, seat of the sexuality from which the object of desire will become separated. (Kristeva, *BS*, 13)

For man and for woman the loss of the mother is a biological and psychic necessity, the first step on the way to becoming autonomous. Matricide is our vital necessity, the sine-qua-non of our individuation, ... I make of Her an image of Death so as not to be shattered through the hatred I bear against myself when I identify with Her, ... I do not kill myself in order to kill her but I attack her, harass her, represent her. (27–8)

With generosity and loss we may conclude this work of recollection.

That which consciousness is aware of in the work of melancholia is thus not the essential part of it, nor is it even the part which we may credit with an influence in bringing the suffering to an end. We see that the ego debases itself and rages against itself, and as little as the patient do we understand what this can lead to and how it can change. We can more readily credit such an achievement to the unconscious part of the work, because it is not difficult to perceive an essential analogy between the work performed in melancholia and in mourning. Just as the work of grief, by declaring the object to be dead and offering the ego the benefit of continuing to live, impels the ego to give up the object, so each single conflict of ambivalence, by disparaging the object, denigrating it, even as it were by slaying it, loosens the fixation of the libido to it. (Freud, *MM*, 168–9)

Freud speaks of the work of grief, of interpretation, and of the work that mourning and melancholia perform. He speaks of clinical work and working, performed by the analyst and the patient, working on life, by indirection and displacement; and he speaks of work and working in relation to the grief and melancholy that haunt the patient, working in life, again by displacement and indirection.

There is always unconscious work to be done, and forgetting may be understood as such work, if not by taking Freud's picture of the unconscious for granted. We do not simply and accidentally forget, nor do we forget intentionally, perhaps because of hidden motives. Forgetting is work, we and others and perhaps the world of things do work in withdrawing and concealing. That is where Freud and Heidegger meet: forgetting is a working of being in indirection, a working from the generosity of being.

That is close in form to what Freud says. The work of mourning and of melancholy guard the unconscious against a violence to it from the object. The work of detachment from the object then is the work that mourning requires, building on that other work. The work of the analyst builds anew, on top of the other work. In this way the sorrow and the loss of death, rage at loss, do the work of displacing what has already been displaced, multiply prolifically and generously.

The generosity allows the work of grief to grant the ego life at the same time that it gives up the dead, the work of melancholia grants the ego peace at the same time that it rages at loss. From the most fixed attachment is given another life, another joy. The generosity of such work remains miraculous. That is why Freud must continually slay the dragons of superstition and myth as delusions. The generosity of being is the invisible work of forgetting beyond attachment to anything to remember.[8]

CHAPTER 10

Diachrony

> A giving which gives only its gift, but in the giving holds itself back and withdraws, ... (Heidegger, *TB*, 8)

> the Forgotten is . . . the Law. (Lyotard, "*HJ*," 147)

> how could this thought (Heidegger's), a thought so devoted to remembering that a forgetting (of Being) takes place in all thought, in all art, in all "representation" of the world, how could it possibly have ignored the thought of [that] which, in a certain sense, thinks, tries to think, nothing but that very fact? . . . to the point of suppressing and foreclosing to the very end the horrifying (and inane) attempt at exterminating, at making us forget forever what, in Europe, reminds us, ever since the beginning, that "there is" the Forgotten? (Lyotard, *HJ*, 4)

> [I]n witnessing, one also exterminates. The witness is a traitor. (Lyotard, *I*, 204)

> The Other becomes my neighbour precisely through the way the face summons me, calls for me, begs for me, and in so doing recalls my responsibility, and calls me into question.
> . . . as if I had to answer for the other's death even before *being*.[1] (83)

Withdrawal, concealment, errancy are the marks of being, the masks behind which being appears, the forgettings in which being is recalled. This is what Heidegger tells us, a telling that bears witness to the forgotten, that calls us to remember forgetting. As difficult as this may seem, it pales next to Lyotard's insistence that Heidegger has forgotten the forgotten, has failed to remember that the forgotten is the law. He has borne witness and has failed to bear witness. Six million and more people died in the name of such a failure. Around the world others continue to die. We might put it this way: such crimes and their victims are the forgotten of a world that insists on possessing truth; every truth bears witness to a murderous forgetting.

Another example of Heidegger's forgetting can be found in his refusal to read the Anaximander fragment as ethical, as testifying to the forgotten injustices everywhere to which we are obligated to bear witness. We must bear witness to what we cannot know, to what it is impossible for us to remember. We must bear witness because we have worked to forget, and that work is justice, the justice in justice, which we always forget. In forgetting the witness betrays the forgotten. As exposition.

> the expression... refers to all those who, wherever they are, seek to remember and to bear witness to something that is constitutively *forgotten*, not only in each individual mind, but in the very thought of the West. And it refers to all those who assume this anamnesis and this witnessing as an obligation, a responsibility, or a debt, not only toward thought, but toward justice. (Lyotard, "HJ," 141)

Lyotard criticizes Heidegger for two different crimes: the first, "Heidegger's political engagement within the National Socialist party in 1933 and 1934 is one thing; his absolute silence (except for one phrase) concerning the *Shoah* right up to his death is another" (Lyotard, "HJ," 137).[2] Lyotard understands this silence to mark another forgetting beyond the forgetting of Being: "of a silent Law that takes the soul hostage and forces it to bear witness to the violent obligation it has undergone" (Lyotard, "HJ," 146). Forgetting is constitutive of thought, of life, of humanity, of Europe, a thought we owe to Heidegger, within another forgetting that he forgets: "remaining anchored in the thought of Being, the 'Western' prejudice that the Other is Being, it has nothing to say about a thought in which the Other is the Law" (Lyotard, HJ, 89).

I might insist that the other is neither being nor the law, but the forgotten human beings, animals, and who knows what else who are sacrificed to identity and being, whose sacrifice constitutes collective, institutional identifications—the West, the State, Europe, humanity, God.

> 38. Some feel more grief over damages inflicted upon an animal than over those inflicted upon a human. This is because the animal is deprived of the possibility of bearing witness according to the human rules for establishing damages, and as a consequence, every damage is like a wrong and turns it into a victim

ipso facto . . . . That is why the animal is a paradigm of the victim. (Lyotard, *DPD*, 28)

Perhaps it is the inability of animals to bear witness, though I believe they expose the pain and suffering caused to them by humans in every movement. Perhaps Lyotard is too captivated by language. The animal is a paradigm of the victim in being made utterly forgotten. And indeed animals are made so, turned into organic factories. Forgetting is something that happens, something that belongs to happening; but it is also work, made to happen by institutional and collective powers. We are made to forget, and we forget that we are made so as well as what we have forgotten.

> Through butchering, animals become absent referents. Animals in name and body are made absent *as animals* for meat to exist. Animals' lives precede and enable the existence of meat. If animals are alive they cannot be meat. Thus a dead body replaces the live animal. Without animals there would be no meat eating, yet they are absent from the act of eating meat because they have been transformed into food. (Adams, *SPM*, 40)

> Just as dead bodies are absent from our language about meat, in descriptions of cultural violence women are also often the absent referent. . . . Women, upon whose bodies actual rape is most often committed, become the absent referent when the language of sexual violence is used metaphorically. These terms recall women's experiences but not women. (Adams, *SPM*, 42–3)

This crime of forgetting—women and animals—can be ascribed to Heidegger, who commits crimes of forgetfulness in the context of calling our attention to forgetting.

> Mortals are they who can experience death as death. Animals cannot do so. But animals cannot speak either. (Heidegger, *OWL*, 107)

> Apes, too, have organs that can grasp, but they do not have hands. The hand is infinitely different from all the grasping organs— paws, claws, or fangs—different by an abyss of essence. Only a being who can speak, that is, think, can have hands and can handily achieve works of handicraft. (Heidegger, *WCT*, 357)

About such a forgetting and such a forgotten Derrida has commented repeatedly on how Heidegger insists on the absolute distinction between the animal kind—in German, *Geschlecht*—and the human kind.

> Here in effect occurs a sentence that at bottom seems to me Heidegger's most significant, symptomatic, and seriously dogmatic. . . . (Derrida, *G2*, 173)

> Man's hand then will be a thing apart not as separable organ but because it is different, dissimilar from all prehensive organs (paws, claws, talons); man's hand is far from these in an infinite way through the abyss of its being. This abyss is speech and thought. (Derrida, *G2*, 174)

> The word [*Geschlecht*, then] signifies the human species (*Menschengeschlecht*) in the sense of humanity (*Menschheit*) as well as the species in the sense of tribes, stocks, and families, all that struck again [*dies alles widerum geprägt*: struck in the sense of what receives the imprint, the *typos*, the typical mark] with the generic duality of the sexes (*in das Zwiefache der Geschlechter*).[3] (Derrida, *G2*, 185)

This insistence on an absolute abyss between human and animal may have many origins—fear of being "natural," a desire to eat meat, Judeo-Christian and Cartesian spirituality. It produces a humanism that insists on defining humanity as separate from the natural world in the least humanistic philosophers.

> Discourses as original as those of Heidegger and Levinas disrupt, of course, a certain traditional humanism. In spite of the differences separating them, they nonetheless remain profound humanisms *to the extent that they do not sacrifice sacrifice.* (Derrida, *EW*, 279)

Perhaps in the name of virility:

> The virile strength of the adult male, the father, husband, or brother (the canon of friendship, as I have shown elsewhere, privileges the fraternal schema), belongs to the schema that dominates the concept of subject. The subject does not want just to master and possess nature actively. In our cultures, he accepts sacrifice and eats flesh. (281)

The subject accepts sacrifice and eats flesh. This is, for some, a recognition and acknowledgment: the hunter who stands face to face with the lion and kills it in the name of virility or food, the farmer who nourishes and loves the baby goat and chick, who kills and eats the adult animal. In today's world this is becoming rarer and rarer. The acceptance of sacrifice is a hidden death, and the flesh that is eaten is made to look as little like a living animal as possible. That is what Adams tells us. Animals are the forgotten of the living whose sacrifice—suffering and death—is required for humanity's dignity. This is not only true in the field or farm, but sanctioned and justified in reason and words. The schema, the exposition, of the virile constitutes the boundaries of the human. In this way, as profound and wonderful are the works of Heidegger and Levinas in relation to the forgotten other, they participate willingly in their own forgetting.

> The "Thou shalt not kill" . . . has never been understood within the Judeo-Christian tradition, nor apparently by Levinas, as a "Thou shalt not put to death the living in general." It has become meaningful in religious cultures for which carnivorous sacrifice is essential, as being-flesh. (279)

With this grim and unsettling beginning before us, constituting for most of us our forgotten, I would now turn to one whose name for many expresses bearing witness to such forgetting. In the case of animals, however, even Levinas does not know.

> I cannot say at what moment you have the right to be called "face." The human face is completely different and only afterwards do we discover the face of an animal. I don't know if a snake has a face. I can't answer that question. a more specific analysis is needed. (Levinas, *PM*, 171–2)

> It is clear that, without considering animals as human beings, the ethical extends to all living beings. We do not want to make an animal suffer needlessly and so on. But the prototype of this is human ethics. Vegetarianism, for example arises from the transference to animals of the idea of suffering. The animal suffers. It is because we, as humans, know what suffering is that we can have this obligation. (172)

Forgetting—obliterating—the animal in us is one of the constitutive acts of humanity. Derrida suggests it is "our" humanism, and indeed it may be humanity's humanism, most if not all. Not because human beings require meat to live or because their dignity requires that they be separate from than animals, but because separation from the Other is the condition of existence. Humanity requires— is—separation. That is the origin of responsibility, given from the Good.

> A guiltless responsibility, whereby I am none the less open to an accusation of which no alibi, spatial or temporal, could clear me. It is as if the other established a relationship or a relationship were established whose whole intensity consists in not presupposing the idea of community. A responsibility stemming from a time before my freedom—before my (*moi*) beginning, before any present. A fraternity existing in extreme separation. (Levinas, *EFP*, 83–4)

A separation extreme beyond the separation of hand from claw, of humans from nature, of one responsibility from another.

I've suggested that the proximity and alterity of animals, intimately linked with the proximity of our own animality, presents this inescapable responsibility to us in the faces and bodies of animals. We are animal, we have animal bodies, animals live, enjoy and suffer, build and destroy, we cannot escape the responsibility that confronts us in the face of the other—human or animal—whose mortality and suffering is in our hands.

> the uniqueness of the responsible ego is possible only *in* being obsessed by another, in the trauma suffered prior to any auto-identification, in an unrepresentable *before*. (Levinas, *S*, 113)

> The proximity of the other is the face's meaning, and it means from the very start in a way that goes beyond those plastic forms which forever try to cover the face like a mask of their presence to perception. But always the face shows through these forms. Prior to any particular expression and beneath all particular expressions, which cover over and protect with an immediately adopted face or countenance, there is the nakedness and destitution of the expression as such, that is to say extreme exposure, defenselessness, vulnerability itself.... Beyond the visibility of whatever is unveiled, and prior to any knowledge about death, mortality lies in the Other. (*EFP*, 82–3)

Levinas says this of the other human, yet we know and feel as intensely as possible that it is true of animals in today's world: the nakedness and destitution of the expression as such, that is to say extreme exposure, defenselessness, vulnerability itself. The defenselessness, vulnerability, mortality, expressibility of animal faces show through all the masks we invent to cover them, all the walls we build to hide them. In a similar way, I would speak of the faces of things before modern human powers: the nakedness and destitution of surfaces, of things that touch each other, bodies exposed to each other: expression as such, that is to say extreme exposure, defenselessness, vulnerability itself. We can kill, destroy, transfigure, disfigure; that is responsibility itself.

All, perhaps, may answer, all may be responsible for death and destruction. Perhaps including animals and nonliving things: volcanoes, hurricanes, too many mice and deer. Human beings alone may know more of this, may care more of it, may have powers to resist. In their capabilities, human beings today may be hostage to suffering and mortality as nothing else we may know.

> The responsibility for another, an unlimited responsibility which the strict book-keeping of the free and non-free does not measure, requires subjectivity as an irreplaceable hostage. This subjectivity it denudes under the ego in a passivity of persecution,

repression and expulsion outside of essence, into oneself . . . without having wished it, I have to answer (s'accuse). (S, 113)

It is one thing to know that the fate of the world, of all unique, expressive, singular things lies in human hands. It is another to repudiate that responsibility on the basis of substitution.

> But is not the diachrony of the inspiration and expiration separated by the instant that belongs to an animality? Would animality be the openness upon the beyond essence? But perhaps animality is only the soul's still being too short of breath. . . . Is man not the living being capable of the longest breath in inspiration, without a stopping point, and in expiration, without return? (OB, 181–2)

One may read this as privilege—the privilege of humanity's subjectivity, expressed in inspiration, guarded against animality. One may read it as a wound—the burden of vulnerability, the persecution of proximity. Human beings bear the weight of responsibility for the things and creatures of the world as nothing else can: not a privilege but a condition of ethics—not just a human ethics, not just ethics for humans, but a responsibility that human beings may bear uniquely, not because they are more inspired but because they are more capable of violence and peace, thereby responsible for bearing witness to the forgotten.

Separation and diachrony are the conditions whereby the face presents the traumas and wounds of inspiration, not its height. It is the ruptures and breaks of a being that cannot be assembled into essence, where the other and I are separate, broken apart by alterity. Each and every other is absolutely other, unassemblable into being together. That is the separation of the other from me and of animals from my animality, the dispossession of the other's identity from mine.

> Heidegger, with the whole of Western history, takes the relation with the Other as enacted in the destiny of sedentary peoples, the possessors and builders of the earth. Possession is preeminently the form in which the other becomes the same, by becoming mine. . . . Ontology becomes ontology of nature, impersonal fecundity, faceless generous mother, matrix of particular beings, inexhaustible matter for things. (Levinas, TI, 46)

> Possession is preeminently the form in which the other becomes the same, by becoming mine. (Levinas, TI, 46)

> It is in generosity that the world possessed by me—the world open to enjoyment—is apperceived from a point of view independent of the egoist position. (75)

The continuity and duration of being are given to us to possess. Generosity and giving take place in separation and diachrony. Rupture, interruption, breaks in time and being are given in the face.

> But, in its expression, in its mortality, the face before me summons me, calls for me, begs for me, as if the invisible death that must be faced by the Other, pure otherness, separated, in some way, from any whole, were my business.... The other man's death calls me into question, as if, by my possible future indifference, I had become the accomplice of the death to which the other, who cannot see it, is exposed, and as if, even before vowing myself to him, I had to answer for this death of the other, and to accompany the Other in his mortal solitude. The Other becomes my neighbour precisely through the way the face summons me, calls for me, begs for me, and in so doing recalls my responsibility, and calls me into question.
> . . . as if I had to answer for the other's death even before *being*. (*EFP*, 83)

Forgetting appears here repeatedly in the exposition of *as if*: as if the death of the other, as if it were my responsibility, as if I had to answer. Anarchic responsibility is as if it were my immemorial responsibility to answer to the forgotten in the diachrony of substitution.

> It is the responsibility of a hostage which can be carried to the point of being substituted for the other person and demands an infinite subjection of subjectivity. Unless this anarchic responsibility, which summons me from nowhere into a present time, is perhaps the measure or the manner or the system of an immemorial freedom that is even older than being, or decisions, or deeds. (84)

It is taken up again by Derrida in the faces of animals—perhaps I mean their whiskers and tails, for I'm sure that bodies are expressive in more ways than we can know:

> How would you ever justify the fact that you sacrifice all the cats in the world to the cat that you feed at home every morning for years, whereas other cats die of hunger at every instant? Not to mention other people? . . . There is no language, no reason, no generality or mediation to justify this ultimate responsibility which leads me to absolute sacrifice; absolute sacrifice that is not the sacrifice of irresponsibility on the altar of responsibility, but the sacrifice of the most imperative duty . . . in favor of another absolutely imperative duty binding me to every other.[4] (*GD*, 71)

No language, reason, generality, or mediation can justify this ultimate responsibility that leads to absolute sacrifice; not the sacrifice of irresponsibility on the altar of responsibility, but the sacrifice of the most imperative duty (that which binds me to the other as a singularity in general) in favor of another absolutely imperative duty binding me to every other.

What binds me and what blinds me, what I am responsible for and cannot be responsible for—it is impossible—is given in the separation of the other from me and the diachrony of a time in which we cannot be assembled. The condition of sociality is difference, rupture, interruption. The condition of possibility for ethical responsibility is its impossibility—impossible to know, understand, assemble, achieve.

> Awaiting without horizon of the wait, awaiting what one does not expect yet or any longer, hospitality without reserve, welcoming salutation accorded in advance to the absolute surprise of the *arrivant* from whom or from which one will not ask anything in return. . . . It would be easy, too easy, to show that such a hospitality without reserve . . . is the impossible itself, and that this *condition of possibility* of the event is also its *condition of impossibility*, . . . But it would be just as easy to show that without this experience of the impossible, one might as well give up on both justice and the event.[5] (*SM*, 65)

There is no continuity of time, no knowledge of the past, no anticipation of the future, and no discipline of history that is not fundamentally unethical, irresponsible, traumatic. That is the diachrony of time for the alterity between the one and the other, animals included, also stones and plants.

It may be time—that is the point, perhaps: it may be time, it is as if we might look after time as if we never have it—to seek diachrony in the face. I mean of course the exposition that is forgetting—in the face, in the hands, in paws, fur, and scales, in the abundance of things themselves—if things have selves.

Time and the Other was published first in 1947, republished with a new preface by Levinas in 1979, and published in an English translation in 1987 with two later essays. I mention this history of a collection to expose the possibility of a diachrony right in the middle of an assemblage. For Levinas treats the text as if it were a continuity, while we who read it, especially in English, know it as a rupture, are able to see it in his preface.

> To write a preface on the occasion of the republication of something one published thirty years earlier is almost to write the preface to someone else's book. Except that one sees its shortcomings more quickly and feels them more painfully. . . .
> . . . The style (or nonstyle) of this writing will surely be, for many, abrupt or maladroit in certain turns of phrase. In these essays there are also theses whose contexts have neither been formu-

lated, nor their openings explored to the end, nor have they a systematic dissemination. Take these remarks as a preliminary note signaling all the flaws that since 1948 the aging of the text has probably accentuated.

If I nonetheless approved the idea of its republication, and in book form, and have foregone rejuvenating it, this because I still adhere to the main project of which it is—in the midst of diverse movements of thought—the birth and first formulation, and because its exposition progressively improves as one advances through its pages written in haste. (Levinas, *TO*, 29–30)

In the midst of a continuity of time, a memory and a recollection of something written many years ago, Levinas tells about its shortcomings and flaws—which surely he has overcome in the interval—but insists that it still says what he meant it to say. It is as if the passage of time exposes the text to its inadequacies, to its errancies, yet even so it is right. One might well imagine that every text—not only canonized texts—would meet such historical conditions: flawed, inadequate, but for all that worth repeating. The repetition presents the work again—in its errancies—and distances the work from us, at least acknowledges the distance.

This is what Derrida calls *iterability*, which for us here expresses the diachrony of time as an erasure or forgetting. The temptation is to forget that "when someone is speaking, in private or in public, . . . some force in him or her is also striving *not* to be understood, . . . not immediately, not fully, and therefore not in the immediacy and plenitude of tomorrow, etc."[6] (Derrida, *PF*, 217–9). Between the past and future, between an exposition and its repetition is a break, an interruption in meaning. Meaning is always in the process of being lost, and that is not its ruin but the production of its meaning. It must always be produced again, meant again, in the caesura of different meanings, different understandings, rememberings and forgettings. In this way forgetting is the condition of memory, the impossibility of remembering is the condition of its possibility. This impossibility is the diachrony of the relation of the one to the other—the break in meaning that is the other; my responsibility as witness to the break, witness to the forgotten alterity of the other.

This is, of course, the theme of *Time and the Other*.

The main thesis caught sight of in *Time and the Other* . . . consists in thinking time not as a degradation of eternity, but as the relationship to that which—of itself unassimilable, absolutely other—would not allow itself to be assimilated by experience; or to that which—of itself infinite—would not allow itself to be comprehended. . . . This impossibility of coinciding and this inadequation are not simply negative notions, but have a meaning in the phenomenon of noncoincidence given in the diachrony of time. Time signifies this always of noncoincidence, but also the always of the relationship, an aspiration and an awaiting, a thread finer than an ideal line that diachrony does not cut. . . . Here there is a relationship without terms, an awaiting without an awaited, an insatiable aspiration. . . .

The "movement" of time understood as transcendence toward the Infinity of the "wholly other" [*tout Autre*] does not temporalize in a linear way, does not resemble the straightforwardness of the intentional ray. Its way of signifying, marked by the mystery of death, makes a detour by entering into the ethical adventure of the relationship to the other person. (31–3)

It is about the impossibility of coinciding in being, where the other in existence is radically other, unassemblable. Alterity is diachrony, the rupture in time that is the other, the call that ruptures me before an infinite responsibility. Infinity here is not immense, grand, very large, but the impossible caesura, and its appearance is by betrayal—that is, in forgetting.

We have been seeking the *otherwise than being* from the beginning, and as soon as it is conveyed before us it is betrayed in the said that dominates the saying which states it. . . . Everything shows itself at the price of this betrayal, even the unsayable. In this betrayal the indiscretion with regard to the unsayable, which is probably the very task of philosophy, becomes possible. . . .

Can this *saying* and this *being unsaid* be assembled, can they be at the same time? In fact to require this simultaneity is already to reduce being's other to *being* and *not-being*. We must stay with the extreme situation of a diachronic thought . . . because a secret diachrony commands this ambiguous or enigmatic way of speaking, and because in general signification signifies beyond synchrony, beyond essence. (*OB*, 7)

Here diachrony appears as the ambiguous and enigmatic saying that signifies the otherwise than being beyond assembling, the anarchic and unassemblable impossibility of saying in the said. Unassembling, betraying, and diachrony are the pre-original, forgotten, otherwise than being. About it, in relation to prophecy as this enigmatic saying, Levinas locates the infinite in the face, before the other, "Thanks to God."

In proximity the other obsesses me according to the absolute asymmetry of signification, of the-one-for-the-other: . . . it is only thanks to God that, as a subject incomparable with the other, I am approached as an other both the others, that is, "for myself." "Thanks to God" I am another for the others. (158)

In other words—and indeed the words themselves are "other"—
it is the other who obsesses me, the other who is neither a god nor
God. The word "god" or "God" is enigmatic, ambiguous, anarchic,
constantly betraying and betrayed.

> The statement of the beyond being, of the name of God, does not
> allow itself to be walled up in the conditions of its enunciation. It
> benefits from an ambiguity or an enigma, which is not the effect of
> an inattention, a relaxation of thought, but of an extreme prox-
> imity of the neighbor, where the Infinite comes to pass.... The
> revelation of the beyond being is perhaps indeed but a word, but
> this "perhaps" belongs to an ambiguity in which the anarchy of
> the Infinite resists the univocity of an originary or a principle.
> (156)

In other words, the word *God* is perhaps *an other word*, enigmatic, ambiguous, as are the infinity and transcendence of anarchy, diachrony, and beyond being—and perhaps *humanity* and *animality*. They
are in virtue of God, but they appear in the face, they come to pass
in the proximity of the neighbor, the Other, and the revelation is received by the inspired subject whose inspiration is alterity.

This language is enigmatic, reminiscent of Blanchot's three levels of ambiguity: always open, never completed, fascinating and fascinated, beyond meaning, thereby as if filled with all meaning.[7] In
Otherwise than Being, God's infinity is not the cause of the infinity of
neighbor and face, but its transcendence. The name of God is betrayal, to bear witness to God is not to say the word or do any particular thing, but is saying itself. Glory cannot be lodged. Witness
betrays, enigmatically and ambiguously. The infinite is glorified by
the voice of the witness that cannot thematize the infinite in the
said. That goes for the word and glory of God.

> "Here I am" as a witness of the Infinite, but a witness that does
> not thematize what it bears witness of, and whose truth is not the
> truth of representation, is not evidence.... The Infinite does not
> appear to him that bears witness to it. On the contrary the witness
> belongs to the glory of the Infinite. It is by the voice of the witness
> that the glory of the Infinite is glorified. (146)

> The Infinite is not in front of its witness, but as it were outside, or
> on the "other side" of presence, already past, out of reach, a
> thought behind thoughts which is too lofty to push itself up front.
> "Here I am, in the name of God," without referring myself directly
> to his presence. "Here I am," just that! ... To bear witness [to] God
> is precisely not to state this extraordinary word, as though glory
> would be lodged in a theme and be posited as a thesis, or become
> being's essence. (149)

In *Time and the Other*, diachrony is the anarchic, nonassemblable relationship with God. I must add immediately that the anarchic and nonassemblable diachrony cannot be named, that naming and speaking is assembling even as the diachrony of saying is its betrayal.

> Language permits us to utter, be it by betrayal, this *outside of being*, this *ex-ception* to being, as though being's other were an event of being. Being, its cognition and the said in which it shows itself signify in a saying which, relative to being, forms an exception; but it is in the said that both this exception and the birth of cognition show themselves. (*OB*, 6)

Betrayal, then, is forgetting, revelation by violation. Every word, including *God*, betrays the otherwise than being, betrays it, violates it, reveals it. The questions for diachrony, then, the rupture and break in time, are of its betrayals, what and how it betrays, how and what is betrayed. And again, the appearance of betraying is its disappearance; the recollection of what cannot be assembled betrays its forgetting; the other is the exception of every rule and every law—exception as the caesura of the forgotten.

Time as continuity and assembling is relation to totality and eternity. Diachrony is a temporal relation to something—almost certainly nothing—unassimilable, absolutely other, that cannot be assimilated by experience, that cannot be comprehended. This impossibility and this inadequation are given as the diachrony of time: always noncoincidence, always in relation. In the caesura of forgotten time.

I must ask, why is time what is always lost, why does time—diachronic and other—define the caesura of inadequation, isn't time but one of the noncoincidences of the otherwise? And of course, I am speaking with Levinas, of subjectivity, materiality, work, pain, suffering, nourishment, enjoyment, absorption, solitude, death, the feminine, the child, fecundity, voluptuosity. In *Time and the Other*,

> There is what is said of subjectivity: the mastery of the Ego over being's anonymous *there is*, forthwith ... the irremissible weight of being in work, pain, and suffering. Next there is what is said of the world: the transcendence of nourishments and knowledge, an experience in the heart of enjoyment, ... Then there is what is said of death: not a pure nothingness but an unassumable mystery and ... the temporality of time where diachrony precisely describes the relationship with what remains absolutely outside. Finally there is what is said of the relationship with the Other, the feminine, the child, of the fecundity of the Ego, the concrete mo-

dality of diachrony, . . . a relationship without relation, an insatiable desire, or the proximity of the Infinite. . . .

Human alterity is not thought starting with the purely formal and logical alterity by which some terms are distinguished from others in every multiplicity. . . . The notion of a transcendent alterity—one that opens time—is at first sought starting with an alterity-content—that is, starting with femininity. . . . This idea should make the notion of the couple as distinct as possible from every purely numerical duality. The notion of the sociality of two, which is probably necessary for the exceptional epiphany of the face—abstract and chaste nudity—emerges from sexual differences, and is essential to eroticism and to all instances of alterity—again as quality and not as a simply logical distinction—borne by the "thou shalt not kill" that the very silence of the face says. (*TO*, 35–6)

It is as if to say that the sociality of the two is the forgotten caesura of the face that says, the diachrony without numerality. It is as if to say that love, femininity, voluptuosity, eros, fecundity, nudity are alterity. Alterity appears right here and now in life, in what before me touches me and moves me away from myself. The sexual couple is the otherwise in the present.

Such a sociality embodies Levinas's relation to Heidegger. It is as if the other's sociality is the forgotten of the subject.

The aim of these lectures is to show that time is not the achievement of an isolated and lone subject, but that it is the very relationship of the subject with the Other.

This thesis is in no way sociological. It is not a matter of saying how time is chopped up and parceled out thanks to the notions we derive from society, how society allows us to make a representation of time. It is not a matter of our idea of time but of time itself. (39)

Time itself—if such a time can be itself—is diachronic, but diachrony resists representation, insists on relation. Sociality is before society, and responsibility is before the other. Here *before* comes before us in its monumental ambiguity. Here I am before you in any immemorial diachrony before any past. *Before* is before solitude.

Solitude lies in the very fact that there are existents. To conceive a situation wherein solitude is overcome is to test the very principle of the tie between the existent and its existing. It is to move toward an ontological event wherein the existent contracts existence. The event by which the existent contracts its existing I call *hypostasis*. (43)

Consciousness is a rupture of the anonymous vigilance of the *there is*; it is already hypostasis; it refers to a situation where an existent is put in touch with its existing. Obviously I will not be able to explain why this takes place. There is no physics in meta-physics. I can simply show what the significance of hypostasis is. (51)

There is no physics in metaphysics—as if these were different disciplines, separate faculties—because physics is the assembling of being in time while metaphysics is its diachrony. Levinas turns the critique of metaphysics on its head—sideways, obliquely, other-wise—in the name of rupture. Traditional metaphysics sought to assemble being and world together under the headings of God and transcendence. Transcendence and God are diachronic, ruptures in the continuity of time made by the otherness of the other.

I do not identify the other or its otherness with consciousness or subjectivity. I think that physics must be transcendent and dia-chronic if there be diachrony and transcendence. I think that being itself is diachronic and transcendent. This is to say that it is enig-matic and mysterious. If this is not evident in physics, that is a shame. And perhaps such a shame attaches to metaphysics. But the greatest shame is that ethics is no longer mysterious and enigmatic, has been assembled into being as if it were possible; not the impos-sible giving of the good, the caesura of diachrony, the insistence of the otherness of the other, but the possibility of achieving goodness as if it were something to have here and now.

> In thus going back to the ontological root of solitude I hope to glimpse wherein this solitude can be exceeded. Let me say at once what this exceeding will not be. It will not be a knowledge, be-cause through knowledge, whether one wants it or not, the object is absorbed by the subject and duality disappears. It will not be an ecstasis, because in ecstasis the subject is absorbed in the object and recovers itself in its unity. All these relationships result in the disappearance of the other. (41)

Let us take this exceeding as fundamental to diachrony. Time is not the succession of one instant after another, events following each other. It is an arrival that exceeds the succession absolutely. It is not the ek-static present that carries with it a past and future. It is the moment and the arrival that carries nothing, that exceeds any carry-ing and assembling, the unassimilable other who (or that) ruptures time.

The ruptures of forgotten time and history that call us into ques-tion are not ideas but violences. First Heidegger, then his master—as terrible as it may be to say it:

I always feel great emotion when I recall my studies with Heidegger. Whatever reserves can be expressed about the man and his political engagement on the side of the Nazis, he is incontestably a genius, the author of an extremely profound philosophical work that cannot be shrugged off in a few words....

Heidegger believes that being is animated by the effort to be. In the being's effort to be, nothing matters but being, above all and at all costs. This resolution makes it as strong and tough as steel when entering into conflicts between individuals, nations, or classes. Heidegger has a dream of blood and sword nobility. Well, humanism is altogether different. It is a response to the other that lets him go first, that gives way to him instead of combating him. There is a connection in Heidegger between the absence of caring for others and his personal political ad-venture. And despite all my admiration for the grandeur of his thought, I could never share that double aspect of his positions....

...one evening...we put on a little sketch portraying the Cassirer-Heidegger controversy. They were both in the audience. I played the role of Cassirer, whose positions were constantly attacked by Heidegger. And to express Cassirer's noncombative and rather desolate attitude, I kept repeating, "I am a pacifist...." (Levinas, *UH*, 134)

I am a pacifist, I am a humanist—themselves no doubt words of violence. It is worth noting the way *Totality and Infinity* begins before continuing with Hitler and Heidegger.

Morality will oppose politics in history and will have gone beyond the functions of prudence or the canons of the beautiful to proclaim itself unconditional and universal when the eschatology of messianic peace will have come to superpose itself upon the ontology of war. Philosophers distrust it. To be sure they profit from it to announce peace also; they deduce a final peace from the reason that plays out its stakes in ancient and present-day wars: they found morality on politics. But for them eschatology—a subjective and arbitrary divination of the future, the result of a revelation without evidences, tributary of faith—belongs naturally to Opinion. (Levinas, *TI*, 22)

Eschatology here is diachrony not destiny, it exceeds history.

Eschatology institutes a relation with being *beyond the totality* or beyond history, and not with being beyond the past and the present.... It is a relationship with *a surplus always exterior to the totality,....*

This "beyond" the totality and objective experience is, however, not to be described in a purely negative fashion. It is reflected *within* the totality and history, *within* experience. The eschatological, as the "beyond" of history, draws beings out of the jurisdiction of history and the future; it arouses them in and calls them forth to their full responsibility. . . . The eschatological vision breaks with the totality of wars and empires in which one does not speak. It does not envisage the end of history within being understood as a totality, but institutes a relation with the infinity of being which exceeds the totality. (22–3)

Messianic peace is a peace that may never arrive but that we must absolutely give to ourselves to believe in if we are to escape the ontology of war. And although the ontology of war lies more with Hegel's dialectic, it recalls Heidegger as well. For Levinas ascribes the term *destiny* to Hitler with Heidegger in mind, who speaks of the destiny (*Geschick*) of being.

The philosophy of Hitler is simplistic. But it smolders with primitive powers that explode its mediocre phraseology under the pressure of an elementary force. They awaken the secret nostalgia of the German soul. Hitlerism is more than contagion or folly; it is an awakening of elementary emotions.

And that makes it terribly dangerous and philosophically interesting. Because elementary sentiments harbor a philosophy. They express the primary attitude of a soul faced with the whole of the real and its own destiny. They predetermine or prefigure the sense of the soul's adventure in the world. (*UH*, 13)

Levinas follows the line of thought we recalled in Arendt, that time and history present action with what is irreparable.

Because history is the most profound limitation, the fundamental limitation. Time, the condition of human existence, is above all the condition of the irreparable. The fait accompli, carried off by a fleeting present, forever escapes man's grasp but weighs on his destiny. Behind the melancholy of the eternal flow of things—the illusory present of Heraclitus—stands the tragedy of an irremovable, ineffaceable past that condemns all initiative to be nothing more than continuation. True freedom, true beginning, would require a true present that is always at the apogee of a destiny, eternally resuming. (14)

Here history, chronology, and destiny join against the wounds of diachrony. Only rupture with this destiny can present a freedom toward the future, only repair of an irremovable, ineffaceable past. Heidegger's ontology and destiny are inescapable and irreparable conditions of historicality.

Judaism appears here twice, first with a radiant answer to this irreparability, then burdened by the weight of its history, German and Christian. Not to mention human and animal.

> Judaism bears the magnificent message that remorse—the painful expression of a radical impotence to repair the irreparable—announces the repentance that generates the pardon that repairs. Man finds in the present the wherewithal to modify the past, to erase it. Time loses its irreversibility. Time, exasperated, collapses at man's feet like a wounded animal. And liberates him. (14)

As if exasperated humanity might not otherwise collapse, wounded, before the hoofs and claws of animals, in another liberation in the forgotten caesura of time.

> Christianity opposes a mystical drama that is as foreign and brutal as a malediction. The cross liberates. And, by the Eucharist, which triumphs over time, this liberation operates every day. . . .
> Thereby Christianity proclaims freedom, makes freedom possible in all its fullness. Not only is the choice of destiny a free choice. The choice, once made, does not become shackles. Man retains the possibility—supernatural, of course, but within reach and concrete—of terminating the contract by which he freely committed himself. He can at any moment recover the nakedness of the first days of creation. (14)

Against this, Hitlerism and National Socialism present a body shackled to its origins, lacking transcendence. Time and history weigh down a body whose diachrony is forgotten in the weight of force. They do so, for Levinas, after secular liberalism has completed its course, after science has done its work.

> Man in the liberalist world does not choose his destiny under the weight of history. He does not know his possibilities as troubled forces churning within, that already orient him on a determined track. He sees them simply as logical possibilities offered to serene reason that chooses while eternally keeping its distance. . . .
> Marxism contests this concept of man for the first time in Western history.
> The human spirit is no longer seen as pure freedom, as the soul soaring above all attachments, as pure reason belonging to a kingdom of ends. The spirit is caught in the grips of material needs. But its concrete, servile existence at the mercy of a matter and a society that no longer obey the magic wand of reason has more importance, more weight, than impotent reason. Decisions that the intelligence did not make are imposed on it by a preexistent struggle. (16)

The biological, with all the fatality it entails, becomes more than an object of spiritual life; it becomes its heart. . . . The essence of man lies no longer in his freedom but in a sort of enslavement. To be truly oneself is not to rise above contingencies, forever foreign to the Ego's freedom; on the contrary, it is to become aware of the ineluctable original enslavement unique to our bodies; it is, above all, to accept this enslavement. (18)

I could not accept this image of liberalism or biology. I do not see the presentation of the past as history in its role as destiny. I do not see the body as anything but the forgotten itself—we might call it the diachrony of materiality. Levinas gives himself over to another destiny, calls it immateriality and subjectivity—and this despite some glorious passages expressing the transcendence of the flesh.

In the form of responsibility, the psyche (*psychisme*) in the soul is the other in me, a malady of identity, both accused and *self*, the same for the other, the same by the other. Qui pro quo, it is a substitution, extraordinary. . . . Such a signification is only possible as an incarnation. The animation, the very pneuma of the psyche, alterity in identity, is the identity of a body exposed to the other, becoming "for the other," the possibility of giving. (Levinas, *OB*, 69)

To hold on to exteriority is not simply equivalent to affirming the world, but is to posit oneself in it corporeally. . . . The body naked and indigent is the very reverting, irreducible to a thought, of representation into life, of the subjectivity that represents into life which is sustained by those representations and *lives of them*; its indigence—its needs—affirm "exteriority" as non-constituted, prior to all affirmation. (*TI*, 127)

Life is a body, not only lived body [*corps propre*], where its self-sufficiency emerges, but a cross-roads of physical forces, body-effect. . . . *To be a body* is on the one hand *to stand [se tenir]*, to be master of oneself, and, on the other hand, to stand on the earth, to be in the *other*, and thus to be encumbered by one's body. (164)

The caress, like contact, is sensibility. But the caress transcends the sensible. . . . The caress consists in seizing upon nothing, in soliciting what ceaselessly escapes its form toward a future never future enough . . . . (257)[8]

The body, bodies in the flesh, erotic, voluptuous, fecund bodies, enter into relations with what is absolutely other, with an alterity that remains other. In the caress, sensible bodies transcend the sensible. The materiality of bodies ceaseless escapes their forms toward a material future never future enough. The diachrony of the other belongs to the other's body, to other bodies.

But force is characterized by a different type of propagation. He who exercises it keeps a tight hold on it. The force is not lost among those who are subject to it. It is attached to the personality

or the society that exerts it. It enlarges them by subordinating the
rest. Here the universal order is not established as a corollary of
ideological expansion; it is the expansion that constitutes unity in
a world of masters and slaves. (20)

The world of masters and slaves is instituted by force, but at its
heart is the demand to own and possess the forces, whatever they
may be. So we may link diachrony again with generosity and dispossession. Reason may insist on possession, may impose the claim
that one can have the truth. But the institution of force and terror,
armies and police, is another violent grasping, one that claims nothing but itself for its inauguration. Intimately related to alterity in the
name of God, it verges on the edge of dogma.

> The problems that dogma attempts to answer are independent of
> it and arise from the simple fact of existence for modern man. For
> modern man, to exist is already to experience solitude, death, and
> the need for salvation. . . . What connects existential philosophy to
> theology is above all its subject—existence—a fact that is at least
> religious, if not theological.
>   . . . Whatever part theology played elsewhere in Heidegger's
> intellectual development, it is undeniable that he did not take the
> secularization of a notion to mean disguising its religious aspect.
> Secularization must signify an operation that results in truly sur-
> passing the theological point of view. . . .
>   In the theological attitude things and beings are envisaged in
> a way that should be called, in Heideggerian terms, ontic. We are
> dealing with that which is, with "beings" who fulfill their desti-
> nies. They are the subjects of narratives. They are treated as indi-
> viduals and take part in a story in which we ourselves are en-
> gaged. Theology is essentially history and mythology. That is why
> in theological matters, authority can guarantee truth.
>   . . . Heidegger breaks with theology precisely in making the
> distinction between ontical and ontological (which he does with a
> radicalism unprecedented in the history of philosophy) and giving
> fundamental transcendence as accomplished not in the passage
> from one "being" to another but from "being" toward Being. (*UH*,
> 65–6)

In the name of Heidegger, not of Hitler, I would like to confront
the truly radical nature of this suggestion that secularization signifies an operation—a word worth another confrontation—truly surpassing the theological point of view, without repudiating its own
spirituality. Is this to surpass the dogma of theology, as many philosophers would insist? Is there no dogma of philosophy, as many
philosophers would deny? Levinas means for us something other
than these familiar alternatives.

The limitation of theology for philosophy is its dogma, but its limits for Levinas are that God is bound to being, whether in this world or not. The being that is God is still ontic, and no matter how transcendent and sublime and mysterious that being may be, it is bound to being as God. In its traditional forms, secularity negates the being of God without in the least negating being. Its questions remain questions of being, one might say bound to Hegel. Beyond being is not nonbeing, and death is not negation.

Secularity in Levinas's sense is more memorable and more forgotten. Nonbeing is something otherwise—not anything at all. There is no being in the otherwise. The radical side of Heidegger is given in the beyond that is being in relation to beings; his betrayal is given in his denial of diachrony, the rupture in which the time of the other is not a time I can join. We cannot share a common sphere of action, even as I am constituted by sociality. This sociality is beyond the being of other beings.

Inside this interruption in the name of Heidegger it is time for another in the name of art. For Levinas contends that such a radical transcendence makes it impossible to take art seriously. Art is not radical enough, never escapes the lure of being, is captured by appearances. Such a view is remarkably close to Kant and Hegel and their followers. For them art's limitations are its superficiality. For Heidegger, art's achievement is its primordiality. Nevertheless, art is bound to truth and its coming to be. Art never escapes the lure of semblance. Levinas does not imagine the diachrony of art in the caesura.[9]

> It is generally, dogmatically, admitted that the function of art is expression, and that artistic expression rests on cognition. An artist—even a painter, even a musician—tells. He tells of the ineffable. An artwork prolongs, and goes beyond, common perception. What common perception trivializes and misses, an artwork apprehends in its irreducible essence. It thus coincides with metaphysical intuition. Where common language abdicates, a poem or a painting speaks. Thus an artwork is more real than reality and attests to the dignity of the artistic imagination, which sets itself up as knowledge of the absolute. (Levinas, *RS*, 130)

It appears—another appearance, another dogma—that art fails twice, first in insisting on reality, being, on its semblance of being, then second in insisting on speaking, and on speaking the truth. Truth and semblance belong to being, and this speaking and expression belong to the said, where truth and appearance and expression are assembled. Form continues to dominate art, so that it must remain on the hither side of being, unable to reach the otherwise, unable to transcend. This is true for Levinas despite his insistence that alterity appears right here and now in life, in what before me touches me and moves me away from itself.

Levinas's scorn is directed in part at another dogma, art for art's sake. But it is driven by the conviction that art is not language, is not open to dialogue.

> One then has the right to ask if the artist really knows and speaks. (130)

> The completion, the indelible seal of artistic production by which the artwork remains essentially disengaged, is underestimated— that supreme moment when the last brush stroke is done, when there is not another word to add to or to strike from the text, by virtue of which every artwork is classical. . . . The artist stops because the work refuses to accept anything more, appears saturated. The work is completed *in spite of* the social or material causes that interrupt it. It does not give itself out as the beginning of a dialogue. (131)

Here is the completion of the work, elsewhere the completion of the concept, there the end of art, science, or philosophy. It is as if completion were the synchronic betrayal of diachrony, as if the wound of time imposed the dogma of completion. What if the disengagement of art were in the caesura? What if the working of art took place in diachrony? Can a work of art be ruptured by alterity as if it might come to conclusion? That art is expression—I mean exposition—means that it is exposure to the other, that its relation to the ineffable is diachronic.

Levinas is unyielding, as if he knows the essence of art, as if art had an essence, walled up in being, as if *art* were not as strange a word as *god* or *other*, as *human* and *animal*; as if he had never read Nietzsche and *The Birth of Tragedy*, Heidegger and *The Origin of the Work of Art*, or Blanchot on the image.

> Art does not know a particular type of reality; it contrasts with knowledge. It is the very event of obscuring, a descent of the night, an invasion of shadow. To put it in theological terms, which will enable us to delimit however roughly our ideas by comparison with contemporary notions: art does not belong to the order of revelation. Nor does it belong to that of creation, which moves in just the opposite direction. (132)

> The notion of shadow thus enables us to situate the economy of resemblance within the general economy of being. . . . The sensible is being insofar as it resembles itself, insofar as, outside of its triumphal work of being, it casts a shadow, emits that obscure and

elusive essence, that phantom essence which cannot be identified with the essence revealed in truth. (137)

If the face is beyond knowledge, if diachrony ruptures every reality, if knowledge is something grasped rather than given, then art's refusal of knowing is a refusal of grasping, its shadowy semblance a refusal of having. It does not reveal but effects (Nietzsche) or happens (Heidegger). The image that refuses to grasp is beyond reality—or, in Blanchot's other words, not beyond.[10]

> The most elementary procedure of art consists in substituting for the object its image. Its image, and not its concept. A concept is the object *grasped*, the intelligible object. Already by action we maintain a living relationship with a real object; we grasp it, we conceive it. The image neutralizes this real relationship, this primary conceiving through action. The well-known disinterestedness of artistic vision, which the current analysis stops with, signifies above all a blindness to concepts. (132)

In the caesura of diachrony, a blindness to concepts is a refusal of grasping, withdrawal from being toward something other, in and beyond the face. In the proliferation of the image lie the ungatherings of the gathering of being, the forgettings of the re-calling of being. *Passivity beyond passivity* in Levinas's later words. Refused as image in the name of art.

> An image marks a hold over us rather than our initiative, a fundamental passivity. Possessed, inspired, an artist, we say, harkens to a muse. An image is musical. Its passivity is directly visible in magic, song, music, and poetry. The exceptional structure of aesthetic existence invokes this singular term magic, which will enable us to make the somewhat worn-out notion of passivity precise and concrete. (132)

Shadowing beyond any shadow I would say in mine, forgotten beyond forgetting.

> There is then a duality in this person, this thing, a duality in its being. It is what it is and it is a stranger to itself, and there is a relationship between these two moments. We will say the thing is itself and is its image. And that this relationship between the thing and its image is resemblance. . . .
>
> A being is that which is, that which reveals itself in its truth, and, at the same time, it resembles itself, is its own image. (135)

In what is the caesura, what is the rupture of diachrony in being, if not this doubling, and the others? It is a resembling, a doubling, that falls into time as if it were being again, as if being could not be again but otherwise. And in this as if of being otherwise we find expression, meaning, exposition as if beyond any containment—the other of all meaning, as Blanchot says, not another meaning. The other of all meaning, infinitely rich, but empty of grasping. The other, for Levinas, of diachrony and time.

There is something of Kierkegaard's view of the aesthetic in Levinas, something of its alleged lightness and irresponsibility. The lack of seriousness of art—that which separates it from the weight of things—is not grave enough, appears as if to be able to escape from death.

> Art then lets go of the prey for the shadow.
>
> But in introducing the death of each instant into being, it effects its eternal duration in the meanwhile, has there its uniqueness, its value. . . . It does not have the quality of the living instant which is open to the salvation of becoming, in which it can end and be surpassed. . . .
>
> . . . Art brings into the world the obscurity of fate, but it especially brings the irresponsibility that charms as a lightness and grace. It frees. To make or to appreciate a novel and a picture is to no longer have to conceive, is to renounce the effort of science, philosophy, and action. (141)

Worst of all, perhaps, in memory of the enjoyment encountered in the home, in hunger and labor, is the pleasingness of art.

> There is something wicked and egoist and cowardly in artistic enjoyment. There are times when one can be ashamed of it, as of feasting during a plague.
>
> Art then is not committed by virtue of being art. But for this reason art is not the supreme value of civilization, and it is not forbidden to conceive a stage in which it will be reduced to a source of pleasure—which one cannot contest without being ridiculous—having its place, but only a place, in man's happiness. Is it presumptuous to denounce the hypertrophy of art in our times when, for almost everyone, it is identified with spiritual life? (142)

The end of art remains on the scene, not because there will be no art but because art is so superficial, finally, that it cannot take on the serious work of being, cannot be responsible enough. Yet the work it does is the diachronic shattering of the buzzing of being. Art repudiates every icon, every boundary, reveals that nothing is to be revealed. And in this refusal opens up infinite responsibilities.

I don't know the supreme value of civilization, or if there could be any. I don't know almost everyone today who identifies art with spiritual life in a world of teeming religions. I don't know because I think these cannot be known—the supreme value of civilization, the identity of spiritual life, the end of happiness. I think this impossibility of knowing is diachrony, realized in the plethora of works and arts, so long as we do not imagine that one work or art might exhaust time. Indeed, the timelessness of works and arts, each a different time, a different lapse, a forgotten death, another loss, each and the multiplicity, marks the diachrony of time at another site than the face. Or perhaps art is the very shadow of the face, forgotten in its appearance?

It is odd that the diachrony that shatters the time of being does not shatter the image of art. What Levinas calls the hypertrophy of art in our times is its insistent shattering: every icon, every grasp, including itself. The veneration—if that is what it is—toward art coexists with the transfiguration of every icon, every monument, the transgression of every limit. One might say that art is parody of itself, that the image does not fix, but proliferates an image of fixity toward itself, that the completion claimed for art is part of the mystique of art. Artists themselves, works of art themselves, are the most visible critics of such a completion. Away from museums art offers an equalizing process in which all are peers.

The two essays included with the English publication of *Time and the Other* take up this vision from the other side, against the assembling of being. I mean to challenge Levinas's dismissal of art from inside his challenge to phenomenology—that is, the preeminence of the "I think" for the ego.

> The *other*, "intentionally" aimed at, invested, and assembled by the apperception of the *I think*, comes through thought as thought, through the *noema*—to fulfill, fill, or satisfy the aim, desire or aspiration of the *I think* or its *noesis*. The other is thus present to the ego. And this "being-present," or this *presence* of the "I think" to the ego, is equivalent to *being*.
>
> Presence or being is also a temporal modality. But it then concretely signifies an ex-position of the other to the ego, and thus signifies precisely an *offering of itself*, a *giving of itself*, a *Gegebenheit*. It is a donation of alterity within presence, not only in the metaphorical sense of the term, but as a donation signifying within a concrete horizon of a *taking* already referred to a "taking in hand." This essential "now" [*main-tenance*], if one can say so, the presence of the present, as temporality, is the promise of a graspable, a solid. It is what is probably the very promotion of the *thing*, the "something;" of the configuration of a *being* [*étant*] in being [*être*], in presence. (Levinas, *DR*, 98)

All this might be said of the artist, whose "I make" is at least as much a grasping and assembling in time and work and being as "I think." But it might be less plausibly said of the happening that is art, in Heidegger's words, even less of the image in Blanchot's, and the proliferation of works and images. The giving of art can be exposed as if not a taking in hand but a giving away, even as institutions like art worlds, galleries, and museums seek to collect and grasp. I mean here anything but the production of monuments that are featured in synchronic installations. I mean the works of art that always move, the products that dismantle and unproduce themselves, the ways in which works of art escape grasping.

> [A] gift is a thing we do not get by our own efforts. We cannot buy it; we cannot acquire it through an act of will. It is bestowed upon us. (Hyde, G, ix)
>
> The only essential is this: *the gift must always move*. There are other forms of property that stand still, that mark a boundary or resist momentum, but the gift keeps going. (4)
>
> works of art exist simultaneously in two "economies," a market economy and a gift economy. Only one of these is essential, however: a work of art can survive without the market, but where there is no gift there is no art. (ix)

I mean not to take this picture of art and gifts as if it were something we can take in hand, hold on to, believe, but as if it were the exposition of diachrony—in giving, as if in art and not only art.[11] The gift—the giving—must always move, yet we know that works of art are bought and sold, collected. So we cannot be speaking of great works of art, of cherished monuments. We cannot be speaking of particular works, but of the *as if* that surrounds the semblance of art as such, the *as if* and *perhaps* that make it impossible to grasp the meaning of the work. This is not unique to art, and art does not own it. Instead it presents it as if in the name of art, as if the name of the *perhaps* and *as if* and *forgetting* were art, when it pertains to all the presence of which Levinas speaks.

It is as if science and representation claimed to grasp the truth, as if the subject controlled the concept, as if truth could be grasped. It is as if art and poetry could not be contained, as if *mimēsis* were beyond having, as if writing wandered in literature as art. But writing wanders as writing, and this wandering is what keeps it from being grasped, what escapes taking. Writing, language, images, exposition escape the conditions that institute grasping—in the modality of *as if*. In science and representation also.

This may make art appear unserious, writing appear frivolous and poisonous. However, the answer to Levinas's critique of the shadow of reality that he takes art to be is that he is taking it as if he could grasp it, while its elusiveness and wandering take the form of

parody and play. It is as if art were unserious because it is play—as
if play were clearly unserious, and as if the serious ones were the
ones to decide. Learn to laugh! Zarathustra says. Learn that no
word—art, philosophy, science, theology, God—and nothing said—I
am, I think, I perform—can escape diachrony. Even the most syn-
chronized performances are performances, present themselves as if
assembled in time, to be dissembled by time. The performance is the
art that disassembles the performative. Every said is a betrayal.
Every performance, every art, betrays that betrayal, in the modality
of *as if*, as if betrayal were not serious, as if responsibility could pass
beyond betrayal.

> Language can pass for interior discourse and can always be
> attributed to the gathering of alterity into the unity of presence by
> the ego of the intentional *I think*. . . . It is the key moment of rep-
> resentation and vision as the essence of thought! And it is this de-
> spite all the time that the reading of a book can take, where this
> gathering, or this texture of presence, returns to duration. (101–2)

Language can *pass for*—perhaps in errancy, perhaps in performativity. The ego can *always attribute to itself* the gathering of alterity—
as if alterity were nothing other, forgotten. The other does not interrupt the gathering, even when present in it. Thought and duration
gather into presence in the key moment of representation, despite
broken, diachronic time. It is as if the ego insists on duration, all the
while present to itself diachronically. Passing and attributing are
modalities of *as if*—the working of diachrony.

> The exteriority of the face is extra-ordinary. It is extra-ordi-
> nary for order is justice. It is extra-ordinary or absolute in the
> etymological sense of this adjective, as always separable from
> every relationship and synthesis, tearing itself away from the very
> justice where this exteriority enters. The absolute—an abusive
> word—could probably take place concretely and have meaning
> only in the phenomenology, or in the rupture of phenomenology,
> which the face of the other calls forth. (107)

Exteriority is extraordinary, beyond the familiar and ordinary,
tears itself away from the abusiveness of any absolute, any gathering. This is diachrony in the tearing and the rupturing—as if by betrayal. This is exposition—exposure beyond exposure, expression
beyond expression.

> The face of the Other—under all the particular forms of ex-
> pression where the Other, already in a character's skin, plays a
> role—is just as much pure expression, an extradition without de-
> fense or cover, precisely the extreme rectitude of a facing, which

in this nudity is an exposure unto death: nudity, destitution, passivity, and pure vulnerability. Such is the face as the very mortality of the other person. (107)

Again, all these roles, all this playing, exposing and extraditing
without defense: where can such expression be found? In one sense
everywhere, but openly in art. Sometimes of course. And always
forgotten in betrayal. But with facing, nudity, exposure, death, destitution, passivity, vulnerability: as if to express and betray the mortality of the other person.

We may think of art as resisting time. Death appears in art as if
it were not death: Hamlet comes back, Antigone buries her brother
again and again. Ozymandias may die but a poem will live forever.
What a performance! It is as if the artist might know and control a
future beyond control. It is as if the most fragile of productions
might be more powerful than the most weighty! It is as if the force
of words were greater than the force of war!

No one is fooled, but everyone insists on playing the fool. Not
because we believe that something painted on canvas might be eternal, but because we know that eternity exists in betrayal, and one of
the visible expressions of this betrayal lies on the canvas, on the
stage. The face and body on the canvas, no matter whose or what,
presents itself in Levinas's words: nude, exposed, long dead, desti-
tute, passive, vulnerable, no matter how vivid or forceful. It is utterly fragile, and we are utterly responsible for it. It offers itself as
the other, of the other, toward the other, in a gesture that cannot
possibly succeed in gathering that other, any other, into its embrace.
It unembraces in its embrace. It ungathers in its gathering. It forgets
in its remembrances. The mortality of the work of art is what gives it
semblance as if it were immortal. In its timeless way it reveals the
diachrony of every time and the mortality of every immortal.

The immemoriality of a past beyond any past, the anteriority in
which responsibility toward the other is beyond any responsibility,
the diachrony before the time of synchrony, can be said and written
only in betrayal. In one sense everywhere, in all writing and speaking, in another sense nowhere, everywhere betrayed. The question is
not so much where diachrony is present—everywhere and nowhere—but which form of writing and speaking is more truthful of,
more torn open to diachrony. The answer has to be none in particular, but here I am before you to attempt that task! Under what
name? Mine perhaps, and yours, and the others.

> In the ethical anteriority of responsibility, for-the-other, in its
> priority over deliberation, there is a past irreducible to a presence
> that it must have been. . . . In this responsibility I am thrown back

toward what has never been my fault or my deed, toward what
has never been in my power or in my freedom, toward what has
never been my presence, and has never come into memory. . . . The
dia-chrony of a past that does not gather into re-presentation is at
the bottom of the concreteness of the time that is the time of my
responsibility for the Other. (111–2)

The diachrony of a past—and present and future—that does not
gather is the forgotten time of my responsibility for the other, realized in every presence, every representation, every retention, every
memory—present by betrayal, forgotten in its traces, as if by ungathering the gathering.

One of its recurrent names is *love*.

Subjection to the order that ordains man—the ego—to answer
for the other is, perhaps, the harsh name of love. Love here is no
longer what this compromised word of our literature and our hy-
pocrisies expresses, but the very fact of the approach of the unique
one and, consequently, of the absolutely other, piercing what
merely shows itself—that is to say, what remains the "individual
of a genus." Love here implies the whole order—or the whole disorder—of the psychic or the subjective, which would no longer be
the abyss of the arbitrary where ontological meaning is lost, but
the very place that is indispensable to the promotion of the logical
category of unicity, beyond the distinction between the universal
and the individual. (116)

But love is not a name, nor are God, art, materiality, forgetting, and
diachrony. Diachrony tears open the naming to its immemoriality, to
a responsibility and betrayal that are present in every representation
of the name as if in betrayal by forgetting. Every word betrays itself
in the said, as if it were the other. Every word expresses itself in
saying, as if it were exposure in the face.

A relationship without correlation, love of the neighbor is love
without eros. It is for-the-other-person and, through this, to-God!
Thus thinks a thought which thinks more than it thinks, beyond
what it thinks. Demand and responsibility are all the more impe-
rious and urgent as they are undergone with the more patience.
The concrete origin or originary situation is where the Infinite is
put into me, where the idea of the Infinite commands the mind,
and the word God comes to the tip of the tongue. Inspiration is
thus the prophetic event of the relation to the new. (137)

On the one hand, the idea of the infinite—in its diachrony—has
been deposited in me by God. On the other, the idea of God is infinite—diachronic—and unassemblable in any place. In both cases,
the key to diachrony is ungathering, even to the point of a unique

reciprocity. Only the singular—and there is no singular, the singular is nothing, but it expresses infinitely—can be infinite and diachronic. Diachrony forecloses nothing but the possibility of foreclosure. The new is more new and the past is more past in virtue of diachrony.

In this way, diachrony is the caesura, the wound of forgetting in which the other is recalled by me—infinite responsibility, endless questioning, beyond responsibility and question, endless betrayals. We never know, never know enough, forget in order to know, forget infinitely to be before the other, all in the modality of *perhaps* and *as if*, infinitely betrayed. Exposition is the recalling and the forgetting in which the other's expression multiplies beyond grasping. Diachrony is the rupture that is forgetting itself, time itself.

In this rupture there must be forgetting, and we are responsible for it and to it. To bear witness to the forgotten, to the immemorial and the law. To bear witness and to exterminate, to bear witness in betrayal. In the caesura of diachrony Levinas betrays, forgets and wounds. In the name of the other, whose human radiance he is more conversant with than almost any other, he insists on humanity in the face of animals, insists on philosophy and the concept in the face of artists who remind us of what we have forgotten, rejects science as if it could maintain a monopoly on being, as if it could forget forgetting. Levinas forgets, as he must, and as we must as well. Heidegger forgets, and remembers, in the midst of extermination.

We must bear witness to their forgetting, perhaps to their violence and wounding, in the face of our own betrayals. We must bear witness as if to know their crimes and to acknowledge our own. Most of all—what is most impossible, if impossibility and infinity can be given in the superlative—we must do so joyfully, must bear witness to violence, death, and loss in the diachrony of traumas and wounds—affirmatively, joyously. It is life itself to remember and to forget. It is life itself to be lived in witness to forgetting and remembering. It is to be lived affirmatively because it is the best we can do, all we can do, doing itself. If we can do so.

CHAPTER 11

Inheritance[1]

How does one desire forgetting? How does one desire not to keep? How does one desire mourning (assuming that to mourn, to work at mourning does not amount to keeping . . .)? (Derrida, *GT*, 36)

Jacques Derrida died Friday night, October 8–9, 2004.

Good morning Jacques.

How can the morning be good, your morning, my morning, now that you are dead?

The bells are ringing, Jacques, morning and evening bells, tolling your death. Do they ring of a new day, a new morning? I hope so. We always hope so. In the face of death.

Good mourning Jacques.

How can mourning be good, how can one mourning be better than another, good in the face of death?

Yet we mourn, we living, in the face of death.

I mourn, I who live, in the face of your death.

I am not your intimate, loving friend. Though we met more than once, we never became friends. And yet, was that without love? We know there can be love between enemies, but can there be love between those who are not friends—might one say impersonally? I will have more to say of love.

I confess I never thought about saying goodbye to Jacques Derrida. I did not imagine that he would always live, nor that I would be the first to die. I simply did not think of his death, what it might mean for him to die. For me, perhaps for you and others.

I learned so much from him about inheritance and ghosts—and perhaps that is what I may try to give to you—but little of death. And then I read *The Work of Mourning* and *Archive Fever*, and I was moved at what he wrote, enthralled at what he said, moved to want to say that I was moved. And then he died soon after. So I am moved again, to speak of him to you, perhaps to speak with him, to him.

To speak to him as he spoke of Louis Marin, of his work without measure.

Who could speak of the work of Jacques Derrida?

Who could speak of the death of Derrida?

Who could speak with Jacques Derrida about his work, now that you are gone?

In what language? With what measure?

I learned so much from you about how to think of the dead, to speak to ghosts, to learn from them how to talk with them. As if they were myself. As perhaps you are yourself.

> If it—learning to live—remains to be done, it can happen only between life and death.... What happens ... can only *maintain itself* with some ghost, can only *talk with or about* some ghost.... No *being-with* the other, no *socius* without this *with* that makes *being-with* in general more enigmatic than ever for us. And this being-with specters would also be, not only but also, a *politics* of memory, of inheritance, and of generations. (*SM*, xviii–xix)

> Could one *address oneself in general* if already some ghost did not come back? If he loves justice at least, the "scholar" of the future, the "intellectual" of tomorrow should learn it and from the ghost. He should learn to live by learning not how to make conversation with the ghost but how to talk with him, with her, not to let them speak or how to give them back speech, even it if is in oneself, in the other, in the other in oneself: they are always *there*, specters, even if they do not exist, even if they are no longer, even if they are not yet.
> *Thou art a scholar, speak to it, Horatio.* (176)

This is life itself, living with the dead, otherwise, with those who are never present, whom we can never be with, and yet a being with ghosts that is not only a work of mourning—if that is what it is—but also a politics of memory, inheritance, and generations.

Memory is the return of ghosts. To remember is to speak with ghosts, with them, to them, enigmatically. To recall them, to call them back as ghosts. Almost certainly forgetting, generations and inheritances of forgetting. And you also taught me about inheritance, again in the name of Marx. To inherit is to remember by forgetting.

> one *must assume the inheritance* of Marxism, assume its most "living" part, which is to say, paradoxically, that which continues to

> put back on the drawing board the question of life, spirit, or the spectral, of life-death beyond the opposition between life and death. . . . That we *are* heirs does not mean that we *have* or that we *receive* this or that, some inheritance that enriches us one day with this or that, but that the *being* of what we are *is* first of all inheritance, whether we like it or know it or not. And that, as Hölderlin said so well, we can only *bear witness* to it. To bear witness would be to bear witness to what we *are* insofar as we *inherit*, and that— here is the circle, here is the chance, or the finitude—we inherit the very thing that allows us to bear witness to it. (54)

Life-death beyond life and death. Remembering-forgetting beyond memory and loss. Is this a universal for all humanity, to bear witness to ghosts? For all life and death? For any future? No future without Marx, without you, without your spirits, and others. How can we be sure? How can we count on it?

> There will be no future without this. Not without Marx, no future without Marx, without the memory and the inheritance of Marx: in any case of a certain marx, of his genius, of at least one of his spirits. For this will be our hypothesis or rather our bias: *there is more than one of them, there must be more than one of them.* (13)

One must assume the inheritance of Marx, assume its living part, we who are heirs of Marx. I have pondered the word *must*, how you could be so sure that we *must assume*, as if we had no choice, as if it were by necessity, as if Marx and Marxism could never be forgotten. I am sure that in a thousand years, or a thousand thousand, Marx and you and I will be forgotten, in the plural. I'm sure that someday it will not be a fault not to read Marx—*always* and *forever* are such enormous, grasping words. I'm sure there can be a future without any marx or marxism. And it may not be a bad thing. We will never know it, and those who inherit may disclaim their inheritance.

For we who are heirs inherit nothing in particular, inherit nothing but inheritance itself, bear witness to inheritance. We receive nothing, have nothing, hold onto and possess nothing in particular. That is what the return of the ghost means, *en arrivant*, always in the plural, always more than one: the arrival of the unheralded, the *parousia* of the event, the coming that marks finitude as our becoming. I mean our mortality. "Only mortals, only the living who are not living gods can bury the dead" (174–5). Only mortals can bury and only mortals can mourn. I recall Polyneices' burial, not even below ground. And I remember mass graves, human and animal remains, buried so deep that no one will ever find them in the limits of historical time.

In the living present, Marx's name has become accursed. And to many so has yours. Perhaps what you say of him will be said of you, now that you have become a ghost, more than one, claimed and disclaimed by many families.

> Marx remains an immigrant *chez nous*, a glorious, sacred, accursed but still a clandestine immigrant as he was all of his life. He belongs to a time of disjunction,.... Between earth and sky.... He is not part of the family, but one should not send him back, once again, him too, to the border. (174)

But then, this seems the best we can hope for, the good morning that follows the work of mourning, even hope itself. And you tell us what it means to lose hope, the absolute loss of hope in the denial of forgetting.

> One must constantly remember that the impossible ("to let the dead bury their dead") is, alas, always possible.... One must constantly remember that it is even on the basis of the terrible possibility of this impossible that justice is desirable: *through* but also *beyond* right and law. (175)

In the absolute disaster that is the impossible act—somehow always possible—in which the dead bury the dead, in which there is nothing more to take place, only the return of the dead. Always more than one. Living as the endless return of death. Perhaps.

But it is impossible, and that is what you insist on when you speak of inheritance and mourning.

> The stake that is serving as our guiding thread here, namely, the concept or the schema of the ghost, was heralded long ago, and in its own name, across the problematics of the work of mourning, idealization, simulacrum, *mimesis*, iterability, the double injunction, the "double bind," and undecidability as condition of responsible decision, and so forth. (184)

Not only the ghost—of past, present, and future. Can there be ghosts of the future? I would think so. And hope so. Not only ghosts but the problematics—and the exposition—of the work of mourning, simulation, *mimēsis*. All exposition and iterability—if these are separable. All uncontainable in the gesture of containment.

Founding and conserving is what you say of iterability. Remembering and forgetting is what I say of *mimēsis*, of the image and the simulacrum. The image is always of another image, a first image, an image that founds the proliferation. There is always an original image, and yet the images that proliferate are also original, also originate, also transfigure and transform, no matter how faithful they would be. Faithfulness to the original, faith in the original, is as if it

were faith in the future, faith to an arrival that cannot be anticipated. That is what faith is, in what will become. That is what
mourning must be, faith in what will arrive in the face of death. As
if it were possible. Perhaps.

I remember—it was just a while ago—reading *Archive Fever*,
wondering about its strange name in English. *Mal d'Archive* becomes
Archive Fever, with its hints of feverishness and frenzy. In French
one might take it simply as bad memories, stored up in the archive.
As if some memories were worse, some better than others. Who is to
say? We all say, we all believe we can tell bad from good, worse
from better. Perhaps that is our fever, our feverishness, our frenzy
to outdo the others in our goodness if not our greed. To outdo the
others, is that not what the archive poses as a possibility? No doubt,
then, the fever is not an illness but the impossibility of this possibility. As you say of psychoanalysis and Freud:

> What is at issue here is nothing less than the *future*, if there is
> such a thing: the future of psychoanalysis in its relation to the fu-
> ture of science. . . .
> The questions which now arise are of at least *two orders*. (*AF*,
> 14–5)

As you repeatedly insist, *il y a pas d'un*—there is not one, there is
more than one. At least two without stopping there, higher and
lower. The dyad is indefinite. And who besides you remembers the
dyad at all?

But I was calling attention to the two orders of questions that
you brought to my attention in memory of Freud, of memory in
Freud:

> 1. . . . Is the psychic apparatus *better represented* or is it *affected
> differently* by all the technical mechanisms for archivization and
> for reproduction, for prostheses of so-called live memory, for
> simulacrums of living things which already are, . . . (microcom-
> puting, electronization, computerization, etc.)? . . .
> 2. . . . in what way has the whole of this field been determined
> by a state of the technology of communication and of archiviza-
> tion? One can dream or speculate about the geo-techno-logical
> shocks which would have made the landscape of the psychoana-
> lytic archive unrecognizable for the past century if, to limit myself
> to these indications, Freud, his contemporaries, collaborators and
> immediate disciples, instead of writing thousands of letters by
> hand, had had access to MCI or AT&T telephonic credit cards,
> portable tape recorders, computers, printers, faxes, televisions,
> teleconferences, and above all E-mail.

> ... [T]he technical structure of the archiving archive also de-
> termines the structure of the archivable content. . . . The archiviza-
> tion produces as much as it records the event. This is also our po-
> litical experience of the so-called news media.
>
> This means that, in the past, psychoanalysis would not have
> been what it was (any more than so many other things) if E-mail,
> for example, had existed. And in the future it will no longer be
> what Freud and so many psychoanalysts have anticipated, from
> the moment E-mail, for example, became possible. (15–7)

I am sorry to have taken so long to get back the scene of mourning, but your words are so memorable it is worth recalling them.
Not only is this scene of the archive doubled and redoubled—who
knows how many times, surely more than once?—in relation to the
history of psychoanalysis and to Freud: one might recall the archive
as the place of memory, repression, writing, and of those *hupomnesic*
techniques that mark psychoanalysis in action. The technique and
theory are theories and techniques of memory, one might say of recovering memories and recovering the forgettings that solicit further
recoveries. In addition to this, Freud himself was an archivist, organized his life in collecting. And on top of this, he engaged in correspondences—the entire school, all the psychoanalytic friends engaged in voluminous writings, personal and public—composing the
vast Freudian archives.

So the question you ask of Freud, whether psychoanalysis and
its history would not have been different with the new archival and
recovery prostheses and techniques that now exist, is a question of
its future, of our future, and of the future of Freud. Will we make
something very different of Freud—and other freuds—now that we
have such different technologies of recording, transcribing, and dis-
seminating? It appears that we already have.

If so, then what will we make of you? With all your words, what
will, what have you already become? I speak of you as if you were
somehow dispersed into your words, as if you were not a living person, an agent, as if you did not act. Yet your own words indicate
that acts here are inscriptions, that the mediums and technologies of
inscribing and transmitting compose a history of memories and forgettings. One might think of the archive, then, if we include archivi-
zation and reproduction, as technologies of forgetting. Archive fever
would be the feverishness of the dissemination of the archive, the
feverishness of the transformation of the archive, the frenzy of the
dispersion of the archive. One might call this the future: the future
of the past, which must come to be in bad memories, bad memoriza-
tions, the *bad past*: not because it contained violent, destructive

events, but because the past itself is a violence and a destruction in relation to the future. That is what death is, and it is what every means—archive or memory—of holding tightly onto it repeats: the badness of the death of the past that is the future.

Right now, already, your life is past. Soon mine will be. Later the rest of us. And in that passing, in that passage, your friends, your readers, your followers and heirs—if there be any—will try to remember. They will inherit, as they must, as they may hope to, and in that inheritance they will find that the memories are bad, to hold onto them too tightly is also bad, that as heirs they must make the future good, must make you good for the future even if everyone in the future forgets you or reviles you.

The reviling and the improvement have begun. I would hold them off. Yet perhaps that is not what mourning can do, not what mourning would hope to do. If I hold them off, do I hold you in an archive of good or bad memories, an archive of stable memories or of frenzied transformations? Can I hold them off? Would I want to? What does it matter?

Is it not better, is it not just that souls and bodies wander after they die, passing away not just by disappearing, leaving traces, but moving rapidly to new places? I don't know what better means, but I would insist that every death including yours—perhaps yours especially—is always more than one death, recalled as more than one life. Who is to decide how many? A work of mourning in this way commits a terrible act of violence, whether it be by a *New York Times* obituary writer who hates you or by Mark Taylor who loves you. It pins you down to a moment that is already past. Alive or dead, you have a future. I would give you your future, give you at least one of your futures—there are always more than one—if it were in my power to do so.

I must speak of what you are to me—and, I'm sure, to others: a gift. Your works, your life, have given me joy, much to think about, to admire, to take up, to inherit. You were not much older than me, our works have overlapped more than they have succeeded each other. I hope I have given to you as well. But here that is no matter.

I would like to take up your gift. I would like to take it up as you have laid it down, as an act of giving beyond any gift. For that is how you have insisted upon gifts, that they are impossible because they become an exchange. When we return a gift, when we insist on returning a gift, when others assume that a gift will be returned, when we think of a gift as a gift, it is not a gift and not a giving. It is an exchange, a reciprocity, a bargain and a deal. I will give to you if you will give to me. I will give to you if I get something in

return from somewhere, if not you. Gifts and giving exceed this exchange, exceed every exchange, most of all exceed remembering the
gift as a gift. To remember the gift, to recall giving, is not to give
and not to have been given. And so we must forget.

The giving of which we are speaking, you and I, not to mention
Heidegger and Levinas, is the *Gabe*, the *es gibt*, the generosity of being. It is the giving that you have suggested haunts Heidegger's
writings. What is the giving of being, and how can it belong to exchange?

> For there to be a gift, it is necessary [*il faut*] that the donee not
> give back, amortize, reimburse, acquit himself, enter into a con-
> tract, that he never have contracted a debt. . . . It is thus necessary,
> at the limit, that he not recognize the gift as gift. If he recognizes it
> as gift, if the gift appears to him as such, if the present is present
> to him as present, this simple recognition suffices to annul the
> gift. . . . The temporalization of time . . . always sets in motion the
> process of a destruction of the gift: through keeping, restitution,
> reproduction, the anticipatory expectation or apprehension that
> grasps or comprehends in advance.
> . . . By its very appearance the simple phenomenon of the gift
> annuls it as gift, transforming the apparition into a phantom and
> the operation into a simulacrum. (*GT*, 13–4)

You and I have written repeatedly on giving and the gift, on a
giving that is the impossibility of the gift, of the giving—of being, of
nature, of art, life, and death—that is the impossibility of taking and
holding and receiving the gift. The gift is nothing, has to be nothing,
it must be possible to receive the gift of nothing, receive the gift as
nothing—yes, giving the gift as if it were nothing is the very possibility of giving. This nothing of the giving exceeds everything: giving is the excess of everything and nothing.

In this way I would affirm your impossible gesture, that to affirm the gift as a gift is for it not to be a gift. It seems that affirmation destroys the gift. But if affirmation belongs to giving, and is
untied from every gift, every thing or act or word bestowed, then
the impossibility is the giving itself. The gift always returns to exchange, but giving does not, cannot, because when it is reciprocated
nothing is given. I give to you—nothing, nothing to remember. You
give to me—nothing, nothing in particular, no word or thing or gift
that would give to someone else. The giving of which I speak—
beyond the gift—is the gift of being in abundance, which is nothing
to remember but to forget. Being, the earth, nature, the world in
abundance is given as if from the good, always in the mode of *as if*:
as if giving, as if received, as if given in gifts, as if forgotten. There

is nothing given to remember, and everything in abundance. That perhaps is what you have given me—as if it were nothing and everything. As if that were love.

I have spoken of what I have received from you—perhaps nothing. Your life is a gift to me, your works have given joy to me—perhaps in no particular way. Here, where I would remember you and mourn you, I would recall what you say of forgetting, returning us to the giving of being beyond beings.

> For there to be gift, not only must the donor or donee not perceive or receive the gift as such, have no consciousness of it, no memory, no recognition; he or she must also forget it right away....
>
> So we are speaking here of an absolute forgetting—a forgetting that also absolves, that unbinds absolutely and infinitely more, therefore, than excuse, forgiveness, or acquittal.... The thought of this radical forgetting as thought of the gift should accord with a certain experience of the *trace* as *cinder* or *ashes* in the sense in which we have tried to approach it elsewhere. (16–7)

I intend to follow the path you have opened much further toward forgetting, absolutely and in absolution, yet I must pause to note that you insist that such forgetting is infinitely beyond and more than forgiveness, which I understand to be infinitely beyond and more than excuse and acquittal. Forgiveness is not absolving sin but giving beyond measure: in our language, absolute, infinite giving beyond gifts. It does not matter if it evokes a god—or does not. What matters is that it is giving and giving knows no gift.

Here is an oblique example:

> The death of a child that was the daily delight of its mother's eyes, and joy of her soul, rends from her heart the whole comfort of her life, and gives her all the torment imaginable: .... Till time has by disuse separated the sense of that enjoyment and its loss, from the idea of the child returning to her memory, all representations, though ever so reasonable, are in vain; and therefore some in whom the union between these ideas is never dissolved, spend their lives in mourning, and carry an incurable sorrow to their graves. (Locke, *E*, 532)

Locke assumes that it would be better if the mother got over her loss. For whom, I would ask, and in what ways? The loss of a child is a terrible loss. Why should we assume that it is better not to grieve.

Yet there is a gift the mother can give—again it is nothing in particular, nothing to hold onto or to exchange. She can give her life back to herself though she cannot give her child's. She can forgive the death, forgive the world, forgive herself, in a giving that accomplishes nothing, has nothing to accomplish, and that cannot be defended. Forgiveness here is what its name says: a giving beyond all limits.

I give you this example in memory of what you say of forgiving as well as in memory of your mother.

> 4 ... why I wonder, confide to the bottom of this book what were my mother's last more or less intelligible sentences, still alive at the moment I am writing this, but already incapable of memory, in any case of the memory of my name, a name become for her at the very least unpronounceable, and I am writing here at the moment when my mother no longer recognizes me, and at which, still capable of speaking or articulating, a little, she no longer calls me and for her and therefore for the rest of her life I no longer have a name, that's what's happening, ... (Derrida, C, 22)

> 12 I have not yet closed her eyes but she will not see me again, whereas I see her eyes wide open, for my mother can no longer see, I had forgotten to say so, she can hardly see now, one can't really tell, her gaze no longer focuses, scarcely following the direction of the voices, less and less every day, ... I always ask what the theory is a symptom of and I admit that I write with the price on, I display, not so that the price be legible to the first-comer, for I am for an aristocracy without distinction, therefore without vulgarity, for a democracy of the compulsion to the highest price, you have to pay the price to read the price displayed, one writes only at the moment of giving the contemporary the slip, with a word, the word for word, you'll see, giving the slip to all those I've just named, ... (C, 12, 60–4)

You speak of price here, facing the death of your mother—a very different work of mourning, Jacques, different for all. Perhaps closer to our own sensibility and mortality than the others for whom you do work. Perhaps we do not do the work of mourning for our mothers, fathers, brothers, sisters, but for ourselves as for them. Perhaps for some death is a gift beyond price.

Your mother does not see, soon she will not speak, alive she will be silent. You will speak, I am speaking, word after word. Are we no more than a family of words, each family for us, of words? Are we always, perhaps, too many words?

One writes only at the moment of giving the slip, with a word, the word for word. Giving the slip—is that the impossible gift, giving beyond gifts, forgiving beyond them all? It does not seem so. Right here before the death of your mother, is it possible that you, like Locke's grieving mother, abandon all justifications and words, replace them with something beyond words, still insisting on words?

Or if not words, insisting on speaking somehow, showing and revealing somehow, the meaningless meaning and priceless price of
death. Of course I mean life. Life goes on in an impossible giving
beyond words, beyond anything and everything, in the caesura between life and death.

> In principle, there is no limit to forgiveness, no measure, no
> moderation, no "to what point?" Provided, of course, that we
> agree on some "proper" meaning of this word. Now, what do we
> call "forgiveness?" What calls for "forgiveness?" Who calls for,
> who calls upon forgiveness? (CF, 27)

> each time forgiveness is at the service of a finality, be it noble and
> spiritual (atonement or redemption, reconciliation, salvation),
> each time that it aims to re-establish a normality (social, national,
> political, psychological) by a work of mourning, by some therapy
> or ecology of memory, then the "forgiveness" is not pure—nor is
> its concept![2] (CF, 31–2)

I'll have more to say of this in another time and place. I'll stay
here with forgetting, not just because my present work is in the
name of forgetting, but because of the question of forgetting you.
Who will remember you and how? How will you be forgotten and
by whom? Who will give you the gift of remembering you, who will
forget you in a giving beyond remembering?

And it is forgetting of which we are speaking, not nothing. If
nothing is anything at all, anything to speak of. As if I did not speak
of it before.

> And yet we say "forgetting" and not nothing. Even though it
> must leave nothing behind it, even though it must efface every-
> thing, including the traces of repression, this forgetting, this for-
> getting of the gift cannot be a simple non-experience, a simple
> non-appearance, a self-effacement that is carried off with what it
> effaces. For there to be gift event (we say event and not act), some-
> thing must come about or happen, in an instant, in an instant that
> no doubt does not belong to the economy of time, in a time with-
> out time, in such a way that the forgetting forgets, that it forgets
> *itself*, but also in such a way that this forgetting, without being
> something present, presentable, determinable, sensible or mean-
> ingful, is not nothing. . . . Far from giving us to think the possibil-
> ity of the gift, on the contrary, it is on the basis of what takes
> shape in the name *gift* that one could hope thus to think forget-
> ting. For there to be forgetting in this sense, there must be gift.
> The gift would also be the *condition* of forgetting. (GT, 18–9)

I apologize again for taking so much space, repeating so many of
your words, which you must know by heart—unless you have forgot-

ten. I needed all these words to say from myself what I would say to you, of you and with you, in your memory. For not only do you speak of absolute forgetting, and of forgetting forgetting, but you link forgetting with the giving of being in the name of Heidegger. So the event of absolute forgetting appears in memory of Heidegger. Perhaps a work of mourning. But you do not stop there, for the absolute forgetting beyond forgetting also appears in memory of Blanchot.

> This detour was meant first of all to remind us that the forgetting we're talking about, if it is constitutive of the gift, is no longer a category of the psyche. It cannot be unrelated to the forgetting of Being, in the sense in which Blanchot also says, more or less, that forgetting is another name of Being. (22)

In its way this return of forgetting to being—absolute, radical, extreme—seems an utter loss. The loss I speak of is not of philosophy, as if we have lost the concepts of forgetting and of Being. We might never have had them, they might never have been something to have, they might be recalled only to be forgotten. The losses I speak of are first the name *Levinas*, for whom the forgotten is the good; and second yours, the name *Derrida*. For it appears very late in your life and under your name for this most radical thought to be the thought of being.

Indeed, what follows this extreme thought in your text—so extreme that I've almost forgotten it—is a repetition of something we've heard before:

> As the condition for a gift to be given, this forgetting must be radical not only on the part of the donee but first of all, if one can say here first of all, on the part of the donor. It is also on the part of the donor "subject" that the gift not only must not be repaid but must not be kept in memory, retained as symbol of a sacrifice, as symbolic in general. (23)

Moreover, at this moment there appears a break between giving and forgetting. For you do not mention forgetting again till thirteen pages later, in the next chapter, with a little madness:

> Only an *atopic* and *utopic* madness, *perhaps* (a certain *perhaps* or *maybe* will be both the modality and the modality to be modified or our meditation), could thus give rise to the gift that can give only on the condition of not taking place, taking up residence or domicile: *the gift may be, if there is any.*
> This madness, let us recall, would also be that of a forgetting, of a given and desired forgetting, not as a negative experience therefore, like an amnesia and a loss of memory, but as the affirmative condition of the gift.... How does one desire forgetting?

How does one desire not to keep?...here we touch on what remains no doubt the unavoidable problem of mourning, of the relation between gift and grief, between what should be non-work,
the non-work of the gift, and the work of mourning)? How does
one desire forgetting or the non-keeping of the gift if, implicitly,
the gift is evaluated as good, indeed as the very origin of what is
good, of the good, and of value? (35–6)

In your spirit, then, some questions:

How does one desire forgetting?
How does one forget forgetting?
How does one desire mourning?
Is it to desire death?
Is mourning keeping or giving?
How does one give beyond gifts?
What is the good that gives?
What is good about giving?
What is the relation between giving and grieving?
Is this the same as between receiving and inheriting?
Is this the caesura between life and death?

I do not think either of us will answer these questions. If we
have not done so already it is probably too late. But perhaps such
questions are not to answer but to give, to keep open, to forget in
the spirit of remembering. Perhaps we need, in the face of death—
and your death stares me in the face—to mourn and to grieve without holding on to death, without holding on to the past. To mourn
and to grieve as if to give the gift of life, as if giving being, to ourselves and to the others. Would this be absolute forgetting?

And if we knew this forgetting, if we knew a gift as a gift, if we
were required—by whom? by what?—to forget it as gift, would forgetting that forgetting be as if to return it as giving? Is this what it
would be to desire forgetting, as if to wish to return to the gifts of
giving, all the while desiring what is beyond any gift?

I would turn from gift and forgetfulness to exposition, to exposure and expression—otherwise to *mimēsis* and art. I don't mean to
turn from you to Levinas. To the contrary, I find myself frequently
recalling Levinas only to remember you in a gesture of forgetting—
which is, of course, a work of mourning. For Levinas and now for
you. For both of you grief and mourning mean something I have not
spoken of till now, that for some time he has not been able to tell me
what he thinks about what I say. And now you are also silent. This
forgetting approaches the absolute of forgetting, forgetting what
you never had a chance to say, never perhaps came to think or re-

member. Forgetting forgetting is in this case living finitely. That is yours. Mine is another forgetting—it cannot be remembering—of the forgetting that you forgot.

Is this death?

Is this mourning?

Is the desire for death and mourning the same as the desire for finiteness, the desire—in Levinas's words again—for the infinite in the finite, still finite? The infinite desire for what in the finite exceeds its finiteness? Mourning then would have to be a repetition—and return—of desire for the finite and for what in it exceeds its finitude. To come, you say so frequently. And always more than one. The work of mourning then is the affirmation—in the grief—of finiteness. And it is affirmative—I mean finiteness itself is affirmative of what in it is beyond it: the other, what is to come, trauma, loss, even death. All this is giving beyond any gifts. The gifts are given—for example, the books and essays and words you have written, the presentations you have given. What is in them is beyond any gifts. Life itself Nietzsche insists. And learn to laugh. Laugh at death, not to make it any less death—that would be another death—but to affirm life.

Is this mourning? Is this the giving beyond being—as the good Levinas reminds us of Plato saying—beyond good and bad, life and death? Giving is not good or bad, life and death are not good or bad. But they are for giving, affirming, acquiescing. In the name of *Zusage*:

> No response, no responsibility, will ever abolish the *perhaps*. The perhaps must open and precede, once and for all, the questioning it suspends in advance—not to neutralize or inhibit, but to make possible all the determined and determining orders that depend on questioning....
>
> For example:
>
> 1. By recalling this acquiescence (*Zusage*) more originary than the question which, without saying *yes* to anything positive, can affirm the possibility of the future only by opening itself up to determinability, thus by welcoming what still remains undetermined and indeterminable.... the perhaps of what *remains* to be thought, to be done, to be lived (to death)....
>
> 2. By specifying recurrently: "if there is one," .... What there is, if there is one or any, *is* not necessarily. It perhaps does not *exist* nor ever *present* itself; nevertheless, there is one, or some; there is a chance of there being one, of there being some. (*PF*, 38–9)

Right here there is one and more than one. Several ways are given as two ways. And in doing this, other figures of *perhaps* and *as if* betray themselves. For example, the *pharmakon*, that word in Greek that means too much, that exceeds any meaning it might be given.[3] Many shaped and colored. Always more than one. The sophist's art is "a great and many-sided art (*technē*)" (Plato, *Sophist*, 223c); the sophist a "many-sided (*poikilos*: many-colored, manifold, diverse, changeable) animal (*thērion*), and not to be caught with one hand, as they say" (226a). This manyness is not a multiplicity but is as if it were indefinitely many—perhaps. Beyond presence, beyond re-membering, there is forgetting, there are one or some with a chance of being forgotten.

And again, this is affirmative, this is affirmation, forgetting is the affirmative not the negative condition of the gift. The gift is good, the giving is good beyond good and bad. Affirmation beyond affirmation. Forgetting is affirmative and it must be forgotten to be affirmed at least once and more.

Does this give us mourning as forgiveness, give the affirmation of death as forgiveness? Here as always you have much to say:

> the question of the gift will never be separated from that of mourning:
>
>> ...I pretend to keep the dead alive, intact *safe* (*save*) in-side me, but it is only in order to refuse, in a necessarily equivocal way, to love the dead as a living part of me, dead *save in me*, through the process of introjection, as happens in so-called normal mourning.... This ques-tion—of the general appropriation or safekeeping of the other *as other*—...does it not at the same time blur the very line it draws between introjection and incorporation, through an essential and irreducible ambiguity? (*GT*, 129n13; quoted from *F*, xvi–xvii)

Let us imagine the work of mourning as forgiveness *in a necessarily equivocal way*; to love the dead *in me*, to recall the dead *as mine*; where the other—and it is a question of the other—must refuse the preservation and the possession. Let us say by forgetting. To mourn is to remember, to grasp, to hold onto the dead and at the same time, inseparably—more than one, more than once—to refuse and to forget.

I must give up the rest of *Given Time* to take on the work of mourning, your work of mourning. So let me summarize the rest of this incredible text. What happens is that forgetfulness—the most radical experience of the gift—is straightaway forgotten. What takes its place is forgiveness. If this is Baudelaire it is also Derrida. In what remains of *Given Time* are extended discussions of forgiveness but fewer than ten references to forgetting, of which the most prolonged remains on the gift and Being—I mean what is beyond Being: *epekeina tes ousias*:

> So as not to take over the other, the overtaking by surprise of the pure gift should have the generosity to give nothing that surprises and appears as gift, *nothing that presents itself as present, nothing that is*; it should therefore be surprising enough and so thoroughly made up of a surprise that it is not even a question of getting over it, thus of a surprise surprising enough to let itself be forgotten without delay. And at stake in this forgetting that carries beyond any present is the gift as remaining [*restance*] without memory, ... (147)

Forgetting is beyond forgiving as it is beyond being. Yet of course, I would say—this is my mark of mourning—that forgiveness is pure giving, not in the sense that it should have no mark and be surprising but in that it be nothing more or less than giving—to the dead, to the living, to you and to me and to the others.

I said that it was time for me to begin the work of mourning with you, to begin to work with your own work of mourning. You do not speak with any of the ghosts you mourn, do not speak to them or with them, but of them. I have spoken of you to you, a presumption I hope you do not mind—I'm sure it is too late for you to mind. I mean to mourn you with you in front of the others. But perhaps I might recall some additional words of yours to ask the question of you yourself. For I have not asked for whom I mourn, for whom I speak, what is the mourning for? Let me ask you who you are? Your oblique answer seems to me to be a remarkable word on the name in mourning, perhaps your name and my mourning. And of course another morning.

This is what you said of Europe:

> I am European, I am no doubt a European intellectual, and I like to recall this, I like to recall this to myself, and why would I deny it? In the name of what? But I am not, nor do I feel, European in every part, that is, European through and through. . . . My cultural identity, that in the name of which I speak, is not only European, it is not identical to itself, and I am not "cultural" through and through, "cultural" in every part.
>
> . . . It is up to the others, in any case, and up to me among them, to decide. (*OH*, 82–3)

Might I say this of you or of me?
You are Jacques Derrida.
Are you he through and through?
Are you he in every part?
Is it up to the others to decide—perhaps to me and to you?

If it is up to any of us, if it is a matter of decision or of memory. Perhaps it is up to us to forget. To forget and to mourn, to forget and to forgive. Under what proper name? More of this later.

Now it is time for me to work with you on mourning. I would begin by asking what you—not Freud—mean by work, why mourning calls for work? I take it you mean *work* and *working* in their many guises, from labor and struggle to building and constructing. Perhaps the work of mourning is an edifice we construct to mourn—in memoriam, a funereal place. If so, then it would seem to be someone's duty to deconstruct the edifice, to unbuild the work, to forget its memory, to bring us back, perhaps, to the death it was built upon, that it covered over.

Perhaps the work of mourning is just that, mourning, grief, loss, death. Less active than working, as excessive as giving. Closer to the terms in which Levinas speaks of our exposure to the face of the other: vulnerability, hostage, passivity beyond passivity, separation, substitution. Here mourning cannot be a work and cannot be the labor of work, but is a generosity of giving in which the other presents itself in its mortality to me in my grief. There is nothing active—no work or working—that I can do or say—you speak repeatedly of the speechlessness of this work—to answer to the other. I would say in suffering as well as mortality, in the pain of the other. The other appears to me in grief and mourning in the heart of friendship. If the other is my friend.[4]

Here is what Pascale-Anne Brault and Michael Naas say of friendship and mourning, beginning with a few of your words, as if in mourning. And while they knew that you were mortal, they did not know when you would die, could not do their own work of mourning:

> *Philia* begins with the possibility of survival. Surviving—
> that is the other name of a mourning whose possibility is
> never to be awaited. (*Politics of Friendship*)
>
> One must always go before the other. In the *Politics of Friendship*, Jacques Derrida demonstrates that this is the law of friendship—and thus of mourning. One friend must always go before the other; one friend must always die first. There is no friendship without the possibility that one friend will die before the other, perhaps right before the other's eyes. For even when friends die together, or rather, at the same time, their friendship will have been structured from the very beginning by the possibility that one of the two would see the other die, and so, surviving, would be left to bury, to commemorate, and to mourn. (*WM*, 1)

It is interesting—to me at least—that this is a law of *friendship* and not of death, that they bring the subject of death—and of philosophy—back to friendship, where philosophy has always maintained it, worked with and contained it—so to speak *carnophallogocentrically*. It is interesting that this is friendship and not community, love, humanity; that it seems personal, singular, ethical where they appear public, affective, universal. For of course they are not, they are as personal, singular, ethical as is friendship, and it is as public, affective, universal—if anything be universal—as are they, including death and mourning.

I would talk of grief in relation to love. I would imagine that mourning and grief take place where there are no friends—and as *The Politics of Friendship* endlessly repeats: *Oh my friends, there are no friends.* Oh my loved ones, who have lived with me, there is no love, and there is no life, there is only death. Oh my dead, there is no death.

Jacques Derrida's work of mourning—his work, his words—is addressed to friends. I am old enough to have seen friends die. I have never been offered the chance to speak, publicly or privately, of my grief toward those I loved most in a work of mourning. I am speaking of my mother and my stepmother, and of my closest friends. I was not there, I did not speak, no one asked me to speak or write, I participated in other ways. And yes, there are other ways, too many to count, and we can be sure there are more than one. If there is one. If there are any.

These last words—if there is one, if there are any, there is always at least one—speak of life and death. They are Derrida's words, yet they do not compose the work of mourning. For example, there was only one Michel Foucault, only one Gilles Deleuze, only one Jacques Derrida. Derrida would say, if there is one, there is at least one, a chance that there is more than one. The one Jacques Derrida may be *plus d'un*, more than, not only one derrida. We mourn you for what in you is more than you. As you say, it is up to us to decide.

How then can there be a *law* of friendship? What kind of law might there be in relation to death that tells us when and how to mourn when we are friends? Is there no mourning, no grief, when enemies die? Is there no loss for us here in knowing that the Sudanese and Ugandans are killing and being killed? Does the bell toll only for my friends?—and are there friends, are you and I friends, am I friends with strangers across the sea? Am I your friend, and if I am not, am I permitted to mourn? May I, must I, work on mourning, work harder on mourning, mourn without working if I am not your friend?

I am struggling with the law of friendship as described by your friends. What you say is the following, reminding us that you have Aristotle in mind:

> (We are striving to speak here in the logic of Aristotle's two *Eth-ics*, ...) . . . .
>
> If *philia* lives, and if it lives at the extreme limit of its possibility, it therefore *lives*, it stirs, it becomes *psychic* from within this resource of survival. This *philia*, this *psukhē* between friends, survives. . . .
>
> . . . This time of surviving thus gives the time of friendship.
>
> But such a time gives itself in its withdrawal. *It comes only through self-effacement.* (PF, 14)
>
> Friendship, the being-friend—what is that, anyway? Well, it is to love *before* being loved. (8–9)

Perhaps there are no friends and yet all of us may be friends, all of us may love each other, love may know no bounds. Not grief and sorrow and loss and mourning. Each death, each life, each bell is mine, and yours, and ours. Not in the sense that we are a community, that we are all human together, not even that we are all going to die. Death and mourning and humanity are not commonalities, even as they may be universalities. They mark the singular and unique reality of each person and thing.

Why do death and grief mark this uniquely? Why not life and work—not just the work of mourning, Jacques, but your work, the work you describe so eloquently?

> By preferring my work, simply by giving it my time and attention, by preferring my activity as a citizen or as a professorial and professional philosopher, writing and speaking here in a public language, French in my case, I am perhaps fulfilling my duty. But I am sacrificing and betraying at every moment all my other obligations: my obligations to the other others whom I know or don't know, the billions of my fellows (without mentioning the animals that are even more other others than my fellows), my fellows who are dying of starvation or sickness. . . .
>
> I can respond only to the one (or to the One), that is, to the other, by sacrificing that one to the other. I am responsible to any one (that is to say to any other) only by failing in my responsibilities to all the others, to the ethical or political generality. And I can never justify this sacrifice, I must always hold my peace about it. . . . How would you ever justify the fact that you sacrifice all the cats in the world to the cat that you feed at home every morning

for years, whereas other cats die of hunger at every instant? Not to mention other people? . . . There is no language, no reason, no generality or mediation to justify this ultimate responsibility which leads me to absolute sacrifice; . . . . (*GD*, 69–71)

Tout autre est tout autre. As you say, every other is altogether other. Always more than one, always wholly other. Every responsibility betrays.

As you also say, in a double gesture toward animals, eating meat and animal sacrifice:

> Discourses as original as those of Heidegger and Levinas disrupt, of course, a certain traditional humanism. In spite of the differences separating them, they nonetheless remain profound humanisms *to the extent that they do not sacrifice sacrifice*. The subject (in Levinas's sense) and the *Dasein* are "men" in a world where sacrifice is possible and where it is not forbidden to make an attempt on life in general, but only on human life, on the neighbor's life, on the other's life as *Dasein*. (*EW*, 279).

And again, a supreme gesture of betrayal:

> The one does violence to itself, and guards itself against the other. (*PF*, ix)

The one, you, your work, every act, every exposition, in betrayal. Remembering, knowing, recalling, being, betray and betray betrayal. Is that not the task of life, with the work of mourning, to sacrifice sacrifice, to betray betrayal, to forget forgetting?

Last chapter I attended to the cats, to the sacrifice of animals you describe as *carnophallogocentrism*, the virility of the *polis*. Here I would attend to the work, your work. It is remarkable work. May I mourn you, in friendship or something else, for your work as well as for your life? Would I turn your life, the singular life of Jacques Derrida, into a work for me to work with? How could I avoid doing so? Would it be to forget you? Might I find a way to forget that forgetting? Would it not be as just an opening—we know that justice cannot be measured, nor the size of the opening here to the future—as hospitality to the *arrivant*?

> Awaiting without horizon of the wait, awaiting what one does not expect yet or any longer, hospitality without reserve, welcoming salutation accorded in advance to the absolute surprise of the *arrivant* from whom or from which one will not ask anything in return and who or which will not be asked to commit to the domestic contracts of any welcoming power. . . . It would be easy, too easy, to show that such a hospitality without reserve . . . is the impossible itself, and that this *condition of possibility* of the event is

also its *condition of impossibility*, like this strange concept of messianism without content, of the messianic without messianism, that guides us here like the blind. but it would be just as easy to show that without this experience of the impossible, one might as well give up on both justice and the event. (*SM*, 65)

> What is going to come, *perhaps*, is not only this or that; it is at last the thought of the *perhaps*, the *perhaps* itself. The *arrivant* will arrive *perhaps*, for one must never be sure when it comes to *arrivance*; but the *arrivant* could also be the *perhaps itself*, the unheard-of, totally new experience of the *perhaps*. (*PF*, 29)

I appear to be digressing, yet perhaps not so far. For would it not be easy to show that mourning—death and grief and loss and wounding—is the impossible of life, and that this condition of possibility is also its condition of impossibility? And, moreover, would it not be easy to show that without the experience of death and mourning one might as well give up on life? Perhaps.

What experience? What death? What mourning? What work? Is that the question? Who is to say? Who is to expose the possibilization of the impossible possible?

The editors—I do not need to repeat their names—say repeatedly that Derrida's work of mourning belongs to a genre.

> While these texts vary greatly in form, from letters of condolence addressed to family members to eulogies read at the grave site, from words of tribute first published in newspapers in the hours immediately following a death to memorial essays read at colloquia a few or even many months after the death, and while any rigorous analysis of these texts would have to reckon with all the differences in tone, style, audience, and context, these texts are nonetheless part of a recognizable genre, even if there is no single apt term to describe it. . . . Eulogizing the singularity of the friend, he has tried to inhabit and inflect both the concept and the genre of mourning differently. He has tried to reinvent, always in public and always in context, that is, always from within, a better politics of mourning. (18)

Perhaps this is what you mean by the *work* of mourning—at least one of its meanings: the genre of the eulogy, the production of a commemoration, perhaps a better politics of mourning? What in the world would that be—a better? politics? of death? As you say,

> *To learn to live*: a strange watchword. Who would learn? From whom? To teach to live, but to whom? Will we ever know? Will we ever know how to live and first of all what "to learn to live" means? . . .

> If it—learning to live—remains to be done, it can happen only
> between life and death. . . . with some ghost. . . . (*SM*, xviii–xix)[5]

If living takes place between life and death, with some ghost,
then what can it be but mourning? And if it is a politics of memory,
inheritance, and generations, what can it be but forgetting? Yet is
this ethics of mourning a better ethics, is this politics of memory a
better politics, is better what we demand from life and death? Is that
what giving and working and forgetting require? Is this what the
genre of funereality solicits?

Is this your work of mourning? I am sure it is not mine. A "better politics of mourning" is not your choice of words.

> Derrida lays out not so much a middle ground as a series of apo-
> rias, ...
>
> Derrida suggests that it is only "in us" that the dead may
> speak, that it is only by speaking of or as the dead that we can
> keep them alive. . . .
>
> Fidelity thus consists in mourning, and mourning—at least in
> a first moment—consists in interiorizing the other and recognizing
> that if we are to give the dead anything it can now be only in us,
> the living. . . . "the image commonly used to characterize mourning
> is that of an interiorization (an idealizing incorporation, introjec-
> tion, consumption of the other)" (159). (9–10)

Under the heading of introjection—if that can be a heading, an
other heading—some of your most poignant observations on mortality and forgetting can be incorporated. I am speaking again of carnophallogocentrism, the space in which pure language, pure memory, join in a tradition in which women and animals are forgotten.
Forgotten here does not mean unremembered, it means recalled as if
to forget their humanity, their subjectivity and mortality, remembered to devour and to kill.

You ask us to unforget them.

> in Heidegger . . . the animal will never be either a subject or a
> *Dasein*. . . . It is from the standpoint of *Dasein* that Heidegger de-
> fines the humanity of man. (*EW*, 261)
>
> I have spoken of the "yes, yes," of the "[to?] come" or of the
> affirmation that is not addressed first of all to a subject. This
> vigil . . . leads us to recognize the processes of differance, trace, it-
> erability, ex-appropriation, and so on. These are at work every-
> where, which is to say, well beyond humanity. (274)
>
> it suffices to take seriously the idealizing interiorization of the
> phallus and the necessity of its passage through the mouth,
> whether it's a matter of words or things, of sentences, of daily

bread or wine, of the tongue, the lips, or the breast of the other. People are going to object: there are ethical, juridical, and political subjects (recognized only quite recently, as you well know), full (or almost full) citizens who are also women and/or vegetarians! But this has been admitted in principle, and in rights, only recently and precisely at the moment when the concept of subject enters into deconstruction. Is this fortuitous? And that which I am calling here *schema* or image, that which links the concept to intuition, installs the virile figure at the determinative center of the subject.

...I would ask you: in our countries, who would stand any chance of becoming a *chef d'État* (a head of State), and of thereby acceding "to the head," by publicly, and therefore exemplarily, declaring him- or herself to be a vegetarian? (280–1)

You ask us to remember animals and women as the forgotten of our culture—and, perhaps, of human culture as such. You ask us to keep in mind that we cannot remember all of them and remember any, cannot feed one cat without not feeding all the other cats of the world. This impossibility is not the same as the inescapability of forgetting—animals in the name of meat, women in the name of virility. And so you wonder, at least for women, what it might be for a culture, our culture, to remember women, for women not to be the forgotten. For example, in *The Gift of Death*, speaking of the story of Abraham and of Bartleby the scrivener:

It is difficult not to be struck by the absence of woman in these two monstrous yet banal stories. . . . Would the logic of sacrificial responsibility within the implacable universality of the law, of its law, be altered, inflected, attenuated, or displaced, if a woman were to intervene in some consequential manner? (75–6)

Where you describe a certain act of hospitality:

In the name of hospitality, all the men are sent a woman, to be precise, a concubine. The guest, the "master" of the woman, picked up his knife, took hold of his concubine, and limb by limb cut her into twelve pieces; then he sent her all through the land of Israel. . . . And all who saw it declared, "Never has such a thing been done or been seen since the Israelites came out of the land of Egypt."

Are we the heirs to this tradition of hospitality? Up to what point? Where should we place the invariant, if it is one, across this logic and these narratives? They testify without end in our memory. (*H*, 155)

Are we heirs to a tradition in which hospitality to men, no matter how terrible, is enacted violently on the bodies of women?

Under the heading of temptation—if that can be a heading, perhaps an other heading—you have something different to say of the
aporia—if it is one, perhaps of the caesura. In *The Politics of Friendship*, if not in the face of death, you say it differently. No aporia, no
choice, no law, the temptation of the madness in the caesura. You
are speaking of the political. Elsewhere I have imagined you to be
speaking of the aesthetic. Here I am sure you are speaking of forgetting.

> 1. *Either* to admit that the political is in fact this phallogocen-
> trism in act. . . .
> 2. *Or else* keep the "old name," . . .
> If there were a single thesis to this essay, it would posit that
> there could be no choice: . . . .[6] (158–59)

Can this be transcribed as a work of mourning?

> 1. *Either* to admit that death is in fact this phallogocentrism
> in act. . . . Women slowly are released from presiding over death
> and become living subjects, living beyond death. Who would
> swear that this is not in progress?
> 2. *Or else* keep the old name of death but understand it dif-
> ferently in relation to life.

Or in witness to forgetting?

> 1. *Either* to admit that forgetting is a crime, and through
> memory establish women and other creatures of the earth as full
> subjects.
> 2. *Or else* keep the old names of memory and forgetting, and
> engage other forms of struggle for human ideals.

In both cases, and between them, there is no such choice. But there
is the temptation to choose:[7]

> [W]e have stressed the performative force which had to prevail in
> both versions of a sentence which in any case, in addressing an-
> other, could not count on any assurance, any purely theoretical
> criterion of intelligibility or accord; it *could not* count on such as-
> surance, but above all *it had to* and *desired not to want* to count on
> such an assurance, which would destroy in advance the possibility
> of addressing the other as such. (217–20)

There is the temptation to imagine a pure memory or forgetting or
humanity free from betrayal, and in that imagination and purity
emerge another betrayal, madness, and impurity.
    In the name of betrayal I would recall some of your other writ-
ings:

The one does violence to itself, and guards itself against the other. (*PF*, ix)

Every other (one) is every (bit) other. (*GD*, 68)

Philosophy has always insisted upon this: thinking its other. Its other: that which limits it, and from which it derives its essence, its definition, its production. To think its other: does this amount solely to *relever (aufheben)* that from which its derives, to head the procession of its method only by passing the limit? Or indeed does the limit, obliquely, by surprise, always reserve one more blow for philosophical knowledge? (*T*, x–xi)

Philosophy, life, and death; you and I; we insist on guarding the limit, thinking the other that limits us, which comes back as the forgotten.

I would speak with you, Jacques, but I am mortal. I must speak to you, of you, after, in my language. I would leave you, Jacques, with the following words—for us, no doubt, and not for you. *We will forget you.* Or at least, *they will forget you.* You will be forgotten, some day, somehow. And that is not after all so bad. Because you may also be remembered. The arrival of what is to come will come as it does, as it must, remembering and forgetting what it can and what it has no control over. That is death. It is what we mourn. And still we laugh.

I will say good night, as well as good morning. I do not know what I have done for you, if anything, but I know what you have done for me and what I would do with you.

Good morning Jacques. Good mourning Jacques. I'm sad that you are gone. I'm glad that you lived. I will miss you.

> Physical pain has no voice, but when it at last finds a voice, it begins to tell a story, and the story that it tells is about the inseparability of these three subjects, their embeddedness in one another.[1] (Scarry, *BP*, 3)

*P*hysical pain has no voice—perhaps psychic pain as well, perhaps joy as well as suffering, perhaps we seek a voice when we have no voice, when voice is inaudible, difficult to hear or know. Perhaps we're never secure in our voice, uncertain of what we have to say, of what others have to say. Perhaps pain gives us—physical, psychic, bodily, mental pain—an urgency to speak, an imperative to remember. We must tell of our pain, of our suffering, we and justice demand it. We may have no corresponding urgency in speaking of love and joy, of *jouissance*. The poet will tell, and if not, that is no injustice, only a lack, if for many a compulsion.

Who would imagine that we could tell all of terrible crimes, that we might remember everything to tell? As "the SS militiamen enjoyed cynically admonishing the prisoners":

> However this war may end, we have won the war against you; none of you will be left to bear witness, but even if someone were to survive, the world will not believe him ... because we will destroy the evidence together with you. And even if some proof should remain and some of you survive, people will say that the events you describe are too monstrous to be believed: they will ... believe us, who will deny everything, and not you. We will be the ones to dictate the history of the Lagers. (Levi, *DS*, 11–2)

> Almost all the survivors, orally or in their written memoirs, remember a dream which frequently recurred during the nights of

> imprisonment, varied in its detail but uniform in its substance: they had returned home and with passion and relief were describing their past sufferings, addressing themselves to a loved one, and were not believed, indeed were not even listened to. (12)

We have encountered this thought before in a different context.[2] This is too strange to be believed, I do not believe it, others will not believe it even if it is true. If it is unfamiliar or shocking enough it will not be believed. Pain and trauma victims face the double wound of horrible suffering that they cannot make others believe. They feel that justice demands that they be believed. They feel that others cannot understand what they say.

Justice demands the truth, but the truth is concealed.

> No one will ever be able to establish with precision how many, in the Nazi apparatus, could *not not know* about the frightful atrocities being committed, how many knew something but were in a position to pretend that they did not know, and, further, how many had the possibility of knowing everything but chose the more prudent path of keeping their eyes and ears (and above all their mouths) well shut. (14)

> At no other place and time has one seen a phenomenon so unexpected and so complex: never have so many human lives been extinguished in so short a time, and with so lucid a combination of technological ingenuity, fanaticism, and cruelty. (21)

Even when well known, it is difficult to believe. At no other place and time did anything comparable occur. Yet torture, murder, terrorization occur every day, every minute, around the world. They occurred for centuries under the heading of slavery and its aftermath. Is it more truthful to emphasize the uniqueness of the Nazi terror or to call attention to widespread violence? Do people want to know what is happening or do they want to forget?

Memory may not be the best source for witness and testimony. It may not be the best way to reveal a difficult and threatening truth. However necessary, it is risky to rely on memory for justice, to provide evidence and documentation. To tell the truth of memories of pain and suffering may be to reveal the most terrible and threatening thing about them, that they do not produce justice. To bring the murderers and torturers to justice may require collecting and organizing evidence in a quiet and unthreatening voice. This is one of the difficulties in bearing witness, one of the ways in which it cannot rely on memory even when memory is all there is. The witness is a traitor, memory is forgetting.

> Human memory is a marvelous but fallacious instrument.... The memories which lie within us are not carved in stone; not only do they tend to become erased as the years go by, but often they change, or even grow, by incorporating extraneous factors. (23)

> the memory of a trauma suffered or inflicted is itself traumatic because recalling it is painful or at least disturbing. A person who has been wounded tends to block out the memory so as not to renew the pain; the person who has inflicted the wound pushes the memory deep down, to be rid of it, to alleviate the feeling of guilt. (24)

> This very book is drenched in memory; what's more, a distant memory. Thus it draws from a suspect source and must be protected against itself. So here then: it contains more considerations than memories, lingers more willingly on the state of affairs such as it is now than on the retroactive chronicle.... As for my personal memories, ... I have examined all of them: time has somewhat faded them, but they are in good consonance with their background and seem to me unaffected by the drifting I have described. (34–5)

Memory is imperfect: we forget, distort, transform; we deceive others and ourselves. We must remember, we are made to forget. Force is destructive, violent, controlling: memories and documents are shredded and rendered suspect. In the case of concentration camps and other hierarchical institutions, those most in a position to know and remember have all the more reason to forget, to distort, to shape memories to their purposes, private or public. One of the reasons why families of those who have been made to disappear cry out for information is that it is so easy for that information to be made to vanish and for the memories of those who might remember to be made obscure. Between secrecy and fallibility, memory gives way to forgetting.

Many years earlier, Levi remembered vividly:

> Sooner or later in life everyone discovers that perfect happiness is unrealizable, but there are few who pause to consider the antithesis: that perfect unhappiness is equally unattainable. The obstacles preventing the realization of both these extreme states are of the same nature: they derive from our human condition which is opposed to everything infinite. (Levi, *SA*, 17)

> It was the very discomfort, the blows, the cold, the thirst that kept us aloft in the void of bottomless despair, both during the journey and after. It was not the will to live, nor a conscious res-

ignation; for few are the men capable of such resolution, and we were but a common sample of humanity. (17)

From the standpoint of forgetting, we might suppose that happiness is possibly only for a mortal, that forgetting haunts the possibility of happiness like a ghost. Imperfection is a much more interesting condition than perfection, as forgetting is much more interesting than remembering.

As terrible as it may be to think it, suffering may be the condition of the greatest accomplishments of the spirit, as forgetting brings them into creation. I do not mean to say that suffering is better than happiness, nor that remembering is worse than forgetting. Better and worse are impossible here. I mean that remembering and happiness are made what they are by the *perhaps* and *as if* of mortality and imperfection, that forgetting in its positive role—to transfigure, transform, and transgress—is what makes memory and life productive.

> The rites to be carried out were infinite and senseless: every morning one had to make the "bed" perfectly flat and smooth; smear one's muddy and repellent wooden shoes with the appropriate machine grease, scrape the mudstains off one's clothes (paint, grease and rust-stains were, however, permitted); in the evening one had to undergo the control for lice and the control of washing one's feet; on Saturday, have one's beard and hair shaved, mend or have mended one's rags; on Sunday, undergo the general control for skin diseases and the control of buttons on one's jacket, which had to be five. (34)

This is the voice of memory, of life, no matter how terrible living may be. This is remembering the past so as to live in the present. It is neither witness nor judgment. Even as evidence for judgment, it does not serve the requirements of justice. Instead it tells those who were not there what it was to be there.

I have never forgotten the following passage and cannot imagine ever doing so. It seems inconsequential as a crime compared with the gassings and beatings, yet it conveys a vivid sense to me of the incredible terror of the inconsequential.

> And do not think that shoes form a factor of secondary importance in the life of the Lager. Death begins with the shoes; for most of us, they show themselves to be instruments of torture, which after a few hours of marching cause painful sores which become fatally infected. Whoever has them is forced to walk as if he was dragging a convict's chain. ... Then only the hospital is left: but to enter the hospital with a diagnosis of *"dicke Fasse"* (swollen feet) is extremely dangerous, because it is well known to all, and

especially to the SS, that here there is no cure for that complaint. (34–5)

In 1958, Levi bears witness, in the tone we will listen to more closely a bit later. The enormity of the events is evident in the facts themselves, recounted almost minimally. One might imagine this to be a fictional strategy. One might imagine it instead as the voice of trauma.

In 1986, 28 years later, Levi is judgmental, as if judgment is permitted now because he is among many. He will and can not judge the prisoners, even those who did terrible things. No one can judge them, not even other prisoners. But he speaks incessantly of judging the Germans, including those who were born much later.

> Now, the network of human relationships inside the Lagers was not simple: it could not be reduced to the two blocs of victims and persecutors. Anyone who today reads (or writes) the history of the Lager reveals the tendency, indeed the need, to separate evil from good, to be able to take sides, to emulate Christ's gesture on Judgment Day: . . . . (36)

We insist on judgment, yet judgment is hard to come by in such terrible conditions. Levi denies that we can judge and yet insists that he must judge.

> It is naive, absurd, and historically false to believe that an infernal system such as National Socialism sanctifies its victims: on the contrary, it degrades them, it makes them resemble itself, and this all the more when they are available, blank, and lacking a political or moral armature. (40)

> Now, one mustn't forget that the greater part of the memories, spoken or written, of those who came back begin with the collision with the concentrationary reality, and, simultaneously, the unforeseen and uncomprehended aggression on the part of a new and strange enemy, the functionary prisoner, who instead of taking you by the hand, reassuring you, teaching you the way, throws himself at you, screaming in a language you do not understand, and strikes you in the face. He wants to tame you, extinguish any spark of dignity that he has lost and you perhaps still preserve. (41)

Including the members of the Special Squad who were responsible for the gas chambers and performed the work of extermination.

> I believe that no one is authorized to judge them, not those who lived through the experience of the Lager and even less those who did not. (59)

> "...what was the point of the humiliations, the cruelties?"
> ..."To condition those who were to be the material executors of
> the operations. To make it possible for them to do what they were
> doing." In other words: before dying the victim must be degraded,
> so that the murderer will be less burdened by guilt. (125–6)

They must be made visible marks of their own degradation.

It is of utmost importance to hear what Levi says here of degradation. It seems entirely evident and yet, for those who have not
been victims, for those who have experienced neither the suffering
nor the mistreatment of which he speaks, it appears to be the most
difficult thing to accept. Why did you not escape? Why did you not
rebel? Why did you not avoid capture "beforehand?"

> In the first place, it is not true that no rebellion ever took place
> in a lager. The rebellions of Treblinka, Sobibor, and Birkenau have
> been described many times, ... others took place in minor camps.
> These were exploits of extreme audacity worth of the deepest re-
> spect, but not one of them ended in victory, if by victory one
> means the liberation of the camp. It would have been senseless to
> aim at such a goal: ....
> In the Lagers oppression was of extreme proportions and en-
> forced with the renowned and in other fields praiseworthy Ger-
> man efficiency. The typical prisoner, the one who represented the
> camp's core, was at the limits of depletion: ....
> ...Why didn't you run away "before?" Before the borders
> were closed? Before the trap snapped shut? Here too I must point
> out that many persons threatened by Nazism and fascism did
> leave "before." ...
> ...To emigrate one needed not only a lot of money but also a
> "bridgehead" in the country of destination: relatives or friends
> willing to offer sponsorship and/or hospitality. (151–62)

The answer, repeatedly, is that many did, and many did not; the
system was powerful, coercive, intimidating, violent, above all degrading. Human beings can be degraded; shame is one of the most
powerful and recurrent reactions during and after such terrible
treatment. One might say that Levi doesn't deal enough with shame,
perhaps because it is too terrible to feel. Shame for the prisoners,
shame for surviving, shame for cooperating, shame at what one has
become, shame, shame, shame. Victims of domestic and civil violence, women who are raped, even in secular societies but especially
in societies where sexual violence makes the woman unclean, all are
made to feel incredible shame.

How did the Nazis know how to make prisoners feel so degraded, how did they know and train their staff to be so effective? I
do not know if anyone has the answer to that question, but after-

ward, around the world, concentration camps have imitated their methods. Perhaps the Germans and Japanese learned from each other. Perhaps the notion of concentration camps in which masses of prisoners are held who have not committed crimes of practice but only of existence and otherness—Jews, gypsies, homosexuals, elderly, women, Koreans, Chinese, other parties, other religions, etc.— allows those in charge to treat them with shame. Here are other possibilities.

> Slaves and domesticated animals exist in relationships of domination, requiring a master as much as a servant. . . .
> The drive for control is so essential—and so similar, whether the object of control is a slave or a domestic animal—as to overwhelm most distinctions between humans and animals. (Jacoby, SN, 92)

> virtually all of the practices cited [toward domestic animals] . . . were ones that humans also applied regularly to human slaves. (92)

> Agriculture is now a mechanized food industry; in essence it is no different than the production of corpses in the gas chambers and death camps, the embargoes and food reductions to starving countries, the making of hydrogen bombs (Heidegger's comment in 1949; quoted in Lyotard, HJ, 85).

Humans treated like animals, animals treated like things—and much worse than things, because they must be degraded, hurt, violated. They must have their spirit cowed; murder is not enough.

Levi insists that at no other time and place did such a phenomenon as the camps exist. I have wondered whether such phenomena can be found in every time and place, no more and no less visible than the Lagers, no less and no more innocent. Concentration camps, murder camps, slave camps. Even the most humane and serene homes were murderous to their slaves. We are made to forget. Some remember.

> "All I knew was I had to get my milk to my baby girl. Nobody was going to nurse her like me. Nobody was going to get it to her fast enough, or take it away when she had enough and didn't know it. . . . Nobody knew that but me and nobody had her milk but me. I told that to the women in the wagon. . . . The milk would be there and I would be there with it." . . .
> "After I left you, those boys came in there and took my milk. That's what they came in there for. Held me down and took it. I told Mrs. Garner on em. She had that lump and couldn't speak but her eyes rolled out tears. Them boys found out I told on em.

Schoolteacher made one open up my back, and when it closed it
made a tree. It grows there still."
        "They used cowhide on you?"
        "And they took my milk."
        "They beat you and you was pregnant?"
        "And they took my milk!" (Morrison, B, 19–20)

What they remember is degradation and shame, the defining qualities of the Lagers. Murder, degradation, and shame, the cruelest violations of humanity.

They held Sethe down and took her milk, then schoolteacher
whipped her. Each of these is a violence and a crime, done to humiliate her. Jews and slaves were unworthy of human respect.

        "It broke him, Sethe." Paul D looked up at her and sighed.
        "You may as well know it all. Last time I saw him he was sitting
        by the churn. He had butter all over his face." . . .
        "What did he say?"
        "Nothing."
        "Not a word?"
        "Not a word."
        "Did you speak to him? Didn't you say anything to him?
Something!"
        "I couldn't, Sethe. I just . . . couldn't."
        "Why!"
        "I had a bit in my mouth." (81–2)

Treated like an animal, as if animals deserved to be degraded, as if
it were necessary to degrade them to make use of them.

        in all of Baby's life, as well as Sethe's own, men and women were
        moved around like checkers. Anybody Baby Suggs knew, let alone
        loved, who hadn't run off or been hanged, got rented out, loaned
        out, bought up, brought back, stored up, mortgaged, won, stolen
        or seized. So Baby's eight children had six fathers. What she called
        the nastiness of life was the shock she received upon learning that
        nobody stopped playing checkers just because the pieces included
        her children. (27–8)

        Chain-up completed, they knelt down. The dew, more likely
        than not, was mist by then. Heavy sometimes and if the dogs were
        quiet and just breathing you could hear doves. Kneeling in the
        mist they waited for the whim of a guard, or two, or three. Or
        maybe all of them wanted it. Wanted it from one prisoner in par-
        ticular or none—or all.
        "Breakfast? Want some breakfast, nigger?"
        "Yes, sir."
        "Hungry, nigger?"
        "Yes, sir."

"Here you go."

Occasionally a kneeling man chose gunshot in his head as the price, maybe, of taking a bit of foreskin with him to Jesus. Paul D did not know that then. He was looking at his palsied hands, smelling the guard, listening to his soft grunts so like the doves, as he stood before the man kneeling in mist on his right. Convinced he was next, Paul D retched—vomiting up nothing at all. An observing guard smashed his shoulder with the rifle and the engaged one decided to skip the new man for the time being lest his pants and shoes got soiled by nigger puke. (127)

No one can doubt that what Levi and Morrison describe is violation and degradation. No one can doubt that such treatment does not benefit the torturers as much as it degrades them. Victimizers force their victims to share the degradation they create, construct a circle in which shame and degradation so completely permeate their lives together that what any of them remember they must forget.

Even so, no level of degradation can eliminate the vitality, creativity, and joyfulness of life, in the lagers or the camps, no matter how bitter.

They chain-danced over the fields, through the woods to a trail that ended in the astonishing beauty of feldspar, and there Paul D's hands disobeyed the furious rippling of his blood and paid attention. With a sledge hammer in his hands and Hi Man's lead, the men got through. They sang it out and beat it up, garbling the words so they could not be understood; tricking the words so their syllables yielded up other meanings. They sang the women they knew; the children they had been; the animals they had tamed themselves or seen others tame. They sang of bosses and masters and misses; of mules and dogs and the shamelessness of life. They sang lovingly of graveyards and sisters long gone. Of pork in the woods; meal in the pan; fish on the line; cane, rain and rocking chairs.

And they beat. The women for having known them and no more, no more; the children for having been them but never again. They killed a boss so often and so completely they had to bring him back to life to pulp him one more time. Tasting hot mealcake among pine trees, they beat it away. Singing love songs to Mr. Death, they smashed his head. More than the rest, they killed the flirt whom folks called Life for leading them on. Making them think the next sunrise would be worth it; that another stroke of time would do it at last. (128–9)

One of the features of this kind of cruelty and degradation is the hypocrisy with which the moments of kindness are offered in a context in which they mean nothing. Levi describes a woman who sur-

vives the gas chamber, whom the Special Squad want to protect.
Even he imagines a moment of hesitation as a gift of compassion.

> A doctor is called, and he revives the girl with an injection:
> yes, the gas has not had its effect, she will survive, but where and
> how? Just then Muhsfeld, one of the SS men attached to the death
> installations, arrives. The doctor calls him to one side and presents
> the case to him. Muhsfeld hesitates, then he decides: No, the girl
> must die. If she were older, it would be a different matter, she
> would have more sense, perhaps she could be convinced to keep
> quiet about what has happened to her. But she's only sixteen: she
> can't be trusted. And yet, he does not kill her with his own hands.
> He calls one of his underlings to eliminate her with a blow to the
> nape of the neck. Now, this man Muhsfeld was not a compassion-
> ate person; his daily ration of slaughter was studded with arbi-
> trary and capricious acts, marked by his inventions of refined cru-
> elty. He was tried in 1947, sentenced to death and hung in Krakow
> and this was right, but not even he was a monolith. Had he lived
> in a different environment and epoch, he probably would have
> behaved like any other common man. (Levi, *DS*, 57)

In the camps such compassion is in complicity with the degradation.

> For years Paul D believed schoolteacher broke into children
> what Garner had raised into men. And it was that that made them
> run off. Now, plagued by the contents of his tobacco tin, he won-
> dered how much difference there really was between before
> schoolteacher and after. Garner called and announced them men—
> but only on Sweet Home, and by his leave. Was he naming what
> he saw or creating what he did not? ... Suppose Garner woke up
> one morning and changed his mind? Took the word away. Would
> they have run then? And if he didn't, would the Pauls have stayed
> there all their lives? Why did the brothers need the one whole
> night to decide? To discuss whether they would join Sixo and
> Halle. Because they had been isolated in a wonderful lie, dismiss-
> ing Halle's and Baby Suggs' life before Sweet Home as bad luck.
> (Morrison, *B*, 260)

> Remembering his own price, down to the cent, that school-
> teacher was able to get for him, he wondered what Sethe's would
> have been. What had Baby Suggs' been? How much did Halle
> owe, still, besides his labor? What did Mrs. Garner get for Paul F?
> More than nine hundred dollars? How much more? Ten dollars?
> Twenty? Schoolteacher would know. He knew the worth of every-
> thing. (268–9)

Seth and Paul D intensely recall the characteristics that define their
inhumanity and the calculations that define their worth. And they
remember.

I was talking about time. It's so hard for me to believe in it. Some things go. Pass on. Some things just stay. I used to think it was my rememory. You know. Some things you forget. Other things you never do. But it's not. Places, places are still there. If a house burns down, it's gone, but the place—the picture of it— stays, and not just in my rememory, but out there, in the world. What I remember is a picture floating around out there outside my head. I mean, even if I don't know it, even if I die, the picture of what I did. or knew, or saw is still out there. Right in the place where it happened.

Can other people see it? . . .

Oh, yes. Oh, yes, yes, yes. Someday you be walking down the road and you hear something or see something going on. So clear. And you think it's you thinking it up. A thought picture. But no. It's when you bump into rememory that belongs to somebody else. Where I was before I came here, that place is real. . . . The picture is still there and what's more, if you go there—you who never was there—if you go there and stand in the place where it was, it will happen again; it will be there for you, waiting for you. (43–4)

What here is telling? What remembering? Why would we want to remember such terrible shame and degradation? Who would we tell, and why would we want to do so? Why not forget? Because of injustice, we may say. Those who suffered monstrous harm deserve a chance to speak, to know, to remember and to tell. Yet they do not. Concentration camp survivors frequently remain silent, even toward their children. Those who tell, those who attempt to speak, frequently feel monstrously inadequate.

The word *monstrous* appears here twice, adjectivally and adverbially, with what may appear to be different meanings. One is the monstrosity of the crime, the other the monstrosity of the victim's silence. These are both experienced as crimes. The victim who cannot speak, who is not heard, cannot find the words, is denied standing; the victim who cannot be a victim visibly and audibly is the victim of another crime. And it is no less a crime for that, if a different one, different perhaps in relation to the offender—individual or institution—but not lesser in relation to the victim. The victim must tell, it must be possible to say, it must be understood by others.

1. You are informed that human beings endowed with language were placed in a situation such that none of them is now able to tell about it. Most of them disappeared then, and the survivors rarely speak about it. When they do speak about it, their testimony bears only upon a minute part of this situation. How can you know that the situation itself existed? (Lyotard, *DPD*, 3)

Lyotard begins with the damage, the harm done in concentration camps, where most were killed and the survivors rarely speak. On top of this, those who follow have political reasons to deny everything. Lyotard describes this as an epistemological problem. "The only acceptable proof that it [a gas chamber] was used to kill is that one died from it. But if one is dead, one cannot testify that it is on account of the gas chamber" (3). If it is an epistemological issue—of what is true, what took place, what can be documented and remembered—it is a strange one because it appears in the form of a court of law, consequently as an ethical and political issue.

That is how Lyotard takes it:

> 9. It is in the nature of a victim not to be able to prove that one has been done a wrong. A plaintiff is someone who has incurred damages and who disposes of the means to prove it. One becomes a victim if one loses these means. One loses them, for example, if the author of the damages turns out directly or indirectly to be one's judge. (8)

Would that it were so simple! If anything is simple. I do not mean that Lyotard is describing anything simple and clear. But he poses the wrong from the side of the judge, as if from the side of victim it would always be possible to tell the truth, to remember. Yet people forget, people want to forget, and even when they remember horribly and vividly, they cannot speak.

> 14. "The survivors rarely speak" (no. 1). But isn't there an entire literature of testimonies...? —That's not it, though.... Not to speak is part of the ability to speak, since ability is a possibility and a possibility implies something and its opposite.... If the survivors do not speak, is it because they cannot speak, or because they avail themselves of the possibility of not speaking that is given them by the ability to speak? Do they keep quiet out of necessity, or freely, as it is said? Or is the question poorly stated? (10)

The question is poorly stated because the ability to speak is not so evident a possibility.

> 15. ... they do not speak because they are threatened with the worst in the case that they would speak, or when in general a direct or indirect attempt is made against their ability to speak. Let's suppose that they keep quiet under threat....
> 16. What is subject to threats is not an identifiable individual, but the ability to speak or to keep quiet. This ability is threatened with destruction. There are two means to achieve this: making it impossible to speak, making it impossible to keep quiet. These two means are compatible: it is made impossible for x to speak about

> this (through incarceration, for example); it is made impossible for him or her to keep quiet about that (through torture, for example). The ability is destroyed as an ability: . . . . (10–1)

Would that it were so simple! Would that it were so clear! If that were possible. Yet Lyotard makes the point that testimony is not only fragile, capable of destruction, but that the harm itself can destroy the ability to speak. Torture takes away the ability to give testimony. Lyotard understands this as the compulsion to tell, to tell all, and tell again. Scarry dwells upon the inability and disability brought by pain, especially the pain of torture. Here is another example:

> Pain is highly localized. Its outermost limit is the boundary of the victim's body. Its inner limit can be as small as a point in one's foot where a nail is being pounded in. And no one pain is like any other. (Daniel, *IT*, 233)

This is from the first a evocation of how difficult it is to speak of pain, perhaps because pain is uniquely localized, perhaps because it is always difficult to speak of any experience without abstraction, without forgetting the experiential qualities of the experience. This is no less true for phenomenology, which insists that it can speak, that it can have a knowledge in words of what is experienced beyond words. Words abstract, even in poems. Words are words, whereas experiences take place in flesh and touch. Pain is where and when it is, precisely what it is, different from every other. No words can express what is what it is unlike any other. No knowledge can express the singularity of the singular, the alterity of the alter.

> For the most part chronic pain patients see their problem as one of "matter over mind" because their intractable pain makes them feel that their bodies are powerfully influencing their minds. Some go so far as to use an idiom of possession, saying that their bodies are taking over, are driving them crazy. Many of these people have found that their lives, their emotions, their spirituality, their personalities, their destinies are dominated by their pain-full bodies, and their role as sufferer has shunted aside previous roles as caregiver, provider, lover, companion, parent, friend, citizen. (Jackson, *CP*, 207)

> Patients speak (and, therefore, we can posit, actually experience) their pain at times in terms of an identification of self apart from pain, with the pain as alien, an intruder, an invader; at other times they use terms revealing an identification of self with pain, or pain experienced as coterminous with the body—the pain-full body, which is, at least intermittently, coterminous with the subject. (209)

> [C]hronic pain sufferers report feeling profoundly misunderstood
> by non-sufferers and profoundly understood by fellow sufferers.
> They are exiles in the province of pain, and they find everyday-
> world language inadequate for communicating about their experi-
> ences there. (223–4)

This suggests what mystics know, that the most powerful experiences are characterized by the urgency to speak of them, to tell
the world about them, joined with a sense of utter inadequacy in
doing so. It also suggests that the corporeality of pain and of other
bodily events and states gives the attempt to speak, portray, imagine
in any but a corporeal form a sense of inadequacy and failure.

I would express this experience of inadequacy in terms of forgetting, understanding the urge to speak and to express as the imperative to remember. To remember the experiential, singular qualities
of lived experiences, especially more vivid, painful, affective experiences, is to forget their singularities and their intensities. To remember the corporeal, material events and conditions of bodies is to forget their materialities and corporealities. This is true even where the
memory is qualitative and affective, material and corporeal; true
where the memory of pain is itself felt as pain, where the body remembers the body by displacement as well as repetition. Memory
here is forgetting in the sense that it substitutes something different
for the singularity and intensity of what would be remembered.
Only the singular event can be the singular event again, which is
impossible. The adequacy of memory is its inadequacy. Remembering the particularities and singularities of events, especially of intense, excruciating, and degrading experiences, is by necessity to
forget.

This is true for all events, painful and joyful, extraordinary and
ordinary. Joy and pain are not unique, but they are more intense in
their affectivities, more singular in their qualities. That is what I
take Daniel and Scarry to assert. The inadequacy of expressing pain
is experienced in the urgency to tell it—to share it with others—and
to know and experience the impossibility of doing so in the singularity of the experience.

Daniel and Scarry take the unsharability of pain for granted. I
take the unsharability of all experiences and things for granted. *Tout
autre est tout autre.* Including pain and joy and love, but also walking, looking, seeing, hearing; rainbows, fogs, sunsets, stars, flowers,
trees, but also rocks, dirt, hills, bones, grass. Each is what it is, infinite in the particularities of its abundance; and if we attend more
closely we get closer to that abundance, to its uniqueness. Of course
these are all sharable, we can speak of them all, say something, ex-

press something of them and through them in image and song. One question is what such exposition means of them. Another is what it does for us. In relation to pain and love and joy our need is to share what is unsharable: the intense localization and corporeality of the affect.

How great is this need? Daniel and Scarry insist that pain seeks a voice, Lyotard insists that victims demand a hearing. Sometimes this appears to be true. Yet I have noted that survivors of concentration camps frequently refuse to speak. Who is to decide that it would be better for them to speak, that they would do better to share their pain and grief with others? And, moreover, who is to decide that the way in which they should share is through speaking, writing, language? In a court of law, to bring criminals to justice, perhaps. But if that is no longer an issue, or is less urgent, why speak and write rather than dance and sing? Why words rather than gestures, why thoughts rather than bodies?

First, then, whether the individual in pain needs to communicate.

> I don't believe that most of the victims I interviewed were unwilling to talk about their experiences because it was too painful to do so. There were no signs of contained passion. Rather, attempts to extract information were met with expressions of utter listlessness. I was later to find out that it was not so much boredom that weighed down on the victim but the overwhelming sense of the sheer worthlessness of all attempts to communicate something that was so radically individuated and rendered unsharable. . . . In court, this disposition of the victim is exploited by the torturers to make lies of the victim's claims of having been tortured. The passionless listings of atrocities committed by the torturer leaves the judge and the court unconvinced. The unbelievable is also unexplainable and the unexplainable the inexpressible. (Daniel, *IT*, 238)

Having experienced something far too terrible to remember, how can repeating and reliving it in court be worth doing, even when one has a chance to bring the torturer to justice? For some this is a necessity, for others an impossibility. Who is to demand that victims share their suffering when they choose not to do so? Why take for granted that victims of trauma and terror want to tell but cannot, are either prevented or feel inadequate? Daniel can put into words *the overwhelming sense of the sheer worthlessness* of doing so. Still he imagines that it is desirable and necessary.

Yet his explicit concern is not with the original pain of torture but the subsequent pain of terror, the terror that memory and reliving evoke. This terror takes hold of the body, shakes it, twists it, shatters it, tears it apart.

> Of course, it is terror (and pain) that hyper-individuate the victim in the first place. But the terror I speak of is a second, therapeutic terror, a seismic after-shock. This terror can take many forms. Of the torture victims I came to know whose pain passed into this terror, terror manifested itself in a variety of ways: in uncontrollable sobbing, in rage, in violent shakings of the body, in visible efforts and restructuring a narrative with conscious self-corrections introduced regarding details and their proper sequences—corrections that even while appearing to be far more confusing to the interviewer than the mechanical recitation of the pre-terrorized torture victim, carried far greater conviction. (238)

Epistemologically, the body knows more than the mind, which copes with this violence through denial. Practically, the body acts, feels, expresses more than the mind, presents the terror and violence of torture as another terror laying hold of the body. Mnemastically, this terror in the body takes place not as recalling but as forgetting. What is forgotten in the mind, forgotten in order to live, takes hold of the body and shakes it, tears it open. The terror lies in the body, the individual's body remembers in terror, remembers what is forgotten. Here is an extreme example:

> With the closeness of one man, whom I could not visually connect as the rapist, explosions of terror similar to those I experienced on the night of the attack permeated and swelled inside my body....
>
> Recognition of that man's face as the rapist's was not possible.... My body's sensibility counteracted part of the terror: I could at least match the body form of the man on the street with the body form of the rapist.... There was no doubt in my mind as to the similarity of those body forms....
>
> Later I asked myself: Why hadn't anyone told me about bodily identification? Why couldn't my mind break down the protective barrier of terror to unable me to recognize that man as the rapist?...
>
> ...Through the re-enactment of the rape terror, my body informed that the man-on-the-street was the rapist.... My mind continued to protect me because the threat of another rape was a major issue: the rapist could still run and hide from the police. (Winkler, *RT*, 258–9)

One could say her body remembers while her mind forgets. One could hope that her mind would forget. Yet the reiteration of the horror in her body as terror—the terror Daniel describes—cannot be understood as memory but as forgetting. It is the way in which she forgot in order to live, forgot in order not to be ready to die, forgot in order to escape from terror. And it is a way in which she experiences another terror.

> Counselors and therapists had explained to me that these body traumas were like emotional upheavals that I would get over. To them, tremors were experiences to live through and forget. These traumas are *not* meaningless residual pain from the attack. Rather, these traumas contain, in this instance, alarm meanings that activist-survivor-victims need to learn about and interpret. (260)

In other words, forgetting is both necessary and impossible; and memory is both impossible and necessary. The necessity and impossibility of the body and the mind bearing the pain and horror requires remembering and forgetting in their impossibility and necessity. That necessity itself is both the repetition and a sign of the terror. This time the terror is not an aftermath or a trace but the work of terror again in the body.

> The identification of trauma with the attack—in its intensity and pervasiveness—is a means by which our bodies give us information. Our bodies provide interpretations by warning us of the pending peril because of the presence of the rapist or another similar abuser. This warning is a notice to remove ourselves from that dangerous context. (259)

It is interesting how Winkler interprets her body's actions—as interpretations and signs, that is as knowledge. Her body knows, her body remembers, her body gives her information that must be understood and decoded. Yet her body moves, shakes in terror, defecates in fear. How can we understand this except as action and sign, state and knowledge? The difficulty with thinking that what pain demands is words—shared knowledge and understanding—is that the body acts to be safe.

> At the Rape Crisis Center, I met the Rape Survivor Advocate. She immediately pulled me from the cliff of insanity and treated me like a person who could deal with that bludgeoning pain. I told her that the rapist had wanted to kill me. She assured me that all rapists threaten their victims, but that few carry through with their threats; besides, the rapist had no weapon.... After three months of numbness and another three months of short spells of crying in private, my body provided the answer....
> ... In an explosive emotional experience, those murderous moments became evident. My body told me that I was now safe to confront that meaning because I was alone, without people to deny my experience. The meaning that I had to accept was that I had had a confrontation with physical death. (260–1)

I am spending this time on Winkler's testimony before returning to Daniel and Scarry to pose one side of their work that may largely be forgotten. The fascinating and urgent question of how to make pain intelligible and sharable takes too much for granted in the context of survivors who do not wish to share, who find their bodies way ahead of them, who have to deal with the fear of being violated again. This pertains to the fact of speaking, saying, expressing: we have to ask the question as if we do not know the answer in advance why survivors of violence and trauma *want* to speak, *must be made* to speak, why *it is better* to speak and share one's pain rather than keeping it to oneself. Many victims find that others do not want to share, do not understand and would rather not find out. We also have to ask the question as if we do not know the answer in advance why survivors of violence and trauma want to and must be made *to speak*, rather than to act, to be, to live and flourish in safety instead of fear. Winkler's activism speaks directly to these two questions from other directions than Daniel's and Scarry's:

> Survivor-victims become activists when they interpret the meanings of rape trauma. If activist-survivor-victims interpret these contexts and sets of meanings, they can better help themselves to deal with the rocky road to recovery. I argue that the following four therapeutic functions affirm this activist approach:
> 1. Protection.... As their bodies react traumatically, survivorvictims learn to guard themselves against the presence of the rapist or another abuser. The body brings to the attention of the survivor-victim, in a dramatic visceral manner, the occurrence of danger....
> 2. Forewarning.... their bodies re-enact horror feelings to warn them of potentially unsafe contexts. Thus, this trauma is important for self-preservation.
> 3. Safety. The non-rape context, while resurrecting past trauma, can also be a context of safety in which survivor-victims can deal with the trauma and its meanings without fear....
> 4. Information. The momentous shock of the rape attack or other rape trauma may contain some devastating meanings for survivor-victims to confront. Denial of these meanings by those people around survivor-victims can further impede an understanding of our feelings.... (262–3)

The key for me here is not the terms *protection, forewarning, safety, information*. These are what people in general require. The key is *bodies reacting traumatically, reenacting horror*. These are memories that cannot be remembered, that must be forgotten, yet that are impossible and dangerous to deny. So perhaps we may close this level of discussion by affirming body memories far beyond obscure bodily traces and the differences between forgetting and denying. I do not mean the force of will in denial that may be missing in forgetting, as if forgetting were passive, but to note the work that denial does, which is to block. Forgetting blocks nothing, lets everything through, takes place anywhere, always in conjunction with remembering. Bodies feel, express, forget, transform—and thereby remember. What do we want to remember of pain? What shall we forget? Daniel answers this question, *in transformation*.

> Even at the brink of language, pain lies stuck, individuated and arrested. . . . Pain can be freed, however. In Sri Lanka, a culturally recognized means of effecting such a freedom entails the experience of remembered terror. Terror remembered, disarticulates and de-individuates. Terror shatters pain, and in so doing makes it available for union with beauty. (Daniel, *IT*, 246)

> of all the pictures he showed, the one that they all liked the most, and had asked him to show them over and over again, on every visit, was that of Christ dying on the cross. "How beautiful! What pain! It gave us peace" he said. (245)

I would wonder if the example of Christ on the cross is predominantly of beauty or something else. I would wonder why the image of pain is required to achieve release from pain. I would think of Buddhism and emptiness and Asian images in relation to release from pain and suffering. More of that later. Here I am interested in how, in Daniel, the bodily terror that tells Winkler that she was at risk of death becomes a redemptive activity.

> I am suggesting that terror shows pain a way out of its static particularity into a domain of inexhaustible virtuality, a domain that is home to beauty as well. But what we do know for certain is that once pain extends into terror, it becomes more understandable to those with whom the victim returns to live, and reflexively, pain becomes more understandable to victims themselves. (239)

Perhaps not more truthful but more salvatory. We do have to go on, even the victims, even in pain. Beauty has always presented the possibility of healing; here it presents the possibility of remembering. I would consider it as the impossible forgetting that constitutes the condition of remembering. It does not make things whole, it makes them other, transforms and transfigures them, brings them back—even in pain and terror—as the wholly other. In other words it does not recall them, does not call them back, but calls them forth in the mode of forgetting, that is, as if in exposition and transgression.

This is the subject of this chapter, the *as if* and *perhaps* that haunt memories of suffering, terror, and death. For Scarry it is the telling of stories. For Daniel it is more corporeal, and for Winkler still more so, bodies show fear and pain in shaking, groaning, vomiting, defecating, show terror in bodily shocks, bodily movements. These are then not just movements—if there be such—not just molecules moving, but signify and express. Bodies are expressive, visibly and auditorily in the context of wounds and trauma. Expression is exposition, that is, tightly linked with exposure, touch, trauma, persecution, vulnerability, wounding. Levinas's terms for exposition, for the ways in which the other's face is present join expression with exposure etymologically and corporeally, still in the modalities of *perhaps* and *as if*, modes of forgetting in remembering.

I will return to Scarry and then to Levinas, a conjunction that might be uncomfortable for each but which, in the modality of *perhaps*, may express something vital of forgetting and recalling. Here I would extend the images of terror and victims into still another place in Asia, joined with another culture's exposition of the social conditions of mutilation.

> My subject is a population of Cambodians who have survived the depredations of Pol Pot's rule and sustained an unusually high number of landmine injuries over the course of a twelve-year guerrilla war that followed the overthrow of the Khmer Rouge regime in 1979. My thesis is that even the most apparently subjective and personal of experiences—the experience of one's own body— is shaped in important ways by the relations of power and domination in which the body is involved. (French, *PEIC*, 69)

> In the Buddhist universe there is a ranked continuum of sentient beings that stretches from the lowliest earthworm up through the animal kingdom to the kings and angels and bodhisattvas, and ultimately to the Buddha himself. Each being inhabits a different position in this hierarchy of virtue according to its karma or destiny, which is the result of all of its actions, good and bad, stretching back through the history of all of its past lives. We accumulate merit through our moral actions, and suffer according to our karma. If our karma is good we will be born rich and powerful, but if it is bad we will be born poor or crippled or orphaned. These are both the signs and the manifestations of our karmic status. . . .
>   . . . Cambodians have a fundamentally pragmatic outlook, and have traditionally accepted as karma those difficult things in their lives which they could do little to change. . . .
>   But in Site II, that sense had been badly shaken. . . . In spite of the Buddha's teaching many Cambodians did ponder why such

bad fortune had been visited upon them, and on the Khmer people as a group. The sense of accumulating bad fortune was hard to reverse in the context of life in Site II, where in practical terms people had very little ability to influence their future in significant ways. They were, in essence, prisoners in the camp until a settlement was reached in the guerrilla struggle, and no settlement was in sight during the time I was recording people's responses. (81–3)

Ideally, suffering leads to reflection and enlightened understanding. But in this situation of scarce resources and overwhelming political priorities, suffering often seemed only to bring more suffering, in a downward spiral. Karma, rather than offering hope through the possibility of change, seemed to close in on amputees with a sense of immutable destiny. Their bodies betrayed this destiny which they themselves read as a sign of their degradation, just as this reading was reflected back in the behavior of the people around them. (92)

French emphasizes that Cambodian Theravada Buddhist teachings call for compassion, but in the wounded social and individual worlds of concentration camps and physical mutilation, suffering is read as a mark of hierarchy, rank, and fortune. Karma, the possibility of release from suffering, contributes to a spiral of degradation and suffering.

Buddhism and Buddhist teachings interrupt us here with suffering and compassion. Let us begin with the noble truths that define the Buddhist world:

1. All is suffering (*Duhkha*): impermanence, imperfection, non-independence (*dharma*).
2. Suffering comes about by grasping, craving, clinging, attachment.
3. Suffering can be overcome by ending grasping.
4. The way to ending grasping is the eightfold noble path.

Suffering is imperfection, comes about by grasping, can be overcome by ending grasping, even grasping after imperfection, and is accomplished through the eightfold path.

(1) Life is suffering. This is more than a mere recognition of the presence of suffering in existence. It is a statement that, in its very nature, human existence is essentially painful from the moment of birth to the moment of death. Even death brings no relief, for the Buddha accepted the Hindu idea of life as cyclical, with death leading to further rebirth. (2) All suffering is caused by ignorance of the nature of reality and the craving, attachment, and grasping that result from such ignorance. (3) Suffering can be ended by overcoming ignorance and attachment. (4) The path to the sup-

pression of suffering is the Noble Eightfold Path, which consists of right views, right intention, right speech, right action, right livelihood, right effort, right-mindedness, and right contemplation. These eight are usually divided into three categories that form the cornerstone of Buddhist faith: morality, wisdom, and samadhi, or concentration. Anatman.

The Eightfold Path (*Atthangika-magga/Astangika-marga*) consists of eight interdependent categories or aspects of proper Buddhism practice, both mental and physical:

1. Right Understanding
2. Right Thought
3. Right Speech
4. Right Action
5. Right Livelihood
6. Right Effort
7. Right Mindfulness
8. Right Concentration (Gard, *B*, 133–4)

Spelled out in still greater detail, suffering and grasping are the conditions to be overcome, dispelled, to be forgotten—that is, by a rightful and rightly forgetting.

If this is, that comes to be; from the arising of this, that arises, that is to say: conditioned by ignorance (*avijh*-a) are the karma-formations; conditioned by the karma-formations is consciousness; conditioned by consciousness is psycho-physicality; conditioned by psycho-physicality are the six (sensory) spheres; conditioned by the six (sensory) spheres is sensory impingement; conditioned by sensory impingement is feeling; conditioned by feeling is craving; conditioned by craving is grasping; conditioned by grasping is becoming; conditioned by becoming is birth; conditioned by birth, ageing and dying, grief, sorrow, suffering, lamentation and despair come into being. Such is the arising of this entire mass of anguish [*dukkha*]. But from the utter fading away and stopping [*nirodha*] of this very ignorance is the stopping of the karma-formations; from the stopping of the karma-formations the stopping of consciousness; from the stopping of consciousness the stopping of psycho-physicality; from the stopping of psycho-physicality the stopping of the six (sensory) spheres; from the stopping of six (sensory) spheres the stopping of sensory impingement; from the stopping of sensory impingement the stopping of feeling; from the stopping of feeling the stopping of craving; from the stopping of craving the stopping of grasping; from the stopping of grasping the stopping of becoming; from the stopping of becoming the stopping of birth; from the stopping of birth, old age and dying, grief, sorrow, suffering, lamentation and de-

spair are stopped. Such is the stopping of this entire mass of anguish. (120–1)

   1. Every element is a separate (*prthqak*) entity or force.
   2. There is no inherence of element in another, ...
   3. Elements have no duration, ...
   4. The elements cooperate with one another (*samskrta*).
   5. This co-operating activity is controlled by the laws of causa-
tion (*pratitya-samuspada*).
   6. The world-process is thus a process of co-operation between
seventy-two kinds of subtle, evanescent elements, and such is the
nature of *dharmas* that they proceed from causes (*hetu-prabhava*)
and steer toward extinction (*nirodha*).
   7. . . .
   8. . . .
   9. The final result of the world-process is its suppression, Absolute Calm: all co-operation is extinct and replaced by immutabil-
ity (*asamskrta = nirvana*).
   Since all these particular doctrines are logically developed out
of one fundamental principle, Buddhism can be resolved in a series of equations:—
   *dharmata = nairatmya = ksanikatva = samskratva = prati-
tya-samutpannatva = . . . anasravatva = . . . vyavadanatva = duhkha-
nirodha = . . . nirvana.* (Gard, *B*, 111–2; quoted from Stcherbatsky
[Stcherbatskoi], *CCB*)

That is, suffering = impermanence = nonself = illusion = phenomenal existence = the middle way = emptiness = sensory dispositions =
relational origination = wisdom = compassion.
   The moments of this equation relevant here are suffering (*dukkha*), emptiness (*sunyata*), and compassion (*karuna*). Suffering comes
about from craving and grasping in a world in which everything is
interconnected, therefore nothing in itself, empty. What we crave,
what we hope to grasp—especially we ourselves, our beings and
identities—is empty, nothing in itself. We learn through meditation
and the eightfold path to release ourselves from grasping, thereby
from suffering, and thereby gain compassion. We learn to forget
what we are attached to, including ourselves, and thereby remember
others.
   Would that it were so simple, both for the Cambodian amputees
and for the rest of us! If this be simple. In the face of devastating
trauma—mutilation, rape, violence, horror—we respond with terror,
not with compassion. We are emptied out by the violence but it can
make us grasp all the more tightly to what we might hope for. Even
worse, others who have not been mutilated recoil as if from a conta-

gious disease, are made to suffer by violence as if they were the victims.

Having said this, having expressed the terrible reality that trauma and wounding carry with them all the more wounding and trauma; that in a world of suffering, domination produces domination, suffering produces suffering; what are we to do? If we cannot feed all the cats in the world, if we cannot take care of wounded children, why try to take care of any?

That is not where Buddhism would take us, nor Daniel and Scarry. To the contrary, if you will. Moreover, it is not that pain and suffering are an ethical obligation for others to remedy, but that in the wounds themselves are resources for transformation. Daniel and Winkler tell us that the most terrible experience of all, the shaking, screaming, violence from the body in its terrors, shakes us loose from too tight a grip on the traumatic experiences. The social reality of suffering does not bring about goodness and hope, but it does present the imperative of compassion in another light.

For it is not that compassion follows suffering without a struggle, but that it must pass through emptiness by means of an intense effort—even if that phrase is not apt. The eightfold path is a regimen through which is cultivated ease and freedom from conflict. It can be ruptured by calamity, as can nearly anything else. But it is a fusion of release, letting grasping go, through meditation, self transformation, and emptiness. Here emptiness links the denial of identity—self and other—with identification and forgetting. Identities and essences are graspings of identifications as if they were stable identities. Compassion is given in the modalities of *as if* and *perhaps*. That is, what things are and what they suffer is forgotten in their exposition.

I'm sure it seems suspect if not mad to seek Buddhist compassion in the midst of the traumas of German concentration camps and rape. Yet there still are Asian concentration camps, and Asian and other women are still raped. On the one hand, then, this is something to remember. On the other hand, I am recalling compassion as forgetting—not to forget wounds and harm and suffering so much as the identifications that compose them, dwelling on the realities of the sufferings, grasping after pain and suffering in such a way that release is impossible.

I have refused to accept the insistence that we must get over pain and death, that it is better to forget and to suffer no longer than to continue in pain. Nonattachment asks us to give up grasping, after grief and after release. In Buddhism, giving up grasping is giving, we give ourselves to life, give life to ourselves, give beyond gifts and beyond grasping. One way to put this is that we must in the end live with our pain, that compassion does not come to one who has never lived or felt pain but to those who have given up grasping it. Another is that compassion emerges from the risk of a remembering that is another grasping to a forgetting that is beyond suffering. It is a forgetting that is a gift, but nothing to grasp; a giving beyond having; forgiving beyond gifts, beyond fault, beyond pain and suffering; empty of grasping, including grasping after release from wounding.

What can this be but a practice beyond thinking and knowing, beyond all familiar categories? With that question I would return to Scarry.

> Whatever pain achieves, it achieves in part through its unsharability, and it ensures this unsharability through its resistance to language.... The merest schoolgirl when she falls in love has Shakespeare or Keats to speak her mind for her, but let a sufferer try to describe a pain in his head to a doctor and language at once runs dry. (Scarry, BP, 4)

> It is part of the work of this book to suggest that achieving an understanding of political justice may require that we first arrive at an understanding of making and unmaking. As in an earlier century the most searing questions of right and wrong were perceived to be bound up with questions of "truth," so in the coming time these same, still-searing questions of right and wrong must be reperceived as centrally bound up with questions about "fictions." (279–80)

Scarry's treatment of pain and the imperative to make, to create and tell, is a landmark for the literature of pain and for literature itself. We write from pain, pain requires that we tell, telling builds a world of language. Pain, trauma, terror, violence, shame—but perhaps other experiences and affects—are solitary and ask to be shared. Why to be shared, why must one speak, why speak rather than paint or sing or dance? And what work does telling do?

Here it is imperative to distinguish therapy from life and to consider the possibility that those who have suffered trauma may need to share and to recover, and that recovery and sharing may not be identical. For example, Eye Movement Desensitization and Reprocessing Therapy (EMDR) is said to offer an effective procedure for patients suffering from post traumatic stress syndrome in recovering from a wide range of damaging medical and psychological effects.[3] To insist that pain calls for storytelling and narration as therapy is perhaps to ignore more effective treatments. It is by no means clear that Levi's books served as therapy, and in some ways may have done him as much harm as good—if we accept the standard story of his death, that he committed suicide. This in no way belies or diminishes the importance of his testimony, for him and for others, his bearing witness to monstrous crimes.

So we may think of pain and trauma from the standpoint of their effects, seeking ways to ameliorate them, to make life easier for survivors. We may think of trauma and pain from the standpoint of the suffering they themselves are, seeking to share such suffering with others. Finally, we may think of them as terrible events and acts, seeking to bear witness to what most people do not know or wish to forget. We must not forget! Yet we cannot bear to remember!

In this space of wounding between forgetting and remembering lies the caesura between two imperatives: to reveal and to hide, to know and not to know, to say and to keep silent. It is a caesura that Scarry fills with creation. If we cannot bear to remember still we must bear witness. If in bearing witness we cause pain again, to ourselves and others, still we must do so. And so the task of witness becomes a task of creation, creating something that speaks or shows without reenacting the suffering that cannot be remembered.

Scarry insists on the inexpressibility of pain. Yet her book is wonderful testimony to its expression.

> When one hears about another person's physical pain, the events happening within the interior of that person's body may seem to have the remote character of some deep subterranean fact, belonging to an invisible geography that, however portentous, has no reality because it has not yet manifested itself on the visible surface of the earth. Or alternatively, it may seem as distant as the interstellar events referred to by scientists who speak to us mysteriously of not yet detectable intergalactic screams or of "very distant Seyfert galaxies, ..." (Scarry, BP, 3)

> First, the phenomenon of creating resides in and arises out of the framing intentional relation between physical pain on the one hand and imagined objects on the other, a framing relation that as it enters the visible world from the privacy of the human interior becomes work and its worked object. . . . Second, the now freestanding made object is a projection of the live body that itself reciprocates the live body: regardless of the peculiarities of the object's size, shape, or color, and regardless of the ground on which it is broken open . . . it will be found to contain within its interior a material record of the nature of human sentience out of which it in turn derives its power to act on sentience and recreate it. Third, as is implicit in the overlay of the first two statements, the created object itself takes two different forms, the imagined object and the

materialized object: that is, "making" entails the two conceptually distinct stages of "making-up" and "making-real." (280)

The body in pain insists on speaking, and if it cannot make its pain known directly it will create something that recalls it mimetically. The body in pain, then, is expressive, and it makes something expressive. In this context one must know that silence is another response to pain, to wounding, and that it is expressive. The world becomes expressive, creative, in its memories of disasters and wounds. And, moreover, each expression is as forgetful—recessive, withdrawing—as it is memorable. It is in the nature of pain to seek expression, and it is the nature of this expression to be mimetic, transformative, creative: indirect yet imagistic. It is in the nature of the image to copy and to diverge, to imitate and to transform, to remember and to forget.

Here it is perhaps useful to distinguish the imperative to speak, to express pain in language, from the way in which it is expressed. I have indicated reservations about the imperative to speak, the demand for language. Some are so wounded that they would remain silent; silence is all they have. This does not mean that they do not build or create, sometimes things, sometimes lives. But they do not speak. And many—Kierkegaard's account of Abraham—have recognized this silence.

However, when and how they speak, when and how they create, are another matter when impelled by pain. Here Scarry is eloquent:

> Why pain should so centrally entail, require, this shattering of language . . . may be partially apprehended by noticing the exceptional character of pain when compared to all our other interior states . . . our interior states of consciousness are regularly accompanied by objects in the external world, . . . physical pain—unlike any other state of consciousness—has no referential content. It is not of or for anything. It is precisely because it takes no object that it, more than any other phenomenon, resists objectification in language. (5)

The phenomenon is not the speaking but the shattering: the cries, moans, groans, twists of voice and timbre. If at one end of its being pain calls creation forth, at the other end it is bound tightly to the practical—not theoretical—impossibility of expression. The pain itself makes expressing it impossible. Its inexpressibility is material, experiential, tangible. It's not that you will not understand what I say, but that I cannot say it wholly. It will make me cry, weep, moan, unable to finish a sentence, a word, without screaming. I am inexpressive to myself as well as to others.

Scarry follows Virginia Woolf to acknowledge that literature too has been impoverished before pain. Yet the key to justice in response to pain, the key to bearing witness, is understanding the *uncreation, unmaking,* and *deconstruction* of the world in torture especially but also in disaster and trauma, and the subsequent *creation* and *making* that are the world again.

> [T]he story of physical pain becomes as well a story about the expansive nature of human sentience, the felt-fact of aliveness that is often sheerly happy, just as the story of *expressing* physical pain eventually opens into the wider frame of *invention*. The elemental "as if" of the person in pain ("It-feels as if . . . ," "It is as though. . . ") will lead out into the array of counterfactual revisions entailed in making.
>
>   This book is about the way other persons become visible to us, or cease to be visible to us. It is about the way we make ourselves (and the originally interior facts of sentience) available to one another through verbal and material artifacts, as it is also about the way the derealization of artifacts may assist in taking away another person's visibility. . . . But the two go together, for what is quite literally at stake in the body in pain is the making and unmaking of the world. (22–3)

The key to both, in relation to remembering and forgetting, is the recurrence of the *as if* that marks both the inexpressibility and the most creative forms of expression. It is because we must remember and cannot bear to remember that the *as if* of remembering becomes forgetting; it is because we remember by forgetting that the *as if* of forgetting becomes creation. This is not true of art and literature alone, but of the expressiveness of the world, made and unmade.

> The appropriation of the world into the torturer's arsenal of weapon is a crucial step in the overall process of torture. . . . Nowhere does language come so close to being the concrete agent of physical pain. . . . Just as the words of the one have become a weapon, so the words of the other are an expression of pain, in many cases telling the torturer nothing except how badly the prisoner hurts. The question, whatever its content, is an act of wounding; the answer, whatever its content, is a scream. (45–6)

Scarry's point is that this is a collapse of world. The torturer unmakes the world of the victim. But of course, as she and Levi also indicate, this is a collapse of the world of the torturer, both in the effects of the violence and in creating the victim's world of pain. The torturer's world is the victim's, and as the latter collapses, so does the former. The SS men tortured and killed. But they created a world in which humanity was unmade, theirs first and then the prisoners'. War too unmakes the world, creates a world in which pain and suffering are given, caused to take place, in the midst of profound denial. This is a world based on the disjunction between what is felt and what is real, between inner and outer, thoughts and objects. It is a world that is not a world, not one that anyone can live in.

Calamities, disasters, floods, earthquakes, as well as torture and war unmake the world. Victims experience similar disjunctions, dislocations, violations. State authorities are too slow, too blind, too inconsiderate, do not understand the victims' suffering. And indeed that is so. They do not, and they do not want to know, there is no way that they can imagine that they want to know. They may want to care or help or take care of the problem, sometimes highly responsively. But the world that is shared by official and victim is no longer whole. Even an anticipated flood or hurricane that washes away one's house shatters the unity of the world into broken fragments.

The one does violence to itself and guards itself against the other. The other as victim, the other in suffering, the other who comes to aid the victim come from different worlds to a world unmade, shattered between them in a violence in which the one may no longer be whole.

Whether or not the world can be whole, a world can be made in response to the unmaking. This is Scarry's major thesis.

> The only state that is as anomalous as pain is the imagination. While pain is a state remarkable for being wholly without objects, the imagination is remarkable for being the only state that is wholly its objects. There is in imagining no activity, no "state," no experienceable condition or felt-occurrence separate from the objects: the only evidence that one is "imagining" is that imaginary objects appear in the mind. (162)

> Physical pain, then, is an intentional state without an intentional object; imagining is an intentional object without an experienceable intentional state. Thus, it may be that in some peculiar way it is appropriate to think of pain as the imagination's intentional state, and to identify the imagination as pain's intentional object. . . . What may . . . be the case is that "pain" and "imagining" constitute extreme conditions of, on the one hand, intentionality as a state and, on the other, intentionality as self-objectification; and that between these two boundary conditions all the other more familiar, binary acts-and-objects are located. That is, pain and imagining are the "framing events" within whose boundaries all other perceptual, somatic, and emotional events occur; thus,

between the two extremes can be mapped the whole terrain of the human psyche. (164)

Scarry's marvelous explanation emphasizes intentionality. Her narrative emphasizes making and unmaking in the modality of *as if*. The worlds expressed, the worlds unmade, the worlds created all take place in the modality of *perhaps* and *as if*. Another way to address the binary of acts and objects, then, is to seek a nonbinary exposition in which—to follow Levinas's language—expression and exposure are bound tightly and inseparably to each other. This takes place in the nonbinary spaces of *as if* and *perhaps*, which are constituted by forgetting. What is forgotten is the binary reality—if reality can be binary, if our thinking of reality as binary is not itself in the mode of *as if*. We create *as if* to create a world, *as if* to rebuild something damaged irreparably. We must remember and we cannot remember; we must not forget yet we cannot help but forget. The *as if* and *perhaps* here are not the substitution of a fictive world for a real one, a whole fiction for a broken reality, but are the reality itself in relation, first, to pain and suffering—the world comes to us as if through a fog of torture and pain—then, second, to reconstitution— not of the world we lost, nor of a world to follow, but of a world whose characteristics are different forms of *as if*: as if destroyed by pain—Levi's world—and then as if reconstituted by witness, inheritance, memory, filled with forgetting.

What we can forget we must remember.

What we cannot remember we must not forget.

In the modalities of exposition.

> pain and the imagination are each other's missing intentional counterpart, and that they together provide a framing identity of man-as-creator within which all other intimate perceptual, psychological, emotional, and somatic events occur . . . . (169)

This is a remarkable thesis on the side of pain seeking its voice, but it is far more expressive on the side of imagination impelled by pain. Taken as if defining necessary and sufficient conditions of the intentionality at the heart of both, Scarry's thesis is difficult to sustain. Taken as an expression of the exposition that pain solicits and that imagination unfolds, as intense crystallizations of the *perhaps* and *as if* that haunt life and being, Scarry's thesis is that pain and suffering call forth in the voice and modality of *as if* and *perhaps* in a more intense way, perhaps, than we ordinarily experience them. Here intentionality gets in the way—intending to create, to build, to say. In the case of pain, *perhaps* and *as if* are torn out of terrible circumstances and intensities. In the case of imagination, *as if* and *per-*

haps bear the same experienced necessity. One imagines *as if* in truth, one seeks a way to express one's wounds *as if* they were something less opaque.

I do not believe that the silence of trauma calls out for imagination, but that it calls out together with all things and all things cry out in return. Such a calling we may name sending; its other name is exposition. It withdraws and forgets as much as it comes forth and recalls. The call of the world, of pain and joy, calls for answers, calls forth answering, in remembering and as forgetting. There is no escape from forgetting, no elimination of betrayal, the witness is a traitor, we will always remember and forget. Always in between, in the caesura. Between life and death, happiness and pain, making and unmaking, the caesura of remembering and forgetting emerges out of itself—to create, to wound, to love.

CHAPTER 13

Disaster

> • The disaster ruins everything, all the while leaving everything intact. It does not touch anyone in particular; "I" am not threatened by it, but spared, left aside. It is in this way that I am threatened;....
>
> The disaster is separate; that which is most separate.
>
> When the disaster comes upon us, it does not come. The disaster is its imminence, but since the future, as we conceive of it in the order of lived time, belongs to the disaster, the disaster has always already withdrawn or dissuaded it; there is no future for the disaster, just as there is no time or space for its accomplishment. (Blanchot, WD, 1–2)

*T*he disaster—as if it were the forgotten, as if our relation to disaster were forgetting—passive beyond passivity, separate beyond separation, impossible to assemble or to remember—perhaps not impossible but accomplished by betrayal. The disaster is forgotten, comes by way of betrayal, in the modalities of forgetting—*as if* and *perhaps*: the endless betrayal of exposition.

Is the disaster *a* disaster—a catastrophe, calamity, destruction? As if the word were enigmatic, ambiguous, anarchic, constantly betraying and betrayed. As if it did not allow itself to be walled up in the conditions of its exposition.[1] As if we were not infinitely open in our exposure.

Why disaster—and not love? Which disaster—what of the image? Why ruin—and not building? Which disaster—of the many? Neither mine nor yours, no one's in particular, archaic, immemorial, before me, or you, but not the other? Is this death, pain, ruination—of the other? Is this falling, fault, destruction—toward the other? Is this infinite calling—from the other? Why not love? Might it be love? Might we affirm the disaster as disaster, not turning away from it as if it were not disaster, wounding, betrayal, death? Might we learn to love disaster without loving pain or loss? What would it be to do so?

Can we live in joy in the midst of disaster? Can we live without forgetting it is disaster, can we affirm absolute loss without denial? Can we find a joyous place in our lives betraying disaster? Is this disaster writing, speaking, exposition: exposure as expression, calling; as *aisthēsis, mimēsis, poiēsis, catachrēsis, technē*; as image, aesthetics, beauty, art; calling as giving; betraying as forgetting?

Perhaps it is as if disaster had no place, as if we could not situate it, as if it were neither past nor future nor in between, but always forgotten, an other. Perhaps it is as if we were always on the edge of what cannot or will not come, yet remains as if to come, perhaps always coming. Perhaps it is as if the arrival that is stopped by disaster were made more present, immanent, more unexpected, imminent. Perhaps disaster is the perhaps.

The future that awaits is forgotten in the immanence of disaster, which accomplishes nothing, which is entirely forgotten, yet which presents itself everywhere. Forgetfully.

> • The disaster is related to forgetfulness—forgetfulness without memory, the motionless retreat of what has not been treated—the immemorial, perhaps. To remember forgetfully: again, the outside.
> • ... it means, not so much what we undergo, as that which goes under. It denotes the *pas* ["not"] of the utterly passive, withdrawn from all sight, from all knowing. Unless it be the case that knowledge—because it is not knowledge of the disaster, but knowledge as disaster and knowledge disastrously—carries us, carries us off, deports us (whom it smites and nonetheless leaves untouched), straight to ignorance, and puts us face to face with ignorance of the unknown so that we forget, endlessly.
> • The disaster: stress upon minutiae, sovereignty of the accidental. This causes us to acknowledge that forgetfulness is not negative or that the negative does not come after affirmation (affirmation negated), but exists in relation to the most ancient, to what would seem to come from furthest back in time immemorial without ever having been given. (3–4)

The disaster is the forgotten beyond remembering and forgetting. Neither moving nor happening, it is the coming of becoming. Becoming—is that disaster? Becoming—is that joy? Yet death cannot be joy, neither mine nor the other's. Loss is never absolute—loss is always absolute: the aporia of disaster. Disaster is never complete— disaster is never incomplete. Death is death, and yet we bury the dead, keep them alive, inherit from them, and mourn. In life. Perhaps mourning becomes us, perhaps our becoming is the forgetting of death. We forget—and yet we *are* memory, we remember and inherit, what we are takes place in the becoming after the disaster.

Why not in the wonder of becoming—not the ruin—of the past? Why in mourning and not in gratitude for death? Should we be grateful for disaster, for death, for loss?

Let us go under in affirmation and joy to the disaster that allows us to be. Let us go under in disaster to the affirmation and joy whose being we are.

With the disaster, Blanchot retraces many of the proper names and improper themes that have defined forgetting for us, repeats them to displace them. Levinas, Deleuze, Heidegger, Derrida, Winnicott, etc. With the disaster he affirms them in the mode of forgetting. For example, Levinas, responsibility, and the other:

> • In the relation of *myself to the Other*, the Other exceeds my grasp. The Other: the Separate, the Most-High which escapes my power—the powerless, therefore; the stranger, dispossessed. But, in the relation of the Other to me, everything seems to reverse itself: the distant becomes the close-by, this proximity becomes the obsession that afflicts me, that weighs down upon me, that separates me from myself—as if separation (which measured the transcendence from me to the Other) did its work within me, disidentifying me, abandoning me to passivity, leaving me without any initiative and bereft of present. And then, the other becomes rather the Overlord, indeed the Persecutor, he who overwhelms, encumbers, undoes me, he who puts me in his debt no less than he attacks me by making me answer for his crimes, by charging me with measureless responsibility which cannot be mine since it extends all the way to "substitution." (19)

The disaster separates me from myself—in proximity, the otherness of the other.

Here in interruption are other separations from oneself, other names in whose memory the self is shattered by forgetting:

> Why are there so many becomings of man, but no becoming-man? First, because man is majoritarian par excellence, whereas becomings are minoritarian; all becoming is a becoming-minoritarian.... Majority implies a state of domination, not the reverse.... In this sense, women, children, but also animals, plants, and molecules, are minoritarian.... It is important not to confuse "minoritarian," as a becoming or process, with a "minority," as an aggregate or a state. Jews, Gypsies, etc., may constitute minorities under certain conditions, but that in itself does not make them becomings. One reterritorializes, or allows oneself to be reterritorial-

ized, on a minority as a state; but in a becoming, one is deterrito-rialized. (Deleuze and Guattari, *TP*, 291)

Let us try to say it another way: There is no becoming-man because man is the molar entity par excellence, whereas becom-ings are molecular. (292)

Music is a creative, active operation that consists in deterritorializ-ing the refrain. Whereas the refrain is essentially territorial, terri-torializing, or reterritorializing, music makes it a deterritorialized content for a deterritorializing form of expression. (Deleuze and Guattari, *TP*, 300)

Becoming is away from oneself, from majoritarian to minori-tarian, shattering the boundaries that guard the self, that perpetuate the name. The disaster here is not death but form.[2] Bordering is the caesura of form. Repetition is for-getting where becoming is re-membering and repetition is dif-ference, multi-plication. Here are several versions of repetition as for-getting if not for-giving. First in the name of Marx:

Marx's theory of historical repetition, as it appears, notably in *The Eighteenth Brumaire of Louis Bonaparte*, turns on the following principle which does not seem to have been sufficiently under-stood by historians: historical repetition is neither a matter of analogy nor a concept produced by the reflection of historians, but above all a condition of historical action itself... historical actors or agents can create only on condition that they identify them-selves with figures from the past. In this sense, history is thea-tre: .... (Deleuze, *DR*, 91)

From this point of view, we must distinguish several repeti-tions which cannot be exactly reconciled:
1. An intracyclic repetition, which involves the manner in which the first two ages repeat one another—or rather, repeat one and the same "thing," act or event yet to come....
2. A cyclic repetition in which it is supposed that, at the end of the third age and at the end of a process of dissolution, every-thing recommences with the first age: ....
3. The problem remains: isn't there a repetition peculiar to the third age, which alone merits the name of eternal return? For the two first ages do no more than repeat something which appears for itself only in the third, but in the third this "thing" repeats it-self. The two "significations" are already repetitive, but the signi-fied itself is pure repetition. (93)

Then in the name of Nietzsche:

The eternal return is a force of affirmation, but it affirms eve-rything of the multiple, everything of the different, everything of chance *except* what subordinates them to the One, to the Same, to necessity, everything *except* the One, the Same and the Necessary. (115)

There has only ever been one ontological proposition: Being is univocal. There has only ever been one ontology, that of Duns Scotus, which gave being a single voice. . . . A single voice raises the clamour of being. We have no difficulty in understanding that Being, even if it is absolutely common, is nevertheless not a genus. (35)

Univocal Being is at one and the same time nomadic distribution and crowned anarchy. (37)

A single and same voice for the whole thousand-voiced multiple, a single and same Ocean for all the drops, a single clamour of Being for all beings: on condition that each being, each drop and each voice has reached the state of excess—in other words, the differences which displace and disguises them and, in turning upon its mobile cusp, causes them to return. (303–4)

In *Thus Spoke Zarathustra*, the question of the eternal return arises twice, but each time it appears as a truth not yet reached and not expressed: . . . Nevertheless, the existing dramatic progression of *Thus Spoke Zarathustra* allows a series of questions and answers.

> 1. Why, on the first occasion, does Zarathustra become angry and suffer such a terrible nightmare when the dwarf says: "All truth is crooked, time itself is a circle?" As he explains later in interpreting his nightmare: he fears that eternal return means the return of Everything, of the Same and the Similar, including the dwarf and including the smallest of men. . . .
>
> 2. Why does Zarathustra undergo a further crisis and become convalescent? Zarathustra is like Hamlet; the sea voyage has made him *capable*, he has reached the becoming-similar or the becoming-equal of the heroic metamorphosis; yet he feels that the hour has not yet come . . . .
>
> 3. Why does Zarathustra still say nothing: why is he not yet "ripe," and why will he become so only in a third unsaid time? . . . The eternal return is the end of the line. . . . The Negative does not return. The Identical does not return. The Same and the Similar, the Analogous and the Opposed, do not return. Only affirmation returns—in other words, the Different, the Dissimilar. . . . How could the reader believe that Nietzsche, who was the greatest critic of these categories, implicated Everything, the

> Same, the Identical, the Similar, the Equal, the I and the
> Self in the eternal return? (297–9)

Not to mention Pierre Menard and Cervantes, in the name of Borges:

> He did not want to compose another *Don Quixote*—which
> would be easy—but *the Don Quixote*. It is unnecessary to add that
> his aim was never to produce a mechanical transcription of the
> original; he did not propose to copy it. His admirable ambition
> was to produce pages which would coincide—word for word and
> line for line—with those of Miguel de Cervantes.³ (Borges, *PM*,
> 48–9)

The eternal return, here, infinite repetition, is the endless return
of difference, re-membering as for-getting, becoming as for-giving—
giving beyond identity and restoration. Not that one can choose
such generosity, though it seems as if that is what is being said, as if
becoming is advocated. One cannot choose giving—it comes. One
cannot choose forgetting—it withdraws and dissembles. One cannot
choose giving except as *what*, one cannot choose forgetting except as
which. Forgiving and forgetting proliferate as the image, in the modality of *as if* and *perhaps*. There can be no such choice and the temptation to choose must be resisted.⁴

This is not to say—anything but—that there is an established
discourse of forgiving and forgetting, that we can understand and
know and live by forgetting. That is the temptation. To the contrary,
every choice reiterates the absence and invisibility and violence of
the choice. Here is another example:

> No Satan
> warmed in the electric coils of his creatures
> or Gunga Din
> will make him come before you.
> To see an invisible man or a missing person,
> trust no Eng. Lit. That
> puffs him up, narrows his eyes,
> scratches him fangs. Caliban
> is still not IT.
> ... (Jussawalla, *MP*; quoted in Bhabha, *II*, 188)

Bhabha reads Fanon from the standpoint of the question in *Black
Skin, White Masks*, "What does the black man want?" (185). The
question, then, is who the black man might be to want? Such a question arrives too late to provoke an answer in any living memory. The
answer is divided by for-getting and dis-appearing.

The representative figure of such a perversion, I want to suggest, is the image of post-Enlightenment man tethered to, *not* confronted by, his dark reflection, the shadow of colonized man, that splits his presence, distorts his outline, breaches his boundaries, repeats his action at a distance, disturbs and divides the very time of his being. This ambivalent identification of the racist world . . . turns on the idea of man as his alienated image, not Self and Other but the Otherness of the Self inscribed in the perverse palimpsest of colonial identity. (187)

> One day I learnt,
> a secret art,
> Invisible-Ness, it was called.
> I think it worked
> as even now you look but never see me . . .
> (Meiling, *SHL*; quoted in Bhabha, *II*, 189)

What remains to be thought is the *repetitious* desire to recognize ourselves doubly, as, at once, decentered in the solidary processes of the political group, and yet, ourselves as a consciously committed, even individuated, agent of change—the bearer of belief. . . . We may have to force the limits of the social as we know it to rediscover a sense of political and personal agency through the unthought of the civic and the psychic. (Bhabha, *II*, 207–8)

Finally, then, a different figure of for-getting, at the extremities, bordering on re-membering as for-getting, disastering at the edge.

> Wind tugging at my sleeve
> feet sinking into the sand
> I stand at the edge where earth touches ocean
> where the two overlap
> a gentle coming together
> at other times and places a violent clash.
>
> Across the border in Mexico
>   stark silhouette of houses gutted by waves,
>   cliffs crumbling into the sea,
>   silver waves marbled with spume
>   gashing a hole under the border fence.
>
>   *Miro el mar atacar*
>   *la cerca en* Border Field Park
>   *con sus buchones de agua,*
>   an Easter Sunday resurrection
>   of the brown blood in my veins.
>
> . . .
>
> 1,950 mile-long open wound
>   dividing a *pueblo*, a culture,

> running down the length of my body,
> staking fence rods in my flesh,
>
> splits me splits me
> me raja me raja
>
> This is my home
> this thin edge of
> barbwire. (Anzaldúa, *B/F*, 23–5)

She has this fear   that she has no names   that she
has many names   that she doesn't know her names
She has this fear   that she's an image   that comes and
goes clearing and darkening   fear that she's the dreamwork
inside someone else's skull   She has this fear   that if
she takes off her clothes   shoves her brain aside peels off
her skin   that if she drains   the blood vessels
strips the flesh from,the bone   flushes out the marrow
          She has this fear   that when she does reach her-
self   turns around to embrace herself   a lion's or
witch's or serpent's head   will turn around swallow her and
grin   She has this fear that if she digs into herself   she
won't find anyone   that when   she gets "there" she
won't find her notches on the trees   the birds will have eaten
all the crumbs   She has this fear that she won't find the way
back
. . .

Her soft belly exposed to the sharp eyes of everyone; they see,
they see. Their eyes penetrate her; they slit her from head to belly.
Rajada. She is at their mercy, she can do nothing to defend herself.
(65)

> Are there lights from all sides shining on me?
> Ahead, ahead.
> curled up inside the serpent's coils,
> the damp breath of death on my face.
> I knew at that instant: something must change
> or I'd die.
> *Algo tenia que cambiar.* (56–7)

Bordering, splitting, doubling. We are *mestizo*, never pure, never
one thing, palimpsests and hybrids of this and that, mixed up, mon-
grels of identity and identification. This bordering, splitting, shatters memory. What are we to remember—which *what, we, image* of
remembrance? Memory on the border is forgetting, the forgotten is
buried in the split, the splitting comes from disastering—not without affirming. Pain, joy; violence, fulfillment; war, peace. Forgotten
disaster.

Returning from this interpolation to Blanchot reading Levinas:

> But there is an ambiguity which the paradox does not elimi-
> nate. If I, bereft of selfhood, withstand (not that I could be said
> even to have experienced it) this passive passivity when the other
> crushes me into radical alienation, is my relation still a relation to
> the other? Is it not rather a relation to the "I" of the master, to ab-
> solute egotistical force, to the dominator who predominates and
> ultimately wields the force of inquisitorial persecution? . . . I must
> come back to knowledge; I must return (if possible—for it may be
> that there is no return) to the I that knows and that knows it is ex-
> posed, not to the Other, but to the adverse I, to egotistical Om-
> nipotence, to murderous Will. (19–20)

Blanchot chooses to speak the language of paradox, that traditional
figure of traditional reason. The other transcends reason to reason,
betrays it in discourse, betrays the saying in the said. Is this not disaster? Is this not disaster itself—if disaster and reason and saying
can have a self? Is not the reversal anything but a reversal? The
other does not become my lord and master, in which I engage in
struggle, but defines the struggle that is myself, here before the
other. Here I am—myself—exposed to the other beyond all calculation. What can this be but disastering?—the other's mortality calling
me to infinity. What can this be but affirmation and joy?—I am
called to infinity.

I am called to infinity as interruption. Interrupting is another
name for paradox, exposure, substitution—all the ways in which the
face of the other signifies beyond signification. Interrupting is another name, and no name. Another name is writing, and no name.
Still another is disastering, still no name.

If the disaster is not disaster, not horror, pain, violence, or suffering, then what is it? It is a phenomenon of bordering, etching the
immemorial forgotten call of that which allows us to speak, to write,
to be—to recall.

> • It is upon losing what we have to say that we speak—upon an
> imminent and immemorial disaster—just as we say nothing except
> insofar as we can convey in advance that we take it back, by a sort
> of prolepsis, not so as finally to say nothing, but so that speaking
> might not stop at the word—the word which is, or is to be, spo-
> ken, or taken back. . . .
> • The interruption of the incessant: this is the distinguishing char-
> acteristic of fragmentary writing: interruption's having somehow
> the same meaning as that which does not cease. Both are effects of
> passivity. Where power does not reign—nor initiative, nor the cut-
> ting edge of a decision—there, dying is living. . . . So it is that men

who are destroyed (destroyed without destruction) are as though incapable of appearing, and invisible even when one sees them. And if they speak, it is with the voice of others, a voice always other than theirs which somehow accuses them, interrogates and obliges them to answer for a silent affliction which they bear without awareness. (21–2)

Is this not the calling of the other?—a voice that accuses, interrogates, and obliges us to answer? Is this not the disastering—fragments, fragmentary speaking beyond speech, words, writing beyond? Is this not forgetting, the ruin without destruction of memory, not *without* memory but beyond? The disaster is exposure beyond memory, beyond pain and suffering, beyond disaster. The disaster is disastering, otherwise.

> • If the Other is not my enemy . . . then how can he become the one who wrests me from my identity and whose proximity (for he is my neighbor) wounds, exhausts, and hounds me, tormenting me so that I am bereft of my self hood and so that this torment, this lassitude which leaves me destitute becomes my responsibility? . . .
> • Here, perhaps, is an answer. If the Other calls me into question to the point of stripping me of myself, it is because he is himself absolute nakedness, the entreaty [*supplication*] which disqualifies the me in me till it becomes sheer torture [*supplice*]. (22–3)

Because the other is disastering—torturing, stripping, disqualifying, entreating—the disaster calls—beyond, in fragments, to and from the other. And in this disastering the entreaty fails, the calling falls into betrayal.

> • I cannot welcome the Other, not even with an acceptance that would be infinite. Such is the new and difficult feature of the plot. The other, as neighbor, is the relation that I cannot sustain, and whose approach is death itself, ...
> • If I cannot welcome the Other by answering the summons . . . I am called to enter it with my selfhood gangrened and eaten away, altogether alienated (thus it is among lepers and beggars beneath the Roman ramparts that the Jews of the first centuries expected to discover the Messiah). (23)

If this is disaster, it must be understood in welcome. The failure of welcome is hospitality itself. I cannot welcome the other except by wounding, through derision and folly. And yet—or because—of this disastrous exposure to and from and of the other the world is filled with joy, I live in bread and love as well as in responsibility. I love in hospitality and need as well as in philosophy.

• Responsibility: a banal word, a notion moralistically assigned to us as a (political) duty. . . . The word "responsible" qualifies the successful man of action. But now responsibility—my responsibility for the other, for everyone, without reciprocity—is displaced. . . . I can no longer appeal to any ethics, any experience, any practice whatever—save that of some counter-living, which is to say an un-practice, or (perhaps) a word of writing.

But then, the word "responsibility" . . . comes as though from an unknown language which we only speak counter to our heart and to life, and unjustifiably, just as we are unjustifiable with respect to every death, to the death of the Other, and to our own, our own ever improper death. One would have thus to turn toward some language that never has been written—a language never inscribed but that is always to be prescribed—in order that this incomprehensible word be understood in its disastrous heaviness and in its way of summoning us to turn toward the disaster without either understanding it or bearing it. That is why responsibility is itself disastrous—the responsibility that never lightens the Other's burden (never lightens the burden he is for me), and makes us mute as far as the word we owe him is concerned. (25–7)

The word *responsibility*, the call of passivity, the language of saying in which we speak and write of death, the summons of and from and toward disaster—all are nameless, transcendent, impossible, beyond. Disaster names—and unnames—this burden of beyond. Yet if it is nameless, why is it a burden rather than a treasure? Why is disaster heavy rather than light if it is beyond the polarities of light and heavy? What is disaster but the wound and cut that cannot be named but must be lived in every moment as trauma, inscribed in every exposition as if in forgetting?

• *The unknown name, alien to naming:*
The holocaust, the absolute event of history—which is a date in history—that utter-burn where all history took fire, where the movement of Meaning was swallowed up, where the gift, which knows nothing of forgiving or of consent, shattered without giving place to anything that can be affirmed, that can be denied—gift of very passivity, gift of what cannot be given. How can it be preserved, even by thought? How can thought be made the keeper of the holocaust where all was lost, including guardian thought?
In the mortal intensity, the fleeing silence of the countless cry. (47)

The unknown name—named holocaust, perhaps Holocaust? The absolute event of history, a date in history—1939–1944? A place in history—Europe? Not Africa or Asia? The movement of meaning, the gift of life, nature, the impossible, beyond forgiving or consent, beyond any given, any keeping, any memory. Is this disaster? Can any disaster be *the disaster*, any holocaust be *the Holocaust*, any memory be so grasped? Is the disaster disastrous, wounding, violent, a violation beyond violation, violence beyond violence, wounds, destruction? Could this be death, the greatest disaster, the wounding loss, the violent separation? Could this be life, unbounded joy, unending exposing, joying, disastering?

> • There is in death, it would seem, something stronger than death: it is dying itself—the intensity of dying, the push of the impossible, the pressure of the undesirable even in the most desired. Death is power and even strength—limited, therefore.... But dying is un-power. It wrests from the present, it is always a step over the edge, it rules out every conclusion and all ends, it does not free nor does it shelter. In death, one can find an illusory refuge: the grave is as far as gravity can pull, it marks the end of the fall; the mortuary is the loophole in the impasse. But dying flees and pulls indefinitely, impossibly and intensively in the flight. (47–8)

Let us recall that it is writing, language, meaning, images, exposition, proliferation in time of which we speak. Death—name and event—is not dying, which is intensely beyond any name. Death is refuge but dying is beyond refuge and illusion. In the same way, the gift is given but giving is beyond any gift and any given. Giving gives nothing, nothing with and nothing as a name. Dying does not die, knows no death, brings nothing to end or cease, nothing with and nothing as a name.

> • The disaster is the gift; it gives disaster: as if it took no account of being or not-being. It is not advent (which is proper to what comes to pass): it does not happen. And thus I cannot ever happen upon this thought, except without knowing, without appropriating any knowledge. Or again, is it the advent of what does not happen, of what would come without arriving, outside being, and as though by drifting away? The posthumous disaster? (Blanchot, *WD*, 5)

Is this disaster—I mean disastering? Not just because of the difference between the nouns *death, gift, disaster* and the verbs *dying, giving, disastering*. Not because, not only because, but *as if*. The verb does work, names becoming, process, repeats disaster, loss, wounding in the affirmation of the unexpected, unexpectable, unanticipatable *perhaps* and *as if*. Dying takes place in order that—anything but orderly—we cannot anticipate, cannot grasp, even in the name of death and gift and disaster, or any other name. What we cannot grasp we cannot name. And still we must live it, give it, expose it, write and speak and imagine and affirm the disaster as if by forgetting.

This giving beyond gift and given, this dying beyond death and loss, this disastering beyond destruction and wounding—is this not exposure beyond remembering, beyond forgetting as forgiving? Is this forgotten the gift of what cannot be given, including the impossibility of giving forgiveness? Is this impossibility the disaster. Is disastering the possibility of being? I mean of holding onto it in grief. "In the work of mourning, it is not grief that works: grief keeps watch" (51). If mourning is work, if death watches, if disastering calls.

> • Do not forgive. Forgiveness accuses before it forgives. By accusing, by stating the injury, it makes the wrong irredeemable. It carries the blow all the way to culpability. Thus, all becomes irreparable; giving and forgiving cease to be possible.
> Forgive nothing save innocence.
> Forgive me for forgiving you. . . .
> I cannot forgive—forgiveness comes from others—but I cannot be forgiven either, if forgiveness is what calls the "I" into question and demands that I give myself, that I subject myself to the lack of subjectivity. And if forgiveness comes from others, it only comes; there is never any certitude that it can arrive, because in it there is nothing of the (sacramental) power to determine. (53)

There is nothing in forgiving that determines, forgiveness calls every determination into question. Is this disastering, traumatizing, wounding? Is it writing, speaking, exposing, imaging? Do these determine as they undetermine, or is the determining itself undetermining, the imaging the multiplying of images? Could this be the writing of the disaster—not *writing of*, nor *writing in*, but *writing as (if) it were disastering, forgetting, forgiving, exposing?*

I would imagine writing as exposition, exposure of and in and from and toward disastering. As betrayal: death and loss and wounding, joy and happiness and affirmation. This does not mean that death is good—it is neither bad nor good. It does not mean that loss is joy, that we are to take pleasure and be happy in suffering. It is that in the disastering of death and loss and time and wounds these are affirmed—there is affirming—*as life*. This is not to enjoy death but perhaps to hate it in the midst of a joyous disastering. After all there is enjoying, and it is unbounded with dying and disastering as if all were giving, forgiving, forgetting. "If it weren't for prisons, we would know that we are all already in prison" (66).

Reminding us of another psychoanalytic moment, repeated in a different register, another forgetting. "Why do men fight *for* their servitude as stubbornly as though it were their salvation?" (Deleuze and Guattari, *A–O*, 29).[5] Returning us to death from servitude and prison, as if there were no salvation for any, as if the names *death, disaster, servitude, salvation* named something no matter how forgotten—perhaps *life, happiness, freedom, immanence*—or something else.

> • Can one say: horror reigns at Auschwitz, senselessness in the Gulag? Horror, because extermination in every form is the immediate horizon. Zombies, pariahs, infidels: such is the truth of life....
>
> Surely, senselessness is at Auschwitz, horror in the Gulag.... Inside was horror at its most extreme. Or again, sometimes concerts were organized. The power of music seems, momentarily, to bring forgetfulness and dangerously causes the distance between murderers and victims to disappear. But, Langbein adds, for the pariahs there was neither sport nor music. There is a limit at which the practice of any art becomes an affront to affliction. Let us not forget this. (82–3)

Let us not forget this. Let us forget this, while remembering. In the name of disaster—and life—let us give Blanchot the closing words on forgetting.

> • If forgetfulness precedes memory or perhaps founds it, or has no connection with it at all, then to forget is not simply a weakness, a failing, an absence or void.... No, forgetfulness would be not emptiness, but neither negative nor positive: the passive demand that neither welcomes nor withdraws the past, but, designating there what has never taken place ... refers us to nonhistorical forms of time, to the other of all tenses, to their eternal or eternally provisional indecision, bereft of destiny, without presence. (85)

> • That there is no awaiting the disaster is true to the extent that waiting is considered always to be the awaiting of something waited for, or else unexpected. But awaiting—just as it is not related to the future any more than to an accessible past—is also the awaiting of awaiting, which does not situate us in a present, for "I" have always already awaited what I will always wait for: the immemorial, the unknown which has no present, and which I can no more remember than I can know whether I am not forgetting the future—the future being my relation with what, in what is coming, does not come and thus does not present, or re-present itself. That is why it is permitted, by the movement of writing, to say: You are already dead. And what is forgetfulness? It is not related to ignorance of the eventual present (the future), any more than it is loss of the memorable from the memory. Forgetfulness designates what is beyond possibility, the unforgettable Other; it

indicates that which, past or future, it does not circumscribe: patience in its passive mode. (117)

• "That forgetfulness exists: this remains to be proved." (Nietzsche.) Exactly: unproven, improbable forgetfulness, vigilance that ever reawakens us. (105)

Forgetting remains to be proved because it is beyond proof, reason, calculation, beyond remembering. Forgetting remains beyond, exposition as if disastering, affirming, joying, loving, giving. Forgetting is for giving beyond any memory, present or future.

The disaster is disastrous, violent, catastrophic.
The disaster is disastering.
The disaster is not disastrous, not disastering, not disaster,
Even as it is violent, catastrophic, betraying, wounding.

Perhaps.

The disaster is forgetting, forgetting is disastrous.
The disaster is the forgotten, the forgotten has no name.
The disaster calls, gives, beyond memory, time, and history.
Time and history are the disaster.
Time and history are beyond memory.

Perhaps.

Calling, responding, giving, forgiving are all forgotten,
Are all forgettings,
Exposure as if not beyond any name.
Ethics, life, being as if not beyond memory, beyond time,
Exposition as if from the borders of the world.
Any world, mine and the others'.

Perhaps.

The image proliferates.
The image is forgotten.
The proliferation is forgetting.
Forgetting is calling, giving, responding, forgiving.
Beyond any truth, beyond truth itself,
If truth can have a self except disastrously.

Perhaps.

Death is forgetting, oblivion, beyond memory,
Loss, wounding, separation, beyond remembering,
Betraying beyond life,
Life beyond life,

Calling beyond calling,
Giving beyond gifts,
Disastering beyond disasters.

Perhaps.

As if disaster were joy.
As if death were life.
As if loss were fortune.
As if giving were nothing.
As if calling were empty.
As if emptiness called beyond fullness.
As if time were empty.
As if the other were myself.
As if I were the other.

Perhaps.

As if the loss of time were its increase.
As if the loss of time were its transformation.
As if the loss of time were death.
As if forgetting were memory.
As if remembering were transgression.
As if the image were its proliferation.

Perhaps.

Between the image and its proliferation,
Between the image and the other images,
Between the one and the other,
In exposition,
There is forgetting,
There is forgiving,
Giving beyond gifts.
The forgotten is generosity beyond gifts.
The forgetting is exposition beyond itself.

Perhaps.
As if.
~~Not~~.
Beyond.

NOTES

Introduction

1 See here chapter 3, p. 61.

2 See the discussions of Plato in my gift series, each the personification of another living creature in the name of Plato.

3 In later chapters, see especially chap. 1, pp. 24–7.

4 Not to mention many others:

In *Being and Time* we purposely and cautiously say, *il y a l'Être*: "there is / it gives" [*"es gibt"*] Being. *Il y a* translates "it gives" imprecisely. For the "it" that here "gives" is Being itself. The "gives" names the essence of Being that is giving, granting its truth. The self-giving into the open, along with the open region itself, is Being itself.
    At the same time "it gives" is used preliminarily to avoid the locution "Being is"; for "is" is commonly said of some thing which is. We call such a thing a being. But Being "is" precisely not "a being." (Heidegger, *LH*, 214)

    We say of beings: they are. With regard to the matter "Being" and with regard to the matter "time," we remain cautious. We do not say: Being is, time is, but rather: there is Being and there is time. Instead of saying "it is," we say "there is," "It gives [*es gibt*]."
    In order to get beyond the idiom and back to the matter, we must show how this "there is" can be experienced and seen. The appropriate way to get there is to explain what is given in the "it gives," what "Being" means, which—It gives; what "time" means, which—It gives. Accordingly, we try to look ahead to the It which—gives Being and time. Thus looking ahead, we become

foresighted in still another sense. We try to bring the It and its giving into view, and capitalize the "It." (Heidegger, *TB*, p. 5)

> Being, by which all beings as such are marked, Being means presencing.... To let presence means: to unconceal, to bring to openness. In unconcealing prevails a giving, the giving that gives presencing, that is, Being, in letting-presence. (Heidegger, 125 *TB*, p. 5)

5 See here chaps. 7 and 8.

Chapter 1

1 See the introduction here, pp. 4–5.

2 Throughout the dialogues Socrates tells tales handed down from old (*palaios*), as if in memory and forgetting, as if he lives with ghosts. See the men and women who know the truths of the gods in this chapter, pp. 24–5. See also *Parmenides*, where being is both older and younger than itself.

3 See the continued discussion of *Phaedrus* in chapter 8, pp. 185–8.

4 These are modeled after the three levels of ambiguity Blanchot describes in his *Space of Literature*. See here chap. 2, p. 45.

5 I offered such a reading of *Meno* in my *LD*. Here I would pass by that reading—though I still pursue it—to emphasize the mysteries of unforgetting in remembering—I mean in every truth, every knowing, every act. Knowing and truth are exposition.

6 See the introduction here and chap. 3.

7 He is understood to be the Anytus who at his trial demanded Socrates' death.

Chapter 2

1 See my *WAP*, especially the introduction.

2 Something of this sort can be found today. Speaking of history as the literature of fact, Ash says the following:

> the truth achieved by the literature of fact is in many ways the same as that achieved by the literature of fiction. If we are con-

vinced that human beings might have acted, thought, or felt in this way, it is in large measure as a result of the writer's art and imagination.

I would suggest that, as well as satisfying all the truth-tests that apply to fiction, the literature of fact must pass two further, special truth-tests: those of "facticity" and of veracity. (Ash, *OF*, 61)

As if facticity and veracity were immune to the *perhaps* and *as if* that make literature literature, as if the tests did not themselves depend on imagination and invention for their plausibility, as if we could ever escape the multiplications and betrayals of exposition. Fact and truth are valuable things, guarded by the betrayals of their expositions.

Chapter 3

1 *La réalité comporte le différend*. Translated by Van Den Abbeele as "Reality entails the differend" (Lyotard, *D*, 50; *DPD*, 90). Reality is constituted by forgetting.

2 See p. 74 for the full quotation.

3 By which men, in an act of sovereign reason, confine their neighbors, and communicate and recognize each other through the merciless language of non-madness. See here chap. 4, p. 109.

4 Concluding with the glorious reading:

We know that Nietzsche gave no exposition of the eternal return, ... In *Thus Spoke Zarathustra*, the question of the eternal return arises twice, but each time it appears as a truth not yet reached and not expressed: .... The first time is enough to make Zarathustra ill, producing his terrible nightmare and leading him to undertake a sea voyage. The second time, after a further crisis, the convalescent Zarathustra smiles indulgently at his animals, knowing that his destiny will be decided only in an unsaid third time (that announced at the end: "The sign has come"). .... Nevertheless, the existing dramatic progression of *Thus Spoke Zarathustra* allows a series of questions and answers.

1. Why, on the first occasion, does Zarathustra become angry and suffer such a terrible nightmare when the dwarf says: "All truth is crooked, time itself is a circle?" As he explains later in interpreting his nightmare: he fears that eternal return means the return of Everything, of the Same and the Similar, including the dwarf and including the smallest of men. ...

2. Why does Zarathustra undergo a further crisis and become con-
    valescent? Zarathustra is like Hamlet; the sea voyage has made
    him *capable*, he has reached the becoming-similar or the becom-
    ing-equal of the heroic metamorphosis; yet he feels that the hour
    has not yet come. . . .
3. Why does Zarathustra still say nothing: why is he not yet "ripe,"
    and why will he become so only in a third unsaid time? . . . The
    eternal return is the end of the line. . . . The Negative does not re-
    turn. The Identical does not return. The Same and the Similar,
    the Analogous and the Opposed, do not return. Only affirmation
    returns—in other words, the Different, the Dissimilar. . . . How
    could the reader believe that Nietzsche, who was the greatest
    critic of these categories, implicated Everything, the Same, the
    Identical, the Similar, the Equal, the I and the Self in the eternal
    return? (pp. 297–9)

See the detailed discussion of this reading of the eternal return in my
WAP, chap. 5.

5 See p. 90.

6 The expulsion of the Jews from Spain in 1492.

7 See the return of the inhuman in the next chapter, p. 104.

Chapter 4

1 See another translation of this passage on p. 199.

2 Kant's word, *Unmündigkeit*, is translated as *immaturity* and *tutelage*
in English, as *minorité* in French. I would hold on to the image of unworldliness, being out of this world. See here pp. 122–3.
    I would also call attention to the lower case in enlightenment, a ges-
ture toward what is forgotten in the capitalization, as if The Enlightenment were something definite to remember.

3 This is a passage I have quoted repeatedly in my recent work as if
all my recent writing took place inside the question posed by the girl and
her fruits, of the Muses and their arts. And perhaps it does, with ghosts,
between life and death, in memory of forgetting.

4 See my *WAP*, pp. 106–7.

5 I am quoting Cixous rather than Lispector. Cixous's reading is
imund.

6 By the Judeo-Christian God, if you will.

7 Again, I am quoting Cixous reading Lispector. The translation says *impure*.

Chapter 5

1 Including Hegel's decay. See chap. 4, pp. 110–1. Perhaps a frog knows life from its perspectives.

2 A question that returns for us in chapter 7.

Chapter 6

1 And everyday practices of resistance. See here chap. 9, pp. 235–7.

2 In Deleuze's words, "the Heideggerian *Not* refers not to the negative in Being but to Being as difference; it refers not to negation but to questioning" (Deleuze, *DR*, 64).

3 "[T]he necessary disappearance of that which is its foundation—of the person it resembles and the person in whose eyes it is only a resemblance. This very subject—which is the same—has been elided. And representation, freed finally from the relation that was impeding it, can offer itself as representation in its pure form" (*OT*, p. 16).

4 Only men, only whites, only wealthy human beings have had rights.

Chapter 7

1 See chap. 2 here, p. 45.

Chapter 8

1 See here chap. 7, pp. 160–1.

2 "Now it seems to me that *The Origin* can also be read as an essay on the gift (*Schenkung*), on the offering: one of the three senses, precisely, in which truth is said to come to its installation, its institution, or its investiture [*Stiftung*]" (Derrida, *TP*, 291–2).

3 See also this chapter, pp. 210–2.

4 See chapter 13.

5 "How could one not evoke the hymn to love proclaimed by Saint Paul in the First Epistle to the Corinthians?" (Ricoeur, *MHF*, 467).

6 See here also chap. 11, pp. 285–93.

7 Even Athena's regard, as we have seen it practiced on the Eumenides. See chapter 2, pp. 71–4.

8 Restricted economies, if you will, substitutions and exchanges; general economy after Bataille as well, extravagance beyond exchange, substitution, and utility.

9 See here chapter 2.

10 As cited in Arendt, *BPF*, n. 3, p. 227: "The story is the last of a series of 'Notes from the year 1920,' under the title 'HE.' Translated from the German by Willa and Edwin Muir, they appeared in this country in *The Great Wall of China*, New York, 1946."

11 *Allegorical etching by Jan Van der Straet for* Americae decima pars *by Jean-Théodore de Bry (Oppenheim, 1619).*

Chapter 9

1 See here chap. 2, pp. 25–31, and my *WAP*.

2 See here chapter 4. There is something odd in both Kant and Freud (repeatedly expressed in its absurdity by Kafka) with this example of censorship in relation to the mind and reason, as if the state controlled what we think. That at least must be the question.

3 See the introduction here, pp. 8–9.

4 See here chap. 6, pp. 149–53.

5 Here is a physicist on the subject:

It turns out that our mastery of the universe is largely a bluff— all hat and no cattle. The argument that all the important laws of nature are known is part of this bluff.

Thus the end of knowledge and the closing of the frontier it symbolizes is not a looming crisis at all, but merely one of many embarrassing fits of hubris in civilization's long history. (Laughlin, *RP*, B8)

He argues that organizations develop their own principles, that

the organization can acquire meaning and life of its own and begin to transcend the parts from which it is made.
...Thus if a simple physical phenomenon can become effectively independent of the more fundamental laws from which it descends, so can we. I am carbon, but I need not have been. I have a meaning transcending the atoms from which I am made. (B7)

Every image transcends and is transcended in the images that it proliferates.

6 See here chap. 4, p. 104.

7 See here chap. 7, pp. 160–2.

8 To be continued here in chap. 11.

Chapter 10

1 See p. 254 for the complete quotation.

2 That phrase is "Agriculture is now a mechanized food industry; in essence it is no different than the production of corpses in the gas chambers and death camps, the embargoes and food reductions to starving countries, the making of hydrogen bombs" (quoted in Lyotard, *HJ*, 85).

3 With respect to *Being and Time*, Derrida remarks that Heidegger dismisses sexual difference as constituting *Dasein*, again in the name of *Geschlecht*:

Dasein in general hides, shelters in itself the internal possibility of a factual dispersion or dissemination (*faktische Zerstreuunt*) in its own body (*Leiblichkeit*) and "thereby in sexuality" (*und damit in die Geschlechtlichkeit*). Every proper body of one's own [*corps propre*] is sexed and there is no *Dasein* without its own body. (Derrida, *G1*, 75)

And he does so repeatedly, under one heading after another.

The friend has no face, no figure. No sex. No name. The friend is not a man, nor a woman: it is not I, nor a "self," not a subject, nor a person. It is another Dasein that each Dasein *carries*, through the voice it hears, with itself.... (Derrida, *G4*, 165)

The animal has no friend, man has no friendship properly so called for the animal. The animal that is "world poor," that has neither language nor experience of death, etc., the animal that has no hand, the animal that has no friend, has no ear either, the ear capable of hearing and of carrying the friend that is also the ear that opens Dasein to its own potentiality-for-being and that . . . is the ear of being, the ear for being. (172)

4 See chap. 11, p. 295, for the full quotation.

5 See chap. 11, p. 296, for the full quotation.

6 See the introduction here, p. 8, for the full quotation.

7 See here chap. 2, p. 45. See also chap. 13 and *the disaster*.

8 Some additional passages:

There is no natural religion; but already human egoism leaves pure nature *by virtue of the human body raised upwards*, committed in the *direction of height*. This is not its empirical illusion *but its ontological production and its ineffaceable testimony*. The "I can" proceeds from this height.
. . . in need I can sink my teeth into the real and satisfy myself in assimilating the other; in Desire there is no sinking one's teeth into being, no satiety, but an uncharted future before me. . . . Need has thus the time to convert this *other* into the *same* by labor. I exist as a body, that is, as raised up, ... For a body that labors everything is not already accomplished, already done; thus to be a body is to have time in the midst of the facts, to be *me* though living in the *other*.
. . . it is the relation with the other, inscribed in the body as its elevation, that makes possible the transformation of enjoyment into consciousness and labor. (Levinas, *TI*, 117)

the body is not only what is steeped in the element, but what *dwells*, that is, inhabits and possesses. (137)

What remains unrecognized is that the erotic, analysed as fecundity, breaks up reality into relations irreducible to the relations of genus and species, part and whole, action and passion, truth and error; that in sexuality the subject enters into relation with what is absolutely other, with an alterity of a type unforeseeable in formal logic, with what remains other in the relation and is never converted into "mine," and that nonetheless this relation has nothing ecstatic about it, for the pathos of voluptuosity is made of duality. (276)

9 I am reading "Reality and Its Shadow." Even in *Otherwise than Being*, Levinas holds onto the betrayal of art in the assembling of being.

> Art is the pre-eminent exhibition in which the said is reduced to a pure theme, to absolute exposition, even to shamelessness capable of holding all looks for which it is exclusively destined. The said is reduced to the Beautiful, which supports Western ontology....
>
> In the inexhaustible diversity of works, that is, in the *essential renewal* of art, colors, forms, sounds, words, buildings—already on the verge of being identified as entities, already disclosing their nature and their qualities in the substantives that bear adjectives—recommence being. (*OB*, 40)

10 See Blanchot, *Le Pas Au-Delà*, translated into English as *The Step Not Beyond*, translated by me *as if not beyond*. See my *GSSEB*. See also the ambiguity of the image, discussed here in chap. 2, p. 45.

11 As general economy. In Bataille's words:

> I insist on the fact that there is generally no growth but only a luxurious squandering of energy in every form! The history of life on earth is mainly the effect of a wild exuberance; the dominant event is the development of luxury, the production of increasingly burdensome forms of life. (Bataille, *AS* 1, "Consumption," 33)

> Changing from the perspectives of *restrictive* economy to those of *general* economy actually accomplishes a Copernican transformation:.... Henceforth, leaving aside pure and simple dissipation, analogous to the construction of the Pyramids, the possibility of pursuing growth is itself subordinated to giving. (25)

> The *general economy*, in the first place, makes apparent that excesses of energy are produced, and that by definition, these excesses cannot be utilized. The excessive energy can only be lost without the slightest aim, consequently without any meaning. (Bataille, *MM*, 233, n. 1)

Chapter 11

1 Written and delivered shortly after Derrida's death. With HC, I hope, on the side of life (Derrida, *HCL*).

2 See here also chap. 8.

3 See here chap. 8, pp. 185–8.

4 The rest of this discussion on friendship and mourning recasts Margalit's account of shared memory, discussed here in chapter 3.

5 See this chapter, n. 1.

6 See the introduction here, p. 8, for the full quotation.

7 See the introduction here, pp. 8–9.

Chapter 12

1 The three subjects are: "first, the difficulty of expressing physical pain; second, the political and perceptual complications that arise as a result of that difficulty; and third, the nature of both material and verbal expressibility or, more simply, the nature of human creation" (Scarry, *BP*, 1).

2 See here chap. 9, p. 221.

3 From the EMDR web site at http://www.emdr.com as of October 2004. First the practice:

Eye Movement Desensitization and Reprocessing (EMDR) integrates elements of many effective psychotherapies in structured protocols that are designed to maximize treatment effects. These include psychodynamic, cognitive behavioral, interpersonal, experiential, and body-centered therapies. EMDR is an information processing therapy and uses an eight phase approach.

During EMDR the client attends to past and present experiences in brief sequential doses while simultaneously focusing on an external stimulus. Then the client is instructed to let new material become the focus of the next set of dual attention. This sequence of dual attention and personal association is repeated many times in the session.

Eight Phases of Treatment

The first phase is a history taking session during which the therapist assesses the client's readiness for EMDR and develops a treatment plan. Client and therapist identify possible targets for EMDR processing. These include recent distressing events, current situations that elicit emotional disturbance, related historical incidents, and the development of specific skills and behaviors that will be needed by the client in future situations.

During the second phase of treatment, the therapist ensures that the client has adequate methods of handling emotional distress and good coping skills, and that the client is in a relatively stable state. If further stabilization is required, or if additional skills are needed, therapy focuses on providing these. The client is then able to use stress reducing techniques whenever necessary, during or between sessions. However, one goal is not to need these techniques once therapy is complete.

In phase three through six, a target is identified and processed using EMDR procedures. These involve the client identifying the most vivid visual image related to the memory (if available), a negative belief about self, related emotions and body sensations. The client also identifies a preferred positive belief. The validity of the positive belief is rated, as is the intensity of the negative emotions.

After this, the client is instructed to focus on the image, negative thought, and body sensations while simultaneously moving his/her eyes back and forth following the therapist's fingers as they move across his/her field of vision for 20–30 seconds or more, depending upon the need of the client. Athough eye movements are the most commonly used external stimulus, therapists often use auditory tones, tapping, or other types of tactile stimulation. The kind of dual attention and the length of each set is customized to the need of the client. The client is instructed to just notice whatever happens. After this, the clinician instructs the client to let his/her mind go blank and to notice whatever thought, feeling, image, memory, or sensation comes to mind. Depending upon the client's report the clinician will facilitate the next focus of attention. In most cases a client-directed association process is encouraged. This is repeated numerous times throughout the session. If the client becomes distressed or has difficulty with the process, the therapist follows established procedures to help the client resume processing. When the client reports no distress related to the targeted memory, the clinician asks him/her to think of the preferred positive belief that was identified at the beginning of the session, or a better one if it has emerged, and to focus on the incident, while simultaneously engaging in the eye movements. After several sets, clients generally report increased confidence in this positive belief. The therapist checks with the client regarding body sensations. If there are negative sensations, these are processed as above. If there are positive sensations, they are further enhanced.

In phase seven, closure, the therapist asks the client to keep a journal during the week to document any related material that may arise and reminds the client of the self-calming activities that were mastered in phase two.

The next session begins with phase eight, re-evaluation of the previous work, and of progress since the previous session. EMDR treatment ensures processing of all related historical events, current incidents that elicit distress, and future scenarios that will require different responses. The overall goal is produce the most comprehensive and profound treatment effects in the shortest period of time, while simultaneously maintaining a stable client within a balanced system.

After EMDR processing, clients generally report that the emotional distress related to the memory has been eliminated, or greatly decreased, and that they have gained important cognitive insights. Importantly, these emotional and cognitive changes usually result in spontaneous behavioral and personal change, which are further enhanced with standard EMDR procedures.

Then the theory:

All humans are understood to have a physiologically-based information processing system. This can be compared to other body systems, such as digestion in which the body extracts nutrients for health and survival. The information processing system processes the multiple elements of our experiences and stores memories in an accessible and useful form. Memories are linked in networks that contain related thoughts, images, emotions, and sensations. Learning occurs when new associations are forged with material already stored in memory.

When a traumatic or very negative event occurs, information processing may be incomplete, perhaps because strong negative feelings or dissociation interfere with information processing. This prevents the forging of connections with more adaptive information that is held in other memory networks. For example, a rape survivor may "know" that rapists are responsible for their crimes, but this information does not connect with her feeling that she is to blame for the attack. The memory is then dysfunctionally stored without appropriate associative connections and with many elements still unprocessed. When the individual thinks about the trauma, or when the memory is triggered by similar situations, the person may feel like she is reliving it, or may experience strong emotions and physical sensations. A prime example is the intrusive thoughts, emotional disturbance, and negative self-referencing beliefs of posttraumatic stress disorder (PTSD).

It is not only major traumatic events, or "large-T Traumas" that can cause psychological disturbance. Sometimes a relatively minor event from childhood, such as being teased by ones peers or disparaged by ones parent, may not be adequately processed.

Such "small-t traumas" can result in personality problems and become the basis of current dysfunctional reactions.

Shapiro proposes that EMDR can assist to successfully alleviate clinical complaints by processing the components of the contributing distressing memories. These can be memories of either small-t or large-T traumas. Information processing is thought to occur when the targeted memory is linked with other more adaptive information. Learning then takes place, and the experience is stored with appropriate emotions, able to appropriately guide the person in the future.

Chapter 13

1 Together with God. See here chap. 10, p. 258.

2 See chap. 7, pp. 171–2.

3 "I am the only one who thinks of himself not as a commentator on Nietzsche but as being the same as he. Not that my thought is always faithful to his: it often diverges from it, especially if I consider the detailed developments of a theory. But that thought is placed under the same conditions as was his" (Bataille, *AS 3*, 367).

4 See the introduction here, pp. 8–9.

5 Ascribed to Spinoza and then to Wilhelm Reich.

BIBLIOGRAPHY

Abbott, Sally. "The Origins of God in the Blood of the Lamb" [*OGBL*]. In Diamond and Orenstein, eds., *Reweaving the World*.

Abram, David. *The Spell of the Sensuous: Perception and Language in a More-Than-Human World* [*SS*]. New York: Pantheon, 1996.

Acker, Kathy. "Against Ordinary Language: The Language of the Body" [*AOL*]. In Kroker and Kroker, eds., *Last Sex*.

Ackerman, Robert John. *Heterogeneities: Race, Gender, Class, Nation, and State* [*H*]. Amherst: University of Massachusetts Press, 1996.

Adams, Carol J. *The Sexual Politics of Meat* [*SPM*]. New York: Continuum, 1992.

Adams, Robert L. "Alain Locke Revisited: The Reconsideration of an Aesthetic" [*ALR*]. In Young, ed. *Art, Culture, and Ethnicity*.

Addelson, Kathryn Pyne. *Impure Thoughts* [*IT*]. Philadelphia: Temple University Press, 1991.

———. "The Man of Professional Wisdom" [*MPW*]. In *Impure Thoughts*.

Aeschylus. *Oresteia* [*O*]: *Agamemnon* [*A*]; *Libation Bearers* [*LB*]; *Eumenides* [*E*]. Trans. Christopher Collard. Oxford: Oxford University Press, 2002.

Agamben, Giorgio. *Language and Death: The Place of Negativity* [*LD*]. Minneapolis: University of Minnesota Press, 1991.

Agar, Herbert, and Allen Tate, eds. *Who Owns America? A New Declaration of Independence* [*WOA*]. Freeport, NY: Books for Libraries Press, 1970.

Allen, Douglas. "Social Constructions of Self: Some Asian, Marxist, and Feminist Critiques of Dominant Western Views of Self" [*SCS*]. In Allen, ed. *Culture and Self*.

Allen, Douglas, ed. *Culture and Self: Philosophical and Religious Perspectives, East and West* [*CS*]. Boulder, CO: Westview, 1997.

Allen, Paula Gunn. *The Sacred Hoop: Recovering the Feminine in American Indian Traditions* [*SH*]. Boston: Beacon Press, 1986.

Allen, Robert. "The Land Monopoly" [*LM*]. *Green Revolution* 9, 10 (October 1971): 7, 16.

Althusser, Louis, and Étienne Balibar. *Reading Capital* [*RC*]. Trans. Ben Brewster. London: NLB, 1970.

Alverson, Hoyt. *Mind in the Heart of Darkness: Value and Self-Identity among the Tswana of Southern Africa* [MH]. New Haven, CT: Yale University Press, 1978.

Ames, Roger T. "Putting the *Te* Back into Taoism" [PTBT]. In Callicott and Ames, eds., *Nature in Asian Traditions of Thought.*

Ames, Roger T., ed. *Self as Person in Asian Theory and Practice* [SPATP]. With Wimal Dissanayake and Thomas P. Kasulis. Albany: State University of New York Press, 1994.

Ames, Roger T., with Thomas P. Kasulis and Wimal Dissanayake. *Self as Image in Asian Theory and Practice* [SIATP]. Albany: State University of New York Press, 1998.

——. *Self as Person in Asian Theory and Practice* [SPATP]. Albany: State University of New York Press, 1994.

Andersen, Margaret L., and Patricia Hill Collins, eds. *Race, Class, and Gender: An Anthology* [RCG]. 2nd ed. Belmont, CA: Wadsworth, 1995.

Anderson, Walt. *The Future of the Self: Inventing the Postmodern Person* [FS]. New York: T. P. Tarcher, 1997.

Andolsen, Barbara Hilkert, Christine E. Gudorf, and Mary D. Pellauer, eds. *Women's Consciousness, Women's Conscience* [WCWC]. New York: Winston, 1985.

Andreach, Robert. *Creating the Self in the Contemporary American Theatre* [CSCAT]. Carbondale: Southern Illinois University Press, 1998.

Anzaldúa, Gloria. *Borderlands/La Frontera: The New Mestiza* [B/F]. 2nd ed. San Francisco: Aunt Lute Books, 1999.

Appelbaum, David. *Everyday Spirits* [ES]. Albany: State University of New York Press, 1993.

——. *The Interpenetrating Reality: Bringing the Body to Touch* [IR]. New York: Lang, 1988.

Appiah, Kwame Anthony. "Racisms" [R]. In Goldberg, ed., *Anatomy of Racism.*

Apter, Andrew: *Black Critics & Kings: The Hermeneutics of Power in Yoruba Society* [BCK]. Chicago: University of Chicago Press, 1992.

Aquinas, Thomas. *Basic Writings of St. Thomas Aquinas* [BWTA]. Ed. Anton C. Pegis. 2 vols. New York: Random House, 1945.

——. *Summa Theologica* [ST]. Trans. Fathers of the English Dominican Province. London: Burns, Oates & Washbourne, 1912–36.

Ardener, E. "Belief and the Problem of Women" [BPW]. In J. La Fontaine, ed., *The Interpretation of Ritual* [IR]. London: Tavistock, 1975. Reprinted in S. Ardener, *Perceiving Women.*

Ardener, S. *Defining Females: The Nature of Women in Society* [DF]. London: Croom, Helm, 1978.

——. Ed. *Perceiving Women* [PW]. London: Dent, 1975.

Arendt, Hannah. *Eichmann in Jerusalem: A Report on the Banality of Evil* [EJ]. Rev. and enl. ed. New York: Viking, 1964.

——. *The Human Condition* [HC]. Chicago: University of Chicago Press, 1958.

Arens, W., and I. Karp, eds. *Creativity of Power* [CP]. Washington, DC, and London: Smithsonian Press, 1989.

Aristotle. *The Basic Works of Aristotle* [BWA]. New York: Random House, 1941.

——. *The Complete Works of Aristotle* [CWA]. Ed. Jonathan Barnes. 2 vols. Princeton: Princeton University Press, 1984. All quotations from Aristotle are from this edition unless otherwise indicated.

——. *On Memory* [OM]. In *Complete Works*.

——. *Poetics* [P]. In *Basic Works of Aristotle*. Reprinted in part in Ross, ed., *Art and Its Significance*.

Armstrong, Isobel. *The Radical Aesthetic* [RA]. Oxford: Blackwell, 2001.

Asch, Michael. "To Negotiate into Confederation: Canadian Aboriginal Views on Their Political Rights" [NC]. In Wilmsen, ed., *We Are Here.*

Ash, Timothy Garton. "On the Frontier" [OF]. *New York Review of Books*, Vol. 49, No. 17 (November 7, 2002): 60–1.

Athanasiou, Tom. *Divided Planet: The Ecology of Rich and Poor* [DP]. Boston: Little, Brown & Co., 1997.

Atkinson, Adrian. *Principles of Political Ecology* [PPE]. London: Belhaven Press, 1991.

Augé, Marc. *Oblivion* [O]. Trans. Marjolijn de Jager. Minneapolis: University of Minnesota Press, 2004. Translation of *Les Formes de l'oubli* [FO]. Paris: Éditions Payot & Rivages, 1998.

Augustine. *Basic Writings of Saint Augustine* [BWA]. Ed. and int. Whitney J. Oates. New York: Random House, 1948.

——. *The City of God* [CG]. In *Basic Writings of Saint Augustine*.

Avalos, David, with John C. Welchman. "Response to The Philosophical Brothel" [RPB]. In Welchman, ed. *Rethinking Borders.*

Baack, Ben. "The Development of Exclusive Property Rights to Land in England: An Exploratory Essay" [DEPRLE]. *Economy and History* 22, no. 1 (1979): 63–74.

Bachelard, Gaston. *The Poetics of Reverie: Childhood, Language, and the Cosmos* [PR]. Trans. Daniel Russell. Boston: Beacon Press, 1969.

——. *The Poetics of Space* [PS]. Trans. Maria Jolas. Boston: Beacon Press, 1964.

——. *The Psychoanalysis of Fire* [PF]. Trans. Alan C. M. Ross. Pref. Northrop Frye. Boston: Beacon, 1964.

——. *Water and Dreams: An Essay on the Imagination of Matter* [WD]. Trans. Edith R. Farrell. Dallas, TX: Pegasus Foundation; Dallas Institution Publications, 1983.

Bacon, Francis. *Novum Organum* [NO]. In Burtt, ed., *English Philosophers from Bacon to Mill.*

Badiner, Allan Hunt, ed. *Dharma Gaia: A Harvest of Essays in Buddhism and Ecology* [DG]. Berkeley: Parallax Press, 1990.

Baechler, Jean. "Liberty, Property, and Equality" [LPE]. In Pennock and Chapman, eds., *Nomos XXII*, 269–88.

Bakhtin, Mikhail Mikhailovich. *Discourse in the Novel* [DN]. Reprinted in part in Ross, ed., *Art and Its Significance*. In *Dialogic Imagination*. Ed.

Michael Holquist. Trans. Caryl Emerson and Michael Holquist. Austin: University of Texas Press, 1981.

Balibar, Étienne. "Paradoxes of Universality" [PU]. In Goldberg, ed., Anatomy of Racism.

Bar On, Bat-Ami, ed. Modern Engendering: Critical Feminist Readings in Modern Western Philosophy [ME]. Albany: State University of New York Press, 1994.

Barnard, Kathryn E., and T. Berry Brazelton, eds. Touch: The Foundation of Experience [T]. National Center for Clinical Infant Programs. Madison, CT: International Universities Press, 1990.

Barrow, John D. The Artful Universe [AU]. Oxford: Clarendon Press, 1995.

Barthes, Roland. The Pleasure of the Text [PT]. Trans. Richard Miller. New York: Hill and Wang, 1975.

Basham, A. L. The Wonder that was India [WI]. London: Sidgwick and Jackson, 1967.

Baskin, Yvonne. The Work of Nature: How the Diversity of Life Sustains Us [WN]. Washington, DC: Island Press, 1997.

Bataille, Georges. The Accursed Share: An Essay on General Economy [AS]. Trans. Richard Hurley. 2 vols. New York: Zone Books, 1988 and 1993. Translation of La Part maudite, L'Histoire de l'érotisme, and La Souveraineté (Consumption [1]; The History of Eroticism [2]; Sovereignty [3]). In Georges Bataille, Oeuvres Complètes. Paris: Gallimard, 1976.

———. Inner Experience [IE]. Trans. Leslie Anne Boldt. Albany: State University of New York Press, 1988. Translation of L'Expérience intérieure [EI]. Paris: Gallimard, 1954.

———. Méthode de Méditation [MM]. In L'Expérience intérieure. Quoted in Derrida, "From Restricted to General Economy."

———. "The Notion of Expenditure" [NE]. In Visions of Excess.

———. Visions of Excess: Selected Writings, 1927–1939 [VE]. Trans. Allan Stoekl, with Carl R. Lovitt and Donald M. Leslie, Jr. Minneapolis: University of Minnesota Press, 1985.

Batchelor, Martine. "Buddhist Economics Reconsidered" [BER]. In Badiner, ed., Dharma Gaia.

———. "Even the Stones Smile: Selections from the Scriptures" [ESS]. In Batchelor and Brown, eds., Buddhism and Ecology.

———. "The Sands of the Ganges" [SG]. In Batchelor and Brown, eds., Buddhism and Ecology.

Batchelor, Martine, and Kerry Brown, eds. Buddhism and Ecology [BE]. New York: Cassell Publishers, 1992.

Batchelor, Stephen. "Buddhist Economics Reconsidered" [BER]. In Badiner, ed., Dharma Gaia.

Battersby, Christine. The Phenomenal Woman: Feminist Metaphysics and the Patterns of Identity [PW]. New York: Routledge, 1998.

Baudrillard, Jean. "Consumer Society" [CS]. In Selected Writings.

———. Forget Foucault [FF]. New York: Semiotext(e), 1987.

———. "Perfect Crime" [PC]. In Selected Writings.

——. *Selected Writings* [*SW*]. Ed. and int. Mark Poster. Trans. Jacques Mourrain and others. Stanford, CA: Stanford University Press, 2001.

——. *Simulacra and Simulations* [*SS*]. Trans. Sheila Faria Glaser. Ann Arbor: University of Michigan Press, 1994.

——. *Simulations* [*S*]. Trans. Paul Foss, Paul Patton. and Philip Beitchman. Semiotexte.

Beard, Henry. *Poetry for Cats: The Definitive Anthology of Distinguished Feline Verse* [*PC*]. New York: Villard Books, 1994.

Beauvoir, Simone de. *4e cahier* [*4c*]. Holographic manuscript. Paris: Bibliothèque Nationale, 1927.

——. *The Ethics of Ambiguity* [*EA*]. Trans. Bernard Frechtman. New York: Citadel Press, 1991.

——. *The Second Sex* [*SS*]. Trans. H. M. Parshley. New York: Knopf, 1971.

Becker, Anne E. "Nurturing and Negligence: Working on Others' Bodies in Fiji" [*NN*]. In Csordas, *Embodiment and Experience*.

Becker, Lawrence C. "The Moral Basis of Property Rights" [*MBPR*]. In Pennock and Chapman, eds., *Nomos XXII*, 187–220.

Bellany, Ian. *The Environment in World Politics: Exploring the Limits* [*EWP*]. Brookfield, VT: Edward Elgar, 1997.

Bender, Barbara: *Landscapes: Politics and Perspectives* [*L*]. New York: Berg, 1993.

Benedict, Ruth. *The Chrysanthemum and the Sword: Patterns of Japanese Culture* [*CS*]. Boston: Houghton Mifflin, 1946. In Allen, ed. *Culture and Self*.

Benjamin, Walter. *Erfahrung und Armut* [*EA*]. Passages quoted in Derrida, "Letter to Peter Eisenman."

——. *Illuminations* [*I*]. Trans. Harry Zohn. New York: Harcourt Brace & World, 1968.

——. "On Language as Such and on the Language of Man" [*LSLM*]. In *Reflections*.

——. *Reflections: Essays, Aphorisms, Autobiographical Writings* [*R*]. Trans. Edmund Jephcott. New York: Schocken, 1978.

——. "The Work of Art in the Age of Its Technical Reproducibility" [*WAATR*]. Reprinted in part in Ross, ed., *Art and Its Significance*. Selections from "The Work of Art in the Age of Mechanical Reproduction." In *Illuminations*.

Bennett, Lerone, Jr. *The Challenge of Blackness* [*CB*]. Chicago: Johnson Publishing Co., 1972.

Benso, Sylvia. *The Face of Things: A Different Side of Ethics* [*FT*]. Albany: State University of New York Press, 2000.

Bergson, Henri. *Laughter* [*L*]. In Sypher. *Comedy*.

——. *Matter and Memory* [*MM*]. Trans. Nancy Margaret Paul and W. Scott Palmer. London: George Allen and Unwin, 1911.

Berleant, Arnold. "Aesthetic Perception" [*EA*]. In Nasar, *Environmental Aesthetics*.

Berman, Morris. *The Reenchantment of the World* [*RW*]. Ithaca, NY: Cornell University Press, 1981.

Bermùdez, José Luis. *The Paradox of Self-consciousness* [PS]. Cambridge, MA: MIT Press, 1998.

Bermùdez, José Luis, Anthony Marcel, and Naomi Eilan eds., *The Body and the Self* [BS]. Cambridge, MA: MIT, 1995.

Bernal, Martin. *Black Athena: The Afroasiatic Roots of Classical Civilization, Volume 1: The Fabrication of Ancient Greece 1785–1985* [BA]. New Brunswick: Rutgers University Press, 1987.

Bernasconi, Robert, and David Wood, eds. *The Provocation of Levinas: Rethinking the Other* [PL]. New York: Routledge, 1988.

Berofsky, Bernard. *Liberation from Self: A Theory of Personal Autonomy* [LS]. New York: Cambridge University Press, 1995.

Berry, Wendell. *Home Economics* [HE]. San Francisco: North Point Press, 1987.

Bhabha, Homi K. "Interrogating Identity: The Postcolonial Prerogative" [II]. In Goldberg, ed., *Anatomy of Racism*.

Binswanger, Ludwig. "Dream and Existence" [DE]. In Hoeller, ed., *Dream and Existence*.

Birch, Thomas H. "The Incarceration of Wildness: Wilderness Areas as Prisons" [IW]. In Oelschlaeger, ed., *Postmodern Environmental Ethics*.

Blake, William. *The Book of Urizen* [BU]. Ed. and comm. Kay Parkhurst Easson and Roger R. Easson. New York: Random House, 1987.

———. *The Complete Poetry of William Blake*. In *The Complete Poetry of John Donne and the Complete Poetry of William Blake* [JDWB]. New York: Random House, 1941.

Blanchot, Maurice. *The Space of Literature* [SL]. Trans. Ann Smock. Lincoln, Nebraska: University of Nebraska Press, 1982. Translation of *L'espace littéraire* [el]. Paris: Gallimard, 1955.

———. *The Step Not Beyond* [SNB]. Trans. and int. Lycette Nelson. Albany: State University of New York Press, 1992. Translation of *Le Pas Au-Delà*.

———. "Two Versions of the Imaginary" [TVI]. In *Space of Literature*.

———. *The Writing of the Disaster* [WD]. Trans. Ann Smock. Lincoln: University of Nebraska Press, 1995.

Blumer, Herbert. "Fashion: From Class Differentiation to Collective Selection" [F]. In Roach-Higgins, Eicher, and Johnson, eds., *Dress and Identity*.

Bockover, Mary I. "Ethics, Relativism, and the Self" [ERS]. In Allen, ed., *Culture and Self*.

Bookchin, Murray. *The Ecology of Freedom* [EF]. Palo Alto, CA: Cheshire Books, 1982.

———. *Post-Scarcity Anarchism* [PSA]. Berkeley: Ramparts Press, 1971.

———. *Re-enchanting Humanity: A Defense of the Human Spirit Against Anti-humanism, Misanthropy, Mysticism, and Primitivism* [RH]. New York: Cassell, 1995.

———. *Remaking Society: Pathways to a Green Future* [RS]. Boston: South End Press, 1990.

————. "Social Ecology versus 'Deep Ecology': A Challenge to the Ecology Movement" [*SEDE*]. In *Green Perspectives, Newsletter of the Green Program Project* 4–5.

Bordo, Susan. "The Cartesian Masculinization of Thought and the Seventeenth-Century Flight from the Feminine" [*CMT*]. In Bar On, ed., *Modern Engendering*.

————. "Hunger as Ideology" [*HI*]. In Scapp and Seitz, eds., *Eating Culture*.

————. *Unbearable Weight: Feminism, Western Culture, and the Body* [*UW*]. Berkeley: University of California Press, 2004.

Borges, Jorge Luis. "The Analytical Language of John Wilkins" [*ALJW*]. In *Other Inquisitions, 1937–1952*.

————. *Collected Fictions* [*CF*]. Trans. Andrew Hurley. New York: Penguin, 1998.

————. *Ficciones* [*F*]. Trans. Emecé Editores. New York: Grove Press, 1962.

————. *Labyrinths: Selected Stories and Other Writings* [*L*]. Trans. Emecé Editores. New York: New Directions, 1962.

————. *Other Inquisitions, 1937–1952* [*OI*]. Trans. Ruth L. C. Simms. Austin, TX: University of Texas Press, 1964.

————. "Pierre Menard, Author of *Don Quixote*" [*PM*]. In *Ficciones*.

Bormann, F. Herbert, and Stephen R. Kellert, eds. *Ecology, Economics, Ethics: The Broken Circle* [*EEE*]. New Haven: Yale University Press, 1991.

Botkin, Daniel. *Discordant Harmonies: A New Ecology for the Twenty-first Century* [*DH*]. Oxford: Oxford University Press, 1990.

Bourgeois, Verne Warren. *Persons: What Philosophers Say about You* [*P*]. Waterloo, ON: Wilfred Laurier University Press, 1995.

Bourdieu, Pierre. *The Logic of Practice* [*LP*]. Trans. Richard Nice. Cambridge: Polity Press, 1990.

Bowden, Ross. "Sorcery, Illness and Social Control in Kwoma Society" [*SISC*]. In Stephen, ed., *Sorcerer and Witch*.

Brace, C. Loring, George R. Gamble, and James T. Bond, eds. *Race and Intelligence* [*RI*]. Washington: American Anthropological Assocation, 1971.

Brennan, Andrew. *Thinking About Nature: An Investigation of Nature, Value and Ecology* [*TN*]. Athens, GA: University of Georgia Press, 1988.

Brown, Jonathon D. *The Self* [*S*]. Boston: McGraw-Hill, 1998.

Brown, Norman O. *Love's Body* [*LB*]. New York: Vintage Books, 1966.

Brueggemann, Walter. *The Land: Place as Gift, Promise, and Challenge in Biblical Faith* [*L*]. Philadelphia: Fortress Press, 1977.

Bryant, Bunyon, ed. *Environmental Justice* [*EJ*]. Washington, DC: Island Press, 1995.

Buber, Martin. *I and Thou* [*IT*]. Trans. R. G. Smith. New York: Scribner's, 1927.

Buddhadâsa, Bhikkhu. *Me and Mine: Selected Essays of Bhikkhu Buddhadâsa* [*MM*]. Ed. Swearer, Donald K. Albany: State University of New York Press, 1989.

Bullard, Robert D. "Anatomy of Environmental Racism and the Environmental Justice Movement" [*AEREJM*]. In Bullard, ed., *Confronting Environmental Racism*.

——. "Conclusion: Environmentalism with Justice" [*EJ*]. In Bullard, ed., *Confronting Environmental Racism*.

——, ed. *Confronting Environmental Racism: Voices from the Grassroots* [*CER*]. Boston: South End Press, 1993.

Bullough, Edward. "'Psychical Distance' as a Factor in Art and as an Aesthetic Principle" [*PD*]. Reprinted in Ross, ed., *Art and Its Significance*. Originally published in *British Journal of Psychology* (1912): 87–98.

Burnett, John. *Plenty and Want: A Social History of Diet in England from 1815 to the Present Day* [*PW*]. London: Methuen, 1983.

Burtt, Edwin A., ed. *The English Philosophers from Bacon to Mill* [*EPBM*]. New York: Modern Library, 1959.

Butler, Judith. *Bodies That Matter: On the Discursive Limits of "Sex"* [*BM*]. New York: Routledge, 1993.

——. *Gender Trouble: Feminism and the Subversion of Identity* [*GT*]. New York: Routledge, 1990.

Callicott, J. Baird. *In Defense of a Land Ethic* [*DL*]. Albany: State University of New York Press, 1989.

——. "Traditional American Indian and Western European Attitudes Toward Nature: An Overview" [*TAIWEA*]. In Oelschlaeger, ed., *Postmodern Environmental Ethics*.

——, ed. *Companion to* A Sand County Almanac: *Interpretive and Critical Essays* [*CSCA*]. Madison: University of Wisconsin Press, 1987.

Callicott, J. Baird, and Roger T. Ames, eds. *Nature in Asian Traditions of Thought: Essays in Environmental Philosophy* [*NATT*]. Albany: State University of New York Press, 1989.

Candrakīrti. *The Entry into the Middle Way* [*EMW*]. In Huntington, Jr., *Emptiness of Emptiness*.

Capra, Fritjof, and Charlene Spretnak. *Green Politics: The Global Promise* [*GP*]. New York: Dutton, 1984.

Caputo, John D. *Against Ethics: Contributions to a Poetics of Obligation with Constant Reference to Deconstruction* [*AE*]. Bloomington: Indiana University Press, 1993.

Card, Claudia, ed. *Feminist Ethics* [*FE*]. Lawrence: University Press of Kansas, 1991.

Caro, Manuel J., and John W. Murphy. *The World of Quantum Culture* [*WQC*]. Westport, CT: Praeger, 2002.

Carrier, David. *The Aesthetics of Comics* [*AC*]. University Park, PA: The Pennsylvania University Press, 2000.

Carter, Alan. *The Philosophical Foundations of Property Rights* [*PFPR*]. New York: Harvester Wheatsheaf, 1989.

Cassam, Quassim. *Self and World* [*SW*]. New York: Oxford University Press, 1997.

Céline, Louis-Ferdinand. *Journey to the End of the Night* [*JEN*]. Trans. John H. P. Marks. Boston: Little, Brown, 1934.

Certeau, Michel de. *The Writing of History* [*WH*]. Trans. Tom Conley. New York: Columbia University Press, 1988.

———. *The Practice of Everyday Life*. Trans. Steven Rendall. Berkeley: University of California Press, 1984.

Chapman, John W. "Justice, Freedom, and Property" [*JFP*]. In Pennock and Chapman, eds., *Nomos XXII*, 289–324.

Chazan, Pauline. *The Moral Self* [*MS*]. New York: Routledge, 1998.

Cheal, David. *The Gift Economy* [*GE*]. New York: Routledge, 1988.

Cheney, Jim. "Eco-feminism and Deep Ecology" [*EDE*]. *Environmental Ethics* 9, no. 2 (Summer 1987): 115–45.

———. "Postmodern Environmental Ethics: Ethics as Bioregional Narrative" [*PMEE*]. In Oelschlaeger, ed., *Postmodern Environmental Ethics*.

Chief Seattle. *The Eyes of Chief Seattle* [*ECS*]. Exhibition Catalogue. Seattle: The Suquamish Museum, 1985.

Christ, Carol P. "Reverence for Life: The Need for a Sense of Finitude" [*RL*]. In Cooey, Farmer, and Ross, eds., *Embodied Love*.

———. "Spiritual Quest and Women's Experience" [*SQWE*]. In Christ and Plaskow, eds., *Womanspirit Rising*.

Christ, Carol P., and Judith Plaskow, eds. *Womanspirit Rising* [*WR*]. New York: Harper & Row, 1979.

Cixous, Hélène. "Birds, Women, and Writing [*BWW*]." In *Three Steps*.

———. *Firstdays of the Year* [*FY*]. Trans. Catherine A. F. MacGillivray. Minneapolis: University of Minnesota Press, 1998.

———. *Hélène Cixous Reader* [*HCR*]. Ed. Susan Sellers. New York: Routledge, 1994.

———. "Laugh of the Medusa" [*LM*]. In Marks and Courtivron, eds., *New French Feminisms*.

———. *Stigmata: Excaping Texts* [*S*]. New York: Routledge, 1998.

———. *The Third Body* [*TB*]. Trans. Keith Cohen. Evanston, IL: Northwestern University Press, 1999.

———. *Three Steps on the Ladder of Writing* [*TS*]. Wellek Library Lectures at the University of California, Irvine. Trans. Sarah Cornell and Susan Sellers. New York: Columbia University Press, 1993.

Cixous, Hélène, and Catherine Clément. *The Newly Born Woman* [*NBW*]. Trans. Betsy Wing. Int. Sandra M. Gilbert. Minneapolis: University of Minnesota Press, 1975.

Cixous, Hélène, and Jacques Derrida. *Veils* [*V*]. Trans. Geoffrey Bennington. Stanford, CA: Stanford University Press, 2001.

Clark, Cedric X. "Some Implications of Nkrumah's Consciencism for Alternative Coordinates in NonEuropean Causality" [*SINC*]. In Ruch and Anyanwu, eds., *African Philosophy*.

Clark, Lorenne M. G. "Women and John Locke; or, Who Owns the Apples in the Garden of Eden?" *Canadian Journal of Philosophy* 7, no. 4 (December 1977): 699–724.

Clément, Catherine. "The Guilty Ones" [*GO*]. In Cixous and Clément, *Newly Born Woman*.

———. *Syncope: The Philosophy of Rapture* [*S*]. Trans. Sally O'Driscoll and Deirdre M. Mahoney. Minneapolis: University of Minnesota Press, 1994.

Clifford, James. "On Collecting Art and Culture" [CAC]. Reprinted in Ross, ed., *Art and Its Significance*. In Russell Ferguson et al. eds. *Out There: Marginalization and Contemporary Cultures*. New York: New Museum of Contemporary Art and Cambridge: MIT Press, 1990, 141–6, 151–65.

Cobb, John, Jr. "Christian Existence in a World of Limits" [CEWL]. In Oelschlaeger, ed., *Postmodern Environmental Ethics*.

Cobham, Rhonda, and Merle Collins, eds. *Watchers and Seekers: Creative Writing by Black Women in Britain* [WS]. London: Women's Press, 1987.

Codiga, Doug. "Zen Practice and a Sense of Place" [ZPSP]. In Badiner, ed., *Dharma Gaia*.

Cohn, Jan. *Romance and the Erotics of Property: Mass-Market Fiction for Women* [REP]. Durham: Duke University Press, 1988.

Cole, Eve Browning, and Susan Coultrap-McQuin, eds. *Explorations in Feminist Ethics: Theory and Practice* [EFE]. Bloomington: Indiana University Press, 1992.

Coleridge, Samuel Taylor. *Biographia Literaria* [BL]. Ed. J. Shawcross. London: Oxford University Press, 1949.

Collingwood, R. G. *The Principles of Art* [PA]. Oxford: Oxford University Press, 1972.

Comstock, Gary. "Pigs and Piety: A Theocentric Perspective on Food Animals" [PP]. *Between the Species* 8, no. 3 (Summer 1992): 121–35.

Conley, Verena Andermatt. *Ecopolitics: The Environment in Poststructuralist Thought* [E]. New York: Routledge, 1997.

Cooey, Paula M. "The Word Become Flesh: Woman's Body, Language, and Value" [WF]. In Cooey, Farmer, and Ross, eds., *Embodied Love*.

Cooey, Paula M., Sharon A. Farmer, and Mary Ellen Ross, eds. *Embodied Love: Sensuality and Relationship as Feminist Values* [EL]. San Francisco: Harper & Row, 1987.

Cook, Francis H. "The Jewel Net of Indra" [JNI]. In Callicott and Ames, eds., *Nature in Asian Traditions of Thought*.

Cooper, David E., and Joy A. Palmer, eds. *The Environment in Question: Ethics and Global Issues* [EQ]. New York: Routledge, 1992.

Cornell, Drucilla. *Beyond Accommodation: Ethical Feminism, Deconstruction, and the Law* [BA]. New York: Routledge, 1991.

———. *The Imaginary Domain: Abortion, Pornography and Sexual Harassment* [ID]. New York: Routledge, 1995.

———. *The Philosophy of the Limit* [PL]. New York: Routledge, 1992.

———. *Transformations: Recollective Imagination and Sexual Difference* [T]. New York: Routledge, 1993.

Cornell, Drucilla, Michel Rosenfeld, and David Gray Carlson, eds. *Deconstruction and the Possibility of Justice* [DPJ]. New York: Routledge, Chapman and Hall, 1992.

Corrington, Robert S. *Nature's Self: Our Journey from Origin to Spirit* [NS]. Lanham, MD: Rowman & Littlefield, 1996.

Cose, Ellis. *A Nation of Strangers* [NS]. New York: William Morrow and Co., 1992.

Court, Elsbeth. "The Self in African Children's Drawings of Persons" [*SACD*]. In Maw and Picton, eds., *Concepts of the Body/Self in Africa*.

Cranny-Francis, Anne. *The Body in the Text* [*BT*]. Melbourne: Melbourne University Press, 1995.

Crawford, M. D. C. "The Eyed Needle" [*EN*]. In Roach-Higgins, Eicher, and Johnson, eds., *Dress and Identity*.

Croll, Elisabeth. "The Exchange of Women and Property: Marriage in Post-Revolutionary China" [*EWP*]. In Hirschon, ed., *Women and Property—Women as Property*.

Crosby, John F. *The Selfhood of the Human Person* [*SHP*]. Washington, DC: Catholic University of America Press, 1996.

Csordas, Thomas J. *Embodiment and Experience: The Existential Ground of Culture and Self* [*EE*]. Cambridge: Cambridge University Press, 1994.

Curley, E. M. *Spinoza's Metaphysics: An Essay in Interpretation* [*SM*]. Cambridge, MA: Harvard University Press, 1969.

Curtin, Deane. "Toward an Ecological Ethic of Care" [*TEEC*]. In Warren, ed., *Hypatia*, 60–74.

Curtiss, Susan. *Genie: A Psycholinguistic Study of a Modern-Day "Wild Child"* [*G*] New York: Academic Press, 1977.

Dalby, Liza. "Geisha and Kimono" [*GK*]. In Roach-Higgins, Eicher, and Johnson, eds., *Dress and Identity*.

Daly, M. Catherine, Joanne B. Eicher, Tonye V. Erekosima. "Male and Female Artistry in Kalabari Dress" [*MFA*]. In Roach-Higgins, Eicher, and Johnson, eds., *Dress and Identity*.

Daly, Mary. "After the Death of God the Father: Women's Liberation and the Transformation of Christian Consciousness" [*ADGF*]. In Christ and Plaskow, eds., *Womanspirit Rising*.

———. *Gyn/Ecology: The Metaethics of Radical Feminism* [*G/E*]. Boston: Beacon Press, 1990.

Daniel, E. Valentine. "The Individual in Terror" [*IT*]. In Csordas, *Embodiment and Experience*.

Danto, Arthur C. "Approaching the End of Art" [*AEA*]. In *State of the Art*.

———. *The State of the Art* [*SA*]. New York: Prentice Hall, 1987.

———. *Transfiguration of the Commonplace: A Philosophy of Art* [*TC*]. Cambridge: Harvard University Press, 1981.

Dawkins, Richard. *The Selfish Gene* [*SG*]. Oxford: Oxford University Press, 1976.

Debord, Guy. *The Society of the Spectacle* [*SS*]. New York: Zone Books, 1995.

———. *The Society of the Spectacle Revisited* [*SSR*].

de Silva, Lily. "The Hills Wherein My Soul Delights: Exploring the Stories and Teachings" [*HWSD*]. In Batchelor and Brown, eds., *Buddhism and Ecology*.

de Silva, Lynn A. *The Problem of the Self in Buddhism and Christianity* [*PSBC*]. New York: Harper & Row, 1979.

de Silva, Padmasiri. *Environmental Philosophy and Ethics in Buddhism* [*EPEB*]. New York: St. Martin's Press, 1998.

de Waal, Frans. *Good Natured: The Origins of Right and Wrong in Humans and Other Animals* [GN]. Cambridge: Harvard University Press, 1996.

Dean, Carolyn J. *The Self and its Pleasures: Bataille, Lacan, and the History of the Decentered Subject* [SP]. Ithaca, NY: Cornell University Press, 1992.

Delacampagne, Christian. "Racism and the West: From Praxis to Logos" [RW]. In Goldberg, ed., *Anatomy of Racism*.

Deleuze, Gilles. *Difference and Repetition* [DR]. Trans. Paul Patton. New York: Columbia University Press, 1994. Translation of *Différence et répétition*. Paris: P.U.F., 1968.

———. *The Logic of Sense* [LS]. Trans. Mark Lester with Charles Stivale. New York: Columbia University Press, 1990. Translation of *Logique du sens*. Paris: Editions de Minuit, 1969.

Deleuze, Gilles, and Félix Guattari. *Anti-Oedipus: Capitalism and Schizophrenia* [A-O]. Trans. Robert Hurley, Mark Seem, and Helen R. Lane. Minneapolis: University of Minnesota Press, 1983.

———. *Expressionism in Philosophy: Spinoza* [EPS]. Trans. Martin Joughin. New York: Zone, 1992.

———. *A Thousand Plateaus: Capitalism and Schizophrenia* [TP]. Trans. Brian Massumi. Minneapolis: University of Minnesota Press, 1987.

———. *What is Philosophy?* [WP]. Trans. Hugh Tomlinson and Graham Burchell. New York: Columbia University Press, 1994.

Deloria, Vine, Jr. *God is Red* [GR]. New York: Dell, 1973.

Depillars, Murry Norman. "Multiculturalism in Visual Arts Education: Are America's Educational Institutions Ready for Multiculturalism?" [MVAE]. In Young, ed. *Art, Culture, and Ethnicity*.

Derrida, Jacques. *Adieu to Emmanuel Levinas* [A]. Trans. Pascale-Anne Brault and Michael B. Naas. Stanford, CA: Stanford University Press, 1999.

———. *Archive Fever: A Freudian Impression* [AF]. Trans. Eric Prenowitz. Chicago: University of Chicago Press, 1996.

———. "Cogito and the History of Madness" [CHM]. In *Writing and Difference*.

———. *Circumfession* [C]. In *Jacques Derrida*.

———. *Dissemination* [D]. Trans. and int. Barbara Johnson. Chicago: University of Chicago Press, 1981.

———. "'Eating Well,' or the Calculation of the Subject" [EW]. Trans. Peter Connor and Avital Ronell. In *Points*.

———. "Economimesis" [E]. *Diacritics* 11, no. 2 (June 1981): 3–25.

———. "Force of Law: The 'Mystical Foundation of Authority'" [FL]. In Cornell, Rosenfeld, and Carlson, eds., *Deconstruction and the Possibility of Justice*. Reprinted from *Cardozo Law Review* 11, nos. 5–6 (July/August 1991): 919–1045.

———. "Fors" [F]. Preface to Nicolas Abraham and Maria Torok. *The Wolf Man's Magic Word*. Trans. Barbara Johnson. Minneapolis: University of Minnesota Press, 1986.

———. "From Restricted to General Economy: A Hegelianism without Reserve" [FRGE]. In *Writing and Difference*.

———. "Geschlecht: Sexual Difference, Ontological Difference" [*G1*]. *Research in Phenomenology* 13 (1983): 65–83.

———. "*Geschlecht* II: Heidegger's Hand" [*G2*]. Trans. John P. Leavey, Jr. In Sallis, ed., *Deconstruction in Philosophy: The Texts of Jacques Derrida.*

———. *The Gift of Death* [*GD*]. Trans. David Wills. Chicago: University of Chicago Press, 1994.

———. *Given Time* [*GT*]. Trans. Peggy Kamuf. Chicago: University of Chicago Press, 1992.

———. *H.C. for Life, That is to Say . . .* [*HCL*]. Trans. Laurent Milesi and Stefan Herbrechter. Stanford: Stanford University Press, 2006.

———. "Heidegger's Ear: Philopolemology (*Geschlecht* IV)" [*G4*]. In Sallis, ed., *Reading Heidegger*. Bloomington: Indiana University Press, 1993.

———. *Jacques Derrida* [*JD*]. *Derridabase* [*D*] by Geoffrey Bennington and *Circumfession*. Trans. Geoffrey Bennington. Chicago: University of Chicago Press, 1993.

———. "Letter to Peter Eisenman" [*LPE*]. In *Assemblage* 12: 7–13. Reprinted in Ross, ed., *Art and Its Significance.*

———. *Margins of Philosophy* [*MP*]. Trans. Alan Bass. Chicago: University of Chicago Press, 1982.

———. *Negotiations: Interventions and Interviews* [*N*]. Stanford, CA: Stanford University Press, 2002.

———. *Of Grammatology* [*OG*]. Trans. Gayatri Chakravorty Spivak. Baltimore: The Johns Hopkins Press, 1974.

———. *Of Hospitality* [*H*]. Trans. Rachel Bowlby. Stanford, CA: Stanford University Press, 2000. Translation of *De l'hospitalité: Anne Dufourmantelle invite Jacquest Derrida à réponde*. Paris: Calmann-Lévy, 1997.

———. *Of Spirit: Heidegger and the Question* [*OS*]. Trans. Geoffrey Bennington and Rachel Bowlby. Chicago: University of Chicago Press, 1989.

———. *The Other Heading: Reflections on Today's Europe* [*OH*]. Int. Michael B. Naas. Trans. Pascale-Anne Brault and Michael B. Naas. Bloomington: Indiana University Press, 1992.

———. "Parergon" [*P*]. In *Truth in Painting*. Reprinted in part in Ross, ed., *Art and Its Significance.*

———. "Passe-Partout" [*P-P*]. Intro. to *Truth in Painting*. Reprinted in Ross, ed., *Art and Its Significance.*

———. "Plato's Pharmacy" [*PP*]. In *Dissemination.*

———. *Points . . . : Interviews, 1974–94* [*P . . .*]. Trans. Peggy Kamuf and others. Stanford, CA: Stanford University Press, 1995.

———. *The Politics of Friendship* [*PF*]. Trans. George Collins. London: Verso, 1997.

———. "The Politics of Friendship" ["*PF*"]. *The Journal of Philosophy* 85 (November 1988): 632–44.

———. "Restitutions" [*R*]. In *Truth in Painting*. Reprinted in part in Ross, ed., *Art and Its Significance.*

———. *Specters of Marx: The State of the Debt, The Work of Mourning, and the New International* [*SM*]. Trans. Peggy Kamuf. Int. Bernd Magnus and Stephen Cullenberg. New York: Routledge, 1994.

———. *The Truth in Painting* [*TP*]. Trans. G. Bennington and I. McLeod. Chicago: University of Chicago Press, 1987.

———. "Tympan" [*T*]. In *Margins of Philosophy*.

———. "Violence and Metaphysics: An Essay on the Thought of Emmanuel Levinas" [*VM*]. In *Writing and Difference*.

———. "White Mythology: Metaphor in the Text of Philosophy" [*WM*]. In *Margins of Philosophy*.

———. *The Work of Mourning* [*WM*]. Trans. Pascale-Anne Brault and Michael B. Naas. Chicago: University of Chicago Press, 2001.

———. *Writing and Difference* [*WD*]. Trans. Alan Bass. Chicago: University of Chicago Press, 1978.

Descartes, René. *Discourse on the Method of Rightly Conducting the Reason and Seeking Truth in the Sciences* [*DM*]. In *Philosophical Writings of Descartes*, Vol. 1.

———. *Early Writings* [*EW*]. In *Philosophical Writings of Descartes*, Vol. 1.

———. *Meditations* [*M*]. In *Philosophical Writings of Descartes*, Vol. 2.

———. *Objections and Replies* [*OR*]. In *Philosophical Writings of Descartes*, Vol. 2.

———. *Optics* [*O*]. In *Philosophical Writings of Descartes*, Vol. 1.

———. *The Passions of the Soul* [*PS*]. In *Philosophical Writings of Descartes*, Vol. 1.

———. *The Philosophical Writings of Descartes* [*PWD*]. Trans. John Cottingham, Robert Stoothoff, and Dugald Murdoch. 2 vols. Cambridge: Cambridge University Press, 1985.

———. *Principles of Philosophy* [*PP*]. In *Philosophical Writings of Descartes*, Vol. 1.

———. *Rules for the Direction of the Mind* [*RDM*]. In *Philosophical Writings of Descartes*, Vol. 1.

———. *Treatise on Man* [*TM*]. In *Philosophical Writings of Descartes*, Vol. 1.

———. *The World* [*W*]. In *Philosophical Writings of Descartes*, Vol. 1.

Devall, Bill. *Simple in Means, Rich in Ends: Practicing Deep Ecology* [*SMRE*]. Salt Lake City: Peregrine Smith, 1990.

Devall, Bill, and George Sessions. *Deep Ecology: Living as if Nature Mattered* [*DE*]. Salt Lake City: Peregrene Smith, 1985.

Devi, Mahasweta, *Imaginary Maps: Three Stories* [*IM*]. Trans. Gayatri Chakravorty Spivak. New York: Routledge, 1995.

Devisch, René. "The Human Body as a Vehicle for Emotions among the Yaka of Zaire" [*HBVE*]. In Jackson and Karp, eds. *Personhood and Agency: The Experiences of Self and Other in African Cultures*.

Dewey, John. *Art and Experience* [*AE*]. New York: Putnam, 1934. Reprinted in part in Ross, ed., *Art and Its Significance*.

———. "Body and Mind" [*BM*]. In *Philosophy and Civilization*.

———. "Context and Thought" [*CT*]. In *Experience, Nature, and Freedom*.

———. *Experience and Nature* [*EN*]. 2nd ed. New York: Dover, 1958.

———. *Experience, Nature, and Freedom* [*ENF*]. Ed. and int. Richard J. Bernstein. Indianapolis: Library of Liberal Arts, 1960.

———. *Human Nature and Conduct* [*HNC*]. New York: Holt, 1922.

——. *Logic: The Theory of Inquiry* [*L*]. New York: Henry Holt & Co., 1938.

——. "Nature in Experience" [*NE*]. In *Experience, Nature, and Freedom.*

——. "The Need for a Recovery of Philosophy" [*NRP*]. In *Experience, Nature, and Freedom.*

——. *Philosophy and Civilization* [*PC*]. New York: Minton, Balch, 1931.

——. *Quest for Certainty* [*QC*]. New York: Minton, Balch, 1929.

——. *Theory of Valuation* [*TV*]. Chicago: University of Chicago Press, 1939.

Diamond, Irene. "Babies, Heroic Experts, and a Poisoned Earth" [*BHEPE*]. In Diamond and Orenstein, eds., *Reweaving the World.*

Diamond, Irene, and Gloria Feman Orenstein, eds. *Reweaving the World: The Emergence of Ecofeminism* [*RW*]. San Francisco: Sierra Club Books, 1990.

Dimen, Muriel. "Power, Sexuality, and Intimacy" [*PSI*]. In Jaggar and Bordo, eds., *Gender/Body/Knowledge.*

Dion, Mark, and Alexis Rockman, eds. *Concrete Jungle: A Pop Media Investigation of Death and Survival in Urban Ecosystems* [*CJ*]. Juno Books, 1996.

Dixon, Vernon J. "World Views and Research Methodology" [*WVRM*]. In King, Dixon, and Nobles, eds., *African Philosophy.*

Dombrowski, Daniel A. *Babies and Beasts: The Argument from Marginal Cases* [*BB*]. Urbana: University of Illinois Press, 1997.

——. *Hartshorne and the Metaphysics of Animal Rights* [*HMAR*]. Albany: State University of New York Press, 1988.

——. *The Philosophy of Vegetarianism* [*PV*]. Amherst: University of Massachusetts Press, 1984.

Dorter, Kenneth: *Plato's* Phaedo: *An Interpretation* [*PP*]. Toronto: University of Toronto Press, 1982.

Dostoevsky, Fyodor. *The Brothers Karamazov* [*BK*]. Trans. Constance Garnett. New York: Modern Library, 1950.

Douglas, Mary. *Purity and Danger: An Analysis of Concepts of Pollution and Taboo* [*PD*]. New York: Praeger, 1966.

Douglas, Mary, and Baron Isherwood. *The World of Goods: Toward an Anthropology of Consumption* [*WG*]. New York: W. W. Norton, 1979.

Drakulić, Slavenka. "The War on People—and on the Truth—in Croatia" [*WPC*]. *The Chronicle of Higher Education* (June 11, 2004).

Dryzek, John S. "Green Reason: Communicative Ethics for the Biosphere" [*GR*]. In Oelschlaeger, ed., *Postmodern Environmental Ethics.*

——. *Rational Ecology: Environment and Political Economy* [*RE*]. New York: Blackwell, 1987.

duBois, Page. *Sowing the Body: Psychoanalysis and Ancient Representations of Women* [*SB*]. Chicago: University of Chicago Press, 1988.

——. *Torture and Truth* [*TT*]. New York: Routledge, 1991.

Du Bois, W. E. B. *A W. E. B. Du Bois Reader* [*WEBDR*]. Ed. Andrew G. Paschal. New York: Macmillan, 1971.

——. "The Concept of Race" [*CR*]. In Hord and Lee, eds., *I Am Because We Are.*

——. "The Conservation of Races" [*CR*]. In *Du Bois Reader.*

Duerr, Hans Peter. *Dreamtime: Concerning the Boundary Between Wilderness and Civilization* [D]. Trans. Felicitas Goodman. Oxford: Blackwell, 1985.

Dworkin, Andrea. *Intercourse* [I]. New York: Free Press, 1987.

———. *Pornography: Men Possessing Women* [P]. New York: G. P. Putnam's Sons, 1981.

Dussel, Enrique. *Philosophy of Liberation* [PL]. Trans. Aquilina Martinez and Christine Morkovsky. Maryknoll, NY: Orbis Books, 1985.

———. "Principles, Mediations, and the 'Good' as Synthesis (from 'Discourse Ethics' to 'Ethics of Liberation')" [PMG]. Trans. Eduardo Mendieta. *Philosophy Today* (Supplement 1997): 55–66.

———. "'Sensibility' and 'Otherness' in Emmanuel Lévinas" [SOEL]. Trans. John Browning with Joyce Bellows. *Philosophy Today* (Summer 1999): 126–34.

Dworkin, Ronald. "Feminists and Abortion" [FA]. *New York Review of Books* 40, no. 11 (June 10, 1993): 27–9.

———. *Law's Empire* [LE]. Cambridge: Harvard University Press, 1986.

———. Review of MacKinnon, *Only Words* [OW]. *The New York Review of Books* 40, no. 17 (October 21, 1993): 36–42.

Eagleton, Terry. *The Ideology of the Aesthetic* [IA]. Malden, MA: Blackwell Publishers, 2001.

Eberhardt, Jennifer L., and Susan T. Fiske, eds. *Confronting Racism: The Problem and the Response* [CF]. Thousand Oaks, CA: Sage Publications, 1998.

Ebrey, Patricia. "Women, Marriage, and the Family in Chinese History" [WMFCH]. In *Heritage of China*. Ed. Paul Ropp. Berkeley: University of California Press, 1990.

Ecker, Gisela, ed. *Feminist Aesthetics* [FA]. Trans. Harriet Anderson. Boston: Beacon Press, 1985.

Eckersley, Robyn. *Environmentalism and Political Theory: Toward an Ecocentric Approach* [EPT]. Albany: State University of New York Press, 1992.

Ehman, Robert R. *The Authentic Self* [AS]. Buffalo, NY: Prometheus Books, 1994.

Ehrenfeld, David. *The Arrogance of Humanism* [AH]. New York: Oxford University Press, 1978.

———. "The Management of Diversity: A Conservation Paradox" [MD]. In Bormann and Kellert, eds., *Ecology, Economics, Ethics*.

Eicher, Joanne B. "Cosmopolitan and International Dress" [CID]. In Roach-Higgins, Eicher, and Johnson, eds., *Dress and Identity*.

Eliade, Mircea. *Shamanism: Archaic Techniques of Ecstacy* [S]. Princeton: Princeton University Press, 1972.

El Sadaawi, Nawal. *The Hidden Face of Eve: Women in the Arab World* [HFE]. Trans. Sherif Hetata. Boston: Beacon Press, 1980.

Engels, Friedrich. *The Origin of the Family, Private Property and the State* [OFPPS]. In Marx & Engels, *Selected Writings*.

Epstein, Richard. *Takings: Private Property and the Power of Eminent Domain* [T]. Cambridge: Harvard University Press, 1985.

Erikson, Erik H. *Identity and the Life Cycle* [ILC]. New York: International Universities Press, 1959 (*Psychological Issues* 1, no. 1).
——. *Insight and Responsibility* [IR]. New York: Norton, 1964.
——. *The Life Cycle Completed* [LCC]. Extended version. New York: Norton, 1997.
Erodes, Richard. *Lame Deer: Seeker of Visions* [LD]. New York: Simon & Schuster, 1976.
Euripides, *Hecuba* [H]. Trans. E. P. Coleridge. In Oates and O'Neill, eds., *Complete Greek Drama*.
Fanon, Frantz. *Black Skin, White Masks* [BSWM]. Trans. Charles Lam Markmann. New York: Grove Press, 1967.
——. *Wretched of the Earth* [WE]. Trans. Constance Farrington. Pref. Jean-Paul Sartre. New York: Grove Press, 1965.
Felski, Rita. *Beyond Feminist Aesthetics: Feminist Literature and Social Change* [BFA]. Cambridge, MA: Harvard University Press Press, 1989.
——. Felski, Rita, *Doing Time: Feminist Theory and Postmodern Culture* [DT]. New York: New York University Press, 1956.
——. "Why Feminism Doesn't Need an Aesthetic (and Why it Can't Ignore Aesthetics)" [WFDNA]. In *Doing Time*.
Feng, Yu-lan. *A History of Chinese Philosophy* [HCP]. Trans. Derk Bodde. Princeton: University of Princeton Press, 1952–3.
Fernea, Elizabeth W., and Robert A. Fernea. "Symbolizing Roles: Behind the Veil" [SR]. In Roach-Higgins, Eicher, and Johnson, eds., *Dress and Identity*.
Ferry, Luc. *The New Ecological Order* [NEO]. Trans. Carol Volk. Chicago: University of Chicago Press, 1995.
Feyerabend, Paul. *Against Method: Outline of an Anarchistic Theory of Knowledge* [AM]. Atlantic Highlands, NJ: Humanities Press, 1975.
Finley, Karen. *Quotes from a Hysterical Female* [QHF]. In *Shock Treatment*.
——. *Shock Treatment* [ST]. San Francisco: City Lights, 1990.
Fortes, Meyer. "Strangers" [S]. In Fortes and Patterson, *Studies in African Social Anthropology*.
Fortes, Meyer and Patterson, Sheila. *Studies in African Social Anthropology* [SASA]. New York: Academic Press, 1975.
Foster, Patrica, ed. *Minding the Body: Women Writers on Body and Soul* [MB]. New York: Doubleday, 1994.
Foucault, Michel. *Archaeology of Knowledge* [AK]. Trans. A. M. Sheridan-Smith. New York: Pantheon, 1981.
——. "The Birth of Biopolitics" [BB]. In *The Birth of the Clinic: An Archaeology of Medical Perception* (1963). Translated by A. M. Sheridan-Smith. New York: Vintage, 1975.
——. *The Care of the Self* [CS]. Trans. Robert Hurley. New York: Pantheon, 1986.
——. *Discipline and Punish: The Birth of the Prison* [DP]. Trans. Alan Sheridan. New York: Vintage, 1979.
——. "Discourse on Language" [DL]. In *Archaeology of Knowledge*.

———. "Dream, Imagination, and Existence" [*DIE*]. In Hoeller, ed., *Dream and Existence*.

———. *The Essential Foucault* [*EF*]. Ed. Paul Rabinow and Nikolas Rose. New York: New Press, 2003.

———. "The Ethics of the Concern of the Self as a Practice of Freedom" [*ECSPF*]. In *Ethics, Subjectivity and Truth*.

———. *Ethics, Subjectivity and Truth* [*EST*]. Ed. Paul Rabinow. Trans. Robert Hurley and others. New York: New Press, 1997.

———. *Folie et déraison: Histoire de la folie à la l'âge classique* [*FD*]. Paris: Plon, 1961.

———. "The Hermeneutic of the Subject" ["*HS*"]. In *Ethics, Subjectivity and Truth*.

———. *History of Sexuality, Vol. 1* [*HS*]. Trans. R. Hurley. New York: Vintage, 1980.

———. *Language, Counter-memory, Practice* [*LCP*]. Trans. Donald F. Bouchard and Sherry Simon. Ed. and int. Donald F. Bouchard. Ithaca, NY: Cornell University Press, 1977.

———. *Madness and Civilization: A History of Insanity in the Age of Reason* [*MC*]. Trans. Richard Howard. New York: Random House, 1965. Translation and abridgment of *Folie et déraison*.

———. "Nietzsche, Genealogy, History" [*NGH*]. In *Language, Counter-memory, Practice*.

———. "On Popular Justice: A Discussion with Maoists" [*OPJ*]. In *Power/Knowledge*.

———. "On the Genealogy of Ethics: An Overview of Work in Progress" [*OGE*]. In *Ethics, Subjectivity and Truth*.

———. *The Order of Things: An Archaeology of the Human Sciences* [*OT*]. New York: Vintage, 1973.

———. "The Political Technology of Individuals" [*PTI*]. In *Ethics, Subjectivity and Truth*.

———. *Power/Knowledge* [*P/K*]. Ed. and trans. C. Gordon. New York: Pantheon, 1980.

———. "A Preface to Transgression" [*PT*]. In *Language, Counter-memory, Practice*.

———. "Questions on Geography" [*QG*]. In *Power/Knowledge*.

———. *Remarks on Marx* [*RM*]. Trans. R. James Goldstein and James Cascaito. New York: Semiotext(e), 1961.

———. "Theatrum Philosophicum" [*TP*]. In *Language, Counter-memory, Practice*.

———. *Technologies of the Self: A Seminar with Michel Foucault* [*TS*]. Ed. Luther H. Martin, Huck Gutman, Patrick H. Hutton. Amherst: University of Massachusetts Press, 1988.

———. "Technologies of the Self" ["*TS*"]. In *Ethics, Subjectivity and Truth*.

———. "Truth and Power" [*TrP*]. In *Power/Knowledge*.

———. "Two Lectures" [*2L*]. In *Power/Knowledge*.

———. *The Use of Pleasure: The History of Sexuality, Vol. 2* [*UP*]. Trans. Robert Hurley. New York: Pantheon, 1985.

———. "What is an Author?" [*WA?*]. In *Language, Counter-memory, Practice*.

———. "What is Enlightenment?" [*WE?*]. In *Ethics, Subjectivity and Truth*.

Frederickson, Owen P. *The Psychology of Ownership* [*PO*]. Washington, DC: The Catholic University of America Press, 1954.

French, Lindsay. "The Political Economy of Injury and Compassion: Amputees on the Thai-Cambodian Border" [*PEIC*]. In Csordas, *Embodiment and Experience*.

Freud, Sigmund. *The Basic Writings of Sigmund Freud* [*BW*]. Trans. A. A. Brill. New York: Modern Library, 1995.

———. *Collected Papers* [*CP*]. New York: Basic Books, 1959.

———. *The Ego and the Id* [*EI*]. Trans. Joan Riviere. Rev. and ed. by James Strachey. New York: W. W. Norton & Co., 1960.

———. "Femininity" [*F*]. In *New Introductory Lectures on Psychoanalysis*.

———. *A General Introduction to Psychoanalysis* [*GIP*]. Trans. Joan Riviere. Garden City, New York: Doubleday, 1953.

———. *The Interpretation of Dreams* [*ID*]. In *Basic Writings*.

———. "Mourning and Melancholia" [*MM*]. In *Collected Works*, Vol. 4: 152–71.

———. "A Mythological Parallel to a Visual Obsession" [*MPVO*]. Trans. C. M. J. Hubbock. In *Creativity and the Unconscious*. First published in *Zeitschrift*, Bd. IV, 1916.

———. *On Creativity and the Unconscious: Papers on the Psychology of Art, Literature, Love, Religion* [*CU*]. Ed. Benjamin Nelson. New York: Harper & Row, 1958.

———. *The Psychopathology of Everyday Life* [*PEL*]. In *Basic Writings*.

———. "The Uncanny" [*U*]. In *Creativity and the Unconscious*.

———. "The Relation of the Poet to Day-dreaming" [*RPD*]. Reprinted in Ross, ed., *Art and Its Significance*. In Sigmund Freud, *Collected Papers*, Vol. 4. Article trans. I. F. Grant Duff. New York: Basic Books, 1959.

———. *The Standard Edition of the Complete Psychological Works of Sigmund Freud*. Ed. James Strachey, 24 vols. London: Hogarth Press, 1953–74.

———. *Totem and Taboo* [*TT*]. In *Basic Writings*.

———. *Wit and Its Relations to the Unconscious* [*WRU*]. In *Basic Writings*.

Freyfogle, Eric T. *Justice and the Earth: Images for Our Planetary Survival* [*JE*]. New York: Free Press, 1993.

Frodeman, Robert. "Radical Environmentalism and the Political Roots of Postmodernism: Differences that Make a Difference" [*REPRP*]. In Oelschlaeger, ed., *Postmodern Environmental Ethics*.

Fry, Tony, and Anne-Marie Willis. "Aboriginal Art: Symptom or Success?" [*AA*]. In *Art in America* (July 1989): 111–16, 159–61. Reprinted in part in Ross, ed., *Art and Its Significance*.

Fuller, Steve. *Controversial Science: From Content to Contention* [*CS*]. Albany: State University of New York Press, 1993.

———. *Philosophy of Science and Its Discontents* [*PSD*]. Boulder, CO: Westview Press, 1989.

———. *Social Epistemology* [*SE*]. Bloomington and Indianapolis: Indiana University Press, 1988.

Fuss, Diana. "A Supper Party" [*SP*]. Scapp and Seitz, eds., *Eating Culture*.

Gaard, Greta. *Ecofeminism: Women, Animals, Nature* [*E*]. Philadelphia: Temple University Press, 1993.

Gadamer, Hans-Georg. *Truth and Method* [*TM*]. New York: Seabury Press, 1975.

Galletti, R., K. D. S. Baldwin, & I. O. Dina. "Clothing of Nigerian Cocoa Farmers' Families" [*CNCFF*]. In Roach-Higgins, Eicher, and Johnson, eds., *Dress and Identity*.

Gallop, David. *Plato:* Phaedo [*PP*]. Oxford: Clarendon Press, 1975.

Gallop, Jane. *Thinking Through the Body* [*TTB*]. New York: Columbia University Press, 1988.

Galsworthy, John. *The Man of Property* [*MP*]. Moscow, Foreign Languages Publishing House, 1950.

Garb, Yaakov Jerome. "Perspective or Escape? Ecofeminist Musings on Contemporary Earth Imagery" [*PE*]. In Diamond and Orenstein, eds., *Reweaving the World*.

Gard, Richard A., ed. *Buddhism* [*B*]. New York: George Braziller, 1962.

Gates, Jr., Henry Louis. "Critical Remarks" [*CR*]. In Goldberg, ed., *Anatomy of Racism*.

——, ed. "*Race,*" *Writing, and Difference* [*RWD*]. Chicago: University of Chicago Press, 1986.

Gates, Paul W. "Recent Land Policies of the Federal Government" [*RLPFG*]. Section 5 in Forest Service, Department of Agriculture and The Land Policy Section, Agricultural Adjustment Adminsitation for the Land Planning Committee of the National Resources Board, *Certain Aspects of Land Problems and Government Land Policies: Part VII of the Report on Land Planning*. Washington, DC: 1935.

Geis, Deborah R. "Feeding the Audience: Food, Feminism, and Performance Art" [*FA*]. In Scapp and Seitz, eds. *Eating Culture*.

Genet, Jean. *Prisoner of Love* [*PL*]. Trans. Barbara Bray. Hanover, NH: University Press of New England, 1992.

Gilbert, Bil. "Crows by Far and Wide, But There's No Place Like Home." *Smithsonian* 23, no. 5 (August 1992): 101–11.

——. *Our Nature* [*ON*]. Lincoln: University of Nebraska Press, 1986.

Gilbert, Jess, and Craig K. Harris. "Changes in Type, Tenure, and Concentration of U.S. Farmland Owners," [*CTTCFO*]. In *Focus On Agriculture*. Ed. Harry K. Schwarzweller. Greenwich, CN: Jai Press, 1984.

Gilead, Amihud. *The Platonic Odyssey: A Philosophical-Literary Inquiry into the* Phaedo [*PO*]. Amsterdam: Rodopi, 1994.

Gilligan, Carol. *In a Different Voice: Psychological Theory and Women's Development* [*IDV*]. Cambridge: Harvard University Press, 1982.

Gillis, Malcolm. "Economics, Ecology, and Ethics: Mending the Broken Circle for Tropical Forests" [*EEE*]. In Bormann and Kellert, eds., *Ecology, Economics, Ethics*.

Glass, James M. *Shattered Selves* [*SS*]. Ithaca, NY: Cornell University Press, 1993.

Glass, Newman Robert. *Working Emptiness: Toward a Third Reading of Emptiness in Buddhism and Postmoern Thought* [*WE*]. Atlanta, GA: Scholars Press, 1995.

Gluckman, Max. *Politics, Law and Ritual in Tribal Society* [*PLRTS*]. Chicago: Aldine, 1965.

Godway, Eleanor M., and Geraldine Finn, eds. *Who Is This "We"?: Absence of Community* [*WW*]. Montréal: Black Rose Books, 1994.

Goldberg, David Theo, ed. *Anatomy of Racism* [*AR*]. Minneapolis: University of Minnesota Press, 1990.

Golding, Sue. "The Excess" [*E*]. In Kroker and Kroker, eds., *Last Sex.*

Goodman, Nelson. *Languages of Art: An Approach to a Theory of Symbols* [*LA*]. 2nd ed. Indianapolis: Hackett, 1976.

———. *Ways of Worldmaking* [*WW*]. Indianapolis: Hackett, 1978.

———. "What is Art" [*WA?*]. In *Ways of Worldmaking.*

Goosens, William K. "Underlying Trait Terms" [*UTT*]. In Schwartz, ed., *Naming, Necessity, and Natural Kinds.*

Gordon, Eleanore, and Jean Nerenberg. "Everywoman's Jewelry: Early Plastics and Equality in Fashion" [*EJ*]. In Roach-Higgins, Eicher, and Johnson, eds., *Dress and Identity.*

Gordon, Mel. *Lazzi: The Comic Routines of the Commedia dell'Arte* [*L*]. New York: Performing Arts Journal Publications, 1983.

Gore, Charles. *Property: Its Duties and Rights, Historically, Philosophically and Religiously Regarded* [*P*]. New York: Macmillan, Co., 1922.

Gottlieb, Alma. "Witches, Kings, and the Sacrifice of Identity or The Power of Paradox and the Paradox of Power among the Beng of Ivory Coast" [*WKS*]. In Arens and Karp, eds., *Creativity of Power.*

Göttner-Abendroth, Heide. "Nine Principles of a Matriarchal Aesthetics" [*MA*]. Trans. Harriet Anderson. Reprinted in Ross, ed., *Art and Its Significance.* In Ecker, ed., *Feminist Aesthetics.*

Gould, Stephen Jay. "The Golden Rule" [*GR*]. *Natural History* (September 1990).

Gramsci, Antonio. *An Antonio Gramsci Reader: Selected Writings 1916–1935* [*AGR*]. New York: Schocken Books, 1988.

———. *Gramsci* [*G*]. Paris: Seghers, 1966.

———. *The Open Marxism of Antonio Gramsci* [*OM*]. Trans. Carl Marzani. New York: Cameron Associates, 1957.

Graves, Robert. *The Greek Myths* [*GM*]. Baltimore: Penguin, 1955.

Gregory, C. A. "The Emergence of Commodity Production in Papua New Guinea" [*ECPPNG*]. *Journal of Contemporary Asia* (1979): 389–409.

Grey, Thomas C. "The Disintegration of Property" [*DP*]. In Pennock and Chapman, eds., *Nomos XXII*, 69–85.

Griebel, Helen Bradley. "The African American Woman's Headwrap: Unwinding the Symbols" [*AAWH*]. In Roach-Higgins, Eicher, and Johnson, eds., *Dress and Identity.*

Griffin, Susan. *A Chorus of Stones* [*CS*]. New York: Doubleday, 1992.

———. *Pornography and Silence* [*PS*]. New York: Harper & Row, 1981.

———. *Woman and Nature: The Roaring Inside Her* [*WN*]. New York: Harper & Row, 1978.

Griffiths, Ieuan Ll. *An Atlas of African Affairs* [*AAA*]. New York: Routledge, 1994.

Grigsby, Eugene, Jr. "Afro-American Culture and the White Ghetto" [*AAC*]. In Young, ed. *Art, Culture, and Ethnicity*.

Grodin, Debra, and Thomas R. Lindlof, eds. *Constructing the Self in a Mediated World* [*CSMW*]. London: Sage Publications, 1996.

Grosz, Elizabeth. *Volatile Bodies: Toward a Corporeal Feminism* [*VB*]. Bloomington: Indiana University Press, 1994.

Gruen, Lori and Dale Jamieson, eds. *Reflecting on Nature* [*RN*]. Oxford: Oxford University Press, 1994.

Grunebaum, James O. *Private Ownership* [*PO*]. New York: Routledge & Kegan Paul, 1987.

Guattari, Félix. *Chaosmosis: an Ethico-aesthetic Paradigm* [*C*]. Trans. Paul Bains and Julian Pefanis. Bloomington, IN: Indiana University Press, 1995.

———. *The Three Ecologies* [*TE*]. Trans. Ian Pindar and Paul Sutton. London: The Athlone Press, 2000.

Guidieri, R. "Les sociétés primitives aujourd'hui" [*SPA*]. In *Philosopher: les interrogations contemporarines*. Ed. Ch. Delacampagne and R. Maggiori. Paris: Fayard, 1980.

Guy-Sheftall, Beverly, ed. *Words of Fire: An Anthology of African-American Feminist Thought* [*WF*]. New York: New Press, 1995.

Habermas, Jürgen. *Communication and the Evolution of Society* [*CES*]. Ed. T. McCarthy. Boston: Beacon Press, 1979.

Hall, David L. "To Be or Not to Be: The Postmodern Self and the Wu-Forms of Taoism" [*TBNB*]. In Ames, ed. *Self as Person in Asian Theory and Practice*.

Hallen, Barry. "Phenomenology and the Exposition of African Traditional Thought" [*PEATT*]. In *Proceedings of the Seminar on African Philosophy/ La Philosophie Africaine*. Ed. Claude Sumner. Addis Ababa: Chamber Printing House, 1980.

Hallen, B., and J. O. Sodipo. *Knowledge, Belief & Witchcraft: Analytic Experiments in African Philosophy* [*KBW*]. London: Ethnographica, 1986.

Hamilton, C. H. "The Idea of Compassion in Mahâyâna Buddhism" [*ICMB*]. *Journal of the American Oriental Society* 70: 145–51.

Hamilton, Cynthia. "Coping with Industrial Exploitation" [*CIE*]. In Bullard, ed., *Confronting Environmental Racism*.

Hamilton-Grierson, P. J. "Strangers" [*S*]. In *Encyclopaedia of Religion and Ethics*. Ed J. Hastings. Edinburgh: T. & T. Clark, 1921. Vol. 11: 883–96.

Hannoosh, Michele. *Baudelaire and Caricature: From the Comic to an Art of Modernity* [*BC*]. University Park, PA: The Pennsylvania State University Press, 1992.

Haraway, Donna. *Simians, Cyborgs, and Women: The Reinvention of Nature* [*SCW*]. New York: Routledge, 1991.

Hardin, Garrett. "The Tragedy of the Commons" [*TC*]. *Science* 162 (December 13, 1968): 1245–48.

Harding, Sandra. "The Curious Coincidence of Feminine and African Moralities: Challenges for Feminist Theory" [*CCFAM*]. In Kittay and Meyers, eds., *Women and Moral Theory*.

———. "The Instability of the Analytical Categories of Feminist Theory" [*IACFT*]. *Signs* 11, no. 4 (Summer 1986): 645–64.

———. *The Science Question in Feminism* [*SQF*]. Ithaca, NY: Cornell University Press, 1986.

———. *Whose Science? Whose Knowledge?: Thinking from Women's Lives* [*WSWK*]. Ithaca, NY: Cornell University Press, 1991.

Hargrove, Eugene C. *Foundations of Environmental Ethics* [*FEE*]. Englewood Cliffs, NJ: Prentice Hall, 1989.

———, ed. *Religion and Environmental Crisis* [*REC*]. Athens, GA: University of Georgia Press, 1986.

Harman, Lesley D. *The Modern Stranger* [*MS*]. Amsterdam: Mouton de Gruyter, 1988.

Harper, Clifford. *Anarchy: A Graphic Guide* [*A*]. London: Camden Press, 1987.

Harris, Cheryl I. "Whiteness As Property" [*WP*]. *Harvard Law Review* 106, 8 (June 1993): 1707–91.

Harris, Daniel. *Cute, Quaint, Hungry and Romantic: The Aesthetics of Consumerism* [*CQHR*]. New York: Basic Books, 2000.

Harris, Leonard. "Postmodernism and Utopia, an Unholy Alliance" [*PU*]. In Hord and Lee, eds., *I Am Because We Are*.

Harrison, Beverly Wildung. "Our Right to Choose" [*RC*]. In Andolsen, Gudorf, and Pellauer, eds., *Women's Consciousness, Women's Conscience*.

Hatcher, Evelyn Payne. *Art as Culture: An Introduction to the Anthropology of Art* [*AC*]. 2nd ed. Westport, CT: Bergin & Garvey, 1999.

Haug, Wolfgang Fritz. *Critique of Commodity Aesthetics: Appearance, Sexuality and Advertising in Capitalist Society* [*CCA*]. Trans. Robert Bock. Minneapolis: University of Minnesota Press, 1986.

Hegel, G. W. F. *Aesthetics: Lectures on Fine Art* [*A*]. Trans. T. M. Knox. London: Oxford University Press, 1975. Introduction reprinted in part in Ross, ed., *Art and Its Significance* as "Philosophy of Fine Art" [*PFA*].

———. *Hegel's Science of Logic* [*L*]. Trans. A. V. Miller. New York: Humanities Press, 1969.

———. *Jenenser Realphilosophie I, Die Vorlesungen von 1803–1804* [*JR1*]. Ed. J. Hoffmeister. Leibzig: 1932. Quoted and translated in Agamben, *Language and Death*.

———. *Jenenser Realphilosophie II, Die Vorlesungen von 1803–1804* [*JR2*]. Ed. J. Hoffmeister. Leipzig: 1932. Quoted and translated in Agamben, *Language and Death*.

———. *The Logic of Hegel, translated from the Encyclopaedia of the Philosophical Sciences* [*EL*]. Trans. William Wallace. Oxford: Oxford University Press, 1892.

———. *The Phenomenology of Mind* [*PM*]. Trans. and int. James Baillie. London: George Allen & Unwin, 1910.

———. *The Phenomenology of Spirit* [*PS*]. Trans. Trans. A. V. Miller. Oxford: Oxford University Press, 1977.

———. *The Philosophy of Right* [*PR*]. Trans. T. M. Knox. Oxford: Oxford University Press, 1934, 1967.

Heidegger, Martin. "The Age of the World Picture" [*AWP*]. In *Question Concerning Technology and Other Essays*.

———. "The Anaximander Fragment" [*AF*]. In *Early Greek Thinking*.

———. *Basic Writings* [*BW*]. Ed. David Farrell Krell. New York: Harper & Row, 1977.

———. *Being and Time: A Translation of* Sein und Zeit [*BT*]. Trans. John Macquarrie and Edward Robinson. New York: Harper & Row, 1962. Translation of *Sein und Zeit* [*SZ*].

———. *Being and Time: A Translation of* Sein und Zeit [*BT(S)*]. Trans. Joan Stambaugh. Albany: State University of New York Press, 1996. Translation of *Sein und Zeit* [*SZ*].

———. *Discourse on Thinking: A Translation of* Gelassenheit [*DT*]. Trans. John M. Anderson and E. Hans Freund. New York: Harper & Row, 1966.

———. *Early Greek Thinking* [*EGT*]. Trans. D. F. Krell and F. A. Capuzzi. New York: Harper & Row, 1984.

———. *Identity and Difference* [*ID*]. Trans. and int. Joan Stambaugh. New York: Harper & Row, 1969.

———. *Introduction to Metaphysics* [*IM*]. Trans. Ralph Manheim. Garden City, NY: Doubleday, 1961.

———. "Language" [*L*]. In *Poetry, Language, Thought*.

———. "Language in the Poem" [*LP*]. In *On the Way to Language*.

———. "Letter on Humanism" [*LH*]. In *Basic Writings*.

———. "Martin Heidegger interrogé par *Der Spiegel*. Réponses et questions sur l'histoire et la politique" (Martin Heidegger interviewed by *Der Spiegel*: Responses and Questions on History and Politics.) Trans. William J. Richardson S. J. as " 'Only a God Can Save Us': The *Spiegel* Interview." In Sheehan, ed., *Heidegger, the Man and the Thinker*.

———. "The Nature of Language" [*NL*]. In *On the Way to Language*.

———. "On the Being and Conception of *Physis* in Aristotle's *Physics* B. 1" [*OBCP*]. Trans. T. J. Sheehan. *Man and World* 9, no. 3 (August 1976): 219–70.

———. "On the Essence of Truth" [*OET*]. In *Basic Writings*.

———. *On the Way to Language* [*OWL*]. Trans. Peter D. Hertz. New York: Harper & Row, 1971.

———. *On Time and Being* [*OTB*]. Trans. Joan Stambaugh. New York: Harper & Row, 1972.

———. "The Onto-theo-logical Constitution of Metaphysics" [*OTLCM*]. In *Identity and Difference*.

———. "The Origin of the Work of Art" [*OWA*]. Reprinted in part in Ross, ed., *Art and Its Significance*. In *Poetry, Language, Thought*.

——. *Poetry, Language, Thought* [*PLT*]. Trans. Albert Hofstadter. New York: Harper & Row, 1971.

——. "The Question Concerning Technology" [*QT*]. In *Basic Writings*.

——. *The Question Concerning Technology and Other Essays* [*QTOE*]. Trans. William Lovitt. New York: Harper & Row, 1977.

——. "Time and Being" [*TB*]. In *On Time and Being*.

——. *Was ist das—die Philosophie* [*WP*], 1955. Quoted in Derrida, "Heidegger's Ear."

——. "The Way to Language" [*WL*]. In *On the Way to Language*.

——. "What Calls for Thinking?" [*WCT*]. In *Basic Writings*.

Hein, Hilda. "Refining Feminist Theory: Lessons from Aesthetics" [*RFT*]. In Hein and Korsmeyer, eds. *Aesthetics in Feminist Perspective*.

Hein, Hilda, and Carolyn Korsmeyer, eds. *Aesthetics in Feminist Perspective* [*AFP*]. Bloomington: Indiana University Press, 1993.

Heller, Morton A., and William Schiff, eds. *The Psychology of Touch* [*PT*]. Hillsdale, NJ: Lawrence Erlbaum Associates, 1991.

Hendrix, Harville. *Getting the Love You Want: A Guide for Couples* [*GLW*]. New York: Pocket Books, 2001.

——. *Keeping the Love You Find: A Personal Guide* [*KLF*]. New York: Pocket Books, 1992.

Herdt, G. *Guardians of the Flutes: Idioms of Masculinity* [*GF*]. Stanford: Stanford University Press, 1980.

Hermann, Anne. "*Passing*" *Women, Performing Men* [*PWPM*]. In Roach-Higgins, Eicher, and Johnson, eds., *Dress and Identity*.

Hester, Jr., Randolph T. "Sacred Structures and Everyday Life: A Return to Manteo, North Carolina" [*SSEL*]. In Seamon, ed., *Dwelling, Seeing, and Designing*. (271–98).

Hirschon, Renée. "Introduction: Property, Power and Gender Relations" [*PPGR*]. In *Women and Property—Women as Property*.

——, ed. *Women and Property—Women as Property* [*WPWP*]. New York: St. Martin's Press, 1984.

Hisamatsu, Hoseki Shin'ichi. *Die Fülle des Nichts* [*FN*]. Trans. Takashi Hirata and Johanna Fisher. Pfullingen: Neske Verlag, 1984.

——. *Zen and the Fine Arts* [*ZFA*]. New York: Kodansha International, 1974.

Hix, H. L. *Spirits Hovering Over the Ashes: Legacies of Postmodern Theory* [*SHOA*]. Albany: State University of New York Press, 1995.

Hoagland, Sarah Lucia. "Lesbian Ethics and Female Agency" [*LEFA*]. In Cole and Coultrap-McQuin, eds., *Explorations in Feminist Ethics*.

——. "Some Thoughts about 'Caring'" [*STC*]. In Card, ed., *Feminist Ethics*.

Hoard, Adreinne Walker. "The Black Aesthetic: An Empirical Feeling" [*BA*]. In Young, ed. *Art, Culture, and Ethnicity*.

Hobbes, Thomas. *Complete Works* [*CW*]. Ed. William Molesworth. English Works, 11 vols., 1839. Latin Works, 5 vols., 1845.

——. *De Cive* [*DCV*]. In *Complete Works*.

——. *Elements of Philosophy* [*EOP*]. In *Complete Works*, Vol. 4.

——. *Leviathan* [*L*]. In *Complete Works*, Vol. 1.

Hoeller, Keith, ed. *Dream and Existence. Review of Existential Psychology and Psychiatry* [DE]. Trans. Forrest Williams and Jacob Needleman. Vol. XIX, no. 1 (1984–5).

Hölderlin, Friedrich. *Friedrich Hölderlin Poems and Fragments* [FHPF]. Trans. Michael Hamburger. Ann Arbor: University of Michigan Press, 1966.

———. "Patmos" [P]. In *Friedrich Hölderlin Poems and Fragments*.

Homann, Margaret. *Bearing the Word: Language and Female Experience in Nineteenth-Century Women's Writing* [BW]. Chicago: University of Chicago Press, 1986.

Hoppe, Hans-Hermann. *The Economics and Ethisc of Private Property* [EEPP]. Boston: Kluwer Academic Publishers, 1993.

Hord, Fred Lee (Mzee Lasana Okpara), and Jonathan Scott Lee, eds. *I Am Because We Are: Readings in Black Philosophy* [IABWA]. Amherst: University of Massachusetts, 1995.

Horovitz, Irving Louis, ed. *The Anarchists* [A]. New York: Dell, 1964.

Hoseki Shin'ichi Hisamatsu, *Die Fülle des Nichts* [FN]. Trans. Takashi Hirata and Johanna Fisher. Pfullingen: Neske Verlag, 1984.

Hubbard, Jamie and Paul L. Swanson, eds. *Pruning the Bodhi Tree: The Storm Over Critical Buddhism* [PBT]. Honolulu: University of Hawaii Press, 1997.

Hume, David. *An Enquiry Concerning Human Understanding* [EHU]. New York: Prometheus, 1988.

———. "Of the Standard of Taste" [OST]. Reprinted in Ross, ed., *Art and Its Significance*.

———. "On National Characters" [ONC]. In T. H. Green and T. H. Grose, eds., *Philosophical Works* [PW]. Vol. 3. Aalen: Scientia Verlag, 1964.

———. *A Treatise of Human Nature* [T]. London: Oxford University Press, 1888.

Huntington, Jr., C. W. *The Emptiness of Emptiness* [EE]. With Geshé Namgyal Wangchen. Honolulu: University of Hawaii Press, 1989.

Husserl, Edmund. *Ideas: General Introduction to Pure Phenomenology* [I]. Trans. W. R. Boyce Gibson. New York: Collier Books, 1962.

Hyde, Lewis. *The Gift: Imagination and the Erotic Life of Property* [G]. New York: Random House, 1979.

Illich, Ivan. *Gender* [G]. New York: Pantheon, 1982.

———. "Toward a History of Gender" [THG]. *Feminist Issues* 3, no. 1 (Spring 1983). Includes symposium on his work.

Inada, Kenneth K. "Environmental Problematics" [EP]. In Callicott and Ames, eds., *Nature in Asian Traditions of Thought*.

Irigaray, Luce. "Any Theory of the 'Subject' Has Always Been Appropriated by the 'Masculine'" [ATS]. In *Speculum of the Other Woman*.

———. "The Culture of Difference" [CD]. In *Je, tu, nous*.

———. *Elemental Passions* [EP]. Trans. Joanne Collins and Judith Still. New York: Routledge, 1992.

———. *An Ethics of Sexual Difference* [ESD]. Trans. Carolyn Burke and Gillian C. Gill. Ithaca, NY: Cornell University Press, 1993. Translation of *Éthique de la Différence sexuelle* [ÉDS]. Paris: Minuit, 1984.

——. "The Fecundity of the Caress: A Reading of Levinas, *Totality and Infinity*, 'Phenomenology of Eros'" [FC]. In *Ethics of Sexual Difference*.

——. "He Risks Who Risks Life Itself" [HR]. In *Irigaray Reader*.

——. *I Love to You: Sketch of a Possible Felicity in History* [ILTY]. Trans. Alison Martin. New York: Routledge, 1996.

——. "The Invisible of the Flesh: A Reading of Merleau-Ponty, *The Visible and the Invisible*, 'The Intertwining—The Chiasm'" [IF]. In *Ethics of Sexual Difference*.

——. *The Irigaray Reader* [IR]. Ed. and int. Margaret Whitford. Oxford: Blackwell, 1991.

——. "Je-Luce Irigaray" [J]. Ed. and trans. Elizabeth Hirsh and Gaëton Brechotte. Interview in *Hypatia* 10, no. 2 (Spring 1995): 93–114.

——. *Je, tu, nous: Toward a Culture of Difference* [JTN]. Trans. Alison Martin. New York: Routledge, 1993.

——. *Marine Lover of Friedrich Nietzsche* [ML]. Trans. Gillian C. Gill. New York: Columbia University Press, 1991.

——. "The 'Mechanics' of Fluids" [MF]. In *This Sex Which Is Not One*.

——. "La Mystérique" [M]. In *Speculum of the Other Woman*.

——. "The Necessity for Sexuate Rights" [NSR]. In *Irigaray Reader*.

——. *L'oubli de l'air: Chez Martin Heidegger* [OA]. Paris: Minuit, 1983.

——. "The Power of Discourse and the Subordination of the Feminine" [PDSF]. In *This Sex Which Is Not One*.

——. "Questions" [Q]. In *Irigaray Reader*.

——. "Questions to Emmanuel Levinas" [QEL]. In *Irigaray Reader*.

——. "Sexual Difference" [SD]. In *Irigaray Reader*.

——. *Speculum of the Other Woman* [SOW]. Trans. Gillian C. Gill. Ithaca, NY: Cornell University Press, 1985. Translation of *Speculum de l'autre femme*. Paris: Minuit, 1974.

——. *This Sex Which Is Not One* [SWNO]. Trans. Catherine Porter. Ithaca, NY: Cornell University Press, 1985.

——. "This Sex Which Is Not One" [TSWNO]. In *This Sex Which Is Not One*.

——. "The Three *Genres*" [TG]. In *Irigaray Reader*.

——. "Volume-Fluidity" [VF]. Translation of "L'incontourable volume" (*Volume without Contour*). In *Speculum of the Other Woman*.

——. "When Our Lips Speak Together" [WOLST]. In *This Sex Which Is Not One*.

——. "Why Define Sexed Rights?" [WDSR]. In *Je, tu, nous*.

——. "Women on the Market" [WM]. In *This Sex Which Is Not One*.

Isasi-Diaz, Ada Maria. "Toward an Understanding of *Feminismo Hispano* in the U.S.A." [FH]. In Andolsen, Gudorf, and Pellauer, eds., *Women's Consciousness, Women's Conscience*.

Jackson, Jean. "Chronic Pain and the Tension between the Body as Subject and Object" [CP]. In Csordas, *Embodiment and Experience*.

Jackson, Michael. "The Man Who Could Turn into an Elephant: Shape-shifting Among the Kuranko of Sierra Leone" [ME]. In Jackson and Karp, eds. *Personhood and Agency*.

Jackson, Michael, and Ivan Karp, eds. *Personhood and Agency: The Experiences of Self and Other in African Cultures* [*PA*]. Washington, DC: Smithsonian Institution Press, 1990.

Jackson, Wes, et al., eds. *Meeting the Expectations of the Land* [*MEL*]. San Francisco: North Point Press, 1984.

Jacobs, Jane. *Systems of Survival: A Dialogue on the Moral Foundations of Commerce and Politics* [*SS*]. New York: Random House, 1993.

Jacobson-Widding, Anita. "The Shadow as an Expression of Individuality in Congolese Conceptions of Personhood" [*SEI*]. In Jackson and Karp, eds. *Personhood and Agency.*

Jacoby, Karl. "Slaves by Nature? Domestic Animals and Human Slaves" [*SN*]. *Slavery & Abolition: A Journal of Slave and Post-Slave Studies* (April 1994): 89–97.

Jaggar, Alison M., and Susan R. Bordo, eds. *Gender/Body/Knowledge: Feminist Reconstructions of Being and Knowing* [*GBK*]. New Brunswick: Rutgers University Press, 1989.

James, William. *Essays in Radical Empiricism* [*ERE*]. New York: Longman's Green, 1912.

Jameson, Frederic. "Postmodernism, or The Cultural Logic of Late Capitalism" [*P*]. *New Left Review* 146, no. 4 (July–August, 1984): 53–93.

Johnson, Mark. *The Body in the Mind: The Bodily Basis of Meaning, Imagination, and Reason* [*BM*]. Chicago: University of Chicago Press, 1987.

Jonas, Hans. "De la Gnose au Principe Responsabilité: Entretien avec Hans Jonas" [*GPR*]. *Esprit* 171 (May 1991): 5–21.

———. *The Imperative of Responsibility: In Search of an Ethics for the Technological Age* [*IR*]. Chicago: University of Chicago Press, 1984.

Jowett, Donna. "Origins, Occupations, and the Proximity of the Neighbour" [*OOPN*]. In Godway and Finn, eds., *Who Is This "We"?*

Jung, Carl Gustav. *Modern Man in Search of a Soul* [*MMSS*]. Trans. W. S. Dell and Cary F. Baynes. New York: Harcourt Brace Jovanovich, 1955.

———. "Psychology and Literature" [*PL*]. Reprinted in Ross, ed., *Art and Its Significance.* In *Modern Man in Search of a Soul.*

Jussawalla, Adil. *Missing Person* [*MP*]. Bombay: Clearing House, 1976.

Kafka, Franz. *The Complete Stories* [*CS*]. Ed. Nahum N. Glatzer. New York: Schocken, 1971.

———. "In the Penal Colony" [*IPC*]. In Kafka, *Complete Stories.*

Kant, Immanuel. "An Answer to the Questin: What is Enlightenment?" [*WE?*]. In *Toward Perpetual Peace.*

———. *The Conflict of the Faculties; Der Streit der Fakultäten* [*CF*]. Trans. Mary J. Gregor. New York: Abaris, 1979.

———. *Critique of Judgment* [*CJ*]. Trans. J. H. Bernard. New York: Hafner, 1951. Translation of *Kritik der Urteilskraft.* In *Kritik der Urteilskraft und Schriften zur Naturphilosophie.* Wiesbaden: Insel-Verlag Zweigstelle, 1957.

———. *Critique of Practical Reason* [*CPrR*]. In *Kant's Critique of Practical Reason and Other Works on the Theory of Ethics.* Trans. T. K. Abbott. London: Longman's Green, 1954.

————. *Critique of Pure Reason* [*CPR*]. Trans. J. M. D. Meiklejohn. Buffalo: Prometheus, 1990. Trans. Norman Kemp Smith [*CPR (NKS)*]. New York: St. Martin's, 1956. Translation of *Kritik der reinen Vernunft* [*KRV*]. 2 Band. Berlin: Deutsche Bibliothek, 1936.

————. *Fundamental Principles of the Metaphysics of Morals* [*FPMM*]. In *Kant's Critique of Practical Reason and Other Works on the Theory of Ethics*.

————. *Lectures on Ethics* [*LE*]. Trans. L. Infield. New York: Harper & Row, 1963.

————. *The Metaphysical Principles of Virtue* [*MPV*]. Indianapolis: Bobbs-Merrill, 1968.

————. *The Metaphysics of Morals* [*MM*]. Trans. Mary Gregory. Cambridge: Cambridge University Press, 1991.

————. *Observations on the Beautiful and the Sublime* [*OBS*]. Trans. John T. Goldthwait. Berkeley: University of California Press, 1960.

————. *Toward Perpetual Peace and Other Writings on Politics, Peace, and History* [*TPP*]. Trans. David L. Colclasure. Ed. Pauline Kleingeld. With essays by Jeremy Waldron, Michael W. Doyle, Allen W. Wood. New Haven: Yale University Press, 2006.

Kasulis, T. P. "Researching the Strata of the Japanese Self" [*RSJS*]. In Ames, ed. *Self as Person in Asian Theory and Practice*.

————. *Zen Action, Zen Person* [*ZAZP*]. Honolulu: University of Hawaii Press, 1981.

Katz, David. *The World of Touch* [*WT*]. Trans. Lester E. Krueger. Hillsdale, NJ: Lawrence Erlbaum Associates, 1989.

Katz, Eric. "The Call of the Wild: The Struggle against Domination and the Technological Fix of Nature" [*CW*]. In Oelschlaeger, ed., *Postmodern Environmental Ethics*.

————. *Nature as Subject: Human Obligation and Natural Community* [*NS*]. Lanham: Rowman & Littlefield, 1997.

Keller, Mara Lynn. "The Eleusinian Mysteries: Ancient Nature Religion of Demeter and Persephone" [*EM*]. In Diamond and Orenstein, eds., *Reweaving the World*.

Kheel, Marti. "Ecofeminism and Deep Ecology: Reflections on Identity and Difference" [*EDE*]. In Diamond and Orenstein, eds., *Reweaving the World*.

————. "The Liberation of Nature: A Circular Affair" [*LN*]. *Environmental Ethics* 7, no. 2 (Summer 1985): 135–50.

Kierkegaard, Søren. *Either/Or* [*E/O*]. Trans. David F. Swenson and Lillian Marvin Swenson. Rev. Howard A. Johnson. 2 vols. Garden City, NY: Doubleday, 1959.

————. *Fear and Trembling/The Sickness Unto Death* [*FT*]. Trans. W. Lowrie. Garden City, NY: Doubleday, 1954.

————. *The Self in Society* [*SS*]. New York: St. Martin's Press, 1998.

Kigunga, Raphael. *The Anthropology of Self—Person and Myth in Africa: A Philosophyical Reflection on Man in South-East Africa* [*AS*]. New York: Peter Lang, 1996.

Kim, Hee-Jin. *Flowers of Emptiness* [FE]. Lewiston, NY: The Edwin Mellen Press, 1985.

King, Deborah K. "Multiple Jeopardy, Multiple Consciousness: The Context of a Black Feminist Ideology" [MJMC]. In Guy-Sheftall, ed., *Words of Fire*.

King, Lewis M. "On the Nature of a Creative World" [ONCW]. In Ruch and Anyanwu, eds., *African Philosophy*.

King, Lewis M., Vernon J. Dixon, and Wade W. Nobles, eds. *African Philosophy: Assumptions & Paradigms for Research on Black Persons* [AP]. Los Angeles: Charles R. Drew Postgraduate Medical School, 1976. Fanon Research and Development Center Publication, Area 8, no. 2.

King, Roger J. H. "Caring about Nature: Feminist Ethics and the Environment" [CN]. In Warren, ed., *Hypatia*, 75–89.

King, Sallie B. *Buddha Nature* [BN]. Albany: State University of New York Press, 1991.

King, Ynestra. "The Ecology of Feminism and the Feminism of Ecology" [EFFE]. In Plant, ed., *Healing the Wounds*.

——. "Healing the Wounds: Feminism, Ecology, and the Nature/Culture Dualism" [HW]. In Diamond and Orenstein, eds., *Reweaving the World*.

Kirkham, Richard L. *Theories of Truth: A Critical Introduction* [TT]. Cambridge, MA: MIT Press, 1992.

Kittay, Eva Feder, and Diana T. Meyers, eds. *Women and Moral Theory* [WMT]. Totowa, NJ: Rowman & Littlefield, 1987.

Klemm, David E. and Günter Zöller, eds. *Figuring the Self: Subject, Absolute, and Others in Classical German Philosophy* [FS]. Albany: State University of New York Press, 1998.

Kline, Linus W. and C. J. France. "The Psychology of Ownership" [PO]. *The Pedagogical Seminary* 6, 3 (September 1899): 421–70.

Kokole, Omari H. "The Political Economy of the African Environment" [PEAE]. In Westra and Wenz, eds., *Faces of Environmental Racism: Confronting Issues of Global Justice*.

Kondo, Dorinne. "The Aesthetics and Politics of Japanese Identity in the Fashion Industry" [APJI]. In Roach-Higgins, Eicher, and Johnson, eds., *Dress and Identity*.

Krell, David Farrell. *Daimon Life: Heidegger and Life-Philosophy* [DL]. Bloomington: Indiana University Press, 1992.

——. "Eating Out" [EO]. In Scapp and Seitz, eds., *Eating Culture*.

——. *Intimations of Mortality* [IM]. University Park: Pennsylvania State University Press, 1986.

Kristeva, Julia. *Black Sun: Depression and Melancholia* [BS]. Trans. Leon S. Roudiez. New York: Columbia University Press, 1989.

——. *Desire in Language: A Semiotic Approach to Literature and Art* [DL]. Trans. Leon S. Roudiez. New York: Columbia University Press, 1980.

——. *The Kristeva Reader* [KR]. Ed. Toril Moi. Trans. Alice Jardine and Harry Blake. New York: Columbia University Press, 1986.

——. *Powers of Horror: An Essay on Abjection* [PH]. Trans. Leon S. Roudiez. New York: Columbia University Press, 1982.

———. "Stabat Mater" [*SM*]. In *Kristeva Reader*.

———. *Strangers to Ourselves* [*SO*]. Trans. Leon S. Roudiez. New York: Columbia University Press, 1991.

———. "Women's Time" [*WT*]. In *Kristeva Reader*. Published as "Le temps des femmes." *Cahiers de recherche de sciences des textes et documents* 5 (Winter 1979).

Kroker, Arthur, and Marilouise Kroker, eds. *The Last Sex: Feminism and Outlaw Bodies* [*LS*]. New York: St. Martin's, 1993.

Lacan, Jacques. *Écrits: a Selection* [*É*]. Trans. Alan Sheridan. New York: W. W. Norton & Co., 1977.

———. *Feminine Sexuality* [*FS*]. Ed. Juliet Mitchell and Jacqueline Rose. Trans. Jacqueline Rose. New York: Norton, 1985.

———. "God and the *Jouissance* of The Woman" [*GJW*]. In *Feminine Sexuality*.

———. "A Love Letter" [*LL*]. In *Feminine Sexuality*.

———. "Seminar on *The Purloined Letter*" [*SPL*]. Trans. Jeffrey Mehlmann. *Yale French Studies*, no. 48 (1972).

LaChapelle, Dolores. *Earth Wisdom* [*EW*]. San Diego: Guild of Tudors, 1978.

Lacoue-Labarthe, Philippe. *The Subject of Philosophy* [*SP*]. Trans. Thomas Trezise, Hugh J. Silverman, Gary M. Cole, Timothy D. Bent, Karen McPherson, and Claudette Sartiliot. Ed. Thomas Trezise. Minneapolis: University of Minnesota Press, 1993. Translation of *Le Sujet de la philosophie* [*Sp*]. Paris: Aubier-Flammarion, 1979.

Lacoue-Labarthe, Philippe, and Jean-Luc Nancy. *Retreating the Political* [*RP*]. Ed. Simon Sparks. New York: Routledge, 1997.

Lafferty, William M., and James Meadowcroft, eds. *Democracy and the Environment: Problems and Prospects* [*DE*]. Cheltenham: Edward Elgar, 1996.

LaFleur, William. "Sattva—Enlightenment for Plants & Trees" [*S*]. In Badiner, ed., *Dharma Gaia*.

Lahar, Stephanie. "Ecofeminist Theory and Grassroots Politics" [*ETGP*]. In Warren, ed., *Hypatia*, 28–45.

Langer, Susanne K. *Feeling and Form: A Theory of Art* [*FF*]. New York: Scribner's, 1953.

Largey, Gale Peter, and David Rogney Watson. "The Sociology of Odors" [*SO*]. In Roach-Higgins, Eicher, and Johnson, eds., *Dress and Identity*.

Laughlin, Robert B. "Reinventing Physics: The Search for the Real Frontier" [*RP*]. *Chronicle of Higher Education* (February 11, 2005): B6–8; adapted from *A Different Universe: Reinventing Physics from the Bottom Down* (New York: Basic Books), 2005.

Lebra, Takie Sugiyama. "*Migawari*: The Cultural Idiom of Self-Other Exchange in Japan" [*M*]. In Ames, ed., *Self as Person in Asian Theory and Practice*.

Lefkovitz, Lori Hope, ed. *Textual Bodies: Changing Boundaries of Literary Representation* [*TB*]. Albany: State University of New York Press, 1993.

Leibniz, G. W. F. "The Exigency to Exist in Essences: Principle of Plenitude" [*EEE*]. In *Leibniz Selections*.

———. *Leibniz Selections* [*LS*]. Ed. P. Wiener. New York: Scribner's, 1951. All references to Leibniz are from this edition.

———. "The Monadology" [*M*]. In *Leibniz Selections*.

Leiss, William. *The Limits to Satisfaction: An Essay on the Problem of Needs and Commodities* [*LS*]. Montreal: McGill-Queen's University Press, 1988.

Leopold, Aldo. *Game Management* [*GM*]. Madison: University of Wisconsin Press, 1986.

———. "The Land Ethic" [*LE*]. In *Sand County Almanac*.

———. *A Sand County Almanac* [*SCA*]. New York: Ballantine Books, 1970.

———. "Thinking Like a Mountain" [*TLM*]. In *Sand County Almanac*.

———. "Wilderness" [*W*]. In *Sand County Almanac*.

Levinas, Emmanuel. "Diachrony and Representation" [*DR*]. In *Time and the Other*.

———. "Ethics as First Philosophy" [*EFP*]. Trans. Seán Hand. In *Levinas Reader*.

———. *The Levinas Reader* [*LR*]. Ed. Seán Hand. Oxford: Blackwell, 1989.

———. "Martin Buber and the Theory of Knowledge" [*MBTK*]. In *Levinas Reader*.

———. "The Old and the New" [*ON*]. In *Time and the Other*.

———. *Otherwise than Being or Beyond Essence* [*OB*]. Trans. Alphonso Lingis. The Hague: Martinus Nijhoff, 1978. Translation of *Autrement qu'être ou au-delà de l'essence* [*AÊ*]. The Hague: Martinus Nijhoff, 1974.

———. "The Paradox of Morality: an Interview with Emmanuel Levinas" [*PM*]. With Tamra Wright, Peter Hughes, Alison Ainley. Trans. Andrew Benjamin and Tamra Wright. In Bernasconi and Wood, ed., *Provocation of Levinas*.

———. "Reality and Its Shadow" [*RS*]. Trans. Alphonso Lingis. In *Levinas Reader*.

———. "Reality and Its Shadow" [*RS2*]. In *Unforeseen History*.

———. "Substitution" [*S*]. In *Levinas Reader*.

———. *Time and the Other (and additional essays)* [*TO*]. Trans. Richard A. Cohen. Pittsburgh: Duquesne University Press, 1987.

———. *Totality and Infinity* [*TI*]. Trans. Alphonso Lingis. Pittsburgh: Duquesne University Press, 1969.

———. "The Transcendence of Words" [*TW*]. Trans. Seán Hand. In *Levinas Reader*.

———. *Unforeseen History* [*UH*]. Trans. Nidra Poller. Chicago: University of Illinois Press, 2004.

Levine, David P. *Subjectivity in Political Economy: Essays on Wanting and Choosing* [*SPE*]. New York: Routledge, 1998.

Levine, Donald N. "Simmel at a Distance: On the History and Systematics of the Sociology of the Stranger" [*SD*]. In Shack & Skinner, eds., *Strangers in African Societies*.

Lévi-Strauss, Claude. *The Elementary Structure of Kinship* [*ESK*]. Trans. James Harle Bell, John Richard von Sturmer, and Rodney Needham. Boston: Beacon Press, 1969.

Lewis, James A. *Landownership in the United States, 1978* [*LUS*]. Washington, DC: Natural Resource Economics Division; Economics, Statistics, and Cooperative Services, U.S. Department of Agriculture, Agricultural Information Bulletin 435, April, 1980.

Liddell, Henry George, and Robert Scott. *An Intermediate Greek-English Lexicon, Founded Upon The Seventh Edition of Liddell and Scott's Greek-English Lexicon* [*IGEL*]. Oxford: Oxford University Press, 1991.

Lingis, Alphonso. "Appetite" [*A*]. In Scapp, ed. *Eating Culture.*

——. *Foreign Bodies* [*FB*]. New York: Routledge, 1994.

Linsky, Leonard, ed. *Semantics and the Philosophy of Language* [*SPL*]. Urbana: University of Illinois Press. 1952.

Lipietz, Alan. *Green Hopes: The Future of Political Ecology* [*GH*]. Cambridge, MA: Polity Press, 1995.

Lipka, Richard P. and Thomas M. Brinthaupt. *Self-Perspectives Across the Life Span* [*SPALS*]. Albany: State University of New York Press, 1992.

Lispector, Clarice. *The Passion According to G. H.* [*PGH*]. Trans. Ronald W. Sousa. Minneapolis: University of Minnesota Press, 1988.

——. *O Lustro* [*OL*]. Rio de Janeiro: Editora Nova Fronteira, 1982.

Locke, Alain. *Negro Art: Past and Present* [*NAPP*]. Washington, DC: Associates in Negro Folk Education, 1936.

——. *The Negro in Art: A Pictorial Record of the Negro Theme in Art* [*NA*]. Washington, DC: Associates in Negro Folk Education, 1940.

Locke, John. *An Essay Concerning Human Understanding* [*E*]. Ed. Alexander Campbell Fraser. New York: Dover, 1959.

——. *Two Treatises of Government* [*TT*]. Student ed. Ed. Peter Laslett. Oxford: Cambridge University Press, 1988.

Loewental, Kate. "Property." *European Journal of Social Psychology* 6, no. 3 (May–June 1976): 343–51.

Lorde, Audre. "Age, Race, Class, and Sex: Women Redefining Difference" [*ARCS*]. In Andersen and Collins, eds., *Race, Class, and Gender.*

Lovelock, James. *Gaia: A New Look at Life on Earth* [*G*]. Oxford: Oxford University Press, 1979.

Lowrie, Robert H. *Primitive Religion* [*PR*]. New York: Boni and Liveright, 1924.

Lozano, Luis-Martin. *The Magic of Remedios Varo.* Trans. Elizabeth Goldson and Liliana Valenzuela. Washington, DC: National Museum of Women in the Arts, 2000.

Lubar, Steven, and W. David Kingery, eds. *History from Things: Essays on Material Culture* [*HS*]. Washington, DC: Smithsonian Institution Press, 1993.

Ludwig, Arnold N. *How Do We Know Who We Are?: A Biography of the Self* [*HDWKWWA?*]. Oxford: Oxford University Press, 1997.

Lugones, Marìa C. "On the Logic of Pluralist Feminism" [*OLPF*]. In Card, ed., *Feminist Ethics.*

——. "Playfulness, 'World'-Travelling, and Loving Perception" [*PWTLP*]. *Hypatia* 2, no. 2 (Summer 1987): 3–20.

Lury, Celia. *Prosthetic Culture: Photography, Memory and Identity* [PC]. London: Routledge, 1998.

Lyon, M. L., and J. M. Barbalet. "Society's Body: Emotion and the 'Somatization' of Social Theory" [SB]. In Csordas, *Embodiment and Experience*.

Lyotard, Jean-François. *Le Différend* [D]. Paris: Minuit, 1983.

———. *The Differend: Phrases in Dispute* [DPD]. Trans. Georges Van Den Abbeele. Minneapolis: University of Minnesota Press, 1988.

———. "Europe, the Jew, and the Book" [EJB]. In *Political Writings*.

———. "German Guilt" [GG]. In *Political Writings*.

———. "The Grip (*Mainmise*)" [G]. In *Political Writings*.

———. *Heidegger and "the jews"* [HJ]. Trans. A. Michel and M. Roberts. Minneapolis: University of Minnesota Press, 1990.

———. "Heidegger and 'the jews': A Conference in Vienna and Freiburg" ["HJ"]. In *Political Writings*.

———. *The Inhuman: Reflections on Time* [I]. Trans. Geoffrey Bennington and Rachel Bowlby. Stanford: Stanford University Press, 1991.

———. *Lessons on the Analytic of the Sublime* [LAS]. Trans. Elizabeth Rottenberg. Stanford, CA: Stanford University Press, 1994.

———. *Libinal Economy* [LE]. Trans. Iain Hamilton Grant. Bloomington: Indiana University Press, 1993.

———. *The Lyotard Reader* [LR]. Ed. Andrew Benjamin. Oxford: Blackwell, 1989.

———. "Oikos" [O]. In *Political Writings*.

———. *Peregrinations* [P]. New York: Columbia University Press, 1988.

———. *Phenomenology* [Ph]. Trans. Brian Beakley. Albany: State University of New York Press, 1991.

———. *Political Writings* [PW]. Trans. Bill Readings and Kevin Paul Geiman. Minneapolis: University of Minnesota Press, 1993.

———. *The Postmodern Condition: A Report on Knowledge* [PMC]. Trans. Geoff Bennington and Brian Massumi. Minneapolis: University of Minnesota Press, 1984.

———. "The Sign of History" [SH]. In *Lyotard Reader*.

———. "What Is Postmodernism?" [WP?]. Reprinted in part in Ross, ed., *Art and Its Significance*. In *Postmodern Condition*.

Lyotard, Jean-François, and Jean-Loup Thébaud. *Just Gaming* [JG]. Trans. Wlad Godzich. Minneapolis: University of Minnesota Press, 1985.

MacKinnon, Catharine A. "Feminism, Marxism, Method, and the State: An Agenda for Theory" [FMMS1]. *Signs* 7, no. 3 (Spring 1982): 515–44.

———. "Feminism, Marxism, Method, and the State: Toward Feminist Jurisprudence" [FMMS2]. *Signs* 8, no. 4 (Summer 1982): 635–58.

———. *Feminism Unmodified: Discourses on Life and Law* [FU]. Cambridge: Harvard University Press, 1987.

———. *Only Words* [OW]. Cambridge: Harvard University Press, 1993.

———. "Sexuality" [S]. Chapter 7 in *Toward a Feminist Theory of the State*.

———. *Toward a Feminist Theory of the State* [TFTS]. Cambridge: Harvard University Press, 1989.

————. "Toward Feminist Jurisprudence" [*TFJ*]. Chapter 13 in *Toward a Feminist Theory of the State*.

Macpherson, C. B. "The Meaning of Property" [*MP*]. In Macpherson, ed., *Property: Mainstream and Critical Positions* [*P*].

————. *The Political Theory of Possessive Individualism: Hobbes to Locke* [*PTPI*]. Oxford: Oxford University Press, 1962.

————, ed. *Property: Mainstream and Critical Positions* [*P*]. Toronto: University of Toronto Press, 1983.

Maddock, Kenneth. "Involved Anthropologists" [*IA*]. In Wilmsen, ed., *We Are Here*.

Malhotra, Ashok K. "Sartre and Samkhya—Yoga on Self" [*SSYS*]. In Allen, ed., *Culture and Self*.

Manderson, Desmond. *Songs Without Music: Aesthetic Dimensions of Law and Justice* [*SWM*]. Berkeley: University of California Press, 2000.

Manes, Christopher. *Green Rage: Radical Environmentalism and the Unmaking of Civilization* [*GRF*]. Boston: Little, Brown and Co., 1990.

————. "Nature and Silence" [*NS*]. In Oelschlaeger, ed., *Postmodern Environmental Ethics*.

Margalit, Avishai. *The Ethics of Memory* [*EM*]. Cambridge, MA: Harvard University Press, 2002.

Margolis, Diane Rothbard. *The Fabric of Self: A Theory of Ethics and Emotions* [*FS*]. New Haven, CT: Yale University Press, 1998.

Marion, Jean-Luc. *Being Given: Toward a Phenomenology of Givenness* [*BG*]. Trans. Jeffrey L. Kosky. Stanford, CA: Stanford University Press, 2002.

————. *Étant Donné: Essai de la phénoménologie de donation* [*ÉD*]. Paris: Presses Universitaires de France, 1997.

————. *Reduction and Givenness: Investigations of Husserl, Heidegger, and Phenomenology* [*RG*]. Trans. Thomas A. Carlson. Chicago: Northwestern University Press, 1998.

————. *Réduction et donation: recherches sur Husserl, Heidegger et la phénoménologie* [*Rd*]. Paris: Presses universitaires de France, 1989.

Marks, Elaine, and Isabelle Courtivron, eds. *New French Feminisms: An Anthology* [*NFF*]. New York: Schocken, 1981.

Martin, James J. *Men Against the State: The Expositors of Individualist Anarchism in America, 1827–1908* [*MAS*]. DeKalb, IL: Adrian Allen Associates, 1953.

Marx, Karl. *Capital: A Critique of Political Economy* [*C*]. 4th ed. 3 vols. Ed. Friedrich Engels. Trans. Ben Fowkes. London: Penguin Books in association with New Left Review, 1976.

————. *Capital: A Critique of Political Economy* [*C3*]. 3rd ed. 3 vols. Ed. Friedrich Engels. Trans. Samuel Moore and Edward Aveling. New York: International Publishers, 1967.

————. *The German Ideology* [*GI*]. In Karl Marx and Friedrich Engels, *Collected Works*, Vol. 5. New York: International Publishers, 1976.

————. "Marx to Schweitzer" [*MS*]. In *Poverty of Philosophy*.

————. *The Poverty of Philosophy* [*PP*]. New York: International Publishers, 1963.

———. *A World Without Jews* [*WWJ*]. 4th ed. Ed. and int. Dagobert D. Runes. New York: Philosophical Library, 1960.

Marx, Karl and Friedrich Engels. *Selected Works* [*SW*]. 2 vols. Marx-Engels-Lenin Institute. Moscow: Foreign Languages Publish House, 1953. London: Lawrence and Wishart, 1953.

Massumi, Brian. "The Bleed" [*B*]. In Welchman, ed. *Rethinking Borders*.

Matilal, Bimal Krishna. "The Perception of Self in Indian Tradition" [*PSIT*]. In Ames, ed. *Self as Person in Asian Theory and Practice*.

Mathews, Freya. *The Ecological Self* [*ES*]. Savage, MD: Barnes & Noble Books, 1991.

Mauss, Marcel. *The Gift: Forms and Functions of Exchange in Archaic Societies* [*G*]. Trans. Ian Cunnison. Glenco: Free Press, 1954. Also *The Gift: The Form and Reason for Exchange in Archaic Societies*. Trans. W. D. Halls. London: Routledge, 1990.

Maw, Joan, and John Picton, eds. *Concepts of the Body/Self in Africa* [*CBS*]. Vienna: Afro-Pub, 1992.

May, Todd. *The Political Philosophy of Poststructuralist Anarchism* [*PPPA*]. University Park, PA: The Pennsylvania State University Press, 1994.

Mbiti, John S. *African Religions and Philosophy* [*ARP*]. London: Heinemann Educational Books, 1969.

McConnell, Theodore A. *The Shattered Self: the Psychological and Religious Search for Selfhood* [*SS*]. Philadelphia: Pilgrim Press, 1971.

McIntosh, Peggy. "White Privilege and Male Privilege: A Personal Account of Coming to See Correspondences through Work in Women's Studies" [*WPMP*]. In Andersen and Collins, eds., *Race, Class, and Gender*.

McLaughlin, Andrew. *Regarding Nature: Industrialism and Deep Ecology* [*RN*]. Albany: State University of New York Press, 1993.

Meiling, Jin. "Strangers on a Hostile Landscape" [*SHL*]. In Cobham and Collins, eds., *Watchers and Seekers*.

Merchant, Carolyn. *The Death of Nature: Women, Ecology, and the Scientific Revolution* [*DN*]. New York: Harper & Row, 1980.

———. *Radical Ecology: The Search for a Livable World* [*RE*]. New York: Routledge, 1992.

Meredith, George. *An Essay on Comedy* [*EC*]. In Sypher, *Comedy*.

Merleau-Ponty, Maurice. *Eye and Mind* [*EM*]. Trans. Carleton Dallery. Reprinted in part in Ross, ed., *Art and Its Significance*. In *Primacy of Perception*, 282–98.

———. *Phenomenology of Perception* [*PhP*]. Trans. Colin Smith. London: Routledge & Kegan Paul, 1962.

———. *The Primacy of Perception* [*PrP*]. Ed. James M. Edie. Evanston: Northwestern University Press, 1964.

———. *The Visible and the Invisible* [*VI*]. Ed. Claude Lefort. Trans. Alphonso Lingis. Evanston: Northwestern University Press, 1968.

Merriam-Webster Dictionary of English Usage [*MWDEU*]. Springfield, MA: Merriam-Webster, 1989.

Meyer, Christine, and Faith Moosang, eds. *Living with the Land: Communities Restoring the Earth* [*LL*]. Gabriola Island, BC: New Society Publishers, 1992.

Mignolo, Walter D. *Local Histories/Global Designs: Coloniality, Subaltern Knowledges, and Border Thinking* [*LH*]. Princeton: Princeton University Press, 2000.

Mill, John Stuart. *On Liberty; with The Subjection of Women and Chapters on Socialism* [*L*]. New York: Cambridge University Press, 1989.

———. *Utilitarianism and Other Essays* [*U*]. New York: Penguin, 1987.

Miller, Mara. "Views of Japanese Selfhood: Japanese and Western Perspectives" [*VJS*]. In Allen, ed., *Culture and Self*.

Milton, Katharine. "Real Men Don't Eat Deer" [*RMDED*]. *Discover* 18, no. 6 (June 1997): 46–53.

Minogue, Kenneth. "The Concept of Property and Its Contemporary Significance" [*CPCS*]. In Pennock and Chapman, eds., *Nomos XXII*, 3–27.

Morgan, Lewis. *Ancient Slavery, or Researches in the Lines of Human Progress from Savagery through Barbarism to Civilization* [*AS*]. London: MacMillan, 1877.

Morgan, Robin, ed. *Sisterhood Is Powerful: An Anthology of Writings from the Women's Liberation Movement* [*SP*]. New York: Random House, 1970.

Morris, Brian. *Anthropology of the Self: The Individual in Cultural Perspective* [*AS*]. London: Pluto Press, 1994.

Morton, A. I., ed. *Freedom in Arms: A Selection of Leveller Writings* [*FA*]. New York: International Publishers, 1974.

Mote, Frederick W. *Intellectual Foundations of China* [*IFC*]. New York: Alfred A. Knopf, 1971.

Mouffe, Chantal. *The Return of the Political* [*RP*]. New York: Verso, 1993.

———, ed. *Deconstruction and Pragmatism* [*DP*]. New York: Routledge, 1996.

———, ed. *Dimensions of Radical Democracy: Pluralism, Citizenship, Community* [*DRD*]. New York: Verso, 1992.

Mudimbe, V. Y. *The Invention of Africa* [*IA*]. In *Invention of Africa: Gnosis, Philosophy, and the Order of Knowledge*. Bloomington: Indiana University Press, 1988. Reprinted in part in Ross, ed., *Art and Its Significance*.

Munzer, Stephen R. *A Theory of Property* [*P*]. Cambridge: Cambridge University Press, 1990.

Murti, T. R. V. *The Central Philosophy of Buddhism: A Study of the Mâdhyamika System* [*CPB*]. 2nd ed. London: George Allen and Unwin, 1960.

Myers, Fred. "Burning the Truck and Holding the Country: Pintupi Forms of Property and Identity" [*BTHC*]. In Wilmsen, ed., *We Are Here*.

Nadotti, Maria. "Karen Finley's Poisoned Meatloaf" [*KFPM*]. *Artforum* 27 (March 1989).

Naess, Arne. *Ecology, Community and Lifestyle: Outline of an Ecosophy* [*ECL*]. Trans. David Rothenberg. Cambridge: Cambridge University Press, 1989.

———. "The Shallow and the Deep: Long Range Ecology Movement" [*SD*]. *Inquiry* 16 (1973): 95–100.

Nagakawa, Keiichirō and Henry Rosovsky. "The Case of the Dying Ki-
mono: The Influence of Changing Fashions on the Development of the
Japanese Woolen Industry" [CDK]. In Roach-Higgins, Eicher, and
Johnson, eds., Dress and Identity.
Nāgārjuna, Elegant Sayings [ES]. Ed. Sakya Pandit. Emeryville: Dharma
Publishing, 1977.
———. The Philosophy of the Middle Way [PMW]. Trans. int., and commentary
David J. Kalupahana. Albany: State University of New York Press,
1986.
Nagel, Thomas. Moral Questions [MQ]. Cambridge: Cambridge University
Press, 1979.
Nancy, Jean-Luc. The Birth to Presence [BP]. Trans. Brian Holmes and Oth-
ers. Stanford: Stanford University Press, 1993.
———. The Experience of Freedom [EF]. Trans. Bridget McDonald. Fwd. Peter
Fenves. Stanford: Stanford University Press, 1993.
———. The Inoperative Community [IC]. Trans. P. Connor, L. Garbus, M. Holland,
and S. Sawhney. Minneapolis: University of Minnesota Press, 1991.
———. Literary Communism [LC]. In Inoperative Community.
———. The Muses [M]. Trans. Peggy Kamuf. Stanford, CA: Stanford Univer-
sity Press, 1996.
———. "Of Divine Places" [DP]. In Inoperative Community.
———. The Sense of the World [SW]. Trans. and fwd. Jeffrey S. Librett. Min-
neapolis: University of Minnesota Press, 1997.
———. "Shattered Love" [SL]. In Inoperative Community.
Nasar, Jack L., ed. Environmental Aesthetics: Theory, Research, and Applica-
tions [EA]. Cambridge: Cambridge University Press, 1988.
Nash, Roderick. The Rights of Nature [RN]. Madison: University of Wiscon-
sin, Press, 1989.
———. Wilderness and the American Mind [WAM]. 3rd ed. New Haven: Yale
University Press, 1982.
Naukkarinen, Ossi. Aesthetics of the Unavoidable: Aesthetic Variations in Hu-
man Appearance [AU]. Saarijärvi: Gummerus Kirjapaino Oy, 1998.
Negri, Antonio. Marx Beyond Marx: Lessons on the Grundrisse [MBM]. South
Hadley, MA: Bergin & Garvey, 1984.
———. Revolution Retrieved: Writings on Marx, Keynes, Capitalist Crisis and
New Social Subjects [RR]. London: Red Notes, 1988.
———. The Savage Anomaly: The Power of Spinoza's Metaphysics and Politics
[SA]. Trans. Michael Hardt. Minneapolis: University of Minnesota
Press, 1991.
Neither Nationalisation Nor Privatisation: An Anarchist Approach [NP]. Lon-
don: Freedom Press, 1989.
Nerburn, Kent, ed. The Wisdom of the Great Chiefs: The Classic Speeches of
Chief Red Jacket, Chief Joseph, and Chief Seattle [WGC]. San Rafael, CA:
New World Library, 1994.
Nietzsche, Friedrich. The Antichrist [A]. In Portable Nietzsche.
———. "Attempt at a Self-Criticism" [ASC]. In Basic Writings. Reprinted in
Ross, ed., Art and Its Significance.

――――. *Basic Writings of Nietzsche* [BWN]. Trans. Walter Kaufmann. New York: Random House, Modern Library Giant, 1968.

――――. *Beyond Good and Evil* [BGE]. In *Basic Writings*.

――――. *Birth of Tragedy* [BT]. In *Basic Writings*. Reprinted in part in Ross, ed., *Art and Its Significance*.

――――. *Ecce Homo* [EH]. In *Basic Writings*.

――――. *The Gay Science* [GS]. Trans. with comm. Walter Kaufman. New York: Vintage, 1974.

――――. *Genealogy of Morals* [GM]. In *Basic Writings*.

――――. *Human, All Too Human* [HATH]. Trans. R. J. Hollingdale. Cambridge: Cambridge University Press, 1996.

――――. *On the Advantage and Disadvantage of History for Life* [OADHL]. Trans. P. Preuss. Indianapolis: Hackett, 1980.

――――. *The Portable Nietzsche* [PN]. Ed. and trans. Walter Kaufmann. New York: Viking Press, 1954.

――――. *Seventy-Five Aphorisms from Five Volumes* [75A]. In *Basic Writings*. From *Dawn* [D]; *Gay Science* [GS]; *Human, Al-Too-Human* [H]; *Mixed Opinions and Maxims* [MOM]; *The Wanderer and His Shadow* [WS].

――――. *Thus Spake Zarathustra* [Z]. In *Portable Nietzsche*.

――――. *Twilight of the Idols* [TI]. In *Portable Nietzsche*.

――――. *The Will to Power* [WP]. Ed. Walter Kaufmann. Trans. Robert Hollingdale and Walter Kaufmann. New York: Vintage, 1968.

――――. *Unfashionable Observations* [UO]. Trans. Richard T. Gray. Stanford, CA: Stanford University Press, 1995.

Nishida Kitarō. *A Study of Good* [SG]. Trans. V. H. Viglielmo. New York: Greenwood Press, 1988.

Nishitani. *Religion and Nothingness* [RN]. Trans. Jan. Van Bragt. Berkeley: University of California, 1982.

――――. *The Self-Overcoming of Nihilism* [SON]. Trans. Graham Parkes with Setsuko Aihara. Albany: State University of New York Press, 1990.

Nodding, Nel. *Caring: A Feminine Approach to Ethics and Moral Education* [C]. Berkeley: University of California Press, 1984.

Nozick, Robert. *Anarchy, State, and Utopia* [ASU]. New York: Basic Books, 1968.

Nussbaum, Martha. *The Fragility of Goodness* [FG]. Cambridge: Cambridge University Press, 1986.

――――. *Love's Knowledge: Essays on Philosophy and Literature* [LK]. New York: Oxford University Press, 1990.

――――. *Poetic Justice: The Literary Imagination and Public Life* [PJ]. Boston, MA: Beacon Press, 1995.

――――. *The Therapy of Desire: Theory and Practice in Hellenistic Ethics* [TD]. Princeton, NJ: Princeton University Press, 1994.

――――. *Women, Culture, and Development: A Study of Human Capabilities* [WCD]. Oxford: Clarendon Press, 1995.

Oates, W. J., and E. O'Neill, eds. *The Complete Greek Drama* [CGD]. New York: Random House, 1938.

Obenchain, Diane B. "Spiritual Quests of Twentieth-Century Women: A Theory of Self-Discovery and a Japanese Case Study" [*SQTW*]. In Ames, ed. *Self as Person in Asian Theory and Practice*.

O'Donovan-Anderson, Michael, ed. *The Incorporated Self: Interdisciplinary Perspectives on Embodiment* [*IS*]. Lanham, MD: Rowman & Littlefield, 1996.

Oelschlaeger, Max, ed. *The Wilderness Condition: Essays on Environment and Civilziation* [*WC*]. San Francisco: Sierra Club Books, 1992.

———. *Postmodern Environmental Ethics* [*PMEE*]. Albany: State University of New York Press, 1995.

Ogunwale, Titus A. "Traditional Hairdressing in Nigeria" [*THN*]. In Roach-Higgins, Eicher, and Johnson, eds., *Dress and Identity*.

Olalquiaga, Celeste. "Vulture Culture" [*VC*]. In Welchman, ed. *Rethinking Borders*.

Olson, Carl. *Zen and the Art of Postmodern Philosophy: Two Paths of Liberation from the Representational Mode of Thinking* [*ZPP*]. Albany: State University of New York Press, 2000.

Omolade, Barbara. "Hearts of Darkness" [*HD*]. In Guy-Sheftall, ed., *Words of Fire*.

Ophuls, William. *Ecology and the Politics of Scarcity* [*EPS*]. San Francisco: W. H. Freeman, 1977.

Osoro, R. *The African Identity in Crisis* [*AIC*]. Hudsonville, MI: Bayana Publishers, 1993.

Otnes, Per. *Other-wise: Alterity, Materiality, Mediation* [*AMM*]. Oslo: Scandinavian University Press, 1997.

Oudshoorn, Nelly. "A Natural Order of Things: Reproductive Sciences and the Politics of Othering" [*NOT*]. In Robertson, Mash, Tickner, Bird, Curtis, and Putnam, eds., *Futurenatural*.

Outlaw, Lucius. *Philosophy, Ethnicity, and Race: The Alfred B. Stiernotte Lectures in Philosophy* [*PER*]. Hamden, CT: Quinnipiac College, 1989.

———. "Philosophy, Ethnicity, and Race" [*PER*]. In Hord and Lee, eds., *I Am Because We Are*.

———. "Toward a Critical Theory of 'Race'" [*TCTR*]. In Goldberg, ed., *Anatomy of Racism*.

Owens, Craig. "The Discourse of Others: Feminists and Postmodernism" [*DO*]. In Hal Foster, ed., *The Anti-Aesthetic: Essays on Postmodern Culture*. Port Townsend, WA: Bay Press, 1983. Reprinted in Ross, ed., *Art and Its Significance*.

Oxford English Dictionary [*OED*]. Compact Edition. Oxford. Oxford University Press, 1971.

Pagels, Elaine H. "What Became of God the Mother? Conflicting Images of God in Early Christianity" [*WBGM*]. In Christ and Plaskow, eds., *Womanspirit Rising*.

Parrinder, Geoffrey. *Witchcraft: European and African* [*WEA*]. London: Faber and Faber, 1970.

Peirce, Charles Sanders. *The Collected Papers of Charles Sanders Peirce* [*CP*]. 6 vols. Ed. Charles Hartshorne and Paul Weiss. Cambridge: Harvard University Press, 1931–5.

———. "The Fixation of Belief" [*FB*]. In *Philosophical Writings*.

———. *The Philosophical Writings of Peirce* [*PP*]. Ed. Justus Buchler. New York: Dover, 1955.

Pennock, J. Roland, and John W. Chapman, eds. *Property: Nomos XXII* [*P*]. New York: New York University, 1980.

Pepper, David. *Eco-socialism: From Deep Ecology to Social Justice* [*E*]. New York: Routledge, 1993.

Picton, John. "Masks and Identities in Ebira Culture" [*MIEC*]. In Maw and Picton, eds., *Concepts of the Body/Self in Africa*.

Plant, Christopher, and Judith Plant, eds. *Green Business: Hope or Hoax?* [*GB*]. Gabriola Island, BC: New Society Publishers, 1991.

Plant, Judith, ed. *Healing the Wounds: The Power of Ecological Feminism* [*HW*]. Philadelphia: New Society Publishers, 1989.

Plato. *The Collected Dialogues of Plato* [*CDP*]. Ed. Edith Hamilton and Huntington Cairns. Princeton: Princeton University Press, 1961. All quotations from Plato are from this edition unless otherwise indicated.

———. *The Dialogues of Plato*. Trans. Benjamin Jowett. New York: Random House, 1920.

———. *Phaedo* [*PP*]. Ed., with int., and notes by John Burnet. London: Oxford University Press, 1963.

———. *Phaedo*. Trans. Harold North Fowler. Loeb Classical Library. Cambridge: Harvard University Press, 1914. All Greek passages from *Phaedo* are from this edition.

———. *Phaedo*. Trans. Benjamin Jowett. In *The Dialogues of Plato*.

———. *Phaedrus*. Trans. Harold North Fowler. Loeb Classical Library. Cambridge: Harvard University Press, 1914. All Greek passages from *Phaedrus* are from this edition.

———. *Protagoras*. Trans. Benjamin Jowett. 3rd ed. London: Oxford University Press, 1982.

———. *Republic*. Trans. Benjamin Jowett. In *The Dialogues of Plato*.

———. *Symposium*. Trans. Benjamin Jowett. In *The Dialogues of Plato*. 3rd ed. London: Oxford University Press, 1982. All quotations in English from *Symposium* are from this edition. Reprinted in part in Ross, ed., *Art and Its Significance*.

———. *Symposium*. Trans. W. R. M. Lamb. Loeb Classical Library. Cambridge: Harvard University Press, 1925. All Greek passages from *Symposium* are from this edition.

Plotinus. *The Philosophy of Plotinus*. Ed. and sel. Joseph Katz. New York: Appleton-Century-Crofts, 1950.

Ponge, Francis. *Things* [*T*]. Trans. Cid Corman. New York: Grossman Publishers, 1971.

Porteous, J. Douglas. *Environmental Aesthetics: Ideas, Politics and Planning* [*EA*]. New York: Routledge, 1996.

Poster, Mark. "Postmodern Virtualities" [*PV*]. In Robertson, Mash, Tickner, Bird, Curtis, and Putnam, eds., *Futurenatural*.

Proudhon, Pierre-Joseph. *What is Property?: An Inquiry into the Principle of Right and of Government* [*WP?*]. Ed. and trans. Donald R. Kelley and Bonnie G. Smith. Cambridge: Cambridge University Press, 1993.

Purchase, Graham. *Anarchism and Ecology* [*AE*]. Montreal: Black Rose Books, 1997.

Quigley, Peter. "Rethinking Resistance: Environmentalism, Literature, and Poststructural Theory" [*RR*]. In Oelschlaeger, ed., *Postmodern Environmental Ethics*.

Quine, Willard Van Ormine. "Natural Kinds" [*NK*]. In Schwartz, ed., *Naming, Necessity, and Natural Kinds*.

———. *Word and Object* [*WO*]. Cambridge: MIT Press, 1960.

Rachels, James. "Why Animals Have a Right to Liberty" [*WARL*]. In Regan and Singer, eds., *Animal Rights and Human Obligations*.

Radin, Margaret Jane. "Market-Inalienability" [*MI*]. *Harvard Law Review* 100 (1987): 1849–1937.

———. "Property and Personhood" [*PP*]. *Stanford Law Review* 34 (1982): 957–1015.

———. *Reinterpreting Property* [*RP*]. Chicago: University of Chicago Press, 1993.

Randall, Jr., John Herman. *Aristotle* [*A*]. New York: Columbia University Press, 1960.

———. *Plato: Dramatist of the Life of Reason* [*P*]. New York: Columbia University Press, 1970.

Random House Dictionary of the English Language [*RHD1*]. Unabridged. New York: Random House, 1966.

———. [*RHD2*]. 2nd ed. Unabridged. New York: Random House, 1987.

Ransaw, Lee A. "The Depiction of Black Imagery Among the World's Masterpieces in Art" [*DBI*]. In Young, ed. *Art, Culture, and Ethnicity*.

Rapaport, David. "A Historical Survey of Psychoanalytic Ego Psychology" [*HSPEP*]. In Erikson, *Identity and the Life Cycle*.

Rawls, John. *A Theory of Justice* [*TJ*]. Cambridge: Belknap Press of Harvard University, 1971.

Reed, A. W. *Myths and Legends of Australia* [*MLA*]. Sydney: A. H. and A. W. Reed, 1971.

Regan, Tom. *All That Dwell Therein: Animal Rights and Environmental Ethics* [*ADT*]. Berkeley: University of California Press, 1982.

———. *The Case for Animal Rights* [*CAR*]. Berkeley: University of California Press, 1983.

Regan, Tom, and Peter Singer, eds. *Animal Rights and Human Obligations* [*ARHO*]. 2nd ed. Englewood Cliffs: Prentice Hall, 1989.

Reich, Charles. "The New Property" [*NP*]. *Yale Law Journal* 73 (1964): 733–87.

Reiter, Rayna R. ed., *Toward an Anthropology of Women*. New York: Monthly Press, 1975.

Richard, Nelly. "The Cultural Periphery and Postmodern Decentring: Latin America's Reconversion of Borders" [*CPPD*]. In Welchman, ed. *Rethinking Borders.*

Ricoeur, Paul. *Memory, History, Forgetting* [*MHF*]. Trans. Kathleen Blamey and David Pellauer. Chicago: University of Chicago Press, 2004.

———. *Oneself as Another* [*OA*]. Chicago: University of Chicago Press, 1992.

Rigby, Peter. *Cattle, Capitalism, and Class: Ilparakuyo Maasai Transformations* [*CCC*]. Philadelphia: Temple University Press, 1992.

Rigterink, Roger J. "Warning: The Surgeon Moralist Has Determined That Claims of Rights Can Be Detrimental to Everyone's Interests" [*W*]. In Cole and Coultrap-McQuin, eds., *Explorations in Feminist Ethics.*

Roach, Catherine. "Loving Your Mother: On the Woman-Nature Relationship" [*LM*]. In Warren, ed., *Hypatia*, 46–59.

Roach-Higgins, Mary Ellen, and Joanne B. Eicher. "Dress and Identity" [*DI*]. In Roach-Higgins, Eicher, and Johnson, eds., *Dress and Identity.*

Roach-Higgins, Mary Ellen, Joanne B. Eicher, and Kim K. P. Johnson, eds. *Dress and Identity* [*DI*]. New York: Fairchild Publications, 1995.

Robertson, George, Melinda Mash, Lisa Tickner, Jon Bird, Barry Curtis, and Tim Putnam, eds. *Futurenatural: Nature, Science, Culture* [*FN*]. New York: Routledge, 1996.

Robinson, John Manley. *An Introduction to Early Greek Philosophy* [*EGP*]. Boston: Houghton Mifflin, 1968. All Greek fragments are quoted from this edition unless otherwise indicated.

Rocheleau, Dianne, Barbara Thomas-Slayter, and Esther Wangari. *Feminist Political Ecology: Global Issues and Local Experience* [*FPE*]. London: Routledge, 1996.

Rolston, Holmes, III. *Environmental Ethics: Duties to and Values in the Natural World* [*EE*]. Philadelphia: Temple University Press, 1988.

———. "Environmental Ethics: Values in and Duties to the Natural World" [*EEVDNW*]. In Bormann and Kellert, eds., *Ecology, Economics, Ethics.*

Rorty, Richard. *Consequences of Pragmatism* [*CP*]. Minneapolis: University of Minnesota Press, 1982.

———. "Philosophy in America Today" [*PAT*]. In *Consequences of Pragmatism.*

Rose, Carol. "Possession as the Origin of Property" [*POP*]. *University of Chicago Law Review* 52 (1985): 73–88.

Rosemont, Henry, Jr. "Classical Confucian and Contemporary Perspectives on the Self: Some Parallels and Their Implications" [*CCCPS*]. In Allen, ed. *Culture and Self.*

Rosenberger, Nancy. *Japanese Self of Self* [*JSS*]. Cambridge: Cambridge University Press, 1992. In Allen, ed. *Culture and Self.*

Ross, Stephen David. *The Gift of Beauty: The Good as Art* [*GBGA*]. Albany: State University of New York Press, 1996.

———. *The Gift of Kinds: The Good in Abundance* [*GKGA*]. Albany: State University of New York Press, 1999.

———. *The Gift of Property: Having the Good* [*GPHG*]. Albany: State University of New York Press, forthcoming.

——. *The Gift of Self: Shattering, Emptiness, Betrayal* [*GSSEB*]. Binghamton, NY: International Studies in Philosophy Monograph Series—Interdisciplinary Studies in Philosophy, Interpretation, and Culture, 2005.

——. *The Gift of Touch: Embodying the Good* [*GTEG*]. Albany: State University of New York Press, 1998.

——. *The Gift of Truth: Gathering the Good* [*GTGG*]. Albany: State University of New York Press, 1997.

——. *Ideals and Responsibilities: Ethical Judgment and Social Identity* [*IR*], Belmont, CA: Wadsworth, 1998.

——. *Inexhaustibility and Human Being: An Essay on Locality* [*IHB*]. New York: Fordham University Press, 1989.

——. *Injustice and Restitution: The Ordinance of Time* [*IROT*]. Albany: State University of New York Press, 1993.

——. *Learning and Discovery* [*LD*]. New York: Gordon and Breach, 1981.

——. *The Limits of Language* [*LL*]. New York: Fordham University Press, 1993.

——. *Locality and Practical Judgment: Charity and Sacrifice* [*LPJ*]. New York: Fordham University Press, 1994.

——. *Metaphysical Aporia and Philosophical Heresy* [*MAPH*]. Albany: State University of New York Press, 1989.

——. *Perspective in Whitehead's Metaphysics* [*PWM*]. Albany: State University of New York Press, 1983.

——. *Plenishment in the Earth: An Ethic of Inclusion* [*PE*]. Albany: State University of New York, 1995.

——. *The Ring of Representation* [*RR*]. Albany: State University of New York Press, 1992.

——. *A Theory of Art: Inexhaustibility by Contrast* [*TA*]. Albany: State University of New York Press, 1983.

——. "Translation as Transgression" [*TT*]. In *Translation Perspectives*, Vol. 5. Ed. D. J. Schmidt. Binghamton: Binghamton University, 1990.

——. *The World as Aesthetic Phenomenon: The Image in Abundance, The Wonder of the Earth* [*WAP*]. International Studies in Philosophy Monograph Series in Interdisciplinary Studies in Philosophy, Interpretation, and Culture, 2 volumes, 2008.

——, ed., *Art and Its Significance: An Anthology of Aesthetic Theory* [*AIS*]. 3rd ed. Albany: State University of New York Press, 1994.

Roszak, Theodore. Introduction to Schumacher, *Small is Beautiful.*

Rousseau, Jean-Jacques. *The Basic Political Writings* [*BPW*]. Trans. Donald A. Cress. Int. Peter Gay. Indianapolis: Hackett, 1987.

——. *A Discourse on the Origin of Inequality* [*DOI*]. In *Basic Political Writings.*

——. *A Discourse on Political Economy* [*DPE*]. In *Basic Political Writings.*

——. *The Social Contract* [*SC*]. In *Basic Political Writings.*

——. *The Social Contract and Discourses* [*SCD*]. Trans. G. D. H. Cole. New York: Dutton, 1950.

Rovane, Carol A. *The Bounds of Agency: An Essay in Revisionary Metaphysics* [*BA*]. Princeton: Princeton University Press, 1998.

Rowlands, Michael. "Accounting for Personal Success in Bamenda" [APSB]. In Maw and Picton, eds., Concepts of the Body/Self in Africa.

Rubin, Arnold. Marks of Civilization: Artistic Transformations of the Human Body [MC]. University of California, Los Angeles: Museum of Cultural History, 1988.

Rubin, Gayle. "The Traffic in Women: Notes on the 'Political Economy' of Sex" [TW]. In R. Reiter, ed., Toward an Anthropology of Women.

Ruch, E. A., and K. C. Anyanwu, eds., African Philosophy: An Introduction to the Main Philosophical Trends in Contemporary Africa [AP]. Rome: Catholic Book Agency, 1984.

Ruether, Rosemary. New Woman, New Earth [NWNE]. New York: Seabury Press, 1975.

Ryan, Alan. Property and Political Theory [PPT]. New York: Blackwell, 1984.

Sachs, Wolfgang. Global Ecology: A New Arena of Political Conflict [GE]. London: Zed, 1993.

Sacks, Oliver. The Man Who Mistook His Wife for a Hat and Other Clinical Tales, published in four volumes as Awakenings [A]; A Leg to Stand On [LSO]; The Man Who Mistook His Wife for a Hat and Other Clinical Tales [MMWH]; and Seeing Voices [SV]. New York: Quality Paperback Book Club, 1990.

Sadler, Barry and Allen Carlson. Environmental Aesthetics: Essays in Interpretation [EA]. Western Geographical Series Vol. 20. Victoria, British Columbia: Department of Geography, University of Victoria, 1982.

Salleh, Ariel. "Class, Race, and Gender Discourse in the Ecofeminism/Deep Ecology Debate" [CRGD]. In Oelschlaeger, ed., Postmodern Environmental Ethics.

Sallis, John, ed. Deconstruction in Philosophy: The Texts of Jacques Derrida [DP]. Chicago: University of Chicago Press, 1987.

———. Reading Heidegger: Commemorations [RH]. Bloomington: Indiana University Press, 1993.

Salomon, Charlotte. Charlotte: Life or Theater?: An Autobiographical Play by Charlotte Salomon [CLT]. Trans. Leila Vennewitz. Int. Judith Herzberg. New York: Viking Press, 1981.

———. Leven? of Theater? Life? or Theatre? [L?T?]. Int. Judith C. E. Belinfante, Christine Fisher-Defoy, and Ad Petersen. Amsterdam: Joods Historisch Museum, 1992.

Sanders, Clinton R. "Drill and Frill: Client Choice, Client Typologies, and Interactional Control in Commercial Tattooing Settings" [DF]. In Roach-Higgins, Eicher, and Johnson, eds., Dress and Identity.

Sartre, Jean-Paul. Being and Nothingness: An Essay on Phenomenological Ontology [BN]. Trans. Hazel Barnes. New York: Philosophical Library, 1956.

———. Nausea [N]. Trans. Lloyd Alexander. New York: New Directions, 1964.

Scapp, Ron, and Brian Seitz, eds. Eating Culture [EC]. Albany: State University of New York Press, 1998.

Schapiro, Meyer. "The Still Life as a Personal Object" [*SLPO*]. In Marianne M. Simmel, ed., *Reach of the Mind: Essays in Memory of Kurt Goldstein*. New York: Springer, 1968. Discussed in Derrida, "Restitutions," in *Truth in Painting*.

Schelling, Friedrich Wilhelm Joseph von. *The Ages of the World* [*AW*], Fragment from the Third Version. Trans. and int. Jason M. Wirth. Albany, NY: State University of New York Press, 2000.

——. *The Ages of the World* [*AWB*], Trans. and int. Frederick deWolfe Bolman, Jr. New York: AMS Press, 1967.

——. *On the History of Modern Philosophy* [*OHMP*]. Trans. and int. Andrew Bowie. Cambridge: Cambridge University Press, 1994.

——. *Philosophical Inquiries into the Nature of Human Freedom* [*NHF*]. Trans. James Gutmann. Las Salle, IL: Open Court, 1936.

——. *Philosophy of Art* [*PA*]. Trans. and ed. Douglas W. Stott. Minneapolis: University of Minnesota Press, 1989.

——. *System of Transcendental Idealism* [*STI*]. Charlottesville, VA: University of Virginia Press, 1978.

Scheper-Hughes, Nancy. "Vernacular Sexism: An Anthropological Response to Ivan Illich" [*VS*]. In *Feminist Issues* 3, no. 1 (Spring 1983): 28–36.

Scherer, Donald, and Tom Attig, eds. *Ethics and the Environment* [*EE*]. Englewood Cliffs, NJ: Prentice Hall, 1983.

Schleuning, Neala. *To Have and To Hold: The Meaning of Ownership in the United States* [*THTH*]. Westport, CT: Praeger, 1977.

Schopenhauer, Arthur. *The World as Will and Representation*. 2 Vols. Trans. E. F. J. Payne. New York: Dover, 1968.

Schor, Naomi. "This Essentialism Which Is Not One: Coming to Grips with Irigaray" [*TEWNO*]. *Differences: A Journal of Feminist Cultural Studies* 2, no. 1 (Summer 1989): 38–58.

Schrag, Calvin O. *The Self After Postmodernity* [*SAP*]. New Haven, CT: Yale University Press, 1997.

Schultz, David A. *Property, Power, and American Democracy* [*PPAD*]. New Brunswick, NY: Transaction Publishers, 1992.

Schumacher, E. F. *A Guide for the Perplexed* [*GP*]. New York: Harper and Row, 1977.

——. *Small Is Beautiful: Economics as if People Mattered* [*SB*]. Pref. John McClaughry, Kirkpatrick Sale. Int. Theodore Roszak. New York: Harper & Row, 1989.

Schutte, Ofelia. *Cultural Identity and Social Liberation in Latin American Thought* [*CISL*]. Albany: State University of New York Press, 1993.

Schutz, Alfred. "The Homecomer" [*H*]. *American Journal of Sociology* 60, no. 5 (1945): 369–76.

——. "The Stranger: An Essay in Social Psychology" [*S*]. *American Journal of Sociology* 49, no. 6 (1944): 499–507.

Schwartz, Stephen P., ed. *Naming, Necessity, and Natural Kinds* [*NNNK*]. Ithaca, NY: Cornell University Press, 1977.

Scott, Charles E. *The* **Question** *of Ethics: Nietzsche, Foucault, Heidegger* [*QE*]. Bloomington: Indiana University Press, 1990.

Scott, G. E. *Moral Personhood: An Essay in the Philosophy of Moral Psychology* [*MP*]. Albany: State University of New York Press, 1990.

Scott, Russell. *The Body as Property* [*BP*]. New York: Viking, 1981.

Seager, Joni. *Earth Follies: Coming to Terms with the Global Environmental Crisis* [*EF*]. New York: Routledge, 1993.

Seamon, David, ed. *Dwelling, Seeing, and Designing* [*DSD*]. Albany: State University of New York Press, 1993.

Seed, John, Joanna Macy, Pat Fleming, and Arne Naess. *Thinking Like a Mountain: Toward a Council of All Beings* [*TLM*]. Philadelphia: New Society Publishers, 1988.

Selfe, Lorna. *Nadia: A Case Study of Extraordinary Drawing Ability in an Autistic Child* [*N*]. New York and London: Harcourt Brace Jovanovich, 1977.

Sen, Amartya. "More Than 100 Million Women Are Missing" [*MMWM*]. *New York Review of Books* (December 20, 1990): 61–6.

Senghor, Léopold Sédar. "Negritude: A Humanism of the Twentieth Century" [*N*]. In Hord and Lee, eds., *I Am Because We Are.*

Serequeberhan, Tsenay. *African Philosophy: The Essential Readings* [*AP*]. New York: Paragon House, 1991.

Serres, Michel. *The Natural Contract* [*NC*]. Trans. Elizabeth MacArthur and William Paulson. Ann Arbor: University of Michigan Press, 1995.

Sessions, Robert. "Deep Ecology versus Ecofeminism: Healthy Differences or Incompatible Philosophies?" [*DEE*]. In Warren, ed., *Hypatia*: 90–107.

Setton, Mark. *Chŏng, Yagyong: Korea's Challenge to Orthodox Neo-confucianism* [*CY*]. Albany: State University of New York Press, 1997.

Shack, William A. "Open Systems and Closed Boundaries: The Ritual Process of Stranger Relations in New African States" [*OSCB*]. In Shack and Skinner, eds., *Strangers in African Societies.*

Shack, William A., and Elioot Skinner, eds. *Strangers in African Societies* [*SAS*]. Berkeley: University of California Press, 1979.

Shantideva. *Bodhicaryavatara* [*B*] 8:114. Trans. Stephen Batchelor. In *A Guide to the Bodhisattva's Way of Life* [*GBWL*]. Dharamsala, India: Library of Tibetan Works and Archives, 1979.

Sharma, Ursula. "Dowry in North India: Its Consequences for Women" [*DNI*]. In Hirschon, ed., *Women and Property—Women As Property.*

Sharper, Stephen D. *Redeeming the Time: A Political Theology of the Environment* [*RD*]. New York: Continuum, 1997.

Shcherbatskoi [Stcherbatsky], Fedor Ippolitovich. *Buddhist Logic* [*BL*]. New York: Dover Publications, 1962.

———. *The Central Conception of Buddhism and the Meaning of the Word "Dharma"* [*CCB*]. Delhi: Motilal Banarsidass, 1970.

———. *The Conception of Buddhist Nirvâṇa* [*CBN*]. New York: Gordon Press, 1971.

Sheehan, Thomas, ed. *Heidegger, the Man and the Thinker* [*HMT*]. Chicago: Precedent Publishing, 1981.

Shepard, Paul. *Nature and Madness* [NM]. San Franciso: Sierra Club Books, 1982.

Shimomura Toratarō. "Nishida Kitarō and Some Aspects of His Philosophical Thought" [NK]. In Nishida, *Study of Good*.

Shiva, Vandana. "Development as a New Project of Western Patriarchy" [DNPWP]. In Diamond and Orenstein, eds., *Reweaving the World*.

———. *Staying Alive* [SA]. London: Zed, 1989.

Shiva, Vandana, and Ingunn Moser, eds. *Biopolitics: A Feminist and Ecological Reader on Biotechnology* [B]. London: Zed Books, 1995.

———. Silko, Leslie Marmon. *Ceremony* [C]. New York: New American Library, 1977.

Shoemaker, Sidney. *The First-Person Perspective and Other Essays* [FPP]. New York: Cambridge University Press, 1996.

Siebers, Tobin. *The Subject and Other Subjects: On Ethical, Aesthetic, and Political Identity* [SOS]. Ann Arbor: University of Michigan Press, 1998.

Sillah, Memuna M. "Bundu Trap" [BT]. *Natural History* (August 1996): 42–53.

Simmel, Georg. *Sociologie* [Soc]. Leipzig: Duncker & Humblot, 1908.

———. "The Stranger" [S]. In Donald N. Levine, *On Individuality and Social Forms*. Chicago: University of Chicago Press, 1971.

Simons, Margaret A. "From Murder to Morality: The Development of Beauvoir's Ethics" [FMM]. *International Studies in Philosophy* 31, no. 2 (1999): 1–20.

Singer, Joseph W. "The Reliance Interest in Property" [RIP]. *Stanford Law Review*, 40 (1988): 611–51.

———. "Sovereignty and Property" [SP]. *Northwestern University Law Review* 86, no. 1 (1991): 1–56.

Singer, Linda. "Defusing the Canon: Feminist Rereading and Textual Politics" [DC]. In *Erotic Welfare: Sexual Theory and Politics in the Age of Epidemic*. Ed. and int. Judith Butler and Maureen MacGrogan. New York: Routledge, 1993.

Singer, Peter. *Animal Liberation: A New Ethics for Our Treatment of Animals* [AL]. New York: Avon, 1975.

Sini, Carlo. *Images of Truth: From Sign to Symbol* [IT]. Trans. Massimo Verdicchio. Atlantic Highlands, NJ: Humanities Press, 1993.

Slicer, Deborah. "Your Daughter or Your Dog" [DD]. In Warren, ed., *Hypatia*, 108–23.

Smith, Adam. *An Inquiry into the Nature and Causes of the Wealth of Nations* [WN]. Ed. R. H. Campbell, A. S. Skinner, and W. B. Todd. Oxford: Clarendon Press, 1976.

Smith, Bradley. "Assimilationism: Learning How to Learn the Beauty of It All" [A]. In Young, ed. *Art, Culture, and Ethnicity*.

Smith, Mick. "Cheney and the Myth of Postmodernism" [CMP]. In Oelschlaeger, ed., *Postmodern Environmental Ethics*.

Soper, Kate. "Nature/'nature'" [NN]. In Robertson, Mash, Tickner, Bird, Curtis, and Putnam, eds., *Futurenatural*.

Sophocles. *Oedipus the King* [*OK*], *Antigone* [*A*], *Oedipus at Colonus* [*OC*]. All trans. R. C. Jebb. In Oates and O'Neill, eds., *Complete Greek Drama*.

Sorabji, Richard. "Aristotle on Demarcating the Five Senses" [*ADFS*]. *Philosophical Review* 80 (1971): 55–79.

Soyinka, Wole. *Art, Dialogue, and Outrage: Essays on Literature and Culture* [*ADO*]. New York: Pantheon, 1994.

——. *The Burden of Memory, the Muse of Forgiveness* [*BMMF*]. New York: Oxford Oxford University Press, 1999.

Spelman, Elizabeth V. *Inessential Woman: Problems of Exclusion in Feminist Thought* [*IW*]. Boston: Beacon Press, 1988.

Spencer, Colin. *The Heretic's Feast: A History of Vegetarianism* [*HF*]. Hanover: University Press of New England, 1995.

Spiegel, Marjorie. *The Dreaded Comparison: Human and Animal Slavery* [*DC*]. Rev. ed. New York: Mirror Books, 1996.

Spinoza, Benedict de. *Collected Works of Spinoza* [*CWS*], Vol. 1. 2nd printing with corr. Ed. and trans. Edwin Curley. Princeton: Princeton University Press, 1988.

——. *Descartes' Principles of Philosophy* [*DPP*]. In *Collected Works*, Vol. I.

——. *Ethics* [*E*]. In *Collected Works*, Vol. I.

——. *Ethics* [*EG*]. Trans. William Hale White. Rev. Amelia Hutchinson Stirling. Ed. and int. James Gutmann. New York: Hafner, 1949.

——. *Ethics and Selected Letters* [*ESL*]. Trans. Samuel Shirley. Ed. and Int. Seymour Feldman. Indianapolis: Hackett, 1982.

——. *A Theologico-Political Treatise* [*TPT*] *and A Political Treatise* [*PT*]. Trans. and int. R. H. M. Elwes. New York: Dover, 1951.

——. *Short Treatise on God, Man, and His Well-Being* [*STG*]. In *Collected Works*.

——. *Treatise on the Emendation of the Intellect* [*TEI*]. In *Collected Works*.

Spretnak, Charlene. *The Resurgence of the Real: Body, Nature, and Place in a Hypermodern World* [*RR*]. New York: Addison-Wesley, 1997.

——. *The Spiritual Dimension of Green Politics* [*SDGP*]. Santa Fe, NM: Bear and Co., 1986.

Stambaugh, Joan. *The Formless Self* [*FS*]. Albany: State University of New York Press, 1999.

Starhawk [Miriam Simos], "Ethics and Justice in Goddess Religion" [*EJGR*]. In Andolsen, Gudorf, and Pellauer, eds., *Women's Consciousness, Women's Conscience*.

——. "Witchcraft and Women's Culture" [*WWC*]. In Christ and Plaskow, eds., *Womanspirit Rising*.

Starr, June. "The Legal and Social Transformation of Rural Women in Aegean Turkey" [*LSF*]. In Hirschon, ed., *Women and Property—Women As Property*.

Stephen, Michele. "Contrasting Images of Power" [*CIP*]. In Stephen ed., *Sorcerer and Witch*.

——. "Master of Souls: The Mekeo Sorcerer" [*MS*]. In Stephen ed., *Sorcerer and Witch*.

————, ed. *Sorcerer and Witch in Melanesia* [*SWM*]. New Brunswick, NJ: Rutgers University Press, 1987.

Stirner, Max. *The Ego and His Own* [*EO*]. Trans. Steven T. Byington. New York: Dover, 1973.

Stone, Christopher D. *Earth and Other Ethics* [*EOE*]. New York: Harper & Row, 1987.

————. "Moral Pluralism and the Course of Environmental Ethics" [*MPCEE*]. In Oelschlaeger, ed., *Postmodern Environmental Ethics*.

Stone, Gregory P. "Appearance and the Self" [*AS*]. In Roach-Higgins, Eicher, and Johnson, eds., *Dress and Identity*.

Strathern, Marilyn. *The Gender of the Gift: Problems with Women and Problems with Society in Melanesia* [*GG*]. Berkeley: University of California Press, 1988.

————. "Subject or Object? Women and the Circulation of Valuables in Highlands New Guinea" [*SO*]. In Hirschon, ed., *Women and Property— Women As Property*.

Strawson, Peter F. *Individuals: An Essay in Descriptive Metaphysics* [*I*]. Garden City, NY: Doubleday & Co., 1959.

Strong, Marilee. *A Bright Red Scream: Self-mutilation and the Language of Pain* [*BRS*]. New York: Viking, 1998.

Sumner, Claude. *The Source of African Philosophy: The Ethiopian Philosophy of Man* [*SAP*]. Stuttgart: Franz Steiner Verlag Wiesbaden GMBH, 1986.

Suzuki, Daisetz T. *The Essence of Buddhism* [*EB*]. Kyoto: Bunko, 1948.

————. "How to Read Nishida" [*HRN*]. In Nishida, *A Study of Good*.

————. *Zen and Japanese Culture* [*ZJC*]. Princeton, NJ: Princeton University Press, 1993.

Swift, Jonathan. *Gulliver's Travels and Other Writings* [*GT*]. Int. Louis A. Landa. Cambridge: Riverside, 1960.

Sypher, Wylie. *Comedy* [*C*]. Baltimore: Johns Hopkins University Press, 1956.

Tanahashi, Kazuaki, ed. *Moon in a Dewdrop* [*MD*]. San Francisco: North Point Press, 1985.

Tannen, Deborah. *You Just Don't Understand: Women and Men in Conversation* [*YJDU*]. New York: Ballantine, 1990.

Tarski, Alfred. "The Semantic Conception of Truth" [*SCT*]. *Philosophy and Phenomenological Research*, 4:341–76 (1944). Reprinted in Linsky, ed., *Semantics and the Philosophy of Language*. All page references to Linsky.

Taylor, Charles. *Sources of the Self: The Making of Modern Identity* [*SS*]. Cambidge, MA: Harvard University Press, 1989.

Taylor, Dorceta E. "Environmentalism and the Politics of Inclusion" [*EPI*]. In Bullard, ed., *Confronting Environmental Racism*.

Taylor, Mark C. *Altarity* [*I*]. Chicago: University of Chicago Press, 1987.

————. *Hiding* [*H*]. Chicago: University of Chicago Press, 1997.

————. *The Moment of Complexity: Emerging Network Culture* [*MC*]. Chicago: University of Chicago Press, 2001.

Taylor, Mark C., and Era Saarinen. *Imagologies: Media Philosophy* [*I*]. New York: Routledge, 1994.

Taylor, Paul. *Respect for Nature: A Theory of Environmental Ethics* [*RN*]. Princeton: Princeton University Press, 1986.

Tellenbach, Hubertus, and Bin Kimura. "The Japanese Concept of 'Nature'" [*JCN*]. In Callicott and Ames, eds., *Nature in Asian Traditions of Thought*.

Theroux, Paul. "Self-Propelled" [*SP*]. *The New York Times Magazine* (April 25, 1993): 22–4.

Thomas, Elizabeth Marshall. "Reflections (Lions)" [*L*]. *The New Yorker* (October 15, 1990): 78–101.

Thompson, Robert Farris. *Flash of the Spirit; African & Afro-American Art & Philosophy* [*FS*]. New York: Vintage, 1984.

Tobias, Michael. "Ecological Aesthetics" [*EA*]. In Tobias and Cowan, eds., *Soul of Nature*.

Tobias, Michael, and Georgianne Cowan, eds. *The Soul of Nature: Visions of a Living Earth* [*SN*]. New York: Continuum, 1994.

Tolstoy, Leo. *What Is Art?* [*WA*]. Reprinted in part in Ross, ed., *Art and Its Significance*.

———. "What is To Be Done" [*WD*]. In Horovitz, ed., *Anarchists*.

Topan, Farouk M. "Body and Self in a Spirit Mediumship Cult of Mombasa" [*BS*]. In Maw and Picton, eds., *Concepts of the Body/Self in Africa*.

Trinh, T. Minh-ha. "An Acoustic Journey" [*AJ*]. In Welchman, ed., *Rethinking Borders*.

———. "Nature's R: A Musical Swoon" [*NR*]. In Robertson, Mash, Tickner, Bird, Curtis, and Putnam, eds., *Futurenatural*.

———. *Woman, Native, Other: Writing Postcoloniality and Feminism* [*WNO*]. Indianapolis: Indiana University Press, 1989.

Trippi, Laura. "Untitle Artists' Projects by Janine Antoni, Ben Kinmont, Rirkrit Tiravanija" [*UAP*]. In Scapp and Seitz, eds., *Eating Culture*.

Trumbull, H. C. *The Threshold Covenant* [*TC*]. New York: Scribner's, 1896.

Tu Wei-ming. "The Continuity of Nature: Chinese Visions of Nature" [*CN*]. In Callicott and Ames, eds., *Nature in Asian Traditions of Thought*.

———. "Embodying the Universe: A Note on Confucian Self-Realization" [*EU*]. In Ames, ed. *Self as Person in Asian Theory and Practice*.

Tuan, Yi-Fu. *Passing Strange and Wonderful: Aesthetics, Nature, and Culture* [*PSW*]. New York: Kodansha America, 1995.

Tucker, Benjamin Ricketson. *Instead of a Book, By a Man Too Busy to Write One; A Fragmentary Exposition of Philosophical Anarchism* [*IB*]. 2nd ed. New York: Gordon Press, 1972.

Turner, Victor. *The Ritual Process* [*RP*]. Chicago: Aldine, 1969.

Tyler, Edward B. *Primitive Culture* [*PC*]. New York: Holt and Co., 1889.

Underkuffler, Laura S. "On Property: An Essay" [*OP*]. *Yale Law Journal* 100 (1990): 127–48.

Valiente, Doreen. *Witchcraft for Tomorrow* [*WT*]. Custer, WA: Phoenix, 1987.

Vattimo, Gianni. *The End of Modernity* [*EM*]. Trans. J. R. Snyder. Cambridge: Polity Press, 1988.

Vale, V., and Andrea Juno. *Modern Primitives* [*MP*]. San Francisco: Re/Search Publications, 1989.

Van Sertima, Ivan. *The African Presence in Ancient America: They Came Before Columbus [APAA]*. New York: Random House, 1976.

Vaughan, Genevieve. *For-Giving: A Feminist Criticism of Exchange [F-G]*. Austin, TX: Plain View Press, 1997.

Veblen, Thorstein. "The Beginnings of Ownership" *[BO]*. *The American Journal of Sociology* 4 (November 1989): 352–65.

———. *The Portable Veblen [PV]*. Ed. Max Lerner. New York: Viking, 1972.

———. *The Theory of the Leisure Class [TLC]*. New York: Modern Library, 1934.

Victoria, Brian (Daizen) A. *Zen at War [ZW]*. New York: Weatherhill, 1997.

Waldron, Jeremy. *The Right to Private Property [RPP]*. Oxford: Clarendon Press, 1988.

Warren, Karen J. "Feminism and Ecology: Making Connections" *[FEMC]*. *Environmental Ethics* 9, no. 1 (Spring 1987): 3–20.

———. "The Promise and Power of Ecological Feminism" *[PPEF]*. *Environmental Ethics* 12, no. 2 (Summer 1990): 125–46.

Warren, Karen J., ed. *Hypatia* 6, no. 1 (Spring 1991). Special Issue on Ecological Feminism.

Warren, Karen J., and Jim Cheney. "Ecological Feminism and Ecosystem Ecology" *[EFEE]*. In Warren, ed., *Hypatia*, 179–97.

Watkins, Susan M. "Stitchless Sewing for the Apparel of the Future" *[SSAF]*. In Roach-Higgins, Eicher, and Johnson, eds., *Dress and Identity*.

Weber, Renée, "A Philosophical Perspective on Touch" *[PPT]*. In Barnard and Brazelton, eds., *Touch*.

Welchman, John C. "The Philosophical Brothel" *[PB]*. In Welchman, ed. *Rethinking Borders*.

———. *Rethinking Borders [RB]*. Minneapolis: University of Minnesota Press, 1996.

Welwood, John, and Ken Wilber. "On Ego Strength and Egolessness" *[ESE]*. In John Welwood, ed. *The Meeting of the Ways: Explorations in East/West Psychology [MW]*. New York: Schocken Books, 1979.

Wenders, William. *Wings of Desire [WD]*. Screenplay by Wenders and Peter Handke. 1988.

Wenz, Peter S. "Just Garbage" *[JG]*. In Westra and Wenz, eds., *Faces of Environmental Racism: Confronting Issues of Global Justice*.

West, Cornel. *Keeping Faith: Philosophy and Race in America [KP]*. New York: Routledge, 1993.

———. "Race Matters" *[RM]*. In Andersen and Collins, eds., *Race, Class, and Gender*.

Weston, Anthony. "Before Environmental Ethics" *[BEE]*. In Oelschlaeger, ed., *Postmodern Environmental Ethics*.

Westra, Laura, and Peter S. Wenz, eds., *Faces of Environmental Racism: Confronting Issues of Global Justice [FER]*. Lanham, MD: Rowman & Littlefield, 1995.

Westwood, Sallie. "'Fear Woman': Property and Modes of Production in Urban Ghana" *[FW]*. In Hirschon, ed., *Women and Property—Women As Property*.

White, Daniel R. *Labyrinths of the Mind: The Self in the Postmodern Age* [*LM*]. Albany: State University of New York Press, 1998.

White, Stephen L. *The Unity of the Self* [*US*]. Cambridge, MA: MIT Press, 1991.

Whitehead, Alfred North. *Adventures of Ideas* [*AI*]. New York: Macmillan, 1933.

——. *Modes of Thought* [*MT*]. New York: Capricorn, 1938.

——. *Process and Reality* [*PR*]. Corrected edition. Ed. D. R. Griffin and D. W. Sherburne. New York: Free Press, 1978.

——. *Science in the Modern World* [*SMW*]. New York: Macmillan, 1925.

Whitehead, Ann. "Women and Men; Kinship and Property: Some General Issues" [*WMKP*]. In Hirschon, ed., *Women and Property—Women As Property*.

Whitman, Walt. *Song of Myself* [*SM*]. In *Works*.

——. *Works* [*W*]. New York: Viking Press, 1982.

Wikse, John R. *About Possession: The Self as Private Property* [*AP*]. University Park, PA: The Pennsylvania State University Press, 1977.

Wilcox, Finn, and Jeremiah Gorsline, eds. *Working the Woods, Working the Sea* [*WW*]. Port Townsend, WA: Empty Bowl, 1986.

Willis, Janice. *On Knowing Reality: The* Tattvârtha *Chapter of Asåga's* Bodhisattvabhûmi [*OKR*]. New York: Columbia University Press, 1979.

Wilmsen, Edwin H. ed. *We Are Here: Politics of Aboriginal Land Tenure* [*WAH*]. Berkeley: University of California Press, 1989.

Wilson, Edward O. *The Diversity of Life* [*DL*]. Cambridge: Harvard University Press, 1992.

Wilson, Peter J. *The Domestication of the Human Species* [*DHS*]. New Haven: Yale University Press, 1988.

Winkler, Cathy (with Kate Wininger). "Rape Trauma: Contexts of Meaning" [*RT*]. In Csordas, *Embodiment and Experience*.

Wittgenstein, Ludwig. *The Blue and Brown Books* [*BB*]. New York: Harper & Row, 1958.

——. *Philosophical Investigations* [*PI*]. Trans. G. E. M. Anscombe. Oxford: Blackwell, 1963.

——. *Tractatus Logico-Philosophicus* [*TLP*]. Trans. D. F. Pears and B. F. McGuinness. London: Routledge & Kegan Paul, 1961.

Wittig, Monique. "The Category of Sex" [*CS*]. In *Straight Mind*.

——. *The Lesbian Body* [*LB*]. Trans. David Le Vay. Boston: Beacon Press, 1973. Translation of *Le Corps Lesbien* [*CL*]. Paris: Minuit, 1973.

——. "The Mark of Gender" [*MG*]. In *Straight Mind*.

——. "One Is Not Born a Woman" [*OBW*]. In *Straight Mind*.

——. "The Straight Mind" [*SM*]. In *Straight Mind*.

——. *The Straight Mind and Other Essays* [*SME*]. Boston: Beacon Press, 1992.

Worster, Donald. *Rivers of Empire* [*RE*]. New York: Pantheon, 1985.

Young, Bernard, ed. *Art, Culture, and Ethnicity* [*ACE*]. Reston, VA: National Art Education Association, 1990.

Young-Bruehl, Elizabeth, and Faith Bethelard. *Cherishment: A Psychology of the Heart* [C]. New York: Free Press, 2000.

Zack, Naomi. *Bachelors of Science: Seventeenth-Century Identity, Then and Now* [BS]. Philadelphia: Temple University Press, 1996.

Zimmerman, Michael E. *Contesting Earth's Future: Radical Ecology and Post-modernity* [CEF]. Berkeley: University of California Press, 1994.

———. "Quantum Theory, Intrinsic Value, and Panentheism" [QTIVP]. In Oelschlaeger, ed., *Postmodern Environmental Ethics*.

Žižek, Slavoj. "Eastern Europe's Republics of Gilead" [EERG]. In Mouffe, ed., *Dimensions of Radical Democracy*.

Mimēsis, imitation, 10, 207, 222, 272, 280, 289, 336; *See also* Art, Exposition

Minds, 26, 30–8, 46–50, 53–5, 58, 61, 65, 78, 90, 93–9, 108, 112, 130, 160–8, 178, 181, 193, 201, 248, 263, 275, 292, 295, 299, 312, 315, 318–9, 327, 331, 356, 361; *See also* Consciousness,

Modernity, 52, 64, 77–9, 100, 115–21, 153–5, 160, 207, 211–2, 234–5, 242, 252, 266

Moments, 2–3, 31, 34–5, 51–2, 58, 83, 97, 100, 109, 112–5, 118–21, 124, 130, 146, 149, 170, 199, 211, 214, 217, 224, 238, 242, 251, 261, 264, 268–9, 273, 282–3, 286–8, 295, 299, 311–2, 319, 323–5, 345–7; *See also* Events, Present

Monuments, 81, 114, 137–8, 146, 153, 156, 242, 260, 271–2; *See also* Art

Morality; *See* Ethics

Mourning, 18, 36, 198, 203, 217, 232, 243–5, 277–301, 336–7, 347, 360; *See also* Death, Grief

Mysteries, 29–30, 53, 103, 114, 233, 257–61, 267, 328, 352; *See also* Enchantment

Name, naming, 1–2, 6–9, 12, 16, 34, 45, 48–9, 64–6, 72–7, 87, 93, 97–100, 104, 107–13, 116–27, 137, 143, 147, 150–2, 172, 187, 190–1, 194, 199, 203, 211–6, 232–8, 248–51, 258–61, 266–9, 272–81, 286–93, 299–300, 333, 337–51, 357; *See also* Exposition, Language

Nancy, J.-L., 78, 110

Narratives, 10, 89, 144, 185–6, 222–3, 266, 299, 318, 327, 332; *See also* Language, Literature, Telling

Nature, 4, 25–8, 34–7, 46–7, 51, 54, 62–7, 74, 81–3, 86–9, 100, 105–10, 113, 127, 137, 144, 150–6, 160–71, 181–2, 192, 197, 201, 206–8, 211–5, 219, 227, 230, 240, 250–3, 266, 284, 301, 305, 314, 323–5, 328–30, 345, 356–60; *See also* Being, Earth, World

Nietzsche, F., 63–4, 113, 129–39, 143–4, 137, 177–8, 187, 206, 216, 223, 268–9, 290, 338–9, 348, 353–4, 363

Nothing, nothingness, 3, 10–1, 14, 17–9, 22–6, 31–40, 43–53, 57–8, 64, 69, 73, 80–2, 85–8, 92–8, 107, 111–2, 115–7, 123–5, 129–33, 136, 142–3, 150, 157, 163–73, 176, 182–3, 190–1, 195–6, 199–202, 206–13, 217, 221–5, 231, 242–4, 247–8, 252–3, 259–66, 270, 273, 276, 279–81, 284–7, 292–3, 310–1, 321, 325–7, 330, 336, 339, 342–7, 350, 354, 358; *See also* Absence

Objects, 6, 23, 32, 43–5, 48–54, 57–8, 82–3, 104, 112, 119, 140, 143, 150, 155, 165, 174, 180–3, 187, 193, 205–7, 211, 214, 227–8, 232–4, 243–5, 261, 264, 269, 299, 309, 328–32; *See also* Beings

Oblivion, 1, 7, 32, 43, 76, 106–9, 122, 125–7, 131–5, 139–41, 154–7, 183, 190, 216–7, 349; *See also* Forgetting

Open, opening, openness, 12, 21, 30–1, 46, 80, 92–43, 127, 142, 151–4, 160–1, 169, 172, 177, 180, 206, 213, 222, 251–3, 258, 268–70, 274–5, 285–6, 289–90, 296, 310, 318, 328, 335, 341, 351–2

Order, 1–3, 7, 16, 33, 46–7, 54, 57–9, 70–2, 75, 91–2, 96, 104, 107, 110, 118–9, 123, 132–6, 142, 148–9, 152–6, 163, 167, 180, 183, 188–9, 192, 196, 199, 204, 217, 221, 228, 238, 244, 266–8, 273–6, 291, 318–9, 335, 345–6, 351; *See also* Disorder